Class Counts

Class Counts

Education, Inequality, and the Shrinking Middle Class

Allan Ornstein

ROWMAN & LITTLEFIELD PUBLISHERS, INC.
Lanham • Boulder • New York • Toronto • Plymouth, UK

71789923

ROWMAN & LITTLEFIELD PUBLISHERS, INC.

Published in the United States of America
by Rowman & Littlefield Publishers, Inc.
A wholly owned subsidary of The Rowman & Littlefield Publishing Group, Inc.
4501 Forbes Boulevard, Suite 200, Lanham, Maryland 20706
www.rowmanlittlefield.com

Estover Road
Plymouth PL6 7PY
United Kingdom

British Library Cataloguing in Publication Information Available

Library of Congress Cataloging-in-Publication Data

Ornstein, Allan C.
    Class counts : Education, inequality, and the shrinking middle class / Allan
Ornstein.
        p.   cm.
    ISBN-13: 978-0-7425-4741-4 (cloth : alk. paper)
    ISBN-10: 0-7425-4741-8 (cloth : alk. paper)
    ISBN-13: 978-0-7425-4742-1 (pbk. : alk. paper)
    ISBN-10: 0-7425-4742-6 (pbk. : alk. paper)
    1. Social classes—United States.   2. Poverty—United States.   3. Wealth—
United States.   4. Education, Higher—Social aspects—United States.   5.
Middle class—United States.   6. Elite (Social sciences)—United States.   7.
Power (Social sciences)—United States.   I. Title.
    HN90.S6O76   2007
    305.5′50973—dc22   2006030859

Printed in the United States of America

Contents

What This Book Is About

1. Class counts. Class differences and class warfare have existed since the beginning of Western civilization, with the Greeks and Romans, and since our nation was founded. It was reflected in the different philosophies of Thomas Jefferson and Alexander Hamilton and presently between liberals and conservatives. It is keenly expressed in who gets admitted to Harvard or Yale and who attends second- or third-tier colleges; only 3 percent of students at the nation's top 146 colleges come from families in the bottom economic quartile (or the lowest 25 percent).

2. The gap in income and wealth between the rich (the top 10 percent) and the rest (the bottom 90 percent) has increased steadily in the last twenty-five years. In 2005 the average worker in the United States earned $43,506. Among Fortune 500 companies, the average executive pay was $11.3 million, not including stock options, which have the potential effect of doubling or tripling the earnings of a CEO. The nation is heading for a financial oligarchy, much worse than the aristocratic old world that our Founding Fathers feared and tried to avoid.

3. In 2005 the bottom 90 percent of the population earned $117,000 or less while the top 0.1 percent earned $16 million or more. From 1950 to 1970 for every additional dollar earned by the lower 90 percent—what I call the "new struggling class"—those on the top 0.1 percent earned $162. From 1990 to 2002, for every dollar earned by the lower 90 percent, these top taxpayers earned an additional $18,000. This kind of income gap is eventually going to shred the middle class and then the democratic process.

4. For the last twenty-five years, real wages of the working class have remained flat at about $15 to $16 per hour. Job loss and job insecurity are at an all-time high in the United States, as reflected in the loss of high-paying jobs and the outsourcing of white-collar jobs, as well as the reduction or elimination of company-funded pensions and health

insurance. Replacement jobs result in a one-third reduction in wages, regardless of retraining and education.

5. Despite continuous growth in the economy since the 2000 stock market bubble, nearly two-thirds of new jobs—more than 5 million in total—pay less than $35,000 a year. The largest U.S. employer is Wal-Mart, where the average worker earns about $7.50 per hour and has minimal health insurance coverage.

6. As many as 85 percent of American families remain in the same class or move up or down one quintile three decades later. During a twenty-five-year period, ending in 2004, 61 percent of families in the lowest income quintile were stuck at the same level. In reverse, 59 percent in the highest income quintile remained at the same level.

7. The middle class is struggling and shrinking. The average consumer debt was more than $9,300 in 2005; the savings rate was a negative .4 percent, the first time since the Depression in 1933 that Americans' spending exceeded disposable income. Educated young Americans are in worse shape. The average debt from student loans among college students graduating with a bachelor's degree was more than $18,000 and among graduate students was approximately $45,000 in 2005.

8. Tuition at private colleges has increased 110 percent in the last decade, compared to 60 percent for four-year state colleges; however, income for the bottom 50 percentile increased 35 percent and, after considering inflation, there was no gain. Measures designed to make colleges more affordable, such as tuition tax breaks and special tax-free savings accounts for college, disproportionly benefit families in the top 40 percentile.

9. Today 23 percent of all people sixty-five to seventy-four years old hold jobs, compared to 16 percent just two decades ago. The number of workers in the sixty-five to seventy-four group grew three times the rate as the overall workforce in 2004 and ten million previously retired people were forced back to work in order to make ends meet. Although most seniors want to keep their homes, 44 percent of homeowners at age seventy will have sold their houses by age eighty-five to pay for living costs and basic needs.

10. The Medicare trust is expected to start running a deficit in 2013 and Social Security is expected to go bust by 2044. Looming deficits in both social programs are forcing the government to curtail benefits. Some 50 percent of the American populace are without pensions and are relying on Social Security for retirement. While hundreds of billions of dollars are passed on yearly to the offspring of the rich (the top 10 percent) and superrich (the top 1 percent), 86 percent of U.S.

households will receive less than $1,000 in cash value or no inheritance at all.

11. Education is no longer the great equalizer. Schools and colleges cannot overcome the difference between those born on third base and those who are struggling to get up at bat. The American dream is slowly evaporating and becoming more unattainable for the under-thirty generation.

12. So long as Americans have the view that the Michael Eisners, Michael Dells, and Michael Jordans of the world, and all their descendants, are entitled to all their wealth because they worked hard, founded highly successful companies, or could shoot a ball through a hoop, then the millions they make will continue to create economic imbalance and doom the rest of us to a bleak future characterized by vast inequality.

13. A democratic society requires some kind of balance between achievement and equality. Endpoints or benchmarks are needed to establish economic ceilings and floors. A moral society, one that is fair and just, sets limits on the accumulation of wealth and inherited privilege and also guarantees a safety net for the less fortunate. Without such limits, social mobility and opportunity become abstract and unachievable ideals, representing nothing more than propaganda derived from a sham notion of a classless society driven by the American notion of equality and the Protestant work ethic.

14. Cultural and social differences and religious views, reflected in red and blue voting patterns, mask important economic and safety net issues such as jobs, pensions, Social Security, and health-care and college tuition costs. New laws and policies are required, including government regulation of Wall Street and the financial and banking industries, as well as increased safety nets for the American people.

15. There needs to be a redistribution of wealth in order to make U.S. society more democratic, fair, and just. Recommended are a host of taxes, including but not limited to luxury taxes, windfall profit taxes, estate taxes, and fuel taxes. Other recommendations include eliminating taxes on food, drugs, and low-cost clothing, free state college tuition for above-average students, and zero tax on the first $50,000 earned in annual wages for all Americans.

16. A strategy is outlined in order to restore the social contract that is supposed to exist between the government and the people. The U.S. standard of living and quality of life for the bottom 90 percent of the economic scale is at stake. The idea is for people to vote for their pocketbook, and not be derailed by secondary or side issues.

Dedication

S ince *Class Counts* is about class, I thought the words below would have
special meaning for most Americans. The book you are about to read
is a 340-page ramble that my old handball, basketball, and baseball buddies might appreciate. We were ordinary guys, growing up in tiny apartments and blighted bungalows during the Cold War and the Bomb. Some
of us were slightly wild and paid the price; some had their lives reduced
to ashes in the jungles of Vietnam, which replaced the Bomb as the
nation's highway to hell. Still others were gripped by amped-up ambitions to break out of their small-town, blue-collar lockup, become organization men, and wear gray flannel or blue-pin stripe suits. None of us was
a class bully or nerd, especially talented or gifted. None was later seduced
by hallucinations, paint spray mishmash, or the new norms. We were
straight shooters; ordinary working-class American children; infatuated
by stories of blood, guts, and glory; liked Ike and Cronkite, and disliked
Allen Ginsberg and Abbie Hoffman (the latter who we construed as loud,
nuts, and off the beaten track).

Many of my old school chums from New York's P.S. 42 did not achieve
the American dream, as they stumbled and mumbled though life as stolid
working-class citizens, considered by their employers as Reynolds wrap
or Kleenex—to be used and discarded. A few of us made it to the solid
middle and professional class. In a nutshell, we were average souls—not
usually different from most middle Americans, just trying to flee from
our surroundings and gain opportunity beyond our small town. Although
we all grew up eager and ambitious, believing in folks in authority and
in the mobility ladder, many of us were humbled and marginalized by
the economic system we thought so highly of.

This book is for all the plain people in America and, the plain people I
grew up with in elementary school, the old gang who called me "Doc" on
the playing field because they thought I was conversational and smart.
Here, then, is a special salute, a quick glimpse into memory lane—a little

like the Everly or Statler Brothers, who anyone under fifty years is not expected to know. The names below have special meaning to me, and they have not been changed to protect the innocent; they are average Americans, what this book in mainly about, known by their friends and family, and unknown by history. So here is the old gang, a small slice of Americana, and what happened to them, fifty-plus years later: To what extent they changed from blue collar to white collar, from working class to professional class.

Jack Alter (small business owner, Coral Springs, Florida)
Alexander Biamonte (status unknown)
Lawrence ("The Babe") Berg (college graduate, retired social worker, New York)
Donald ("Bossy") Bethell (gas station owner, deceased)
Harold ("Blockhead") Blacher (college graduate, accountant, somewhere in California)
Alfred Chapnick (retired manufacturer, New York)
Howard Cohen (clothing sales representative, Miami, Florida)
Stan ("The Man") Eckstein (college graduate, accountant, semi-retired, W. Palm Beach, Florida)
Robert ("Bell") Feldman (tuxedo store owner, deceased)
Alan ("The Toe") Fitleson (retired newspaper printer, New York)
Gilbert Kerry (college graduate, management, public utilities, Houston, Texas)
Bernard ("Bee Bee") Miller (college graduate, retired engineer, New York)
Marvin Rostolla (retired police officer and detective, New York)
Fred ("Muscles") Serge (butcher, New York)
Mike ("Blue Eyes") Sitler (gas station owner, New York)
Harry ("The Greek") Sophos (management, airline flight scheduling, Dallas, Texas)
Leonard Zafonte (soldier, deceased)

It is worth noting that none of us as P.S. 42 had any pedigree, legacy, or inherited power and privilege to set the course for our future, to guide our way toward achieving the American dream, or to help move us from the base toward the top of the socioeconomic ladder. It would be a mistake to under estimate such factors, even though they rarely, if ever, are considered as variables to control in sociological and economic studies of class and rank. But then we were all innocent and idealistic. We were so naïve that we did not even know what we didn't know: How the system works, that executives such as H. Lee Scott of Wal-Mart earns roughly 850 times the average pay of a Wal-Mart sales clerk—the kind of person we knew as the next-door neighbor. Despite all our aspirations and ambitions, we were limited in just how far we could move up the class structure. Although this perspective may seem uncomfortable for many

Americans who whole-heartedly believe in the system, or even slightly un-American, these facts are born out in the pages you are about to read.

Now the flip side is, there is still no better country than America, where the guys from P.S. 42 could have had a better chance to rise from the base of the socioeconomic structure and improve their living standard and status. The problem is, today, the chances of the economic base improving their condition and becoming better off from one generation to the next is diminishing, evidenced by growing inequality in America. Allow me to cite just one of the many facts and figures you are going to read in this book. In the last fifteen years, real household income rose 2 percent for the bottom 90 percent of Americans, but rose 57 percent for the top 1 percent, climbed 85 percent for the top 0.1 percent and sky rocketed 112 percent for the top of the top .01 percent.[1] In other words, the super rich are getting richer almost as twice as fast as the rich and about one hundred times faster than the rest of us. If the kids from P.S. 42, now in retirement age, had to begin again, and given the same starting conditions, they would most likely be in worse economic shape.

It is this factor, *inequality* in America, which my old classmates and friends had to face and were handicapped from the starting gate. The problem is considerably worse today, leaving more people behind— creating a growing loss of motivation at the bottom, a smaller pie to divide, and a shrinking middle class. Extreme differences in income and wealth, a growing gap between rich and common people, is the number one social and economic issue facing America; it is the most important long-term problem confronting the country with the equally rival problem of terrorism.

NOTE

1. Erick Konigsberg, "The New Class War: The Haves vs. the Have Mores," *New York Times*, November 19, 2006.

Introduction: For Readers with Intellectual Pizzazz

As the author sees it, I have grown up in two worlds, a full-fledged citizen of neither, a stranger in both. The clash is primarily one of culture, listening to Johnny Cash or Sarah Brightman, scoffing up a Budweiser or Pabst Blue Ribbon or sipping on Ketel One or eighteen-year-old Glenfiddich, ordering the $9.95 blue-plate special at the local diner or choosing the prix fixe menu (with wine, tax, and tip) at *Le Bernardin* or *Daniel* per couple is equivalent to the annual earnings of nearly half the world's inhabitants.

I have come to know the world outside of heaven and hell, in an upper-class bubble in Winnetka, Illinois, and Manhasset, New York, as I once lived in a working-class bubble in some tiny town, a little pimple on the map, that is known for nothing, except possibly for its beach. This is where the ocean waves rose twenty-five or thirty feet high and met the bay in September, and where rats and weeds outnumbered people and trees. It was a teeming peninsula, sunny and somewhat stormy, that always seemed about to slip into the ocean. Of course, it would have been nice to have grown up "prosperous," "affluent," or just "plain rich," but that would have been vaguely undemocratic; moreover, I would have not known, cared, nor understood what afflicts most Americans today, nor how it feels to have a boss or big business devour your family when you're a child.

Always in exile in Winnetka, I returned after thirty-two years to the place where I grew up as a child, when I came back to New York in 1999, just in advance of the bulldozers. The journey to Arverne, my old neighborhood, was not easy. It was always a small town, trapped by time and going nowhere, but it had a collective conscious, a center to provide benchmarks and values—a place where youthful dreams could be born and old-timers with modest means could spend their winter years on the beach or by the waterfront. The homes were now tired and boarded up, the trees were crooked and lifeless, and the streets were beaten and broken. P.S. 42, my alma mater, was partially in ruins—five floors high and still towering over a sea of surrounding small and shanty-looking bungalows.

In the lost world of the 1940s and 1950s, growing up in a small working-class town had dignity; it was an age of innocence when the future seemed bright. What happened to that lost world, my class of '58, with names I have forgotten, old friends and old memories? Alas, I remember my hero Jackie Robinson—stealing bases, fighting the odds, and paving the way for Martin Luther King and thousands of black athletes. Now, my hero is Johnny Cash—singing about the common man's plight, about being alone on the road, waking up on a Sunday morning, hung over with unarticulated thoughts and unexpressed emotions about dead-end relationships, broken lives, lost memories, about getting older but not necessarily smarter.

Perhaps I've seen too many leaves fall from the trees, or I'm a little too angry because of the scars of class warfare, which started for me when I was about six years old and made my first hour-long drive to K-Mart to shop with my mother for lower prices and start school. Maybe I'm all mixed up—slowly drifting from reality—what the Polish poet, Czelaw Milosz, another one of my heroes, calls "moving away from the fairgrounds of the world." Ah, age has a way of creeping up on you—sometimes clouding your thoughts and stealing your mind or sometimes making you aware of the thicket of history. Here I would like to think that Cicero, the ancient Roman orator, was right: "old age especially an honored old age, has such great authority that it is of more value than all the pleasures of youth."

Today, we live in a tragic world where, as the Greeks knew, there can be no easy answers. We are surrounded by poverty and human misery, by inequality and injustice, by greed and materialism. The genre of tragedy points to centuries of human folly and suffering that defy rational thought and religious philosophy. By historical accident and geography, Americans have been spared much of the world's problems and poverty, and there are fanciful phrases describing our land as the "new Athens" and "new Rome." But these words mask our approaching decline, the dark hole in which we find ourselves, slipping downward as a nation and people. Like all great civilizations that have declined before us, we are a nation that needs to reexamine its values and social and economic institutions.

For all the citizens of the world, *class* reaches back to antiquity and stretches across the globe. It is a defining element throughout history, shaping political, economic, and social attitudes and behavior. Class is the foundation for understanding human thought and the human condition. The choices are vividly portrayed in Victor Hugo's *Les Misérables:* whether you are willing to steal a loaf of bread or use the law to put someone in prison for trying to survive—whether you are a Jean Valjean, one of billions who are hungry, poor and desperate—or an Inspector Javert, just another ordinary person following the orders of the rich and powerful. For myself, class serves as the great divide: People like Jean Valjean (lower- and working-class people), Inspector Javert (middle-class bureaucrats), and those whom the Javerts work for (the rich and powerful).

"Class" is a metaphor for exploitation. Today's workers in some respect are indistinguishable from yesterday's sweatshop workers, the medieval serfs who tilled the soil, or the Greek and Roman slaves. They are the same people that fight all the wars from time immemorial. They are the world's workforce, the common people, the unknown names that built our railroads, bridges, and tunnels, that built the great churches and castles for Charlemagne, Peter the Great, and King Arthur, that built the Acropolis and Coliseum, and before them pushed the stones uphill to build the Pyramids. Sadly, we do not know one of them by name, though they number in the hundreds of millions. They are the faceless people of the earth who for centuries have survived through sweat and toil. Alexander Hamilton labeled them the *herd*. Marx called them the *proletariat*. Eugene Debs organized them as *union workers*. Ben Wattenberg, more recently, referred to them as the *silent majority*. I call them the "massline" and/or "multitude."

"Class" on a worldwide basis invokes the transformation of the landscape into unnatural categories of inequality at the expense of fairness, tolerance, and morality—an assembly of peasants and workers in farms and factories trying to put food on the table. "Class" in America has come to mean a setting aside of the political and social order in ruthless pursuit of profit, a rigged economic system based on money and subsequent privilege and power, an exploited and dislocated mass population, and a random disorder of moral priorities. To be sure, this nation needs to be healed, and to be healed it needs first to find its political center.

Everything is mighty fine so long as we don't have to think about or deal with poverty and human misery around us, or why the vast majority of U.S. high school students cannot locate Laos, Rwanda, or even Iraq and Afghanistan on a map, or why U.S. workers cannot compete on a global basis, or why the world is increasingly anti-American. It's a wonderful world in a rich man's world. Everything is "A-Okay" so long as Dad can get you into Harvard or Yale, that is if you are a member of the privileged and powerful club. It does not hit home that the middle class is struggling and shrinking, not if you drive around in a Mercedes-Benz CL 600 coupe (cost $125,000) or carry around a Fendi handbag (cost $5,000).

It's "peachy keen" if your mom or dad manipulate markets and prices in business posts and live the life in F. Scott Fitzgerald's *The Great Gatsby*. Everything is "sunny" and "rosey" in the wonderful world of *Ozzie and Harriet* and *Mr. Rogers' Neighborhood*, the latter on which my contemporaries grew up. Its great to live in Kansas and recall that July 26 is "Turnip Day" and travel on the yellow-brick road, searching for brains, heart, and courage. It's a little like a Billy Graham or Pat Robinson Sunday sermon—talking about the mind, body, and spirit. On a secular basis, its a little like *Ragtime*, people coming to America with hopes and dreams and clawing their way from the bottom to the top. Perhaps the best antidote is escape: being old and overweight and cruising the Mediterranean Sea on a luxury liner, eating and drinking to your heart's content—or being rich and spoiled and sunning on Southhampton Beach or the French Riviera—ignoring the world that we are leaving our children and their children. No wonder why so many people feel indifferent to the plight of so many other people within our borders and across the oceans.

I would rather be less sharp elbowed and more hopeful, and think about the sensual pleasures of youth and not that Cicero was assassinated at sixty-three (and I'm sixty-five). I prefer not to think about *Class Counts* or some other book about the struggles of the working and middle class. I would rather believe in a fictionalized world: War is over, there was no 9/11, and there is no person in charge with a questionable IQ who can wreck the world. I would rather think of Mozart and Michelangelo and thank Gandhi, King, and Pope John Paul II for trying to make a better world. I would rather say that we are a community of people who can take care of one another, especially the less fortunate, and we can take political action to resolve our economic and social problems. I prefer to believe that through education great minds and hearts are nurtured, the world we live in can change for the better, and the soul can be reborn.

As in life, the meaning you find in the books you read depends on the author's social and political lens and whether he writes as an advocate (subjective) or scholar (supposedly objective). Here I profess to be more concerned about people than property, which makes me somewhere left of center on social and political issues. My writing is fairly charged and is not meant to be neutral, nor taste or look like vanilla ice cream. But readers must understand that no one lives with a calculator in his hand or a camera strapped to his head for research purposes. My writing is also abrasive and critical of people, pundits, and politicians who fabricate different statistics and sound bites, and who are governed by a different sense of truth than mine. Just how abrasive or critical the reader judges my writing will depend on his own experiences and echoes of time, for they do influence the reader's social and political lens and judgment.

Although I believe my book is stuffed to the brim with facts and figures, my writing is slanted and breaks scholarly conventions. Thus, I am well aware of the potential for criticism from my academic colleagues, and from people who fall right of center and are intent on preserving their prosperity—or the social, economic, and political world in which we live. However, my aim is to appeal to a larger audience: Those who were once called the common people or plain people are now called the working- and middle-class people.

The secret story revealed in this book is that government plays a key role in America's class structure and whether the American dream runs on or off track. The story involves more than just tax rates, minimum wages, and medicaid benefits, but which political party is in power—which philosophy or doctrine controls human services and safety nets for people, whether the party supports and protects labor or business, and what kind of policies and regulations govern finance, technology, and globalization. We would like to think that we are alive and well and we have it all under control, and the stuff we overlook or cannot control doesn't matter. But it does matter! It's just that we don't realize it or don't want to face up to it. We would like to think there is very little difference between Democrats and Republicans, between liberal and conservative thought. But there is a difference, and it is bigger than most of us think. What we need is a government that cares more about people than property, more about rising inequality and the shrinking middle class then denying it or arguing that what is good for the rich is good for the country.

The meaning you find in this book also depends on where the author chooses to start and stop—and what is omitted from the passages. This story has a well-defined beginning, but a blurry ending because it is still evolving as the coming decades unfold. I start the message with the Greeks and Romans, then journey to the New World with the American spirit, and the founding of a small number of outposts for European countries that four hundred years later has become the richest and most powerful nation in the world. This is the story of America: Class counts and it has always counted; it counts more today than yesterday, and gaps are growing between the rich (top 10 percent) and super rich (top 1 percent) and the rest of us (bottom 90 percent). The principles of democracy, the very foundation of America, are being threatened by increasing inequality and a diminishing middle class. Moreover, education is no longer the great equalizer it once was. We have reached the point—the economic divide—where education cannot easily compensate nor overcome economic inequality.

As the most affluent society on the face of the map, we have reached the zenith of our military and economic power. All roads now lead to Washington, D.C., and New York City. When we hiccup, the rest of the world hears and feels it. America has been exceptionally fortunate in the past centuries, but the years ahead will be more difficult. Under the guise of protecting or spreading democracy, we have become the most militaristic nation in history (a hard pill for some Americans to swallow). Might makes right in the world of realpolitik, but it inspires world opinion to resent and even despise Americans. Our 2005 military budget was $460 billion (not counting the war in Iraq and Afghanistan) and represented 50 percent of the world's weaponry spending. These costs are unsustainable and result in curtailed spending for real social and human needs.

As we barrel ahead with unaccounted military spending we are being threatened by these issues: hypereconomic competition from Asian-rim countries and resource nationalism and energy intimidation from Russia and Middle Eastern and Latin American countries; U.S. corporate downsizing, layoffs, and outsourcing of jobs; consumer and government overspending; and huge budget and trade deficits. Adding to our problems, giant corporations dominate the American political and economic landscape and supersede the interests of the people. Society is being divided into separate estates, and catch phrases harshly sort people into "winners" and "losers," suggesting a struggling and shrinking middle class. A growing gap between the rich and the rest of Americans has been fostered by a newly imposed tax system designed so that the children's children of super millionaires (the top one-half to 1 percent of the population) have the chance to become billionaires while the masses shoulder the monetary burden. As we squeeze the average American household (earning approximately $46,000 in 2005), we are transforming American democracy into a financial oligarchy.

The American people are in denial, swayed more by cultural warfare and blue-red voting patterns than economic issues, and whether our president was reborn and found God or is he right or wrong when he calls freedom "a gift from the Almighty." We are at the crossroads of American society and, as we look at the facts, there is only one conclusion. All directions point to difficult and bumpy roads ahead. There is no rule, no formula, for predicting the level and rate of decline. An American trait is the yearning for a new president as the Moses to lead the people out of troubled waters and through turbulent times, to find the way toward the rising sun. But America has had its day in the sun. It reached its *belle epoque*, what the French called it, during the Cold War period (when Europe and Asia were in shambles). Since 9/11, however, it has witnessed the emergence of new economic powers, China, India, and oil-rich nations, all challenging U.S. power. Even worse, our enemies believe we have become a "paper tiger." When the going gets tough, the American public will pressure its political leaders to change course or withdraw.

Bogged down by disagreement with our European allies and in Iraq, and consumed by antiterrorist measures, America doesn't even have a viable climate control and energy policy, which in the long run will have more influence on the economy than terrorism. Unquestionably, we are faced with a host of dilemmas and choices, and as we face the future there seems little chance to escape an inevitable decline in military and economic power and prestige. As the twenty-first century marches on, we must accept the fact there will most likely be a redistribution of wealth on a worldwide basis—from the United States to other industrialized and developing countries.

1

✛

Historical Thoughts of Equality and Inequality

Rather than attempting to present the "bare bones" of history and social science in this book, I shall supply an analysis and offer the reader more meat on which to chew. I believe that facts alone tell only a small part of the story and that a neutral position, typical of most textbooks, leaves many readers unsatisfied, and sometimes even hungry. It also insults the readers' intelligence. I do feel that many readers long for a *compass* to direct them across the pages and a *context* to put the facts together for greater understanding. I prefer to think most readers have the ability to think critically about what they read, and can successfully deal with a little tinkering and splicing of ideas. Moreover, it is every reader's prerogative to disagree or argue that the analysis is squeezed to one side of the political spectrum.

The reading audience will quickly come to realize that my ideas do not fit into neutral territory, and that the emotional tone in which the facts are put into evidence represents a political position like that of an attorney advocating a case before a jury. I clearly swing more to the left on the subject of class, and in this regard the book should be considered a political, social, and economic treatise. The words and paragraphs nip and bite you in some places and require some thought and counterthought on the part of the reader. To be sure, mine is hardly a new approach. The best authors in all fields of social science have a distinctive political and social message. They do more than accumulate data; rather they engage their readers and take sides in some political or philosophical struggle.

Now, if I had to categorize my writing, I would like to say it borders on that of what I call a "Social Democrat."[1] In today's world a Social Democrat advocates a fair and just society and the redistribution of wealth in order to achieve his ends. In education, the old reconstructionist ideas of George Counts and Harold Rugg coincide with this philosophy, as do the more recent ideas of Christopher Jencks of Harvard University and Henry Levin of Columbia University. In philosophy, the moral ideas of Columbia professor Brian Barry and Harvard professor John Rawls and their quest for justice have a similar ring. In the field of economics, professors Paul Krugman of Princeton University and Robert Reich of the University of California at Berkeley fit this type of thinking.[2] In fact, as you turn these pages and become more involved with my view of class and how it counts in society, it shall become evident that I would enjoy a few dinners with Krugman or Reich in years to come, before one of us fades into ambiguity.

That said, we cannot compartmentalize historical periods, people, or events, and treat them separately, as we try to do when we segment books into specific time periods or themes without recognizing that our pasts are our present. To put it in different words, our present is connected to all our pasts. There is no single timeline, no specific historical period, separate from another time period. All our eras and epochs, all our times, are alive and with us now. As the present is merely the accumulation of the past, I intend to highlight certain periods of time to show the building blocks of ideas, permitting the reader to think and rethink the idea that in America class counts, inequality is growing, and the achievement of more equality is impossible unless those in power are willing to set floors and ceilings of poverty and wealth, revise the tax code, and redistribute wealth. In simple terms, the issue is how much present levels of inequality of income and wealth should be reduced, and just how much equality is feasible within our political and economic system. The flip side is that if we fail to modify the skewed income and wealth curves, along with rising college tuition and diminishing pensions and health-care trends, we may very well surrender many of the principles of democracy that require a strong and vibrant working and middle class. Shared communal and economic interests are a strong antidote to the dark dimensions of a financial oligarchy—a money class running the government.

PERSONAL COMMENTS ON INEQUALITY

Allow me the moment to make a personal comment to the reader in an honest and open way. My interpretation of society is much less optimistic than most of my academic peers, and more interlaced with social and economic theory. I do not share the liberals' faith in people and feel there are many -*isms* that we succumb to that dethrone individual reason and individual rights and permit power and greed to shape society. Sadly, I believe there is more tyranny than justice in the world, more "captive minds" than free minds, more plunderers than peacemakers, and more people driven by selfish interests than noble interests.

Once we leave the Anglo world, the wealthiest 1 percent of the people have gobbled up more than 50 percent of the remaining world's income and assets for the last two thousand years, while the poorest 50 percent have received less than 1.5 percent. In fact, the gap between the rich and poor has been the rule of order since the Pharaoh's days when the working class were pushing stones uphill. Aspirations and abstractions don't have the same meaning for the majority of the world's populace, who live in an environment that is cold, desolate, and impoverished. Poverty, poor health, and limited education have created a gulag in many parts of the world, where the concepts of equality and equal opportunity don't exist, where society requires a major social and economic transformation.

Here I am inclined to accept Franz Kafka's and Hannah Arendt's world full of irony and tragedy, rather than Johann Goethe's and Robert Louis Stevenson's world where people laugh and live and rejoice in life. Only in the New World, in America, and possibly in England and other Anglo countries, is there hope for the common person to find, as Thomas Jefferson put it, "life, liberty, and the pursuit of happiness," to find modes of morality and truth, and to fulfill individual dreams and visions. On the other hand, the nightmares of the twentieth century, highlighted by Nazi Germany, Japan's militarism, and the Soviet Union, and more recently in Cambodia, Bosnia, Rwanda, and Darfur all testify to unspeakable acts committed by *common people*, who given certain circumstances are capable of committing terrible and sadistic acts to their neighbors.[3] Throughout history, the so-called educated and culturally sophisticated people have supported and even cheered morally wrong and unjust causes. The mass of people, so-called normal, average, everyday, "good" people, observe perverted and evil acts committed by government officials and complicit bureaucrats and could care less about the fate of others so long as they have food on their table and are personally unaffected.

As the Bible reminds us, it only takes the majority of good people to sit on the sidelines or do nothing for evil to raise its ugly head. Similarly, the torments of people who work all day to survive, to whom we owe our luxuries, are never able to reach our hearts. We listen—cool and without emotion—to the accounts of poor and working people, sick people, and disabled people just as we listen to the stories of slavery and how black Americans were tyrannized and brutalized. We cannot fully understand their history unless we have known it ourselves as members of the wrong tribe or ethnic group that once experienced the whip, boot, or gun barrel. Once we analyze a nation and its people on this level, we learn that the idea of equality and equality of opportunity take second place to survival.

People need to be fed, clothed, sheltered, and cared for before there can be a legitimate discussion about moral or democratic principles (which some U.S. policymakers understand and others ignore in their attempt to spread the gospel).

Satisfying basic human needs is more important than an abstract idea dealing with philosophy, theory, or principles of righteousness (or equality). Most people will sell their hearts and minds to a cause, even the wrong cause, so long as they have food on the table and a roof over their heads; they will even switch causes, if needed, to survive. There are only a few good people, a small percentage in history, like Patrick Henry or Joan of Arc, who are willing to die or be burned at the stake for their beliefs—abstract ideas that reflect what is fair and just in the human condition. Tom Cruise in *Mission Impossible* and Kiefer Sutherland in the TV program *24* are heroes because they are willing to risk their lives for their country.

In so many parts of the world, and throughout history, people are more concerned about basic needs and staying alive for the next dawn. They go to bed at night and fall asleep and wake up the next day and start all over again—just hoping to survive; they earn one or two dollars a day. Here I'm describing some 50 percent of the world's populace, living in rural fields, urban roof tops and alleys, and next to garbage heaps. It is also naive to believe that more stories on the front page of any newspaper or on CNN will change the course of history. There are seven thousand years of Western history, since the age of pharaohs—when people in power knew better—yet the masses have been engulfed by atrocity stories, ranging from severe poverty and malnourishment, to rape and plunder, and mass murder. Hence, the world has been skewed and victimized by moral collapse, and those who have been poor and powerless have suffered from all forms of coercion and oppression from the rich and powerful. This history is not accidental or marginal; it is an intrinsic and indispensable part of human's inhumanity to humans.

POVERTY EXPRESSED THROUGH THE NOVEL

How does someone explain the grinding effects of poverty to people who are accustomed to eating three square meals a day and who have been sponsored by their parents through their youth and young adult life? How do students, who have always had their diapers changed and noses kept clean since they were little kids, come to understand those who have been sealed off by the tyranny of poverty—poverty that saps the individual's strength, the person's mind and body? There is no way the anecdotes of sociologists or indicators of social class reveal how poverty turns people into dots and amoeba—people wasted by the wrenching process of no hope, no choice, no future. So, how does a beginning teacher, with a working-class or middle-class background, full of idealism and seeking a larger purpose to the daily act of teaching, get to understand boys and girls who have been left behind by society, who society has always regarded as less than worthy, nothing more than a number to a government bureaucrat or politician? How does the average suburban or small-town student come to understand how for centuries poverty has destroyed the hearts and minds of people?

Allow me to provide you a short glimpse into the life of Mr. Potter, an illiterate taxicab driver living in Antigua. He could also be living in Harlem, New York, South Side Chicago, or Watts, California. Mr. Potter is an uneventful, nondescript person. He has been beaten down by loss and suffering that comes with poverty and lack of education. He created the author of the book titled *Mr. Potter*, but he played no part in raising her and in fact scarcely knew her. Ms. Kincaid was his illegitimate daughter, living among other half-sisters and half-brothers. Mr. Potter is speechless; he has nothing to say. His favorite expression is "eh"; at times, when he shows strong feelings, he remarks "ooohhh!" He is more sensitive to the variations of the sun (the repetitive sameness of the Caribbean) than to the needs and interests of his children or other people. He notices nothing else, for this person who "said nothing to himself . . . and thought nothing to himself. . . . Nothing crossed his mind and the world was blank and the world remained blank."[4]

There is no possibility for Mr. Potter to become self-actualized or to rise from "rags to riches." He routinely eats, sleeps, grunts, and fornicates once a week. (He fathers numerous illegitimate children.) His pleasures are a clean shirt, an open window, and a breeze rippling on his face. It is impossible for him to harbor a novel thought, or to be interesting in a philosophical or literary way. He has been reduced to nothingness, a disconnected person, a prisoner of poverty. Mr. Potter has never been in love, doesn't dream, doesn't express feelings, and doesn't ponder or question political or social issues—a middle-class luxury. He hardly cares about anything, so it is hard to care for him, to worry about him, or to try to improve his life. His story is a tale of sameness, uselessness, and futility. He has been beaten down, like a pancake.

For Mr. Potter, there is no need to escape, no journey to a promised land, as in Harriet Beecher Stowe's *Uncle Tom's Cabin* (1852); no sense of bitterness, as with Frederick Douglass's *My Bondage and My Freedom* (1855); no sense of hope as with Booker T. Washington's *Up from Slavery* (1901); no independent spirit, as with W. E. B. DuBois's *The Soul of Black Folks* (1903); no fire or sense of rage, as with James Baldwin's *The Fire Next Time* (1963); no potential for violence or rebellion, as with Frantz Fanon's

The Wretched of the Earth (1963); no need for a revolution or power struggle, as with Stokely Carmichael and Charles Hamilton's *Black Power*
(1967); no need to honestly address the vexing issues of race and justice,
as with Randall Kennedy's *Race, Crime and the Law* (2000). Mr. Potter has
no emotions, nothing to say, nothing to look forward to other than his
death.

The world of the novel is often incomplete and open to different perspectives and interpretations. Given this construct, and the consideration
of time and place, Mr. Potter is a pathetic figure; he might as well sleep
through life. He is a man erased by the misfortunes of poverty, neglected
and obscured by the power structure. He exists as an appendix to society.
He is a "no-hoper." He has no personality, no status in the family, the community, or the church. Potter doesn't think of the future; he has no heroic
designs. There are hundreds of millions of people like him in the third
world, particularly in Latin America, Africa, and Asia—wasting away with
no voice, no representation, no power, and no opportunity. There are tens
of millions of poor people like him living in the slums of America. Some
clean floors or toilets, some wash dishes or change bed sheets in hotel
rooms, some cut grass or pump gas, some sell drugs, and some sell their
bodies. Some travel downtown, others uptown, to forget all their troubles,
all their cares. For the greater part, these people have been rendered hopeless by society, and their goal is to survive daily and stay clear from the
arm of the law—the boot and whip, the gun, or the prosecutor's fury. As
for most Americans, they prefer not to face this reality, to ignore or withdraw from it, to say it doesn't exist; yet these seething forces, these growing numbers, threaten our way of life.

THE SUBJECTIVE VALENCE

The narrative provided so far purposely avoids the clinical use of statistics, numbers that often appear dry and matter of fact, without feelings
and emotions. In such a cool and objective world, there is no place for
overripe or colorful prose, only a world built on such qualifiers as "if,"
"may," "it appears," or "the data suggest"—words and phrases that do
not leap at you but put you off and blur your memory and imagination.
The point is, collections of facts and figures can bog down the reader and
easily can be tossed to the wayside. The difference in zeros (100,000 or
1,000,000) numbs and blurs the reader's sense of reality and hides the
human element and force of poverty. Now no one is perfect! Maybe I
should have provided more statistics of poverty, the data and tools that
my colleagues relish. Maybe I should have defined my terms in social science jargon to appease my academic friends. However, I thought I would

be more effective in providing the flesh and soul of a person living in squalor, a taste of humanity, a piece or glimpse of what it means to be poor.

Some people may be made uncomfortable by the sufferings of one person, and write it off as an extreme case or as a liberal bias. But class and snobbery have distorted the writings of all social sciences, from the ancient times to the present. The academic world is no different. Despite where professors might start in life's race, with a host of handicaps or privileges, once they gain their degrees they develop clean, pudgy hands and middle-aged pot bellies. In reality, the stories they tell, myself included, can only pretend to know the Mr. Potters of the world or the other litany of horrors that shape the human experience. We are all limited by our own discourse, our own words and methods, and the continuing influence of our own experiences. Some of us are more limited than others. Some of us get our news from the *Boston Globe*, others from the *Beloit News*. Some of us watch CNN or Fox News, and still others regularly turn to the local news channels.

From the perspective of a teacher enrolled in "Education 101," or a rookie policeman enrolled in "Principles of the Law" or a young committed clergyman taking his vows, it is questionable if such a person—or the pillars of society—can grasp the full force of poverty. It is doubtful if grossly underfunded schools, managed by bureaucratic and sometimes cruel policies and staffed by many unprepared teachers, can make a dent. It is doubtful if someone dressed in a shiny blue uniform, with a shield and gun, or someone with a bible and pulpit offering salvation or damnation, can fully grasp Mr. Potter's wasted life—the unsurfaced rage this person has toward the system, a system that has rendered him helpless—whereby despair and depression, eventually nothingness, grip the body, mind, and soul.

Can Mr. Potter, or his offspring, find the "golden ring" or "yellow brick road?" Can his children rise from "rags to riches?" Or, will they be rendered useless for life, beaten down by the institutions of society? How? By the law as in Victor Hugo's *Les Misérables*, by the dictums of church as in Nathaniel Hawthorne's *The Scarlet Letter*, or by the customs and mores of society as in Thomas Hardy's *Jude the Obscure*? The question arises: Can we reverse the culture of poverty that squashes and victimizes the less fortunate, to enable poor children on a large scale to realize their potential talents and skills before they grow up and become the Mr. Potters of America? Here, in this land, the dream still exists, although it is beginning to fade and become more difficult to achieve, not only for poor and working people but also among the shrinking and struggling middle class. The bottom 80 to 90 percent of us is at risk. The vast majority, obviously, are not like Mr. Potter, and will never become like him, but our lifestyle and way of life are heading downhill. We need to understand that more Americans are struggling and working harder and longer hours to make

ends meet—and will continue to do so unless we reexamine and reconceptualize the economic and social system within this country.

Good Morning America!

Here in America we have a real chance of affirming the "natural rights"
of people, including some form of equality and opportunity. But this
nation has its contradictions and heartaches. You have to admire American song writers. They say it with robust style and substance—a country
roadmap, north and south, east and west, and a landscape high and low.
Listen to Johnny Cash's "Big River," the mighty and majestic Mississippi,
from St. Paul, Minnesota, down to Davenport, St. Louis, and Memphis,
then on to the city of New Orleans; Woody Guthrie's "This Land Is Your
Land," a vast and beautiful landscape, from the New York Harbor to the
Redwood Forest; and John Denver's "Rocky Mountain High," where the
eagles fly, and "Country Roads," a picaresque portrait of people and
places. All these hard-boiled words kindle emotions and provide us with
renewed faith in America.

But there is another America, consisting of broken lives and broken
hearts, poor people and dispossessed people who experience pain and
dislocation and "know their land in the dark." (You have to be pretty
down and out to know the land in the dark.) Listen to Bruce Springsteen's
"Youngstown" and "Darkness on the Edge of Town"; Billy Joel's "Allen-
town" and "Down Easter Alexa"; and Johnny Cash singing "How High
Is the River?," "Sunday Morning Coming Down," and "Country Boy."
Here we crisscross to another world: Dusty roads and small towns, row
houses and slums, job displacement and natural disaster, loneliness,
depression, and people down and out—on the edge—all the half-forgot-
ten people, living away from the eyes and ears of the media and middle-
class people, that no one seems to know or want to know.

Tomorrow will never right all the wrongs. Which person or politician
really cares? So long as these Depression-like families and their children
and youth remain withdrawn or lifeless, silent and invisible, away from
the highways and byways, on the other side of the tracks, who will speak
for and organize them? For every outspoken pop star like Bruce Springsteen or Bono, for every liberal educator like Jonathan Kozal and Ted
Sizer, or for every liberal news writer like Frank Rich of the *New York
Times* and Tom Ricks of the *Washington Post*, there are tens of thousands
of Americans who care more that there is bread on the table, a roof over
their head, and that their kids, if they have any, have the proper posture,
vocabulary, and table manners to possibly join one day the ranks of the
rich in Palm Beach, Aspen, or the Hamptons. Achievement is important
in America, and most people want others to know their achievements,

and the hell with the less fortunate. They weren't aggressive enough, or sufficiently smart or strong enough, to win the race. It's "their" fault, a modern echo of Social Darwinism and the Gilded Age, wrapped up now in one big scream: "Money, money, money. . . . It's a rich man's world," so say ABBA, the Swedish rock group of the 1970s.

Ted Turner and Warren Buffett, two of the wealthiest Americans, warn that the concentration of wealth and growing inequality is bound to weaken meritocracy and lower economic growth—and ultimately threaten our democracy. You cannot wipe out the middle class and expect democracy to flourish. But the conservative response, what I would refer to as doublethink and doubletalk, is that extreme wealth is good because people who work hard are being rewarded, which will encourage more people to work hard. Moreover, wealth generates investments which lead to jobs, and everyone benefits. Some people might refer to this as the "trickle-down" theory of economics, and conclude that it is "mighty fine," even good, for people to make lots of money, exploit the environment, and trounce the weak through shrewdness or strength, so long as jobs are provided for people who want to work. Some business people will even argue that it is good to keep a lid on wages to "starve inflation" or keep American companies competitive.

And so the pendulum swings back and forth—at the muse of others. Conservatives now claim the mantle of "victimhood" at college campuses and with the media—a swoop of speech that once belonged to liberals. Then, again, academic life on many campuses, along with printed words and media sound bites, often invokes a political war. We have a steady stream of ideologues and true believers, from the political Left to the Right. Edward Kennedy, Michael Moore, and Maureen Dowd duking it out with Newt Gingrich, Rush Limbaugh, and Ann Coulter. At the education level, there is William Bennett, Chester Finn, and Diane Ravitch on the right mincing words with liberals (and radicals) such as Henry Giroux, Alfie Kohn, and Peter McLarin.

Because educators lack celebrity, most readers will not be acquainted with the thoughts and ideas of the aforementioned educators. To my knowledge, there has never been an education superstar, an appealing and charismatic figure, that turned his or her life into a successful biography. There are no vivid portraits of educational statesmen and leaders smoking their pipes or sipping fine wine and telling people how schools work or making references to "education realities." Outside education circles, and among the general populace, there are no legends in education—no great men or women who speak with authority in the public arena. Perhaps for this reason education is near to last place in the news or television cycle, and last place in the number of best-selling books. No one seems to care, for example, that "in contrast to the peak of access when the top quartile of families, in terms of income, were six times more likely than the bottom group to send their children to college, the rate is [now] ten to one."[5] Part of the reason has to do with the federal government's reduction of scholarships and grants to poor and working-class college students, a loss of more than 50 percent of value (in terms of the consumer price index) between 1980 and 1996[6] and 75 percent between 1980 and 2004 due to shortfalls in human service spending and attempts to reduce budget deficits which are looming in the trillions.[7]

So long as people think they have a chance of getting to the top, hitting the jackpot, or getting a piece of the rock, they don't seem to care that the rich are getting richer and they are leaving the common people—now called the working and middle class—further behind. Hence, we have a new *struggling class* that in my view represents close to 80 or 90 percent of the American populace. There is a tick-tock resonating through American society, a countdown to social and economic disaster—certainly not a well-calibrated machine where the majority of the people have real choices and chances for success. You have to be very optimistic or naive not to hear the ticking of the clock. Of course, if you are from the Brahmin or patrician class, or far Right, you would rather wear ear plugs and not have to deal with the vulgar masses.

OUR WESTERN HERITAGE

The fact that the vast majority of Americans are struggling to make ends meet is something new for Americans but nothing new in the context of world history. Inequality has been part of our Western heritage, as far back as to the Greeks and Romans who devised a way of life with rights of citizenship (but they had more slaves than citizens), as well as differences in income and wealth, education, and opportunity to obtain goods and services (which go with the formation of society). To this extent, Ancient Greece and Rome were class-based societies, and on an abstract, philosophical level, Americans are both Greek and Roman or at least we have a long tradition in tracing our heritage to these ancients.

In a broader sense, all the major Western scientific and artistic achievement from Newton and Einstein to Darwin and Freud can be traced to the Greeks and Romans. Man can reshape and remake the world, not only by war or conquest (the Roman ideal), but by application of reason and the laws of nature (the Greek ideal). Freedom of thought and education are the key to human achievement, and the American ideals of free thought and universal education also have roots in ancient Greece. It is here, however, where the multitude managed to silence Socrates.

The Greeks

Conservative thinkers, from Aristotle to Alexander Hamilton to Leo Strauss, University of Chicago professor and "father philosopher" of the "neoconservatives" and "foreign policy hawks," have condemned "extreme democracy." Philosophers who tell the awful truth will meet the fate of Socrates. The sons of the wealthy or gentleman class invariably run the government, even in democratic countries, and can and usually do enact harsh laws, according to Strauss "to keep the multitude in line and make the world safe for philosophers."[8] Our Founding Fathers represented the manufacturing and plantation class; they were sensitive to class differences and the history of slavery, which characterized the ancient world, including Greek civilization. Ironically, both liberal and conservative philosophers in the Western world trace the ancestry of their ideas to the Greeks, including the idea of the liberal arts in education, reverence for philosopher-kings, and the need to discuss eternal truths and values.[9]

Part of the Greek liberal education included gymnastics, which consisted of functional activities useful for building physical strength and military training. The Greeks were notable athletes, paving the way for the Olympic Games. The games were held at various cities, the oldest and best known at Olympia. Great prizes and honors were bestowed to the winners of the games, and poems were written and statues were erected for favorite athletes. The games extended beyond the notion of competition and involved nationalistic and ethnic spirit among the cities, historical grudges, and were considered an offshoot of military warfare.[10]

For those who know their ancient history, gymnastics were an essential part of the classical curriculum, and adult physical fitness was considered a civic duty and part of military service. (Plato also included rules of diet and hygiene in his school curriculum.) It was at the gymnasium where the most promising youth were selected to be trained to represent their cities at the Greek Olympics. It was here where students first learned to wrestle, run, jump, discus and javelin throw, row, and horseback ride—activities which were originally viewed as part of self-preservation and subsequently—along with chariot races, became the core sports of the ancient Olympics.

With the exception of the chariot races, the athletes competed naked and women were barred from attendance.[11] Without the distinction of clothing or jewelry, every man was looked upon as equal in the arena of competition. Class and privilege did not define this part of Greek life, and those who worked with their hands and trained regularly returned home with privileges and honors. The public officials, philosopher-kings, and members of the privileged upper class were too soft to compete, and their role was relegated to organizing the games and providing the source of honors and prizes for the winners, such as jars of olive oil, bottles of wine, and bushels of wheat.

In the spirit of the modern Olympics, spectators came from a distance, pitched tents, and slept in nearby fields for several nights and attended the games in the days. Here was the chance for boys to act as boys, for men to retreat into the camaraderie of other men, and fathers to bond with sons as if they were on a fishing or camping trip. The games, before and after, were accompanied by food and festivals and occasioned by drinking and fighting in a way that characterizes modern-day European soccer fields. These kind of celebrations were no place for the prim and proper, upper-class boys or men who were used to caretakers and attendants. Today, the world is very different. Only the rich and famous, and comfortable class, can *afford* to attend the modern Olympics and pay the inflated hotel charges, food costs, and tickets.

Greek History and Philosophy

Of course, the Greeks love their philosophy and history, not only because there is so much of it, but also because it is so vivid, influential, and everlasting. Socrates and Aristotle walked the streets of Athens before the times of Jesus and Mohammed, before Caesar and Napoleon, and before Shakespeare and Cervantes. At least for Western civilization, it all started with the Greeks—our philosophy, values, and educational ideas— although a few European-born historians might say the ancient Hebrews form the basis of our political and religious thought and way of life.[12] Still, today, at the foot of the Acropolis and at Delphi (the center of the world, according to Greek mythology), you feel the ancient Greeks and their world passing by you. But it should be noted that Americans do not have an exclusive claim on the Greek influence. Most Western cultures see themselves in the Greek tradition, including the Germans under the rule of Hitler.[13]

Even now, classical historians and educators, both liberal and conservative, love to make comparisons between the ancient Greeks and our Western heritage.[14] To some extent, we are all Greeks—at least in terms of our culture and education. Americans, I believe, are more likely to agree with a dead Greek than the most sophisticated lawyers or social scientists of the modern world to bolster an argument or advocate a point of view. We think the ancient scholars from the Greek mountains and islands spoke with less spin (and more virtue) than modern politicians and policymakers. (This view is especially seen in the writings of traditional educators who advocate the classics and great books approach to education.)

I personally prefer to avoid comparisons between events in the ancient world and the dawn of the twenty-first century; much has transpired to cloud our judgment. Nevertheless, if we must engage in parallel stories between the prior and present world, our Western heritage comes in two or three flavors. While we are quick to compare ourselves with the ancient Greeks (and we have been doing so since colonial times), we are quick to forget about Sparta—and the warrior image of the Western world. We also love to compare American democracy with Athenian democracy and overlook their hubris and godly traditions.[15]

We compare American education to Greek education, to their cultivation of knowledge and rationality, and overlook their elitist traditions in education, which focused on philosopher-kings and distinguished between a liberal education and technical education, reflecting the same issues today about who should work with their minds and who should work with their hands. We overlook the fact that Greek (and Roman) society was built on the backs of slaves, and only a minority of Greeks (and Romans) had the rights and privileges of citizenship. We love to trace our philosophical thoughts to Aristotle and Plato, but we ignore the fact they both resisted democracy and believed it led to mob rule; in the final analysis, both men believed in a government run by a well-educated and property class—nothing more, if I may be honest, than an oligarchy and what later would be called the European nobility, and then what I call the American "superrich" or wealthiest 1 percent.

The Romans

Most important, we are also heirs of the Roman Republic. No one of liberal bent, including Thomas Jefferson and present-day politicians and policymakers, wants to identify with Romans and their well-oiled war machines, imperial ambitions, and fanatic Caesars, who were not much different than the czars of modern Europe. Only the "hawks" today want to be Romans with their "Pax Americana" belief in foreign policy and supposed ability to build democracies, somewhat opposite of the Cold War "domino" theory that suggested, if one country went Communist in a particular part of the world, another would follow.

Like it or not, contemporary America has deep roots in Roman civilization. John Adams and James Madison, the main architects of the U.S. Constitution, were more influenced by Rome and Cicero's opinion of three branches of government to check and balance excessive power than they were influenced by Athens and Plato's concepts of politics and the perfect society. We inhabit a republic, like Rome, not a direct democracy like Athens. While Jefferson envisioned American democracy and the American citizen in Athenian terms, most of his political contemporaries viewed him as radical and saw themselves more like Romans (as did the Federalists) or British monarchs (as did the Tories) in colonial America. Even the picture of George Washington crossing the Delaware, standing erect on his boat, can be viewed as evoking more Roman splendor than a Greek warrior.[16] And Anglo law, which we often cite as the basis of our laws, really stems from Roman law, when the British island was conquered by the Romans, which is the reason why so many of our statutes are phrased in Latin.

It would be nice to always envision America in the Greek mode—to be optimistic, humanitarian, and reflective, to be a champion of balance (Aristotle's golden mean), moral virtue, and democracy. No one of liberal persuasion, from Jefferson's period to the present, would want to trace American history, philosophy, or education to Rome, especially with the parallels between Rome and the Third Reich, the Caesars and the Fuhrer, and the war machine and imperial view of Rome and Nazi Germany still fresh among the democracies of the West.

Although our military policies at the dawn of the twenty-first century may not be in the shambles of the Roman Republic, we have overreached, and our allies are abandoning us. America is still a superpower and more powerful than Rome at the height of its empire. But like the Romans, our society is deeply divided. We have an ever deepening divide between haves and have nots. The idea that public education is the great equalizer is all but dead, given this ever increasing divide between the wealth of the nation. If we can stretch comparisons, the barbarian tribes sacked Rome somewhat like the terrorists attacked the United States nearly two thousand years later. The Republic became unglued and fell from within, similar to the way the U.S. social and economic fiber is slowly unraveling by the seams and becoming divided by cultural and class warfare.[17]

Like the Romans, the American rich dominate politics; they indulge in luxurious holidays and parties, sometimes costing $1 million or more (what 50 percent of Americans will not earn in a lifetime),[18] and feast on gourmet meals costing $1,000 per couple (equal to more than what 75 to 80 percent of the world's populace annually earns). As a nation, Americans annually consume 25 percent of the world's resources, although we represent four percent of the world's population. As with the Romans, our military involvement in other parts of the world is beginning to take its toll on the economy with huge budget deficits and cutbacks on human services. Although we are the nation that most of the world's population looks to for hope and inspiration, like Rome we are also the nation most feared and despised by the world. Even worse, our last president was originally appointed by five judges, despite the popular vote of millions of people—not much different than how the Caesars were appointed.

Class and Culture

Most writing, including history, is dominated by the "Great Man" theory. From the age of Socrates, Aristotle, and Plato, the great Greek philosophers, and Cicero and Cato, the great Roman orators, and Virgil, the Latin poet, the universal concepts of beauty, truth, and justice and the unchanging order of knowledge, values, and reality have all been dominated by upper-class snobbery and not by labor—by people who sit and think and get soft and not by people who rely on muscle power. Class counted in ancient times, like it counts today. Laborers were "generally held in bad repute," Xenophon wrote some twenty-three hundred years ago. "Their work keeps them too busy to be good companions or good citizens, so that men engaged in [labor] must ever appear to be both bad friends and poor defenders of their country." While we honor great men (and now women) in the arts and sciences, from da Vinci to Darwin, from Galileo to Gates, few of us appreciate the anonymous masses, the manual laborers, and the plain people whose work and knowledge as peasants, farmers, hunters, sailors, factory workers, miners, artisans, and technicians formed the bases for our knowledge of nature, tools, scientific discoveries, and the arts. It is the unknown faces and unknown names of people, the sum of human capital, that form the bases of history; their collective skills and knowledge are what operate the political and economic institutions needed for society to prosper and create the building blocks that followed. We forget these ordinary people and do not celebrate such faceless and nameless souls.

The same cultural snobbery is keenly expressed in the history of wine making. The Romans were the first to use wine as a social yardstick—and thus create a world of snobbery built around fine wines. Depending on their social and economic position in Roman society, people served various grades of wine, from third- and fourth-rate wine for manual laborers and slaves to first-rate wine for friends and relatives (for those who could afford it). Ancient records reveal that the Italian region of Campania was considered to be the home of the best wines, and 121 B.C. was decreed the best vintage year. The emperors and senators of Rome used wine for medicinal use; the finer the wine, the greater the curative properties.[19] Lower ranks could not afford good wine nor good medical care. Ah, certain things just don't change, despite the ticking of time.

The notion of class was paramount in the pride and terror of the gladiator's world, for only those accustomed to a hard life with muscle, speed, and agility could expect to survive in the arena. Manual laborers, slaves, prisoners of war, and soldiers lured by the prospect of prize money made up the names of those who fought to the death, while well-born Romans flocked to the arena to witness Rome's most popular "sport." The upper class sat on marble benches in the front and the lower classes sat on wooden benches in the rear, watching and cheering more than one hundred thousand humans perished in the arena over four hundred years. This was the Roman form of television, to amuse the masses, only the violence and blood were real.

According to one historian, those gladiators that demonstrated strength, courage, and a winning record in combat were considered celebrities. If they lasted long enough, that is into their forties and fifties, some were given their freedom and often found work as bodyguards for noblemen. In general, the gladiators lived a harsh life, doomed to death, and like modern boxers were exploited by coaches and managers as the "sport" became professionalized with rules, schedules, and training centers.[20]

The gladiator life was brief and brutal. As the lower ranks on the Roman totem pole, they were easily discarded and considered more dispensable than slaves, the lowest of the low, while citizens with soft hands and soft midsections sat on the sidelines, some on cushions, and were entertained. The same land that gave us Cicero and Virgil, and forged the foundation of the laws of our land, forced humans to square off against wild animals. But, then, Americans are not 100 percent innocent. We glorify the gladiator in movies like *Spartacus, Ben-Hur,* and *Gladiator* with rugged and virile male actors; today, we recruit and train our own gladiators from the lower ranks; we pay them large sums of money and consider them to be heroes as we watch them crush their opponents in various forms of combat on playing fields in large coliseums and stadiums across the country.

How different the Romans were from the Scots and Swedes, whose ancestral lineage is linked to warrior Celts and Vikings, with conquests that rivaled the Romans and exploration that far exceeded imperial Rome. It is in Scotland where there is more nobility, family crests, and castles per square mile than anywhere in Europe. To be Scottish or Swedish means to abhor wastefulness and to find a use for almost everything, a determination to save and preserve, meaning that nothing should be discarded and no one is dispensable. Perhaps it is because the landscape is so cold and brutal, and thus so few countrymen remain and so many leave, that the Scots and Swedes are so rational—concerned about life, preaching austerity and discretion, rather than death and destruction. I emphasize the Scots because their number-one export is brain power, not muscle power, and so many of our Founding Fathers had Scottish blood in them—not Greek, not Roman, blood. I also mention the Swedes because of their social-welfare philosophy, with the hope that present-day political leaders might remember the ABCs of a community of people looking out and providing for one another. Roman gladiator combat was riveting, but it promoted Social Darwinism and the survival of the fittest, the opposite of the social-welfare state.

AMERICA: THE NEW ATHENS, THE NEW ROME

We play the fool in thinking we are only the heirs of Athens. We are also Romans. Like them, we are engaging in conspicuous consumption and military overreach, and we have lost our sense of self-restraint and sense of fairness. I am not alone in my belief that we are witnessing the slow decline of America and evaporation of the American dream—where education and excellence play less and less of a factor in the achievement and reward systems. Sadly, the heredity, privilege, and nobility of the Old World have come back to haunt the New World in revised fashion and form, maybe more extreme than the Old World. Like some two thousand years ago, there is the hint that we are setting in motion the replacement of Greek democracy and freedom with Roman autocracy and nepotism.[21]

We sometimes forget that the Greeks and Romans built a society based around individual and family comfort for its citizens, along with the expectations for security and duty to the nation-state, and for striving and self-improvement. But their societies were flawed: Citizenship was limited to 20 to 25 percent of the populace, and differences in citizenship and noncitizenship, income and wealth, led to a resignation to inequality, a major gap between the patrician class and plebeian class (what eighteenth-and nineteenth-century America often called the *common people,* what twentieth- and twenty-first-century America often called the *working* and *middle class*). Only in an egalitarian society, where the people share political rights as full citizens, what our Founding Fathers referred to as the "natural rights" of man, can stratified societies and class warfare be reduced, can the interests of the public common good become a reality, and can there be a closing gap between peoples' aspirations and expectations.

Only when enough citizens have a political voice can they share sufficient interests so that their basic social needs are considered public ones. Only in a truly democratic society will individual achievement count, some sorting-out process where people can go as far as their abilities and ambitions take them. The Greeks and Romans were relatively more enlightened, advanced, and democratic than other societies of their period, but they were still highly stratified. They certainly did not make the most of bright children and youth who began life in lower-class surroundings. The amount of education and opportunity received by a child depended upon his parents' status in society, which in turn was based on citizenship and property ownership. (Women's formal education was limited in Athens. Rome had education opportunities for upper-class women, but they were educated at home, not in schools, like their upper-class male counterparts.)

The Greek philosophers and Roman senators, in short, the leadership of ancient Greece and Rome, did not trust the multitude. However, in 1776 America declared to the world that "all men are created equal," and it was reaffirmed by Lincoln's Gettysburg address and the Civil War. I don't think it takes a genius to understand that not until 1954, when *Brown v. Board of Education* achieved its place in history, and not until 1964, with the passage of the Civil Rights Act, could people think about the possibility that all of us should be judged by the "content of their character," and not by their race or skin color. Can Americans be true to their ideals? Can whites criticize or condemn their own history? If the answer is no, and I suspect it is for many Americans, then "black Americans must do it,"[22] or at least they should have this option for their own mental health and economic well-being.

So the question is: Have the vestiges of stratification and inequality been eliminated? What counts more: Capability or legacy? Performance or nepotism? Achievement or "old family" connections? You can chew on these questions all you want, but the answers are clear to me. Is the age of meritocracy coming to a halt? Can education continue to enhance social mobility? Assuming most of us can use a little chuckle or entertainment every so often, Stanley and Danko, in their recent book *The Millionaire Next Door*, maintain that a net worth of $1 million would put you in the top 7 percent of American households. But you should not assume that it will make you deliriously happy or give you sufficient security to quit your boring job. Ironically, the authors found that thrift, inheritances, and social class had stronger correlations with money than did intelligence or education.[23]

During the Gilded Age of the 1880s and 1890s, when the Astors, Carnegies, Morgans, and Rockefellers reigned supreme over society, the people of old money who really counted were the so-called Four Hundred; not more than one or two of this ballroom and celebrity club were college graduates. Today the American superrich counts nearly four hundred billionaires, with little more than half having a four-year college education. More sophisticated statistical analysis by University of California, Santa Barbara, professor Otis Duncan and Harvard's Christopher Jencks suggests that schooling represents about 10 to 17 percent of the variance related to income, not an impressive amount for two-thirds of college graduates to assume large debt, in some cases amounting to $50,000 or $100,000 plus interest.[24] This piece of information contradicts our traditional notion of education and social mobility.

The Fall of Rome

Edward Gibbon's work, *The History of the Decline and Fall of the Roman Empire*, remains a classic for its monastic writing style, depth of information and insights, and the dead-on authenticity to the dialogue and the atmospherics of the twelve hundred-year period. In what was originally published as six volumes, Gibbon's *History* was condensed to one volume in 1960 in order to reach a wider audience. Originally published between 1776 and 1788, it took more than one hundred and fifty years to be appreciated as the most important book about Rome, serving as a bridge from the ancient world to modern: "A narrative which began when Rome was revered and the reign of Hadrian and Antoninius Pius offered the prospect of universal peace," to the fall of Rome and the "triumph of barbarism and of religion."[25]

There was a period in which the Roman empire was "governed under the guidance of virtue and wisdom. The armies were restrained by the firm and gentle hand of [four successive] emperors . . . who delighted in the image of liberty, and were pleased with considering themselves as accountable ministers of the laws of the caesars," wrote Gibbon. But absolute power leads to arrogance and avarice, to folly and failed virtues. The "restraints of the senate and laws . . . could never correct the vices of the emperor, and the corruption of Roman manners would always supply flatterers eager to applaud, and ministers prepared to serve, the fear or avarice, the lust or cruelty of their masters."[26] A series of all-powerful emperors, with no checks and balances of any substance, proceeded to abolish Roman liberties and laws and plunged the empire into a series of unnecessary and costly wars. Rome was exhausted; and, by the end of the sixth century, the barbarians were at the gates and sacked the city. A once prosperous and potent Rome, the seat of the empire and the center of the civilized world, was reduced to a second-rate power and subsequently during the next five hundred years became a third-rate power propped up by the increased strength of the Catholic Church.

Gibbon's description of the rise and fall of Rome is a classic story, and it is natural to make comparisons between Rome and that of modern history: the fall of the British Empire and the Soviet Union in the twentieth century, and all the other great empires of Europe since Charlemagne's Holy Roman Empire, Portugal, Spain, the Netherlands, and France during the sixteenth and seventeenth centuries; the Napoleonic Empire and Austria-Hungarian Empire; and the other empires including the Egyptian, Persian, Mongolian, Turkish, Aztec, and Mayan empires in an earlier age. Following Gibbon's work, we now have Arnold Toynbee, the English historian, and Oswald Spengler, the German historian, claiming the rise and fall of all civilizations; they either wither away, crumble from within due to false values and virtues, or self-destruct because of overreach.[27]

Constancy and change are tides that guide us, that set the moment against what might have been and what endures or dies. If we are reflective, they cause us to think and rethink what kind of people we are, what might have been, and what ought to be. If we are blind, or submit to over-zealous ideology, then we become easy prey to the forces of change and enemies that challenge our way of life.

Americans are an optimistic people and believe in reason, morality, and the rights of people as guiding principles, rooted in the Enlightenment and the ideas of John Locke and Jean-Jacques Rousseau and the belief in the perfectibility of society through its government and institutions. This is all well and good, but it can lead to flights of fancy in which we think everyone around the world wants to or expects to live in this state of being. It takes a certain amount of gusto to create a diplomacy of big ideas and fanciful language, but it is folly to assume that all nations and people want democracy, that America is the only agent to these abstract principles, or that we have the moral right or duty to export our principles to other lands. Thanks to our own hubris, unilateralism, and delusional march to war, very much like the Greeks and Romans at the height of their power, the concept of "Americanization" has come to mean little that is good. The word "globalization" has become synonymous. Sadly, our own government policies and propaganda have come to represent the dark side of globalization.

While America has been considered the foundation of hope to the rest of the world, it is questionable if it has the right to spread its values around the globe, and it is also questionable if it has always lived up to its preferred values. Few inhabitants of the global village accept the right of Americans to intervene or to reconfigure the world order (Charlemagne, Napoleon, and Hitler all tried unsuccessfully), but it enjoys enthusiastic support among conservatives and evangelist followers. The idea is rooted in the same vision and ambitions of Woodrow Wilson, like Bush, another presidential evangelist, both of whom, if I may add, considered fools by their European counterparts. In fact, both Wilson and Bush believed they could talk to Jesus and were agents of Christian principles. After Caesar, many of the Roman emperors also thought they had the blessing of the church, but it did not help arrest Rome's decline.

What are the limits of American power? At what point does the rickety architecture of civilization begin to collapse? Is it when the leaders speak to God? Is it when they divide the world into those for or against the American way? Or is it simply when the people have as president some rich and well-connected kid who cannot finish a formal sentence without stuttering, unless the words are scripted? The reader can make his or her own pithy judgment, and without my sarcasm. In this connection, Robert Merry, the president of the *Congressional Quarterly*, maintains that our optimism and view of the world can lead to delusion and decline. He further asserts that civilizations rise and fall in cycles, and there will always be multiple power centers and civilizations that will clash. In *Sounds of Empire*, Merry argues a "hawkish" or neoconservative view that wars are inevitable in a world where cultures and ideals clash.

The war on terrorism is related to an intractable conflict between religious ideals of the Western and Islamic worlds. The Cold War conflict with the Soviets cannot be compared to the clash between Western Christianity and the Islamic world, because religious differences lead to a deeper clash than did political differences with communism. Americans should not be deluded into thinking their civilization is omnipotent. Although our civilization is rooted in democratic principles, the Islamic world combines religion and politics and therefore will take on a more zealous clash than communism ever did. Merry warns that much of America's intervention in world politics is based on a combination of humanitarian and economic interests, but it also rests on hubris and arrogance, which can be fatal. In a world where there will always be civilizational strife, his view reminds us of an old Hobbesian world, where the strong take advantage of the weak, and, if I may add, a contemporary world of Darth Vader, where the dark forces become part of the landscape.

THE FUTURE OF PAX AMERICANA

Today we have a host of liberal commentators, as well as a number of ex-generals such as Wesley Clark, Colin Powell, and Anthony Zinni, making comparisons with Rome, finding themselves embedded in Pax Americana, living as strangers in a country that was once called the new Eden, the new Athens, the nation on the Hill, a land of hope where dreams come true. Rome lasted more than one thousand years. America is less than two hundred and fifty years old and presently characterized by military overreach, diplomatic arrogance, cultural strife, circumvented liberties and laws, global trade problems, and economic depletion. Military involvement in far-off, inhospitable lands, coupled with the neoconservative view that the United States should impose its will on the market economy and belligerent nations while it can spread capitalism and defend democracy, has created an enormous drain on American resources. By 2005 the war in Iraq and Afghanistan was costing American taxpayers $100 billion a year or about $273 million a day; it is estimated to cost another $1.3 trillion (or $11,300 per household) over the next five years, plus $7 billion a year for the next forty-five years for military disability and health payments (which will need to be financed by adding to the federal debt).[28]

The neoconservative argument is that America (like Rome) must use its unprecedented power to make the world a better place, along with the bold assertion that America is more powerful than Rome was at its height of power. It cannot sit idle, engage in appeasement or isolation, or watch history take its course. Economic and military strength go hand-in-hand, we are now told by "hawkish" policy thinkers, and the nation's military must be mobilized to defend and spread the so-called gospel—democracy and capitalism.[29] This is not much different than Rome mobilizing the armies to spread its way of life and increase its power.

The Cold War adhered to a simple paradigm: Contain communism, led by the Kremlin, and defend free societies, led by the United States. But for all of Bush's attempts to frame the current conflict with Islamic terrorism as one of equal epochal proportions, it is clear that the world has resisted such a single, overarching policy, and it tends to isolate us as a nation, as Rome became isolated from its allies. In defense of its borders and interests, the United States has escalated the wars it has begun. In defense of the Bush administration, the United States had to whack someone after 9/11. Afghanistan was too small, so Iraq was chosen because of its size and oil and because "hawkish" policymakers thought they were flirting with destiny. Conservatives warn us that the world's memory is short. Twice we have had to go to war to save democracy; some free-wheeling libertarians and free-market enthusiasts might even quote one of George Orwell's ditties: "People sleep peaceful in their beds at night only because rough men stand ready to do violence on their behalf."

President George Bush, with his air force fatigues and no-nonsense talks with troops on naval ship decks and at graduation commencements at West Point and the Naval Academy, gives this impression as the price of war and the price to defend democracy—an obsession the world doesn't share and even mocks. In the meantime, conservatives have trouble understanding why other nations distrust the United States and are unwilling to support our "Big Stick," intervention policies. The only explanation must be they are morally weak, ill formed, all led by dumb or weak leaders who cannot recall history.[30]

As a nation, we are more than just trying to shape the world and spread our ideology. With the collapse of the Soviet bloc, our Cold War mentality has shifted to Pax Americana—a new global policy with an "imperial" president who has sent American troops into battle halfway around the world, absent an active invasion or threat and without formally declaring war. Stripped of partisan politics, this is what I call a Roman military decision, or what one commentator refers to as the "Rise of the Vulcans"—policy advocated by neoconservatives steeped in Straussian politics.[31] In doing so, we have been abandoned by most of our allies, and we have created self-inflicted, massive debt, which has impacted negatively on social, health, and education spending at the expense of our lower-, working-, and middle-class populace who depend on social programs and social safety nets. The new foreign policy highlights the nation's growing inequality among its people. Wars are usually fought by lower-class and working-class youth, and paid by taxes that disproportionately fall on the working and middle class.

Fareed Zakaria, an American Muslim and editor of *Newsweek International*, discusses the fate of democracies in *The Future of Freedom*. He points out that there is a direct correlation between economic growth, the rise of the working and middle class, and democracy—the greater the per capita income, the stronger the democracy. The problem is we are being economically drained, due to military overreach, and experiencing increasing trade deficits, globalization, and an aging society that needs more social services for a quality life. Real income for the bottom 50 percent of the populace over the last twenty-five years has remained relatively flat, and the bottom 20 percent has experienced a slight decline, which could be argued (using Zakaria's logic) is threatening the democratic system.

Zakaria further argues that taxation of the rich is essential for democracy to flourish, to provide necessary services as *a reciprocal bargain* between government and the people, to prove representation. (This is what Rousseau would refer to as part of the *social contract* between government and the people.) But taxation today falls on the shoulders of the nonrich, more precisely on labor and not on assets, wealth, or investments, which is taxed at a much lower rate than salaries. In addition, Americans no longer trust their government. Voter turnout is consistently at around 50 percent (plus or minus 10 percent), and Americans feel big government and big business are tied together by new elites (Ivy League college graduates), new money, and a host of lobbyists and special interest groups who have their own agendas and self-interests at heart—at the expense of the people.

OLD HISTORY LESSONS

Gary Hart, one of the liberal ghosts of the Democratic Party (a presidential candidate in the 1980s), headed a commission on national security in the 1990s. Known as the Hart-Rudman Commission and ignored by the Bush administration, many of the recommendations were later published by Hart as the *Fourth Power*, referring to American principles of morality and democracy. In the book, former Senator Hart warns against a crusading foreign policy of preemption and the spread of democracy at the point of a gun.[32]

Recalling the overreach and subsequent decline of Rome, Hart argues that the first casualty will be America's own national interests, as more people see us as the "big bully" in the image of imperial Rome and we become isolated from the rest of the world. He warns that there is "a vast difference between advocating that America live up to its own principles and advocating, as the Bush administration [did], that the rest of the world live up to America's principles." That kind of hubris, under the guise of spreading democracy or making the world safe for American interests is interpreted, I would say, by many nations as nothing more than old-fashioned militarism, imperialism, and colonialism and by the Muslim community as another Western invasion or means for spreading the Christian Gospel harkening back to the Crusades. This is exactly what Osama bin Laden drums home to his followers as part of his "defensive jihad" and his justification for targeting civilians.

If the Roman connection or Crusades seems out of place, illogical, or a stretch of historical circumstances, then there is always the Greek connection to ponder. Victor Hanson, an American historian, sees the United States as sharing the Athenian hubris and inviting disaster like the Greeks by trying to export democracy to other parts of the world including Afghanistan, Iraq,[33] and Palestine. The point is, third-world countries do not need Western guidance or missionary advice on how to live or implement democracy, not when it conflicts with local customs and traditions.

The Peloponnesian War between Athens and Sparta and its allies lasted twenty-seven years, from 431 B.C. to 404 B.C., and drained Athens of its power and wealth (a little like Iraq is draining America after just a few years). At the beginning of the war, Athens was the richest city of the world, the most cultured and most democratic. It had everything going for it, as the sole superpower of the ancient world with the most powerful navy. The war was fought because Sparta, a military oligarchy, felt pushed by Athens, in its attempt to export its democracy and cultural values.

Thucydides, the great Greek historian of the era, warned that the war would cost Athens dearly and have long-term, detrimental effects on its citizens and society. Socrates also had doubts about the wisdom of the war. Ironically, as citizens of Athens, both were dragged into the war in command posts. The war resulted in the death of its political and military statesmen, as they either were killed in battle or by disease, which swept through Athens. But Athens regrouped and regained her prestige, partly because there were no other super military and cultural powers during that period, and Aristotle and Plato lived through a revival of its power and glory.

History has many lessons to provide, so long as we don't push the comparisons to the absurd or paint them as ironclad. Of course, the longer we stretch timelines, the more likelihood there is noise in the statistics, fault lines in the analysis, and the thinner the implications for the present. Then there is A. J. P. Taylor, the preeminent British historian of the twentieth century, who warns: "The only lesson of history is there are no lessons of history."

Although Hanson does not believe that the Peloponnesian War can be used today as an argument against encouraging the spread of democracy, there is still much with which to compare Athens and the United States, in terms of democratic ideals, military power, cultural and technological accomplishments, and desire to export institutions and way of life to other parts of the world. When it comes to comparisons, ironically, the Americans are the ones that stretch the timelines and force the remote past as guidance to the present. Since Cotton Mather compared Boston and Athens, as great cities on the hill, and Thomas Paine, one hundred years later, wrote "what Athens was in miniature, America will be in magnitude," we have noted where we came from.

Athens—minus its many slaves—was a democracy and superpower that took on more than it could achieve—and failed. Nonetheless, when it comes to power, war, and the spread of American political and economic systems, we more often look to Rome, not Athens. It is the Roman empire where we have what may be called the Western world's foremost example of imperialism and globalization, and the clash between civilizations—both Western and non-Western. It is at this point in history, where overreach and the reasons for war come into play, where there are real historical lessons to learn, despite Taylor's dictum, which was geared to a British audience so it could understand the rise and fall of their own world empire.

Given its lasting fling as a superpower under the reign of Queen Victoria, which ended at the turn of the twentieth century, the British have been reduced to America's trans-Atlantic "cousin" and "ally" or, in the words of Europhile critics, "America's poodle" with Tony Blair as "Bush's appointee."[34] One can remember a better day, when Britain had considerable political and military power and was the most imperialistic nation on the face of the map; its influence reached to the four corners of the world. Despite all this glory, one can also remember when the British were nothing more than an outpost of the Roman Empire, in the way many Europeans today view the British and Americans. Time has a way of changing the political and economic landscape, creating new allies and enemies, and formulating new ideologies and new swaths of public opinion, which in a democracy suggests new leadership and heads of government.

The Bush and Blair approach to globalization is coming to an end, and hopefully there will be new efforts to reduce the clash of civilizations and the notion that the U.S. hegemony is desirable and sustainable for infinity or that it has the unlimited power to remake and reengineer other nations alien to its principles or way of life—an idea full of folly that the Greeks and Romans took hundreds of years to learn. But we don't have hundreds of years, much less scores of years, to learn that lesson lest we be financially and militarily drained and reduced to the same decline that has swept across other great empires, even before the Greeks and Romans, as the Hebrews, Phoenicians, Egyptians, Persians, and others sought to extend their culture, religion, and/or borders to "lesser" civilizations and "barren" parts of the world.

From the days of Solomon to Aristotle and Plato to Gandhi and Martin Luther King, Pope Benedict XVI and the Dalai Lama, over the course of seven millenniums and right down to the present, the "best and brightest" humanitarians have cautioned people that war analogies cannot be extended or defended where imperialism, colonialism, and other forms of materialism and greed enter into the picture. Though the judgment of the masses may be fickle and easy to sway, those who lead us in secular or religious affairs should have a high regard for peace and the important contribution of knowledge and the arts, not blood and iron.

The lessons of history repeatedly provide evidence that imperial powers and empires that wage war, regardless of the reasons—principles or plunder; racial, ethnic, or religious—eventually exhaust themselves and fall. But if those like Bush lead us into war have no clue to understanding foreign policy, as suggested by Bob Woodward's latest book, *State of Denial*, then the people who follow are in deep trouble. In the book, Bush is portrayed as a once proud and resolute leader in the early days of his presidency, but Woodward later saw him, as did others in the administration, as passive, unsure, in denial[35]—and a symbol of American retreat and scorn around the world. Tom Ricks's book, *Fiasco*, paints a similar, sad story—how dysfunctional the Bush administration was, both as individuals and as a group, in guiding American foreign policy and in implementing their bold ideas and pronouncements.[36]

Whereas Bush preferred to see himself as a second Gipper, in a noble bid to transform the Middle East, his critics saw him as one of the most ignorant presidents and a threat to world stability (fueling, not stifling, fundamentalist Islam). In classic terms, Bush often made reference to Winston Churchill, another one of his heroes, envisioning himself as defending the West against the forces of evil. I would liken him to Don Quixote, possessed by moral and religious righteousness, fighting windmills (the wrong fight and wrong place) and refusing to seek alliances and confronting the reality of the Iraq insurgency. Thus he would stand in front of the red, white, and blue and announce "Mission Accomplished," "Things Are Improving," and "Stay the Course."

The outcome is that Bush refused to listen to critics and retreated to his inner circle of neoconservatives who engineered the war in their so-called attempt to bring democracy to the Middle East. After the 2006 election, he was forced to listen to more pragmatic voices (his father's men), consider bipartisan policies in the wake of Democratic victories (the same people he branded in previous years as "squirrels," "unpatriotic," and "cut-and-run politicians"), and even unofficially open a dialogue and secretly negotiate with countries like Iran, Syria, and North Korea, which he had labeled as terrorist nations or part of the "Axis of Evil."

Sadly, the Bush era may likely signal the decline of the West, particularly the United States, once proud and forceful, now stumbling and disenchanted—foiled in its attempt to spread democracy in the Middle East and unable to grasp the rise of China as its next economic and military threat. Returning to Woodward, he points out that back in the good old days when Bush was thinking of running for president, Bush admitted he had no ideas about foreign policy, much less knew who were the major players of the undeveloped and developing countries. Now I ask how can the American people be expected to understand the world they inhabit if the presidential candidates cannot figure it out?

Are we doomed because of mass global ignorance? George Orwell, the author of *1984*, should probably say yes—and so would many of our western European friends who Rumsfeld dubbed as "Old Europe"—or as outdated and irrelevant. In short, the oceans no longer protect us. So can we last one thousand years as Rome did? Will the lessons of history or the dark forces prevail? Like all great civilizations that have experienced peaks and declines before us, is the United States destined to become a second- or third-rate power, as terrorism produces the twenty-first century horrors and China and India loom in the distant horizon?

CURRENT HISTORY LESSONS

The Romans cherished their democracy, but economic exhaustion caused by foreign wars and domestic corruption (politically and economically) brought a mighty power to its knees. Americans are spending enormous amounts of money and going into debt for costly planes and missiles to fight their wars, while on the home front the nation is forced to "pinch pennies" on social, health, and education needs for American families. Tax policies favoring the wealthy have become "extreme and unrelenting" since the 1980s; now, with America's "imperial" policy, the nation is dismantling social programs that have allowed the elderly, poor, and working class to live with dignity. This bottom 50 percent of the nation's populace is living day to day, mostly in debt, and the middle class is at a point where, according to Paul Krugman, the Princeton economist, "all it takes is a bit of bad luck in employment or health to plunge a family that seems solidly middle class into poverty." It is further argued that, because of new tax policies that favor the rich, "class warfare" is at an all-time high, inequality is growing, and, coupled with growing business greed and fraud, we are marching backward to the "robber baron" era. Krugman maintains that "working class families aren't sharing in the economy's growth, and face economic insecurity"; even worse, there is reason to conclude that the middle class is disappearing.[37]

We have not yet approached Rome's economic slide, but the United States borrows $2.1 billion everyday to keep the economy afloat, and the average American household is carrying more than $9,000 in credit card debt. Today's so-called middle-class families, with two working spouses, are in worse shape financially—they save less and owe more—than a single-income middle-class family of thirty years ago.[38] The problem related to deficits and debt on a national and personal level is manifested in the lives of Americans everyday with the loss of jobs overseas, lower wages at home, college tuition debt and underemployment among college graduates, soaring health costs, and growing vulnerability from Chinese and Indian entrepreneurs. It is serious enough for economists to argue that America is going broke, with publication by economists of such recent books as Laurence Kollikoff and Scott Burns's *The Coming Generational Storm* (2004) and Peter Peterson's *Running on Empty* (2004).

As for comparison between the military might of Rome and America, we are approaching military overreach, isolation from our allies, and ill-feeling and even hatred from large segments of the globe that resent America's so-called imperial and colonial policies and corporate and capitalist interests. In defense of Pax Americana, the global village has changed. American security is threatened by the decline of international organizations with the ability to maintain peace, the proliferation of weapons of mass destruction, and anti-American terrorism. Still others would say we are forced into the role of an international policeman. But there is a difference between regional interests and alliances or American hegemony and an American Empire. The distinction is important for Americans who have to fight and pay for wars and for the world, which would prefer a more balanced power structure that includes nations with a regional stake in the world.

What we need to do is to reverse two trends, without getting into partisan politics and ideological chasms. First, we need to do something about Pax Americana—eliminate the notion of preemptive military strikes and be less deceptive about the reasons for war. Of course, presidents have lied in the past about matters of war and peace, since the days of Roosevelt's lend-lease policy with Britain and at Yalta with Russia,[39] which Americans were told were undertaken for the public good. But the politics of war discriminate against the poor and working class who fight the nation's wars, and against blue-collar and white-collar workers alike, as spending on human services also diminish. Indeed, the lessons of ancient

Greece and Rome clearly show that superpowers engaged in long wars and multiple police actions economically exhaust themselves.

Second, we need to do something about the politics of greed, which cater to the rich and create inequality. The Greeks and Roman taught us, at the height of their civilizations, that a middle-class society is the most productive society and more likely to function as a democracy. If the middle class severely shrinks in size or influence, then the life blood of the nation-state is at stake and the government will likely become an oligarchy. Before we lose our middle class, we need to elect politicians who will not cater to business lobbyists (some thirty-four thousand strong) who have their own selfish agenda, nor to big business and the wealthy interests that work against the interests of most Americans. Despite the likes of free-marketers such as Bruce Bartlett and David Frum, an unregulated market does not serve the interests of the general public. At best, it leads to tax reductions and huge profits for corporate America. More often, it leads to corporate malfeasance and fraud at the expense of employees, stockholders, and the general public.

The old alliance of old money and new dollars has taken on new meaning. The free market system, advocated by conservative economists (from classic John Maynard Keynes to Milton Friedman's theories of capitalism and productivity growth), has replaced liberal notions of the need for social programs and safety nets for Americans in the areas of health, education, employment, and Social Security (rooted in the politics and morality of Locke and Rousseau, and highlighted by the Roosevelt and Johnson administrations). These programs reflect basic benchmarks most Americans accept as necessary for increasing equality and a decent life for the common people, yet they are being eroded by a free-market system based on money, money, money. The rich and superrich disproportionately suck up most of the wealth and gains in economic productivity, at the expense of the masses who need to work harder and longer to keep afloat. Gone are the days when dad was the sole breadwinner and mom could afford to stay home and take care of the children.

As the race widens and one becomes more advantaged than the other runners, the differentiation increases between the potentially successful and unsuccessful. It not only widens in the education arena (commonly called the intellectual deficit), culminating in skewed access to who goes to college and which college, but also in other social and economic areas such as in inequality of earnings and assets, as well as health-care treatment. The different starting points in the race, at the early stages of life, affect how we think, how we dress, how we speak, who we meet socially and marry, who we make contacts with, and who we need to know to get a free walk to first base when we come up to bat or when we need a helping hand.

The bottom line is that education does not have the same effect on social mobility because of growing inequality between the rich (top 10 percent), the superrich (top 1 percent), and the vast majority of the populace who are forced to scramble and struggle for less and less of the nation's wealth and gross domestic product. And critics who reject the view that the influence of education is dwindling, or that inequality is growing, may actually be more Roman than Greek in their thinking, more patrician than plebian in their views of culture and class, more conservative than liberal, more prone to accumulate wealth at the expense of those who get up early in the morning and go to work every day.

In the end, it all comes down to denial, a refusal to face facts, and whether the average American continues to believe in the virtues of American militarism and unrestrained capitalism or whether the "mass line" will rethink the policies of Pax Americana and free-market economies—and vote blue. In terms of history, it comes down to whether you are more Greek or Roman, whether you seek the golden mean—some political center and economic restraint—or wish you had a box seat at the Coliseum to witness the savage battle and blood of humans and animals. Sit back and breathe the free air! The American voter has the power to change the course of history and effect political and economic change at the home front. And, remember, we are all Americans; we are all in the same boat.

NOTES

1. In Europe, after World War I, Social Democratic parties were formed in Germany, Austria, Czechoslovakia, and the Scandinavian countries. They supported a moderate, democratic approach to government and a social-welfare state in which social, education, and health-care services were provided for the people.

2. In American terms, a Social Democrat is an outgrowth of our nineteenth-century populism and twentieth-century muckraker legacy, both movements which sought to curb the excess and corruption of the Gilded Age, the politics of party bosses who sought more money and more power, and the rich who thought they were plain *better* than the masses. Franklin Roosevelt's New Deal legislation was in part based on American populism and European Social Democratic ideals.

3. Here I am thinking of Adolf Eichmann, although it is premature to try to analyze him in one sentence. Eichmann had disdain toward Jews from early childhood; he was a joiner, follower, and low-level bureaucrat caught up in his career opportunities, who allowed his prejudices and hate to diminish any sense of morality and humanism he might have had. In Victor Hugo's *Les Misérables*, Inspector Javert is nothing more than a conformist and low-level bureaucrat following orders, as were the guillotine executioners in Merry Old England (and France), and as were the guards who employed the whip and boot on the backs of the slaves of ancient Egypt, Greece, and Rome. They were ordinary people, corrupted by the moment in history and their need to survive.

4. Jamaica Kincaid, *Mr. Potter* (New York: Farrar, Straus & Giroux, 2002).

5. Gary Orfield, "Policy and Equity," in *Unequal Schools, Unequal Chances*, ed. F. Remiers (Cambridge, MA: Harvard University Press, 2000), 412.

6. Orfield, "Policy and Equity," 412.

7. Edmund L. Andrews, "Fearing That a Gap Will Become a Chasm," *New York Times*, March 2, 2004; William C. Symonds, "Leaving Harvard Greener," *Business Week*, January 24, 2005, 44.

8. David Luban, "Lessons from the Glory of Greece," *New York Times*, May 11, 2003.

9. For example, the liberal view in education, which can be traced to the Greeks, is exemplified by Ernest Boyer, John Gardner, and Ted Sizer. The conservative view in education, which can also be traced to the Greeks, is exemplified by Mortimer Adler, Allan Bloom, and Robert Hutchins.

10. Nigel Spivey, *The Ancient Olympics* (New York: Oxford University Press, 2004).

11. Stephen G. Miller, *Ancient Greek Athletes* (New Haven, CT: Yale University Press, 2004).

12. Hans Kohn, *The Idea of Nationalism* (New York: Macmillan, 1961); Simon Schama, *The Embarrassment of Riches* (New York: Random House, 1987).

13. In the play *Hannah and Martin*, Arendt, the Jewish political scholar who is best known for her analysis of totalitarianism as evil, has an expanded dialogue with Heidegger, her former professor and lover. Heidegger, the German existentialist philosopher and Nazi sympathizer, says: "All great ages seek bridges to the heroic past." Hitler sought to "burn away the weak and corrupted and inconsequential thinking that history is littered." It boils "down to a thin, splendid thread from them to us, from what is Greek to what is German." (What Heidegger is trying to do is to legitimatize Nazism by linking Greek history to German society.)

Arendt responds: "When you say the Greek tradition is the destiny of Germany, you say the rest of us are worth nothing. We interfere and pollute! Why not gas us and be done with it?" (What Arendt is saying is that the Greek-German comparision distorts and trivializes Western civilization. By co-opting the Greek tradition, Germany is mocking Western values and trying to condone mass killings.)

14. This includes liberals such as Jacques Barzun, John Gardner, and Paul Goodman and conservatives such as Mortimer Adler, Allan Bloom, and E. D. Hirsch. The fact is Mortimer Adler's *The Paideia Program* (1983) is based on the Greek word *pals*, meaning "the upbringing of a child." Like Hutchins he was highly influenced by Aristotle—the belief that people are rational and that reason is the human's greatest power.

15. In Homer's *Odyssey*, Odysseus slays Cyclops, the son of Zeus, and boasts and exhibits hubris. The outcome is that Zeus casts him to the seas, to roam for twenty years. Tragedy slowly falls upon his crew, and Penelope, his wife, knits and waits for his return. Sometimes when I daydream about the flesh and blood of humanity, and think about what the ancient Greeks knew, I feel that American foreign policy has a hint of arrogance and Zeus is still passing judgment on us mortals.

16. Laura Miller, "My Favorite War," *New York Times Book Review*, March 21, 2004. See David H. Fischer, *Washington Crossing* (New York: Oxford University

Press, 2004). On the front cover of the book, the spirit of the events is evidenced by Washington's posture and clothing—looking like Caesar or Napoleon.

17. Since the Gore-Bush election in 2000, American politics has hardened, it appears, into two uncompromising camps: a 50-50 split and a clash in values, based on demographics, taxes, gay rights and abortion, geopolitics and patriotism, and spirituality. We are a nation divided, South and North, red and blue, rich and poor. For many, the 2004 election was seen as a rant of uncompromising extremes in which the working- and middle-class population were economically bewildered (while conservative "experts" claimed the economy was on the upswing) and felt they were being squeezed off the map—a concern that Greek advocates or "moderates" would voice—and the number-one concern for Americans was foreign policy and the war with terrorism, what Romans or "hawks" would contemplate.

18. Twenty-eight million Americans earn less than $10 per hour.

19. Tom Standage, *A History of the World in Six Glasses* (New York: Walker & Co, 2005).

20. Fik Meijer, *The Gladiator: History's Most Dangerous Sport* (New York: St. Martin's, 2005).

21. Roman lineage, pedigree, and family surnames were important distinctions among the Roman patrician class. It formed the basis for much of Rome's political, social, and economic institutions and customs.

22. Kwame Ture (formerly Stokely Carmichael) and Charles V. Hamilton, *Black Power: The Politics of Liberation*, 2nd ed. (New York: Vintage, 1992), xvii.

23. Thomas J. Stanley and William D. Danko, *The Millionaire Next Door* (New York: Pocket, 1998).

24. Otis D. Duncan, David Featherman, and Beverly Duncan, *Socioeconomic Background and Achievement* (New York: Seminar Press, 1972); Christopher Jencks, *Inequality: A Reassessment of the Effect of Family and Schooling in America* (New York: Basic, 1972).

25. Edward Gibbon, *The Decline and Fall of the Roman Empire* (abridgement by D. M. Low) (New York: Harcourt Brace, 1960), xi.

26. Gibbon, *The Decline and Fall of the Roman Empire*, 1.

27. Oswald Spengler, *The Decline of the West*, rev. ed (New York: Modern Library, 1962); Arnold Toynbee, *Civilization on Trial* (New York: Oxford University Press, 1948); Arnold Toynbee, *The World and the West* (New York: Oxford University Press, 1953).

28. Linda Bilmes, "The Trillion-Dollar War," *New York Times*, August 20, 2005; "Funny Money in Iraq," *Times Digest*, May 8, 2006.

29. See Niall Ferguson, *The Cash Nexus: Money and Power in the Modern World* (New York: Basic, 2002); Robert D. Kennedy, *Warrior Politics: Why Leadership Demands a Pagan Ethos* (New York: Random House, 2001); and Todd S. Purdum, *A Time of Our Choosing* (New York: Time Books, 2004).

30. Andrew Kohut and Bruce Stokes, *America against the World* (New York: Henry Holt, 2006); Stephen M. Walt, *Taming American Power* (New York: Norton, 2005).

31. James Mann, *Rise of the Vulcans: The History of Bush's War Cabinet* (New York:

Viking, 2004); Ann Norton, *Leo Strauss and the Politics of American Empire* (New Haven, CT: Yale University Press, 2004).

32. Gary Hart, *The Fourth Power: A Grand Strategy for the United States in the Twenty-First Century* (New York: Oxford University Press, 2004).

33. Victor D. Hanson, *A War Like No Other: How the Athenians and Spartans Fought the Peloponnesian War* (New York: Random House, 2005).

34. Con Coughlin, *American Ally: Tony Blair and the War on Terror* (New York: Harper Collins, 2006); Chris Patten, *Cousins and Strangers: America, Britain, and Europe* (New York: Holt, 2006).

35. Bob Woodward, *State of Denial* (New York: Simon & Schuster, 2006).

36. Tom Ricks, *Fiasco* (New York: Penguin Press, 2006).

37. Paul Krugman, "Losing Our Country," *New York Times*, June 10, 2005.

38. Elizabeth Becker, "Quarterly Trade Gap Hits $195 Billion," *New York Times*, June 18, 2005; Robert Samuelson, "A Deficit of Seriousness," *Newsweek*, May 16, 2005; and Elizabeth Warren and Amelia Warren Tyagi, *The Two-Income Trap* (New York: Basic, 2003).

39. Eric Alterman, *When Presidents Lie* (New York: Viking, 2004).

2

✛

1776—And Beyond: Elitist versus Enlightened Thought

Although America has been described "as a nation of equals and a classless society, this is a myth."[1] While we have never had the well-defined classes or estates that have existed in Europe, we have always been a nation of unequals, originally in terms of who could vote (about 10 percent of the adult populace was eligible, white males who owned property) and in terms of income and wealth, and who attended college (children of the rich). In 1776, for example, the richest 10 percent owned more than 90 percent of the property in New York, Philadelphia, Baltimore, and Charleston.[2]

Nearly two hundred years later, the poorest one-fifth of the American population owned 2 percent of the wealth and the richest one-fifth owned 77 percent of the wealth; the top 1 percent (what I call the "super rich") owned 33 percent of the wealth.[3] Optimistic readers would say there is more equality today; pessimists would argue that the economic pie is much bigger so the gap between rich and poor is wider. If we take the long view and consider two hundred and fifty years of political and economic spin (America is the City on the Hill, the foundation of hope, the land of opportunity, etc.), then the record is less than impressive.

REVOLUTIONARY ICONS

Prior to the Revolution, America was in flux. Henry Adams, a descendent of the Adams family and one of America's first historians, described the land as a backwater, uncultured place, consisting of parochial wrangling and treasonous and scheming people.[4] But this remote, miniscule, and provincial place was to meld into a new nation, based on the principles of the Enlightenment, that was to lift the social level and souls of the average man to the most favored position—a free man endowed with certain inalienable rights and liberties. The nation was to be guided by a government of the people with safeguards built into laws against unlimited despotic governments. This new faith in people, founded on egalitarian and humanitarian principles, would become translated into the idea of *democracy* and subsequently serve as a beacon of light for transforming the Old World.

Because of immigration and geographical expansion, it was much easier for those in the thirteen colonies to move up the social and economic ladder, or to fall down, than in England where the population was static, the national boundaries limited, and a paternal monarchy had existed for centuries. Although a class structure evolved in the colonies, it was socially and economically based, not ascribed heredity; there was no aristocracy based on birthright or bloodline. Americans felt more equal in social and economic status than their English counterparts. Despite the deference for privilege, power, and rank among the manufacturing, banking, and plantation class, the vast majority of Americans had a sense of independence and freedom not expressed by the average Englishmen. The Revolution that was to come was intellectually based on Enlightenment theories, but the military struggle was to be fought by an emerging working- and middle-class—a refinement on the historical class struggle. The battles on the field were to be fought by common people, from the village and farm, from below, and not by a professional army, not by paid warrior-masqueraders wearing shining suits and emblems and carrying shining swords and guns.

The Founding Fathers as a group never thought of the coming Revolution as a fight for democracy. All men were not created equal; so was the majority opinion. Some people by birth or intellect had more talent than others and a government based on truth and virtue (Plato's dictum) would put the "natural aristocrats" (philosopher–kings) in charge of government. Pulling on the other side, in the background, was the thirst for equality, ideas based on the Enlightenment and divorced from elitist and aristocratic ideas that had plagued ancient Greece and Rome, and later most of Europe, what was to be defined as part of the Old World. Royal patronage had dominated early colonial government affairs, defined in terms of Tory position and rank. Ultimately, the coming Revolution would lead to a schism within the colonies, or battle between "monarchs" and "radicals," "courtiers" and "patriots," over the hearts and minds of the American people. Eventually what would emerge in the colonies would be an aristocracy of talent, based on merited rank and performance, rather than ascribed, based on birth (and bloodline) into an aristocratic family.

Washington: The Nation's Leader in War and Peace

Class differences have always counted. When Washington took command of the colonial army, the Virginian patrician owned thousands of acres of land and repeatedly complained that the men he led were "exceeding dirty and nasty" and "afflicted by an unaccountable kind of stupidity." At times, he felt he was in "command of an armed mob" who were often drunk and ate like slobs.[5] The slaveowner, then commander-in-chief of the Continental Army, took offense at the presence of many of his officers who he complained were "indecisive, incompetent," and uneducated compared to the British officers who were more disciplined, more tidy and neat in their uniforms, and more refined.

Washington "was not a topnotch tactician or strategist, and many of his soldiers found him cold and aristocratic."[6] Repeatedly, he had to be rescued by his so-called mob-like, working-class soldiers and inept subordinates. The British generals, all from the upper-class ranks, originally likened the rebellion to a fox hunt in which they failed to "bag" their prey when they had the chance first at Lexington and Concord and then at Fort Ticonderoga and Saratoga. The colonialists didn't play by the rules of war! How unsportsmanlike! They hid behind trees and fought and ran instead of standing firm and dying on the battlefield.

Washington took command of the Army to fulfill a "consuming passion . . . to gain honor and respect" and to be "the best known and admired man in the colonies." He fed on patrician needs for rank and fame, to project the image of a great military and political leader, just as he wanted to be known as the "most graceful ballroom dancer and finest horsemen."[7] It all had to do with a feeling of superiority and snobbishness and desire to show he was above the common stock and represented the best virtues of Roman republicanism, elitism, and fashion, as well as the patrician view of serving the public and pursuing the public good (a little like Carnegie, Rockefeller, and Kennedy). To be sure, there is a class consciousness that filtered through Washington's personality, as well as many of the Founding Fathers who envisioned they were superior to the common stock, and thus more than equal.

I realize there have been many attempts to debunk or criticize Washington, but that misses the point. When events called for it, he rose to the occasion and led the nation in war and peace at a fragile period in its history and at the creation of the United States. He was the most respected man in the colonies, later considered by many to be the Father of the Country, the most influential president, and the greatest American. Washington gave power away, when he could have seized power like Caesar or Napoleon. When the war ended, he told his troops to disband and go back to their farms and shops. After the war, he "held the government together until the people could learn to be loyal to the government itself."[8] Then, again he stepped down and gave power away, when many Americans wanted him to stay on as president, or even become king.[9]

Adams: Not So Liberal

The idea of democracy and equality at no time engaged unanimous approval among the Founding Fathers. Even John Adams, a staunch believer in liberty and the principles and rights of the Revolution, had his doubts and suspicions of the people. Although he came from blue-collar and modest surroundings and needed financial support to attend Harvard, and although he was described as an abundantly human person and idealist by David McCullough, in the recent work *John Adams*, he believed in a natural aristocracy of talent and intellect. Such people were entitled to cultural and economic privileges and should direct the affairs of the new nation. "The people of all nations," he wrote, "are naturally divided into two starts, the gentleman and the simple men. . . . The poor are destined to labor, and the rich, by the advantages of education, independence and leisure, are qualified to superior stations."[10]

With the exception of a few radicals, Jefferson being the most famous one, the vast majority of the Founding Fathers had little intention to share government affairs or property interests with the common people, as they considered themselves the proper guardians. They likened themselves to be more like philosopher-kings, right out of the pages of Plato's *Republic*, with the right to govern the common people who they felt, according to Merle Curti, were "ignorant" and "dangerous." In this view, Adams attacked egalitarian principles of government and property as a "false and untenable conception of human nature."[11]

It can be argued that Curti was kind of super liberal and therefore biased in his views of Adams and the Founding Fathers. But even James Madison, an intellectual elitist and moderate Federalist, labeled Adams as a *closet monarchist*. When it came to class differences, Adams stressed the inequality of men. From this starting point, he deduced that certain people are destined to rise to the top and others to sink into poverty. Biologically, individuals were physically and intellectually unequal. Society cannot keep a strong man or educated man down, and it cannot prop up a weak or uneducated man, unless through artificial means.[12] Here then lie the seeds of Social Darwinism or survival of the fittest, a defense for the future robber-baron behavior, and the basis for the principles of heredity and IQ determining the outcomes of life. Even worse, Adams argued in the *Essay on Davila* that society had the right to "establish other inequalities it may judge necessary and good." Here, then, lies the future rationale for promoting business interests at the expense of the common people, shifting the burden of taxation on labor instead of wealth, and expounding "trickle down" theories of economics, which favor the rich under the guise that they provide jobs for the masses.

Although John Adams was good friends and sometimes on the same political wavelength with Boston radicals like Sam Adams (his cousin), Sam Otis, and Tom Paine, in his early volume, *The True Sentiments of America*, he expressed concern for mob action and the Boston "rabble," similar sentiments expressed by the more conservative minds of colonial America. Despite that he spoke in favor of justice, both as a lawyer and a politician, he believed (like many of his contemporaries who signed the Declaration of Independence) that the common people were inclined to be shiftless, vulgar, and unreliable and had to be restrained and disciplined by legal and judicial authority. To his credit, however, he rejected kings and queens, and maintained that "the love of power is insatiable and uncontrollable. . . . The only maxim of a free government ought to be to trust no man living with power to endanger the public trust."[13]

His solution was to devise a system of checks and balances in government, a view similar to James Madison's, not only to curb the instincts of the powerful but also to curb the instincts of the mob. Although Adams consistently argued that Americans had a right to their own destiny, supported by British law, he shared the same conservative legalism of Edmund Burke, the British political scholar, and same conservative judicial thought of John Marshall, the first chief justice of the Supreme Court. He feared the rise of an unprincipled financial oligarchy if the rich were allowed full reign, but he supported property interests and naively believed the "well-born, and educated and disciplined to be free from the crudest temptations for self-advancement."[14] He failed to understand that kind of reasoning, if unchecked, invites massive abuses and inequality.

In the final analysis, Adams believed (like most of the Founding Fathers) that democracy (one person, one vote) would ultimately lead to anarchy. Property rights must be preserved and government must be devised to ensure that the common people, who Hamilton would later call the "mob" and "herd," do not strip the upper class of their wealth and assets or interfere with their economic enterprises, which he felt was part of a sacred social contract. Adams was skeptical of the lower and working classes, feared mob rule and used the French Revolution and Jacobin radicalism as an example of the dangers of egalitarianism.

Despite his working-class and humble start in life, Adams lacked the ability to appreciate and communicate with the small farmer, shopkeeper, and soldier—each who shared their own common experiences and who put their lives on the line for the birth of the nation. Adams forgot the spirit of the Revolution and retreated into the arms of his wife, Abigail, for advice and consolation. On the other hand, Jefferson, despite his upper-class upbringing not only understood but also folded himself into the arms of the people and pushed the principles of the Revolution into practice. Adams saw the masses' potential breath of violence, especially as the French Revolution unfolded, whereas Jefferson knew they were grunts but welcomed the power of the people and appreciated their creative endeavors and loyalty to the new nation. The outcome is Adams was defeated by Jefferson in an attempt for a second term as president, and retreated to his farm in Massachusetts to live out his life, whereas Jefferson continued to affirm his greatness as a thinker and president.[15]

Madison: A Roman Form of Government—A Republic

It rested on James Madison, the chief architect of the Constitution, to devise a republican form of government that would protect property interests and curb the ignorance and dangerous behavior of the masses. Madison is considered by many historians to be one of the two greatest statesmen of the revolutionary period, the other being Jefferson. Both were good friends who wrote thousands of letters (1,250 have been preserved) to each other over a fifty-year period, lengthy discussions about political affairs and government.

Madison was concerned that the government, under the Articles of Confederation, could transform into a monarchy as it lacked a bill of rights and rotation for the office of president. His main purpose was to establish stability in the government, with checks and balances to prevent political mischief and corruption. But he rejected all proposals that would enhance power to the people, which he felt would substitute disorder for tyranny. In a republican government, fashioned by Roman ideas, the people would delegate their power to a few to exercise for them.

The advantage of a representative government over direct democracy (a Greek idea) would allow "people to delegate power to persons as unlike most of themselves, . . . to persons distinguished by their abilities and talents, by the very talents that would lead voters to favor them." Hereditary privilege and power was a bad thing, agreed, but it was the "people with greater virtue, greater talent, and perhaps incidentally, greater wealth than their neighbors . . . whom the people should trust their government." He sincerely believed that this intellectual and economic elite would not be overcome by "irregular passion" and would resist popular pressure "until reason, justice, and truth [could gain] authority over the public mind." Along with other conservative minds, he believed that "the only thing the people by themselves could do about government was to destroy it."[16]

Madison did not trust the common people and thus rejected the idea of direct democracy. He sought a representative republic, a larger electoral process with fewer representatives to make it "more difficult for unworthy candidates to practice with success the vicious arts, by which elections are too often carried." The idea was that, with fewer elected posts, the people would elect "men who possess the most attractive merit, and the most diffusive and established characters."[17] All well and good, unless you believe the common people are irresponsible and stupid and unable to discern the personalities and policies of one candidate from another.

Madison failed to recognize that not only are smart, refined, and wealthy people corruptible, but they cannot always connect closely to the interests of the poor, working and middle classes. In the end, people most often vote according to their self-interests, not the common good as Madison thought. The experience of the Roman Empire with the patrician and plebian class, and the experience of the British parliament with the property class and the common class, are good examples where the rich and powerful draw a line to protect their own interests and where political power conforms to economic power.

Like Jefferson, Madison believed in the natural rights of man, and in order to govern himself he must form a government of the people. But the people who hold power are capable of corruption and evil, and so government must be limited. "If men were angels," he wrote in the *Federalist*, "no government would be necessary. If angels were to govern men, neither external nor internal controls on government would be necessary." His method for limiting and constraining government was reflected in his view of the separation of powers, and by a host of checks and balances.

Government should be powerful enough to make laws and protect its people, and, according to Madison (and his good friend Jefferson), the church and state must be separated to protect civil and religious freedom. Religion was construed as another form of politics, to be avoided because it would most likely arouse dangerous zeal. Although government was to be limited (or balanced) to protect the people, so was the church in civil matters, and thus individual rights could be protected in society. The idea was to cut down on all forms of political and religious zealousness and ideology of which many of our Founding Fathers were fearful, based on the history of the Old World. However, never forgetting his favorable sentiments toward the property class, Madison also maintained that, by limiting both the government and church, there would be room left for people to accumulate property and wealth without having to forcefully surrender it to the government or church. In a free society, people had the right to prosper by the fruits of their labor which would later be translated by modern-day conservatives as part of the theory of "free-market systems," "property rights" and "ownership society."[18]

For Madison, the rights of ownership of property and the accumulation of wealth were considered inherent rights, by the new natural order, along with "life, liberty, and the pursuit of happiness," words embedded in the Declaration of Independence. Such *pursuits* involved property and wealth, and both were to be protected by the Constitution and Bill of Rights, which Madison was instrumental in framing. As the Fifth Amendment maintains: "Nor shall private property be taken for public use without just compensation."

Although Madison was not a Federalist, but a member of the Republican/Democratic Party, he helped write the Federalist Papers. Like the Federalists, Madison urged that a strong national government be formed that could put down rebellious movements that defied government. In this regard, Madison believed both the Shays's Rebellion in 1786 and the Whiskey Rebellion in 1794 were both populist rebellions by the debtor class and small farmers against the creditor class and property owners. He labeled the rebellions as "distressing" and "odious" and the rebels as "enemies of Republican Government." He described the participants, who had to be suppressed by government troops, as "nothing more than riotous."[19]

Jefferson, in one of his famous letters to Madison, argued that "a little revolution now and then is good . . . and necessary [to express] the rights of the people"[20] and to prevent government from becoming too entrenched. (The reader must understand that Jefferson was a champion of the small farmer and states' rights.) Madison, always looking for national stability, would have certainly put down most future populist, labor, and civil rights movements that threatened the political and social order or the authority of the government. But in the end, to his credit, he managed to rescue the American Constitution from the hands of the conservative wing of the Federalists, who were intent on preserving privilege, rank, and inequality, as well as class differences between the manufacturers, bankers, and property class and those who were destined to labor and live off their sweat. Along with his good friend Jefferson, he drafted the Virginia and Kentucky Resolutions during the Adams administration (Adams tried to censure the newspapers), which protected freedom of assembly and the press against the Federalists.

PATRICIAN PRINCIPLES
AND PROPERTY RIGHTS

The critics of democracy enjoyed a significant measure of influence before and after the signing of the Declaration of Independence in 1776 and the Constitution in 1787. The natural rights of man and the principles of liberty were constantly under attack by the ideas of the past, English legalism and American theocracy, by property rights and the landed gentry. These conservative ideas were rooted in well-known British theorists of government such as Thomas Hobbes and David Hume, who were *absolutists* and who set forth a traditional interpretation of human nature, condemned democracy, and associated the rise of the common man with an increase in anarchy. Both men felt that chaos and civil strife would grip society if the new barriers of rank and heredity were broken down. Hume, in particular, sought to check the lower classes, fearing that they would become a beast or mob that would destroy the government.

The doctrine of natural rights of man, "the right of life, liberty, and the pursuit of happiness," the idea that "all men are created equal," a belief in a government consisting of checks and balances to help prevent the abuse of power, the equal right to own land, the right to assemble, to protest and express opinions, the devotion (and right) to education and self-improvement for plain people—all these principles that we taken for granted today—did not come easy, and it was an uphill battle of ideas and for the minds of people. To be sure, the nobility and clergy had always felt superior to the common folk. It was the abstract ideas of the Enlightenment, with its emphasis on freedom, liberty, and tolerance, that broke the control of these twin classes and orthodoxies.

We are lucky ones. Over the course of two hundred and fifty years, this nation has grown from a small cluster of colonies, consisting of a ragtag collection of people, who transformed ideas of the Enlightenment from the "Old Order," where a permanent inequality of condition prevailed, to abstract truths and laws that were never before enacted in principle. Here a free, mighty, and wealthy nation arose, forming a "crucible of democracy" where there has been expectation of full citizenship for all people, and a faith in government by and for the people. In less than two hundred and fifty years, we have become the most influential nation in history and in the present world stage. How was this possible? Does it boil down to accident, luck, or design?

The eighteenth century in America saw the sweeping change from an *absolutist* conception of government, controlled by the aristocratic and theocratic class, to a *republican* ideal of government, based on democratic principles, representative government, and the "natural rights of man." In the process, the outdated concept of loyalty to the Crown and the notion of special rights of inherited nobility and property were overthrown for a government of the people. During this century, three political groups emerged: (1) aristocratic *Tories* with loyalty to England, who felt the "gentleman" class who owned property were superior beings and should control government affairs, and in doing so maintain social stability; (2) *Federalists* and *Whigs*, conservative business people and professionals who supported the Revolution, but opposed a wide extension of democracy and were more concerned about their own businesses and capitalistic interests than the interests of people; and (3) *Republican/democratic* party who were concerned with expanding the natural rights of *all* white men, as well as the potential for education opportunity and self improvement. They were able to translate their ideas into stirring calls to action such as "Give me liberty or give me death."

The Tories

Tory thought was extremely conservative, linked to the spirit of the Anglican Church, the monarchy, and feudal vestiges of landholding. They were an influential minority who resented the growing body of farmers, mechanics, and other plain folks who were struggling for liberty. They were well bred, educated, and rich. They believed in the monarchy and envisioned the Revolution as a revolt against the mother country and against the Crown's authority. They had little respect for democratic principles and the notion of equality, or that privilege and power could or should be eliminated or checked from the natural order of society. They had no inclination to share wealth or property, or even "the intellectual and aesthetic values of which they considered themselves the proper guardians and patrons."[21]

The Tories favored a two-tier system of education based on class, not necessarily on merit, where the sons of property owners and the wealthy commercial class would be favored for Harvard, Yale, or William and Mary, and the multitude would receive the rudiments of an elementary education, so a literate workforce would be available for an expanding economy. The Tories were obviously instrumental in squashing the democratic plans of Benjamin Rush and Thomas Jefferson, who favored a state plan of education to ensure the education of *all* children in their respective states, Pennsylvania and Virginia.

The worst and most infamous of the Tories were Thomas Hutchinson, the last royal governor of Massachusetts, and Daniel Leonard, a Harvard graduate and lawyer, who like Hutchinson allied himself to the Crown, English Constitution, Bible, and divine authority of God and the church. Hutchinson was a descendent of Anne Hutchinson, but there was not the faintest spark of liberalism and idealism left in him. The historian Vernon Parrington describes him as a "cold, arrogant, dogmatic, unimaginative, self-righteous individual," marked by reactionary politics, and with all "the enthusiasm of Mistress Anne washed clean out of the Hutchinson blood."[22] He was the spokesman of New England gentry, always on the side of the monarch, resented liberal forces, and saw no reason to compromise or change. He realized Parliament did not represent the people, that it was controlled by the aristocratic and landed gentry, and espoused the Tory interpretation of the English law for the colonialists, which he knew was a sham. But that's the way he wanted it, and that's the way it is with people who have excess power. "He knew what was at stake in America—whether political control should remain in the hands of 'gentlemen of principle and property . . . or whether it should pass into the hands of the majority,'"[23] which he labeled as the mob and unfit to govern.

Hutchinson's goal was to remake and merge the colonies into the British Empire along Tory lines, which would foster a "nobility appointed by the King for life," which he felt in the end, "would give strength and stability to the American government."[24] As royal governor, he often dispatched mail to England. Here is one of his memos written in 1770, just before the Revolution. He describes a town meeting as a source of democratic dissatisfaction with the Crown, organized by "inferior people [who] meet together" in a mob-like atmosphere. "This has given the lower part of the people such a sense of their importance that a gentleman does not meet with what used to be common courtesy, and we are sinking into perfect barbarism. . . . The spirit of anarchy which prevails in Boston is more than I am able to cope with."[25]

The more the people of Boston petitioned and organized for their freedom, the more letters he wrote complaining about his fellow countrymen. The more political ground he lost, the more he pleaded for help from the Crown. He was convinced that the future welfare of America was linked to the subordination of the colonies to the mother country and to the subordination of the multitude to the few. Boston radicals like Sam Adams, John Hancock, Sam Otis, and Tom Paine would ruin the country and their petitions and acts represented "the madness of mobocracy."

To the end, Hutchinson held to his feudal beliefs, ingrained with aristocratic snobbery: Gentlemen with good manners over good wine resolve all matters of the state. When bricklayers and carpenters, vulgar in their appearance and habits, discussed such matters, over their beer or cider, the atmosphere was ripe for anarchy. Hutchinson could sense the coming Revolution, but he refused to compromise or recognize the fresh air of freedom. He was out of step and out of place in the new world; he grew more frantic, with fits of rage, as his feudal world collapsed.

Daniel Leonard saw the rebellious spirit of the colonialists as unlawful, wicked, and groundless, "dangerous to the peace and well-being of society." Influenced by Thomas Hobbes, who saw man in a state of anarchy, in need of government to protect both person and property, Leonard felt that the ferment of rebellion was "the mischief-maker that unlooses all the evils of Pandora's box."[26] For Leonard, "rebellion is the most atrocious offence, that can be perpetrated by man," which he saw as a cruel act against God and the Crown. The goals of the Federalists and Whigs were clear treason, he argued, and "postage . . . and duties imposed for regulating trade and even for raising a revenue to the crown" were appropriate."[27]

Leonard, until his death, argued that "the king and Parliament" had only purest "intentions of justice, goodness, and truth. . . . They can only repeal their own acts, [and] there would be an end of all government, if one or a number of subjects, or subordinate provinces . . . refuse obedience."[28] By such logic, Leonard opposed all natural rights of the common person. He left the colonies in 1774, was rewarded with a post as chief justice of Bermuda, and died in London in 1829, as one of the last of the Loyalists.

Federalists and Whigs

If the Tories were a "10" in their belief of a natural aristocracy, a class structure based on hereditarian principles, a reverence for good upbringing and good manners, and a belief that the masses were stupid, vulgar, and destined to toil and had limited use for an education other than the ABCs, then the Federalists were an "8" or "9" and the Whigs were a "6" or "7." Now that is a harsh analysis of early America, but it is rooted in five thousand years of history where in every society power has always been concentrated in the hands of a very few people. The more man has struggled to sweep away his bondage, the more resistance he has encountered from the people who already have power and privilege.

The Federalists, led by Alexander Hamilton and John Adams, was the opposition party to the Republican/Democrats, the party of Jefferson. They disintegrated in the early 1820s, to be replaced by the Whigs who had gained increased influence by the turn of the nineteenth century and eventually became the opposition part to Andrew Jackson's Democrats. The Federalists and Whigs were gentlemen, perhaps not as well-bred as the Tories, but they were well-educated professionals and/or businessmen—who preferred a good political jingle or verse to the preaching of a sermon. Their politics ranged from moderately to clearly conservative, not liberal or progressive, but many were willing to join with the Republicans/ Democrats in the struggle for independence to protect their own economic interests. They were driven not by political idealism, but rather by their opposition to stamp taxes and British trade restrictions because such policies interfered with their commercial and merchant interests. They attacked aristocratic Tory philosophy, the British imperial government, and the notion of royal and landowner superiority, which attempted to keep them from owning their own property and restricted their businesses and their ability to accumulate wealth (that is, by imposing taxes). They accepted the traditional interpretation of man, a mix of Thomas Hobbes and Edmund Burke, in the context that democracy could lead to mob rule and that social class differences were largely based on innate intelligence and family background.

Most Federalists and Whigs felt the political writings of Sam Adams, John Hancock, Sam Otis, and Tom Paine were too radical, and they were concerned that the plebian mass might vulgarize government. Whereas radicals like Adams appealed to the yeoman, tradesman, and mechanic—the multitude of people—both the Federalists and Whigs rejected the concept of equality. They were in favor of overthrowing the monarch, and separating the church and state, but they wanted to limit democratic ideals by imposing a strong national government that would maintain order, limit taxes on profits, and favor business—sort of a stepping stone to the Republican platform of the twentieth century. Whereas Thomas Jefferson and the radicals from Boston were concerned about expanding democratic principles, the Federalists and Whigs were more concerned about economic class interests and how the new economy would function within the new government apparatus.

The two classes—Federalists/Whigs and Republicans/Democrats—might work together to overthrow British rule, but they were pretty much on opposite ends of the political and economic platform when it came to individual rights, education, and opportunity. The merchant and commercial class (Whigs) and aristocratic planters and seaboard manufacturers (Federalists) might welcome the support of the shopkeepers, artisans, and mechanics against grievous taxes, but the "high-born" would try to prevent the working class from voting, holding office, or sending their children to the Latin School and Harvard. Thus Sam Adams, who worked closely with Jefferson in securing the Bill of Rights, welcomed the election of his friend as a return to democratic principles after an unhappy period of Federalist/Whig control of the government, which he dubbed as the era of "prejudice and passion." In a letter, written to Jefferson in 1802, he warned: "You must depend upon being hated . . . because they hate your principles."[29]

Colonial liberalism is hard to define, simply because there was such a wide group of diverse geographical and economic interests, social behavior, religious thought, and political ideas, just like twentieth-century progressivism and liberalism are hard to define because of so many competing wings, subgroups, and interpretations. Only a small group of Revolutionary leaders was consciously democratic. Our Founding Fathers were from gentlemen stock and mainly from the Federalist and Whig class. The politics that united the southern planter and yeoman and the Boston seaboard manufacturer and fisherman had more to do about British imperialism than political idealism.

THE SPIRIT OF '76

In works like the Declaration of Independence, the Federalist papers, the Constitution, and the Bill of Rights, our Founding Fathers laid the foundation of the nation's freedoms and liberties. In doing so, they purposely separated religion from the public sector while providing a respectable place for morality and ethics in its place. Their intention to curtail religious ideology and dogma was based on European history and a respect for Greek philosophy and the Roman legal system, as well as ideas of the Enlightenment that underscored the need to design institutions and laws based on tolerance, pluralism, and respect for the common good. Kings and priests would not be allowed to influence the public sector in the New World.

More to the point, our Founding Fathers were influenced by the Greek notion of truth, virtue, and justice, the Roman political system of checks and balances, and the seventeenth- and eighteenth-century British ideas of science and reason (Francis Bacon), commerce and industry (Adam Smith), liberty (John Locke), protection of both individuals and minority rights in the face of the tyranny of the majority (John Stuart Mill), and separation of church and state as designed to protect the government and people from the power of religion (John Milton).

Crossing Swords

What follows is a brief survey of the ideas and thoughts of the leading Founding Fathers. Their secular humanist dispositions, abstract and radical voices about natural rights, and ideology of reason and morality reflect the best of European ideas. Raised as British subjects, they combined ancient Greek and Roman thought about human life and intellectual liberation with British social virtues of reason and progress to form a new nation, a new government, and new laws.

From the beginning two sets of ideas would emerge, ideas that would form the basis for modern life's ideological balance sheet consisting of the political Right and political Left: the federalist and antifederalists, intellectual elitists and egalitarians, and conservatives and radicals. The battle lines of the "best and the brightest" were drawn. As the nation plunged into debate about its place in the world and its moral obligations to its people, the two opposing camps quickly emerged, dividing as to whether the new nation should be run by an aristocracy of the smart and well-bred money class or whether decisions should rest in the hands of the general mass that could not fully understand all the abstract and radical ideas being proposed and debated. Each of the opposing camps had its champions, with Hamilton (and, to a lesser extent, John Adams) emerging as the chief spokesman on the political Right and Jefferson along with Paine (who was much more radical and controversial) representing the ideas of the political Left. Somewhere in the middle of the intellectual divide, that slippery and elusive term, were the likes of Ben Franklin and John Hancock. Whereas most historians would place Madison somewhere on the Left/Center, I would push his label more to the Right/Center; however, I am somewhat of a contrarian when it comes to the Founding Fathers.

The conservatives put their faith in the elitist ideas of statesmen, bankers, and manufacturers—the powerful and prestigious—in linking voting to property rights and in gradual change. The radicals wanted to push "the spirit of '76," insisting on an egalitarian agenda—a nation run by the working class and yeoman farmers, exactly what Hobbes and Hume and later Hamilton feared, a quasi-Marxist polity. The debate came down to whether the new nation should create and foster an economic pyramid with inherited privilege at the top or create and foster a sociology of virtue and egalitarianism.

The promise of America, for the radical or left wing of our Founding Fathers, was that the Enlightenment, with its stress on human rights and human dignity, could emerge and fully blossom in the New World. They believed there was a *natural order* of rights and freedom, as well as liberty and equality (words that sparked the American and French Revolutions), that had been hijacked for centuries by the monarchy and church. But, metaphorically, we were "the chosen people." The natural order of the rights of man, as embodied in the principles of the Revolution and the framing of the Constitution and Bill of Rights, could gain a new birth in the New World. But the conservative or right wing had an affection for property, commerce, and competition, and in the modern world they represented the birth of corporations that rendered Jefferson's small businessman shopkeeper and yeoman farmer powerless. Jefferson would have opposed the Wal-Mart and Kmart landscape, not only because it conflicts with nature but also because these giants threaten small businesses and shop owners.

To be sure, the American Right has always drawn its inspiration from Hamilton, and to a lesser extent from Madison and Adams. The American Left has always drawn its inspiration from Jefferson, and to a lesser extent from Paine. In fact, it can be reasonably argued that the roots of intellectual radicalism, common today in academic circles, can be traced to the ideas and vocabulary of Jefferson and Paine. But history sometimes makes strange bedfellows. In the last forty-plus years, since the Barry Goldwater era right up to Newt Gingrich, Dick Cheney, and George Bush, the conservative side of the political aisle has selectively paraphrased Jefferson and Paine to vent their suspicions of a highly centralized government and support their claim that democratic values are universal and are to be defended throughout the world. The ideas of Jefferson and Paine were so radical and forbidding among the Tories and Federalists; nonetheless, they have gradually become part of the common coin of academic discourse and among some conservative thinkers today. Two cheers for Jefferson and Paine!

When it comes down to who's on first or second, that is whose ideas were most favored or most influential, it boils down to Jefferson and Hamilton. Henry Adams, perhaps the first American historian to work with archival documents, and Richard Hofstadter, perhaps the premier liberal historian of the twentieth century, both saw Jefferson as the early champion of democracy whereas Hamilton "considered democracy a fatal curse."[30] Jefferson was human and thus flawed. Based on his Southern roots and political ambitions, he mildly supported slavery, despite the fact that he sensed it would become a curse on the American landscape. In metaphorical terms, he wrote: "We have the wolf by the ear, and we can neither hold him, nor safely let him go." The remark is not forgotten by his critics, but it also reflects the predicament of the Old South; the South could not or would not free the slaves and the North would not permit them to hold on to them.[31] Nonetheless, Jefferson had faith in the people to govern themselves, a radical and revolutionary idea at the time, whereas Hamilton wanted to hold on to the past and hold down the people, who he considered ignorant and did not trust.

Jefferson is also considered to be "the author of America," the most influential polemicist in shaping the nation's ideas and opinions.[32] Hamilton is considered to be the first and foremost American banker and chief proponent of centralization and business efficiency, as well as critic of state governments (Jefferson's position), which he believed would lead to political problems and fragmentation. For conservatives, today, states' rights is another way of expressing their libertarian view of economics and disdain toward government regulation. Conservatives also reject a strong federal government, fearing federal regulations, audits, and checks on big business. In varying degrees, America's political Right are partial-throated Jeffersonian-style political populists.

Alexander Hamilton: Limiting the "Mob"

Alexander Hamilton was perhaps the most influential Federalist; he had significant influence on the early birth of the nation because of his friendship and military staff relationship with George Washington. He believed in the worst of man, and supported the *Leviathan* state, Hobbes's theory that supported aristocratic and property interests over democratic interests. He was against local government such as town meetings, agrarian legislatures, and village politics, for he felt they would reduce the power of the federal government. He sought a strong central government to enhance business and financial interests, at the expense of the masses, and to keep the common people in check, who he labeled as the "anarchistic forces unleashed by the Revolution."

Hamilton is best known for establishing a national banking system, borrowing and credit system, and a tariff policy to help expand business interests—all of which he associated with the growth of America. As a champion of manufacturing, he welcomed the idea of taxing the farmers and backwoodsmen, rather than taxing the business class, to raise money for the nation, thus precipitating Shays's Rebellion, which was a revolt led by farmers against the government. He encouraged long hours of labor, from sunrise to sunset, as well as child labor, arguing that the mills and factories were "nurses of virtue for lower class children and women." He also proposed the idea of a militant Christian society to check the "Jacobian" influence on "American towns."[33]

For Hamilton, if there was no rank, no authority, then there was no order; where there is no order, there is no society, and no government. Hamilton believed in the principle of hereditary and class domination; historically, the strong dominate the weak and they form into a master group. (The next leap is perhaps a little excessive, but the Nazis would call it a master race.) The master group will come to control the social, economic, and political institutions, "not only to further their interests, but to prevent the spread of anarchy which threatens every society." In the old days, the "master group was a military order," then it "became a landed aristocracy," and in modern times it rests with commercial interest groups. "The economic masters of society of necessity become the political masters." It was unthinkable for the government to go against the wishes of the property class, for historically it would destroy government and lead to anarchy, for "no man or group of men will be ruled by those whom they can buy and sell."[34] Here, then, is a perfect description of how money and politics are intertwined, and how people who control both the purse and power will resist the popular will and promote their own capitalistic interests. Thus we have a near perfect rationale for Marx to later advocate the worldwide revolt of the proletariat against the capitalistic class.

Hamilton argued that government must serve the property class and the interests of big business and capital; otherwise, who would invest, how would labor find employment, and how would the multitude in the cities feed themselves? "If the economic masters do not organize society efficiently, how shall the common people escape ruin?"[35] His explanation was that the common people possessed limited human capacities and were stupid, and, therefore, he had no faith in them. While practical businessmen, Federalists and Whigs bought into Hamilton's philosophy because it promoted their interests, the Republicans and Democrats would strongly oppose his ideas. For such opposition to big business, America remains thankful it had a sufficient number of political leaders who believed in the democratic process and were willing to curtail some of its abuses.

Here are Hamilton's own words: "All communities divided themselves into the few and the many. The first are the rich and well born, the other the mass of the people." The Republicans (Jefferson's party) think God represents the people. Nonsense. "The people are turbulent and changing; they seldom [can] judge or determine right." For government to function, "the first class [must have] distinct, permanent share in the government . . . to check the unsteadiness of the second." Coming close to the idea of an oligarchy, Hamilton argued that the mass would never pursue the public good, and "nothing but a permanent body [of bankers and industrialists] can check the imprudence of democracy. Their turbulent and uncontrollable disposition require checks."[36] In a nutshell, Hamilton's views are pretty scary and mean spirited, dividing society in a way that the vast majority remain outside its borders and creating a permanent division between high and low humans. But, then, there has always been economic divisions in society; that is why *class counts*.

Thomas Jefferson: Natural Rights and Humanitarianism

If there is any one person we have to thank, for his wisdom and writing ability, it is Thomas Jefferson, who was the ultimate Renaissance man—a violinist, surveyor, architect, scientist, gentlemen farmer, expert horseback rider, wine connoisseur and collector of fine art and figurines, intellectual, lawyer, writer, and reluctant politician with a voice so soft you could hardly hear him from the podium. At thirty-four years old, he was entrusted by the Founding Fathers (who were putting their lives and fortunes at stake)[37] to draft the Declaration of Independence. He had a significant say in representing states' rights, or balancing the powers of the federal government, in the Articles of Confederation and Bill of Rights.

Jefferson's basic thoughts were revolutionary: "We hold these truths to be self-evident, that all men are created equal."[38] Here is the man that found the words to express the greatest aspirations of humanity, a few hundred words that are still debated today and inspire people around the world to rise up against monarchs, dictators, and tyrants. Here were the sentiments that expressed the most important truths about civilization—a philosophy of freedom rather than of predestination, one which believed in the basic rights of man and assurance that reason and natural law enabled man to control his universe and mold his destiny, as opposed to being coerced by government or religious doctrine.

Indeed, the ideas of the Enlightenment were congenial among the

American common folk, the farmers, traders, and merchants—largely working class and middle class in composition. The ideas saw the good of the human spirit; they preached a freedom of the mind, not to obey the dictates of the church or state without considering the rights of people, to consider the moral implications and other rational choices—what democracy is about, at least from my vantage point. But it was Jefferson who put it all together, who put his trust in the people, maintaining they had the most to gain or lose in the final analysis. In his notes to the people of Virginia, he maintained that the man with the plow had more "common sense" than members of the natural aristocracy or intellectual elite. Similarly, he felt the common person and small farmer, what he called the "yeoman," had an innate sense of *morality* (the concept that John Dewey would later fuse with education and democracy) and *justice* (the concept that John Rawls would later link to a good society), and could distinguish right and wrong just as well and "often better than the [political leader], because he had not been led astray by artificial rules,"[39] and, if I may add, political compromise and temptation of power and payoff.

Jefferson was the most intellectual and best-read American president; his library consisted of 6,500 books, an immense number for the period and equivalent to hundreds of thousands today if we consider the number of books now available. He was fluent in Latin, Spanish, and French, and he had the advantage of being influenced by both Locke and Rousseau, who were the driving force of the Age of Enlightenment. Both Locke and Rousseau had disdain toward the aristocracy, and both believed that the political order should be based on a contract between the people and the government, which would rule by the consent of the majority. It was Locke in the *Two Treatises of Government*, in 1689, who first argued that all persons possessed inalienable rights of "life, liberty, and prosperity," and it was Jefferson who used the first two words and changed prosperity to "pursuit of happiness" to frame the Declaration of Independence.

Rousseau argued for a secular society against an established church, which became one of the cornerstones of the U.S. Constitution and the driving force for a secular system of public education. It was Rousseau who objected to distinctions based on wealth and property and preferred "noble savages," or common folk, free and uncorrupted by urban strife and social inequality. Although Jefferson would put greater faith in agrarian society than urban life, he would not condemn the accumulation of wealth, and linked it to the establishment of government and national prosperity. He would also argue, as Locke and Rousseau had, for the national rights of citizens.

Jefferson's ideas went against the grain of many of his contemporaries who were politically influential and determined to limit the rights of the people, the masses who they felt could not be trusted. In the South, where plantation life and social elitism prevailed, and where there was emphasis on private schooling, the idea was to keep the black population ignorant and maintain a white working underclass. The libertarian and prevailing view was illustrated by Virginia Governor William Berkley, who, in 1671, argued in a public document to the authorities that educating the poor would result in "disobedience and heresy" and bring conflict and "sects into the world . . . aimed at bringing down the government and property classes."[40]

Few Americans in colonial America were qualified to vote at that time, with voting limited to those white males who were of the property class. Jefferson was willing to turn the prevailing system upside-down, emphasizing the natural rights of man and noting that human nature was not, as Thomas Hobbes insisted, egotistical and selfish, but on the contrary imbued with moral sense, humanitarianism, and the dignity of individual thought. Make no mistake, these ideas were revolutionary, given historical precedent of lack of universals that protected the common person and concentrated power in the hands of small elites with preservation of wealth and property uppermost on their minds (not much different than today).

And, in the North, there were several conservative thinkers—a mix of Tories and Federalists—who felt Jefferson's ideas of equality written in the Declaration of Independence and the Articles of Confederation were high-sounding, unrealistic sentiments that contradicted common knowledge and Puritan scripture. Obviously, some people were not and never had been equal to others. So John Adams "attacked equalitarianism of both American and French leaders as unrealistic and based on a false and untenable conception of human nature." Democracy, for Adams, was "unworkable and considered a step toward anarchy." Hamilton defended the need for "a strong central government to better serve the interests of the bankers and industrialists" against what he called the "mob." James Madison, another political giant and "Founding Father," stressed the innate diversities in the faculties of men," which explained the rise of people with superior abilities and "the accumulation of property by the well-born and educated."[41]

Some fifty years later, even Alexis de Tocqueville, the champion of American democracy, qualified its merits and had a basic reservation toward excessive freedom and rights of the people. His aristocratic upbringing filtered through his political and social lens, leading him to believe that equalitarianism tended to promote some despotism—the despotism of the masses—and also had the potential to limit property rights. And Plato, who for many philosophers and scientists is considered the father of rational thought, more powerful in his ideas than Zeus, was suspect of the masses and relied on philosopher-kings in administering and shaping society. Plato did not believe the people had the knowledge or virtue to govern themselves; rather they should be educated as warriors or workers, depending on their temperament and abilities. He put his trust in the state (seeds of fascism), whereby the state would take children away from parents to be educated in state-run schools (similar to Nazism and Communism). Plato, like Hamilton and Voltaire (Rousseau's alter-ego in the sense that Voltaire was a rationalist and Rousseau was a romanticist), mistrusted the "herd" (Hamilton's expression) and believed that the spirit of a nation always resides in a small number who put a large number to work and tell them what to do (similar to the thoughts of free-market economists today).

Jefferson, who read Plato, disagreed and went against the tide of the times. He forcefully argued in "A Bill for the More General Diffusion of Knowledge," introduced in the Virginia legislature in 1779, a plan to educate both boys and girls and both common people and landed gentry "at the expense of all," and of the need for the talented to attend college"[42]—and so was born the seeds of universal education. In the final analysis, Jefferson had great faith in educating the common citizen as a means for promoting democracy, for it was "the people [who] are the ultimate guardians of their own liberty."[43] It is the kings and queens and nobility that cannot be trusted to promote the interests of the ordinary people, and it was Jefferson who understood that Europe was flawed by its aristocratic beliefs, and that the hope of a new Athens laid on the shores of a wilderness called America, with its new breed of people—diverse in religion, ethnicity, class, and occupation.

Jefferson and Hamilton Yesterday and Today

Although Jefferson's reputation has been rapidly sinking from the twin leaks of Sally Hemings (who he supposedly slept with) and the larger issue of slavery, his defenders and those who know him well enough need to throw away their gags and make sure the American people are reminded what they owe him. Abe Lincoln put it most aptly: "The principles of Jefferson are the definitions and axioms of free society." On the other side of the political divide were Hamilton and the majority of Tories (and some Federalists) who were monarchists in disguise but knew this type of royalty was unacceptable to their countrymen. Nevertheless, their polemics came from the antidemocratic side and were motivated by fear of the multitude and a conviction that the "riff raff" could not govern. If given power, the common people would tax the wealthy and destroy all rank and privilege throughout the country.

Whatever lessons humankind learned from the little band of revolutionists who we call our "Founding Fathers," Jefferson best represents the enlightened wing, not only Greek democracy but also the Age of Reason, the natural rights of man, and faith in a government by and for the people. According to the well-known American historian Bernard Bailyn, by condemning Jefferson for his human flaws we commit suicide—tough words from an aging historian whose books on the origins of the nation are considered classics.[44]

In mathematical terms, if I may venture an educated guess, without Jefferson there is more than a 50 percent chance there would be less democracy and more oligarchyism, less enlightenment and more elitism, characterizing American history. Whatever habits or compromises Jefferson made as a person, slaveowner, or statesman, there would be no America as we know it without him—possibly no Revolutionary victory in the first place and no Constitution with teeth to protect the people. Most important, there would be no lessons learned from it by and for the rest of the world. Without Jefferson's diplomacy and writing ability, the more conservative convictions of Hamilton and his Federalist/Tory friends would have won the day.

Democracies are more fragile than we realize, and all we need to do is look at Latin America, Africa, or the Middle East to fully grasp how difficult it is to plan, implement, and maintain. It does not take a great genius to understand that democracy involves continuous vigilance and both protection and participation of the citizenry. The liberal ideas of Jefferson favored an appreciation of the common and less educated people who Hamilton and his rich friends considered the "inferior species." Jefferson believed that a favorable environment, such as the American countryside, nourished the best virtues of humankind and was an important ingredient for a democratic society and greater opportunity for plain people. Hamilton, as well as John Adams, George Cabot, John Jay, and Chief Justice John Marshall—all dyed-in-the-wool aristocrats snickering at the idea that environment might be more influential than heredity in determining merit and talent—attacked the egalitarianism of both the American and French Revolutions as unrealistic expressions of the masses.

Jefferson realized democracy was a messy process and involved give and take among different people and the natural rights of people built around the spirit of the Enlightenment. He wanted to humble the aristocracy and wealthy class in the New World and eliminate all vestiges of absolutism of both the monarch and church of the Old World. He wanted to free the common people from the rule of a few people despite whether they were kings or clergymen. Hamilton's friends "loathed the mob," believed democracy led to anarchy, and agreed with his remark: "Your people, Sir, is a great beast."[45] Given the dark side of historical interpretation, Hamilton and his buddies would have divided America into haves and have nots, elites and lower echelons working for cheap wages and churning out new goods for society—what free marketing and profiteering is all about.

There were many more wealthy elites and conservatives than liberals who participated in the framing of the Declaration of Independence, Constitution, and Bill of Rights. But Jefferson was the grandmaster chess player, who with the help of John Adams, who was almost twice his age and who he never knew until they both arrived in Philadelphia in the summer of 1776, and later in 1787 with the help of his friend and neighbor James Madison, was able to outwit and outmaneuver the conservative Federalists. Madison was the principle architect of the Constitution, but Jefferson was able to address the fears of his contemporaries and win their confidence by asking a simple question: Having thrown off one ornamental and onerous government, would the people who met in Philadelphia saddle it with another?

The *Federalist* papers, chiefly authored by Alexander Hamilton, John Adams, James Madison and John Jay, advanced the debate between the Federalists (who wanted a strong central government) and the anti-Federalists (who promoted the rights of the states and individuals) and who argued, as Thomas Paine did in 1788 (and as Reagan claimed in the 1980s), "that government is best which governs less."

The polemics came from the conservative (and anticonstitutional side), led by Alexander Hamilton whose members felt they were superior to the masses who they considered an inferior lot; checks had to be devised to restrain the "rabble." It was considered fitting and proper for government to favor the wealthy business and merchant class in order to promote economic growth; the more restraints on business, the less growth. (Sounds like today's Republicans are familiar with Hamilton's ideas.) Nearly all the convention delegates sent to the ratification of the Constitution were men of wealth and property, thus John Adams (one of the more liberal Federalists) argued there was a "physical inequality . . . and intellectual inequality of the most serious kind," and thus society had the right "to establish any other inequalities it may judge necessary and good." Madison, who gets most of the credit for writing the Constitution, also emphasized "the innate diversities in the faculties of men" and the resulting "reasons for inequality of property and wealth."[46]

Jefferson labeled the conservative delegates at Philadelphia as "monarchists" and "pro British"; in fact, Adams at one point during the early ratification stages of the Constitution wanted to call the president "His Elective Majesty" and provide special titles for cabinet members of the government. Jefferson and other liberals were labeled as "pro French" and "Jacobins" (or radicals), ignorant of human nature and unrealistic in their egalitarian beliefs that man had natural and basic rights in legal, political, and social matters. In order to try to discredit Jefferson and his ideas, the

Federalists and conservatives spread rumors and insulted him about his alleged intimacies with slave women (not much different than what the opposition did to Clinton's character and how his liberal policies became sidetracked).

Once his critics mixed race and sex, Jefferson knew his response would be a lost cause and he remained silent; the allegations continued into his presidency.[47] Just as the clergy, mainly conservative, attacked Jefferson for his loose morals and vomitous behavior, the religious Right of the 1990s defamed Clinton. Jefferson refused to respond to his critics. Had he responded, he could have taken down two-thirds of the Southern aristocracy and half the Founding Fathers, who owned plantations and "messed with women." Clinton responded and was almost impeached. Like it or not, Jefferson is the spirit of American democracy (and universal education). His legacy stands despite his alleged intimacies with one or more slave women or his position on slavery (which he repeatedly warned his neighbors and legislators was contradictory to democratic principles and would come to haunt future legislators and eventually cause the second revolution).

The republican form of government that emerged became a fight between aristocratic and patrician beliefs and a much larger number of ordinary "yeomen" and plebian ideas; between gentility and civility on one end of the social ladder and vulgar and routine people on the bottom; between those representing the business and money interests and those committed to the public welfare; between the Federalists who sought a strong national government and the anti-Federalists who opted for states' rights and local interests. The political and intellectual conflict could be summed up as a debate between Hamilton and Jefferson.

As the Revolution gained momentum, and as the Founding Fathers filed into Philadelphia (it took about two weeks on horse to ride from Boston to Philadelphia) and formed the government, there was an assault on privilege and rank that had never been experienced in humankind and on the social bonds that characterized the early royal ties of the Tories with England and monarchial society. The notion of the natural rights of man, with liberties and laws and a sense of justice and equality, became embedded in the discussion of the new republic. It competed with the idea that the freedom won in the Revolution meant freedom to make as much money as possible and to restrain the irresponsible and plain people that Hamilton and other conservative Federalists and Tories feared would foster anarchy and bring down the republic.

Class differences did not die or become submerged after the Revolution; in fact, it might be argued by revisionist and radical historians that it increased as people competed for the riches of the country. But everyone had the opportunity, at least if you were white and male, to acquire property and improve one's station in life. Social distinctions (not necessarily economic differences) began to disappear. Every American citizen, including the most common and lowly, thought himself equal to the next person in terms of natural rights and before the law. Regardless of birth or rank, anyone who did not work was suspect and lost favor in the public eye. As the yeomen class worked and prospered (Jefferson's ideal American), the business and banking class (Hamilton's ideal citizen) realized that the new government had moved beyond traditional republicanism to a belief in equality that would transcend and become part of the nation's fiber.

Gordon Wood, professor of history at Brown University, summed up the new social and economic situation: "Equality became so potent for Americans because it came to mean that everyone else was really the same as everyone else, not just at birth, not in talent or property or wealth. . . . Ordinary Americans came to believe that no one in a basic down-to-earth . . . manner was really better than anyone else."[48] The dignity of the common man had been elevated to a status that was unknown and never as high that any other nation had ever had it.

The Revolution and new government did not do away with social and economic distinctions, but it gave the common man a new pride and power, new opportunities, and multiple chances to succeed. The new experiment, the United States of America, amazed foreign visitors who came to observe the social conditions and institutions of the nation. The two most famous were the French scholar Alexis de Tocqueville who between 1835 and 1840 contrasted the "nobility class and permanent inequality" of Europe with the principles of democracy and equality in the New World[49] and the British scholar Lord James Bryce who wrote fifty years later that the United States had reached "the highest level, not only of material well-being, but of intelligence and happiness which the race has yet attained."[50]

The new nation was never supposed to be a perfect or utopian society; it retained a host of inequalities and inequities which have and still do shape the American populace. The ideas of Jefferson, rooted in the Enlightenment, could only go so far in a world where the human condition is susceptible to flaws, weakness, and temptations, but it did generate a new form of equality and respect for talent, hard work, and merit. It is these intellectual and social ingredients that have provided fuel for the American engine—for the nation's optimism and hustle, invention and innovation, productivity, and standard of living which cannot be matched anywhere in the world or in history.

We shall never escape from the historical clash between Jefferson and Hamilton, for their opposing ideas still filter through today's sentiments and language in the political arena, the media, and on college campuses,

simply under the labels of liberal and conservative. Rather than try to sanitize the sentiments of Jefferson and Hamilton, and defend or praise liberal or conservative beliefs, it is safe to say that the Revolution and the
government that was formed has had the most-far reaching effects on the
world stage. It still does, as the Paul Krugmans and Robert Reichs of contemporary America cross swords with the David Brooks and William
Kristols in newspapers, on cable television, and in college classrooms.
The compromises that resulted among the Founding Fathers represented
by the ideas of Jefferson and Hamilton set in motion the most important
series of events since the rise and fall of ancient Greece and Rome, affecting more people and more nations than any other nation in history.

A Final Comment

One more thought—one more comparison—between Jefferson and, this
time, Lincoln, as these presidents shaped American history more than any
other president. And, as you know, it is always more interesting when
writers go out on the limb and make comparisons of people we all know
and have opinions about, and we all know what happened and how they
influenced history. Regardless of the version of the story you prefer and
which gray-haired expert you listen to, I would say Jefferson and Lincoln
rank among the greatest presidents—agents of their time and America's
destiny. Both men consciously sought power, possessed a rare sense of
timing, and were able to accomplish their political purposes. Jefferson
sought to forge the nation and Lincoln sought to preserve it. Both were
politically savvy men and able to outmaneuver other men who sought to
stymie their causes and ideals. The two presidents read Machiavelli's
Prince, a basic text of the Renaissance period on how to obtain power and
hold on to it, and in their own way, ironically, they were Machiavellian in
their approach to politics and getting things accomplished for the good
of the nation.

Jefferson and Lincoln were America's two greatest communicators,
unsurpassed then and now. Jefferson put his ideas in writing and Lincoln
set them forth in speeches, both appealing to the American principles of
justice, freedom, and democracy. Both men wrote masterpieces without
the assistance of others. Jefferson wrote the Declaration of Independence
in Philadelphia in three days and Lincoln, four score and seven years
later, referred to these principles and wrote the Gettysburg Address in
two days. Jefferson's Declaration takes about three or four minutes to
read and Lincoln's Address (267 words) takes about two or three minutes
to read, yet they represent America's premier documents—providing an
inspirational and most influential message for ordinary people around
the world. To be sure, language is the lever that moves the enormous

weight of the fickle and humdrum world; it's free, universal, and highly portable, more potent than guns or bombs.

Jefferson tended to paraphrase John Locke and Jean-Jacques Rousseau, and Lincoln often quoted Shakespeare and the Bible. Both men were agnostic or religious skeptics, but both nourished the belief in their writings and speeches that Americans were God's "chosen people." Jefferson and Lincoln wrote numerous public letters to news editors and churchmen and private letters to politicians and friends, especially when they thought it would advance the causes and ideals. Both men were very capable in judging the mood of the country and were elected twice to the presidency, even though both had their political rivals and were considered radical and threatening to opposing political forces who sought to overturn their policies. Both presidents went out on the limb and risked their political careers for ideals they held sacred. Both men had the ability to talk and appeal to the plain people—the yeoman farmers, backwoods and rough and tumble persons, small shopkeepers, and soldiers—which enabled them to gauge the mood of the country and build support for their policies. In fact, Lincoln reached out to the common soldier and constantly visited the battlefront, their camps, and hospitals, and displayed a sense of sincerity and sympathy that touched the troops and shaped their spirit.

Whereas Jefferson was direct and more to the point, Lincoln was influenced by English literature and passages from the Bible and relied on metaphorical, allegorical, symbolical, and analytical realms of meaning. In the end, both presidents relied on philosophy and reason, not religion or faith, to achieve their purposes and communicate to the people. Whether they believed or disbelieved, they both sought a calmer, more measured conversation about religion and faith than we have seen in recent years as the faithful today attack skeptics and push forward their brand of religious orthodoxy on to the nation's mind. For Jefferson, there was the philosophy of Rousseau, who was always provocative and outlandish and saw religion as a form of tyranny. For Lincoln, there was the secular interpretation by Hamlet: "There are more things in heaven and earth, Horatio, than are dreamed of in your philosophy." Allowing for the existence of a "superior agent" or transcendent order, as Lincoln did, somehow seems sounder than flatly denying the possibility altogether.[51] Perhaps Jefferson did not fully reason it out: Reason itself assumes faith. Jefferson had serious doubts about religious doctrine but subscribed to its moral principles. One must understand that the majority of the Founding Fathers were deists, which in a nutshell meant Jefferson and his contemporaries could attend church without believing in its teachings, as someone today could join the PTA without fully supporting the schools (as they exist) or its teachers.

It would be another seventy years before another president would fully understand and communicate with ordinary Americans in the same way that Jefferson and Lincoln were able, and who displayed the same resolve in serving the country. His name was Franklin Roosevelt, but that's another story for another book.

NOTES

1. Herbert J. Gans, *More Equality* (New York: Vintage, 1973), 17–18.
2. Gans, *More Equality*; Marcus W. Jernegan, *Laboring and Dependent Classes in Colonial America, 1701–1783* (Chicago: University of Chicago Press, 1931).
3. Richard Hofstadter, *The American Political Tradition and the Men Who Made It* (New York: Knopf, 1951).
4. Gary Wills, *Henry Adams and the Making of America* (Boston: Houghton Mifflin, 2005).
5. David McCullough, *1776* (New York: Simon & Schuster, 2005), 47.
6. Merle Curti, et al., *History of American Civilization* (New York: Harper & Bros., 1953), 89.
7. Richard Brookhiser, "The Genuine Article," in *The Genuine Article: A Historian Looks at Early America*, ed. E. S. Morgan, 252–53 (New York: Norton, 2004); Paul Longmore, *The Invention of George Washington* (Berkley: University of California Press, 1988), 47.
8. Longmore, *The Invention of Washington*, 96.
9. Washington was asked to be king, then President for Life. Perhaps because he had no son he refused to rule for life or consider the presidency a hereditary position. He stepped down after two terms, although the public wanted him to stay on as president.
10. Charles F. Adams, *The Works of John Adams*, vol. 3 (Boston: Little Brown & Co., 1851), 458.
11. Merle Curti, *The Growth of American Thought*, 2nd ed. (New York: Harper & Bros, 1951), 140, 190.
12. Adams, *The Works of John Adams*.
13. Citation from the *Gazette*, cited in David McCullough, *John Adams* (New York: Simon & Schuster, 2001), 70.
14. Curti, *The Growth of American Thought*, 91.
15. During this period Adams and Jefferson rekindled their old friendship built around 1776 and the fermenting years before, and wrote hundreds of letters to each other describing their personal feelings and political views. For those of us who believe in fortune cookies or fate, they both died on the same day, July 4, 1826.
16. Bernard Bailyn, "Power to the People?" in Morgan, ed., *The Genuine Article*, 229.
17. Bailyn, "Power to the People?" 130–231.
18. Larry P. Arnn, "Whatever Happened to the Ownership Society?" *Imprimis*, November 2005, 1–7.

19. James Morton Smith, "The Fixers," in Morgan, ed., *The Genuine Article*, 202.

20. W. W. Abbott, et al., *Diaries, Colonial, Revolutionary War . . . and Presidential*, vol. 1 (Charlottesville: University of Virginia Press, 1976), 84.

21. Curti, *The Growth of American Thought*, 140.

22. Vernon E. Parrington, *The Colonial Mind: 1620–1800* (New York: Harcourt, Brace, 1927), 195.

23. Parrington, *The Colonial Mind*, 198.

24. Hutchinson, cited in H. A. Cushing, ed., *Works of Samuel Adams*, vol. 1 (New York: G. P. Putnam's Sons, 1904), 201.

25. J. K. Hosmer, *Life of Thomas Hutchinson* (Boston: Houghton Mifflin, 1896), 189.

26. Parrington, *The Colonial Mind: 1620–1800*, 108–9.

27. Daniel Leonard, "Letter of February 6, 1775," in J. Adams, ed., *Novanglus* (Boston: Hews & Gross, 1819), 187; "Letter of December 19," 147.

28. Leonard, "Letter of January 9," 171.

29. Cushing, *Works of Sam Adams*, vol. 3 (New York: G. P. Putnam's Sons, 1906), 305.

30. Hofstadter, *The American Political Tradition and the Men Who Made It*; Wills, *Henry Adams and the Making of America*.

31. Melvin P. Ely, *Israel on the Appomattox: A Southern Experiment in Black Freedom from 1790s through the Civil War* (New York: Knopf, 2004).

32. Christopher Hitchens, *Thomas Jefferson: Author of America* (New York: Harper Collins, 2005).

33. Merle Curti, *The Growth of American Thought*, 2nd ed. (New York: Harper & Bros., 1951), 196, 199.

34. Parrington, *The Colonial Mind: 1620–1800*, 299.

35. Parrington, *The Colonial Mind: 1620–1800*. Also see Charles E. Merriam, *A History of American Political Theories* (New York: Macmillan, 1930).

36. Jonathan Elliot, *Debates . . . on the Adoption of the Federal Constitution*, vol. 1 (Washington, DC: Elliot, 1827), 422.

37. Had the outcome of the war gone the other way, King George would have made sure to hang and torture the rebel leaders. The English had a tradition of torturing and hanging all the "Brave Hearts," not just Mel Gibson.

38. John Adams from Boston was originally asked to coauthor the draft with Jefferson, but he declined. Adams claimed that the Declaration should come from a Virginian (the largest colony at that time) or a Southerner (to ensure a union in arms). He also felt that he was too caustic, and the young Virginian was better liked by his peers. Steeped in the words of protest, liberation, reason, and the dignity of man, Jefferson wrote the Declaration in three or four days while he was in Philadelphia.

39. Thomas Jefferson, "To Peter Carr, with Enclosure," in *Crusade against Ignorance: Thomas Jefferson on Education*, ed. G. Lee (New York: Teachers College Press, Columbia University, 1961), 146.

40. Henry Steele Commager, *Documents of American History*, vol. 1 (New York: Crofts, 1934), 114. Also see Daniel J. Boorstin, *The Americans: The Colonial Experience* (New York: Random House, 1993).

41. Curti, *The Growth of American Thought*, 188–90.

42. Thomas Jefferson, "A Bill for the More General Diffusion of Knowledge," in *The Writings of Thomas Jefferson*, ed. P. L. Ford (New York: Putnam, 1893), 221.

43. Jefferson, "A Bill for the More General Diffusion of Knowledge," 96.

44. Bernard Bailyn, *To Begin the World Anew* (New York: Alfred A. Knopf, 2004).

45. Quote by Hamilton, cited in Roger Kennedy, *Burr, Hamilton, and Jefferson* (New York: Oxford University Press, 2000), 179.

46. Curti, *The Growth of American Thought*, 190–91; David McCullough, *John Adams* (New York: Simon & Schuster, 2000), 436.

47. See Joseph L. Ellis, *American Sphinx: The Character of Thomas Jefferson* (New York: Knopf, 1997); Jan Ellen Lewis and Peter S. Onuf, eds. *Sally Hemings and Thomas Jefferson* (Charlottesville: University Press of Virginia, 1999); and Lucia Stantan, *Slavery at Monticello* (Richmond, VA: Spencer, 1993).

48. Gordon S. Wood, "The Second American Revolution," in Morgan, ed., *The Genuine Article*, 244.

49. Alexis de Tocqueville, *Democracy in America*, 4 vols. (New York: J. & H. G. Langley, 1841).

50. James Bryce, *The American Commonwealth*, 2 vols. (New York: Macmillan, 1888).

51. See Brooke Allen, *Moral Minority: Our Skeptical Founding Fathers* (New York: Ivan Dee, 2006); David L. Holmes, *The Faiths of Our Founding Fathers* (New York: Oxford University Press, 2006).

3

+

Patrician Influence and Social/Educational Thought

A s I get older, I don't necessarily get wiser, but I do realize we all have our brand of truth. My political and philosophical views are embedded in the Enlightenment, in the natural rights and freedom of humans, where people in power are guided by a sense of fairness and justice—vividly articulated in the writings of Locke, Rousseau, and Jefferson (and other Founding Fathers). Thus, I am highly suspicious and critical of rulers who come to power as anticolonialist or anticapitalist leaders, though almost invariably given to democratic rhetoric, and end up betraying the liberties and rights they fought for, becoming worse tyrants than the "imperialists" they bravely defeated. I am just as skeptical toward an oligarchy—that is, a select group of people who by birth, class or position, race, or religion feel they are superior, privileged, or "chosen" persons. This makes my ideas incompatible with more than half of the nations of the world, especially in Asia, Africa, and Latin America, and with our own legacy, that is with the Puritan stewards of colonial New England who resented the plain people, stifled free speech and press, performed multiple cruel acts, and relied on coercive rules of order to maintain conformity.

WORLDS APART

Because of my affinity to the Enlightenment, I am against all -isms that drown out the individual, squash rational thought, and rely on zealous or twisted logic to support their ideology. When someone or some group believes they are God's viceroy, and chosen to carry out God's will, certain assumptions are going to follow about the nature of law, authority, and divine custodianship that whittle away the rights of people. In New England's case, there was uniformity of expression, whereby "idolatry, blasphemy, heresy, and venting of corrupt and pernicious opinions . . . [were] punished by civil authorities."[1] One should not be so surprised about the coercive spirit and witch hunts of the Puritans, however. When religion is mixed with politics, as it was in New England, the expected outcome is religious and/or political tyranny, as well as excessive church/police powers. The goal is absolute conformity in the populace, which is to become well trained in subordination and fear.

Old Time Religion

All of us who perceive ourselves as members of a religious, racial, or ethnic minority group understand the meaning of subordination and suffering. We experience our own transitoriness and mortality everyday as we read in the news or see on television the acts of violence committed toward other people in the name of religion, race, tribal identity, or nationalism. The wisdom of the Bible and the virtues of religious leaders provide us with elements of faith and with comfort and hope that bind us together, but sometimes the preachers who teach us are burdened by their own biases and prejudices toward other people who summon up different interpretations of the past and present.

To be sure, Puritan New England was inhospitable to democracy and freedom. The lesson to be learned is that the power of rational thought and free thought can be dwarfed by almost any ideology that appeals to the collective thought of the masses. Not that I'm one of Alexander Hamilton's fans, but the crowd (Hamilton described the people as the "mob") is considerably dumber than its smartest members and usually drowns out individual thought. Democratic politics must find a way of curtailing racial, ethnic, and religious extremism for the benefit of the common good. The idea, according to eighteenth-century rationalist intellects and secular thinkers, as well as twenty-first-century progressives and liberals, is to keep racial, tribal, and religious passion far from politics. This, of course, is not the Bush style of leadership. He uses the theme "City on the Hill," as a metaphor that the United States is a Christian nation, and has a *mission* to spread the gospel and bring its version of American democracy to the world, including Iraq.[2] And, as a fresh insight or bogus argument, depending on your philosophical perspective, the Bush camp claims that First Amendment provisions were added to the Constitution to protect religious institutions from the political interference of the federal government, not to protect the states from the interference of religion.[3] Not only are religious symbols permitted in the public square, but also ideas formed by faith can and should influence public life and policy.

Although there is much wisdom in our religious scriptures, if my memory is correct, the history of religion is full of harsh determinism and conquest. Our New England church leaders can be cheered for their humanitarianism, pacifism, and charity, but they can also be chastised for their absurdity, mysticism, and for imprisoning the minds of their followers with irrational thinking that was antithetical to the values of the Enlightenment. They can also be criticized for their economic precepts and "arrangements" with the rich and well-to-do, claiming that the poor should be content with their station in life and the rich should be sustained in theirs. If you believe in the Scriptures, then the world is made for suffering. Why else did God make so many poor and powerless people, so many malnourished and sickly people? Jesus, Muhammad, Moses, and Buddha did not have rich friends or followers. They walked with and preached to those who Victor Hugo labeled as *Les Misérables* and who Frantz Fanon, a hundred years later, called *The Wretched of the Earth*. They understood the despised and dispossessed, the people of the world who "know their land in the dark" and who rarely see the sky.

Stretched Thin, Today

If you are a Marxist of some sort, or even a liberal, you have a different explanation for why so many people suffer on earth; and why in America we have so many shameful social deficits such as decaying schools and neighborhoods and tens of millions of citizens without health care and/ or a decent job; and why so many working people have to hold down two or three jobs to make ends meet. It's a serious problem, masked by the American dream, which our children and youth don't recognize or fully understand because they have been seduced by the dream. To be sure, ideologies divide us; dreams bind us together. Both require an immense amount of energy and both lead to the classic journey—into the mind of a true believer. So long as we deal with the dream, everything is possible: The sky is the limit and the individual can come from below and move up the mobility ladder.

But there is a real concern that the network of public and private social and health protection, started during the Roosevelt era (1930s), is unraveling. There are fewer safeguards against downward mobility in a world pulsating with economic insecurity for the bottom 80 to 90 percent, characterized by creeping unemployment, limited employment opportunities, and low wages; loss of retirement investments and pensions; soaring medical bills and health insurance costs; a strain in Medicare coverage to cover seniors' bills; and an uneasiness that Social Security is being depleted so that the retirement age will be bumped up or benefits will be reduced. Economic analysts warn that the flood of retiring baby boomers will cause federal spending on Social Security and Medicare to eventually "consume as much of the nation's economy as the entire federal budget does now."[4] Budget deficits that exist now, measured in the hundreds of billions, are forcing the government to borrow from (and some might say rape) Social Security and Medicare funds to finance current deficits.

It is not only the working and middle class that feel the strain and feel stretched thin. Upper-middle-class babies of the baby boomers, the under-thirty generation, who have finished their MBAs, also feel the pinch—from corporate downsizing, global outsourcing, and vanishing pensions. Their moms and dads, with their two-earner households, feel the same pressure—often borrowing on their home equity. (As many as 44 percent of American homeowners have refinanced and increased their mortgage or have taken a second mortgage, called a home equity loan.) The popularity of interest-only and low-rate adjustable loans is rapidly increasing, which suggests more and more buyers are straining to qualify for housing loans. This makes more people vulnerable to rising interest rates, especially those who have balloon or adjustable mortgages. New loans are quickly running into trouble, reflecting hard times among homeowners. Even worse, personal bankruptcies have increased five-fold from 1980 to 2002, largely due to loss of jobs or high medical costs.[5]

Corporations, attempting to keep competitive in a global market, have shifted health costs and pensions to employees. Even worse, conservative policymakers see the need to dismantle social and health programs to balance budgets, as part of the new economic realities and the desire to diminish and decentralize the role of the federal government. They dismiss safety net proposals as a form of welfare, and as subsidizing people who don't want to work or prefer to play the system to their own benefit at the cost of the public good. The traditional lifetime employment arrangement, with health and pension benefits, often referred to as the old GM model, is out the window—replaced by what Jacob Hacker in his new book calls a "less stable, less secure" marketplace and what he labels in his subtitle as "The Assault on American Jobs, Families, Health Care and Retirement."[6] I would argue that the model of GM (once the largest U.S. employer) has been simply replaced by the model of Wal-Mart (now the largest U.S. employer), consisting of low wages and minimal benefits.

What we have, today, is a growing number of working-class and middle-class Americans spiraling downward, what I call "struggling Americans," trying to make it on a daily basis, often in hock, while conservative policymakers lobby hard to shift the tax burden from the rich to the non-rich, from wealth and assets to labor and earnings, from income to consumption (sales tax). The rich, obviously, do not need government help. They are rich because they know how to take care of themselves and know how to make money. The rich need to be impeded, brought down a notch or two—to try to level the playing field. Of course, conservative pundits would argue that the rich pay most of the taxes and their taxes need to be further reduced to stimulate the economy.

The harsh fact is that tens of millions of Americans live in the shadow of prosperity—either in poverty or between poverty and well-being, what both David Shipler and Barbara Ehrenreich call the "working poor" and "forgotten Americans," what Louis Uchitelle labels the "disposable" Americans, laid off, out of work, or underemployed and "silenced Americans,"[7] similar adjectives to those Michael Harrington used forty-five years ago, in his book *The Other America*, to describe what he called "invisible" Americans.

In this compact book, Harrington asserted there were some forty to fifty million Americans living in poverty, on the wrong side of the tracks and away from the highways we travel—invisible to other Americans,[8] including policymakers and patricians who should have known better. Conservative critics argued that his figures were inflated and quoted government statistics that put the poverty number at thirty-three to thirty-five million. We can use whatever number suits our political fancy, as it all boils down to what basis or criteria we want to establish as an index of poverty and what agenda we want to push. Harrington's main point was that poverty was no longer cyclical or temporary; nor was it accurate to talk about "pockets of poverty" to imply it was not serious or limited to a few Americans. Poverty was now affecting some 25 percent of the nation's populace; the condition was becoming permanent in the midst of general prosperity, and it was a scandal that the richest nation in the world was blind to the problem when it had the financial ability to solve it.

Some of the harshest critics would have preferred to squash or burn Harrington like a witch, but the reviews of the book were a call to the American conscience and witch burning was no longer considered cricket. In an economy drowning with data, Harrington was able to influence policymakers by showing that the character of poverty extended beyond immigrant groups and minority groups. His book influenced both John Kennedy and Lyndon Johnson and helped spark the War on Poverty.

Today we are told by government economists in Washington that the poverty class is defined by a family of four with an income of less than $17,000 and there are some thirty-five million Americans falling into this category. As the American population has almost doubled since 1960, the argument can be made that poverty has been reduced on a percentage basis. Again, it goes back to the definition or cut-off point that we are willing to accept for being poor, and what political agenda someone is advancing. In a nutshell, it may simply boil down to whether we prefer having dinner with the likes of Jefferson or Hamilton, or whether we drink Miller Light or XO cognac with dinner.

Without confounding the discussion with the cost of living in big-city U.S.A. or small-town U.S.A., anyone with half an ounce of brains and a smidgen of compassion recognizes that $17,000 for a family of four in 2005, reduced by taxes to $12,000 or $13,000, is kind of skimpy—nothing more than a made-up figure or best guess by a few economists in Washington. Actually, 69 percent of American taxpayers (92.1 million people) earned less than $50,000 in 2003. The average adjusted income, after expenses and line-item deductions, for this group was $19,512[9]—not much money left to pay for food, transportation, or clothing. An argument could be made that everyone in this group is poor, hovering around poverty, or struggling. It's all a matter of definition or the numbers we use to categorize poverty. It's also a matter of morality, how compassionate we are as a people, whether we are guided by heart or the bottom line, and whether we are more interested in knowing people's insides than their outsides.

Times haven't changed much for those on the bottom of the heap, but now there is an increasing number of middle-class people teetering and trying to stay afloat. Increasingly, more people are being left behind, men and women with nothing more than a high school diploma who once had decent blue-collar jobs, earning $20 to $25 per hour in the 1970s and 1980s, now earning half the amount. These are people who are products of bad judgment and bad luck, wrong decisions and wrong choices. According to Michelle Kennedy, many middle-class people have lost their jobs and are forced into low-paying jobs, or are divorced with children, or have experienced huge medical bills. These people are now waiting in unemployment lines, searching for affordable housing, and/or applying for food stamps.[10] It's not a pretty sight, given the fact many of these people once considered themselves middle class. Just a few wrong turns, a few bad choices, or some burst of bad luck, and the world shifts abruptly toward poverty. I don't think I'm telling you anything new. Increasingly, more Americans are treading dangerous waters and hardly keeping afloat.

Fat Cats: The Rich and the Super Rich

Some of us may feel poverty is a temporary condition, and most of us would like to think it is, but the facts tell us otherwise. Americans are becoming victims of corporate greed and job loss,[11] illegal immigrants working for low wages,[12] and a groundswell of low-paying service and retail jobs.[13] We are living in an "upside-down" economy where new inventions and technology have increased productivity on a national level and lowered the standard of living for most Americans, because the economic gains have been gobbled up by the wealthy top $1/2$ percent of the populace—the group of taxpayers earning $500,000 or more per year.[14] The rich don't care, so long as we don't "storm the Bastille" or bang down their doors. F. Scott Fitzgerald, the early twentieth-century American novelist, put it aptly: "The rich are different from you and I." It's more than money; it deals with attitude, lifestyle, social connections, nepotism, and the fact they know how to play the system for their own gain.

In the 1950s, Consuelo Vanderbilt, a symbol of American wealth, published the best-selling autobiography *The Glitter of Gold*, which described her miserable marriages, commonly arranged as a "link in the chain" among aristocratic families to cement their wealth through marriage. She was indoctrinated by her mother Alva to believe that happiness is reached through "practical arrangements of marriages" rather than romance, what Old Europe would refer to as the "protocol of marriage," in order to build an alliance or enhance wealth between ultrarich families. Fifty years later, in the biography *Consuelo and Alva Vanderbilt*, the mother in a moment of cynicism referred to wives as "paid legitimate prostitutes" who design their lives around finding "suitable" spouses,[15] even if it means traveling across countries or oceans, to hold on to their elite statuses. The goal is to not dilute their wealth among "lower orders" of society, that is you and I. In modern corporate terms, marriage is like a hedge fund. If it works, great. If not, there is always the daughter or son of the Duke of Marlborough or King of Sardinia. Everyone in a rich man's world is fungible.

Although some of the titles and symbolic alliances of superwealthy families have disappeared over the last one hundred years, they still retain much of their privileges and continue to manipulate the corporate world and financial markets for their own benefit, as well as domestic and foreign policies of nations though private clubs and social and business relationships. (Given a worse-case scenerio, the U.S. Supreme Court *appointment* of Bush to the presidency in 2000 is an example of this well-concealed web of favors and how "things" work behind the scenes, despite what the people say or how they *vote*.) Although not all of the elite families today are descendents of maligned monopolists or political scoundrels, they manage to live a life of splendor in places like Southampton, NY, Martha's Vineyard, MA, Kennebunkport, NH, Kenilworth, IL, or on some huge Texan ranch, five hundred or more acres, in the style of the old Spanish hacienda from when El Zorro roamed the Mexican countryside and robbed from the rich and gave to the poor.

The ordinary person has no comprehension of the superrich lifestyle and the only contact they have with these kinds of families is that they serve as their workers or soldiers as these elites effect business mergers, make trade alliances, determine war, or make peace treaties. To be sure, a few thousand families have much more to do than we realize with run-

ning the entire industrialized world, and indirectly through world economic organizations, international banks, and paramilitary and spy
groups have a lot to say in determining the fate of third-world governments. This is a hard pill to swallow; it shakes the foundation of our faith,
especially if we were brought up believing in the spirit of democracy and
loyalty to the nation.

The fact is a small number of families dominate business and political
interests in the United States and Europe. They are in the position to provide lucrative favors for each other and amass wealth, more than the old
robber barons dreamed during the Gilded Age. Their key to their fortunes
is not excellence nor individual genius; it has to do with family ties and
social and political clout, who they know and who they do business with.
It is what one insider calls "corporatocracy," the bond that ties together
families, corporations, and government in the United States and other
parts of the world.[16]

Economics 101/ Education 101

Americans accept the fact that communism is antidemocratic, but they
fail to grasp the idea that capitalism can be also antidemocratic. If left
unchecked and unrestrained, it leads to vast inequalities, augmented by
Social Darwinism, survival of the fittest, and a host of get-rich schemes,
as well as by the perverted notion that greed is good as in a free-market
orthodoxy—the latter ideology supported by a host of nineteenth-century
theories and twentieth-century "scientific" models that few people comprehend but have accepted with a faith bordering on religion. In simple
terms, it means affluence accrues only to the top, just as cream rises to
the top, and that big business needs no checks and controls. It took the
Depression, followed then by the lowly Harvard instructor, John Kenneth
Galbraith, to challenge these theories and remedy the economy by government interference and regulation. Thanks to Galbraith's longevity
with many administrations, from Roosevelt to Kennedy and then Clinton,
his advice and books (more than fifty) became the enemy of financers,
bankers, and Wall Street manipulators—and the hope for the little guy.[17]

Once we lived in a world of believers and sinners, those who were
destined for salvation and those who were damned; now we live increasingly in a world of believers and infidels, those who are with
us and those who are not. If we need, still, another compass to direct our
thinking, then we live in a divided world of unbridled materialism, consumerism, and excess on one end of the spectrum and massive slosh of
poverty, deprivation, and blight on the other end. It's not much different
than how the patricians see the world: Those who belong to a blue-blood,
old boys club and those who do not; those who believe their ancestors
amassed great fortunes from their brains and guts and those on the other

side who are convinced the captains of industry, yesterday and today, made their money by trampling on the downtrodden and ripping off the consumer; those who get their first job with major investment firms and those who are relegated to small, local banks; people who are welcomed in the stateliness of the Episcopalian church and other people who listen to the sermons of the untutored clergy of the less prestigious dominations and sects; rich children who are connected by birth to Harvard or Yale and working-class kids who wind up at state colleges across the country.

According to Harvard President Lawrence Summers, "just 3 percent of students at the nation's top 146 colleges come from families in the bottom socioeconomic quartile," that is, the bottom 25 percent.[18] These figures are echoed in a recent report that less than 10 percent of the students in the most selective colleges come from the bottom half of the income scale, whereas 74 percent come from the top quarter, evidencing marked disparities based on income.[19] The inference here is that the bottom half of the student population is either stupid, a rehash of the genetic school of thought that dominated the early twentieth century, or that prestigious institutions of higher learning discriminate against students on the basis of tuition and price out the majority of applicants because of financial need.

Tuition at private colleges has increased 110 percent in the last decade, compared to 60 percent for four-year state colleges; however, income for the bottom 50th percentile increased 35 percent and, after considering inflation, there was no gain. Measures designed to make colleges more affordable, such as merit-based assistance, tuition tax breaks, and special tax-free savings accounts for college, disproportionately benefit families in the top 40th percentile.[20] The Pell Grants, the federal government's main need-based aid program, has slowly declined in the midst of rising tuition costs. In 2004–2005, the maximum Pell Grant covered 33 percent of tuition (including room and board) costs at four-year public institutions. Four years ago, it covered 42 percent.[21]

All these figures can be reduced to the simple fact that private colleges are too expensive for students at the bottom half of the income scale, and possibility the bottom 80 to 90 percent of the scale or those households earning less than $100,000 annually. The public or state colleges are becoming the forced choice among such students. We have created a two-tier system of higher education, one for high-income students who attend prestigious colleges and one for lower- and moderate-income students who attend public colleges. The challenge is for private colleges to provide more *need-based* assistance, while balancing the competitive advantages of awarding *merit-based* assistance, without exhausting their resources to attract a superior faculty.

Still another problem is for selective colleges to come to the realization that they have overlooked a large part of low-income students who comprise the vast majority of two-year state colleges. Tuition at these community colleges averaged $2,191 in 2005–2006, and they enrolled six million students or 46 percent of all undergraduate students attending college. Contrary to popular opinion, nearly 75 percent of these community college students fall in the traditional college age, the eighteen- to twenty-four-year-old cohort, and the majority are interested in transferring to four-year colleges.[22] Increasingly, students attend community colleges because of low tuition or because of the need to work and support themselves. These institutions have attracted students whose family income falls within the bottom 50th percentile. The selective colleges have been remiss in helping out or attracting this student pool, evidenced by the fact that only one out of every one thousand students at selective private colleges started his or her college education at a two-year college, and the ratio is only slightly better, four out of one thousand, at selective public colleges.[23]

Obviously, graduating from a selective college increases a low-income student's income potential more than it does for a high-income student who does not attend such an institution, all other factors being equal. Rather than give low- and moderate-income students a better chance to compete and succeed, high-income families would prefer for selfish reasons the status quo—continuing to have selective colleges enroll and graduate upper-income students.

Private and public institutions intent on enhancing education equity must offer scholarships to top-performing, needy students from two-year institutions. Although two-year colleges provide the education for nearly 50 percent of the nation's 13 million undergraduate students, "their fund raising accounts for less than one half of one percent of all private funds donated to colleges."[24] One likely reason is a class bias exists in the business and philanthropic community, which writes off these institutions as third-rate and generally not worth the efforts since they serve low- and moderate-income students. On the other end of the higher education totem pole are the elite private colleges with beautiful campuses and endowments. In 2006, twenty-five universities were conducting billion-dollar fund-raising campaigns to add to their billions, another example of the rich getting richer because they have the power and ability to do so.[25]

The community colleges must become more proactive in raising money, given the fact that some $41 trillion is expected to transfer between generations by 2050.[26] They must also press selective colleges to reverse the narrowing of higher education opportunity for low- and moderate-income students. Educational reformers have overlooked community college students, focusing on K–12 students and four-year college students. By their silence, the reformers remain grotesquely elitist—ignoring low-income and "less intellectual" students. Despite their often professed liberalism, these reformers unwittingly play into the hands of and help those who live with the protection and privilege of their class.

The Economics of Teaching and Schooling

The affluent of America believe in and advocate a free market, in the spirit of Milton Friedman, because they are already on the top of the heap, whereas the common people who should be voting for John Kenneth Galbraith's ideas don't understand his language. But, then, how many college graduates understand the language of economics—its tables, equations, and models? The irony or failing is that we have a critical mass of people in this country, enough to change history and implement reform, who either don't vote or whose vote is based on a thirty-second soundbite on television—and not on hard data or facts and figures.

The masses are too busy trying to make ends meet to get involved in political or economic issues. Their minds have been conquered by the corporate world and the idea of the self-made man and the American dream, which ideas promulgate rugged individualism and eternal optimism. Similarly, most of their souls have been captured by a white man with a long beard in the sky, and thus cultural and religious issues (dealing with school prayer, religious symbols in public places, intelligent design, and antigay marriage and antiabortion positions) have more importance to them than economic issues. Meanwhile, the Jeffersonian heirs, today's liberals and Democrats, are identified as antireligious and antitraditional values and family. The fact is that the orthodoxies of religion are in place in many red-voting states, preventing any hope of breaking the taboo against questioning faith and shifting attention to the wit of reason and the pocketbooks of the American populace. Eventually, history will break religion's spell on voters, but it may come too late to effect the lives of today's baby boomers who are retiring and could make a change as their numbers dominate the election polls.

Given the fact we can fool most of the people much of the time, coupled with the rise of the University of Chicago school of economics (free-market ideology), we have minimal government regulations of commerce and industry. The outcome is the rise of corporate scandals, stock manipulation, fake accounting, off-shore corporations and tax evasion, bribery, etc., at the expense of those who work hard and play by the rules. Given a weakening progressive and liberal spirit, there is now a growing repeal of school spending and student scholarships, social welfare, health care, disability and unemployment insurance, the ruin of the environment, and our crumbling infrastructure. Then there is the plot to trim Social Security through privatization and to shift the responsibility of a pension from employer to employee, the latter of which is fast becoming a fait accompli.

Average workers don't get the picture. They are divided, just as the country is divided, into liberals and conservatives, blue and red voters, secularists and true believers. It does not take a genius to understand conservative economics, that is, serving oneself and accumulating wealth at the expense of a shrinking middle class and growing struggling class, which sadly bears down hard on the bottom 80 to 90 percent of American families.

In education terms, I would add that, given American affluence, we need to pay our teachers more money, equalize spending between rich schools and poor schools, and ensure that a student qualified to go to college is not saddled with debt—thus creating a new underclass or at minimum a struggling class of college-educated adults. Anyone who studies advanced science, math, and engineering should attend college for free, or reduced tuition, because the future of our economy and national security is based on producing people who can work with new ideas and innovations in science and technology. This has nothing to do with antiglobalism, antitrade, or technophobic thinking. It deals strictly with economic and education policy, that we are losing our technical and scientific edge to China and India and the sad fact that we have always had a two-tier system of education, dating back to colonial America, one for rich kids and one for students of the common people.

Historically, the schools have earmarked students into college preparatory and vocational, or labor class, tracks. This has helped the patrician class to first control and now dominate college education for their children. When Jefferson tried to whittle away at the American two-tier system of education by providing free high school and college education for bright and talented children of modest income, he was voted down by patrician forces that controlled the Virginia legislative body. His liberal ideas could be traced to the ancient Greeks who sought educational opportunities for students, rich and poor, who were intellectually competent to master abstract studies. (See chapter 4.) The problem was that his patrician "buddies" were more Roman in outlook and feared a democratic system—one person, one vote, with common people running for government office.

There is a lingering patrician (Hamiltonian) view that quality education and mass education are mutually exclusive. We all know, or at least suspect, that the people arguing most adamantly for *education quality* are those that were never really reconciled to the idea of *education opportunity*. I am not advocating that everyone should attend college, but a democracy must foster excellence from all its citizens; moreover, it should pay special attention to and provide extra help for the ranks of its less-fortunate populace.

In 1900, only 4 percent of our eighteen to twenty-one-year-old cohort was enrolled in college. By 1950 only 27 percent were enrolled in college. Well, times have changed. Americans link their dreams and opportunities to a college education. Most of us believe that high-tech, high-wage industries on which the future of the American economy depends are linked to a college and post-college education. We believe that every person should be afforded the opportunity to go as far as his or her abilities and ambitions will take him or her, without limitations of class, race, or gender. Today, more than 54 percent of Americans aged eighteen to twenty-one years attend a two-year or four-year college.[27]

But the value of a college education has leveled off because the increasing proportion of youth attending and graduating from colleges and universities has raised job qualifications across the marketplace. Still, only 15 percent of children whose parents are working class attended college in 2002, compared with 81 percent of children of professionals.[28] Because of increased college and university enrollments, the goal is not to go to *a* college, but to get accepted into the *right* college. Indeed, the bid for prestige has helped create a billion-dollar-a-year tutoring and testing-preparation industry, together with guide books and magazines identifying the "best" colleges and the "dos" of college admissions. Due to family resources the upper class has the advantage of grooming their children for college and moving into a neighborhood that has academic quality schools; in other words, local school districts and their neighborhoods foster educational inequality.

With a good schooling, coupled with family connections and alumni networking, affluent children have the advantage of attending the *right* colleges. Attending high-ranking colleges is a means for obtaining better jobs, thus reinforcing a cycle based on patrician advantage. Actually, the frenzy over college admissions begins for some at the prekindergarten age, when highly affluent parents jostle and plead to get their children into exclusive, private schools (at $15,000 to $20,000 a year) to position their children for the race to Harvard and Yale, or at least to take second place at Stanford or University of Pennsylvania. Certain people look far down the road and start to expose their sons and daughters to violin lessons, Mandarin, and computer classes early in the college admissions game.

A further example of privilege and class is private tuition. Upper-middle and upper-class children overwhelmingly attend private schools and colleges; the assumption is private schooling is better than public schools and state colleges or universities. Now that an increasing number of students seek a college education, there is no need to undercut their efforts by imposing high tuition and government debt. (Those not in debt have the lucky gene, and most likely parents with a high net worth.) Moreover, college tax benefits and the growing trend toward non-need-based institutional aid benefit middle- and upper-class students more than working and low-income students.

But don't worry. There is no need to panic! If you need hope, and if you are optimistic, Robert Reich, the former Secretary of Labor under the Clinton administration, has resurfaced and has published such books as *The Resurgent Liberal* and *Reason: Why Liberals Will Win the Battle for*

America, along with the political commentator E. L. Dionne, who has published *They Only Look Dead: Why Progressives Will Dominate the Next Political Era* and *Stand Up Fight Back*. They assail patrician society and conservative economics as ruthless (I call it antidemocratic) and assert that liberals, moderates, and "progressives" will unite and reclaim America. The winds of change will target the rich patricians whose children are shepherded to the Ivy colleges and the cheats who fleece the public and steal money from working people through manipulation of markets and tax advantages. In short, government needs to protect the small person from the rich and powerful, otherwise, the privileged will take advantage of the miniscule muscle of the masses.

Despite the so-called wisdom of free marketers such as Milton Friedman (who recently died), Steve Forbes (CEO of Forbes Inc. and chief editor of *Forbes* magazine), and Alan Greenspan[29] (a youthful disciple of Ayn Rand and a free-market purist), capitalism cannot work without regulations and laws (which updates Galbraith's thesis about money).[30] Americans who work hard should not be poor or struggling, unless you believe in the free marketers' theories of supply and demand and the right for selfish and unscrupulous business executives to crush labor under the guise of progress.

A TRIP DOWN MEMORY LANE

Unquestionably, the past is a foreign land. The people think differently and do things differently. Like most good clichés, these words have the disadvantage of being useful, and they seem especially so in thinking about the people described in this book. We shall, in the pages that follow, discuss many American giants in schools and society, from colonial America to neoconservative America, and raise several questions about their motives and behavior and in some cases reinterpret historical and social events.

For example, why did Thomas Jefferson refuse to free his slaves whereas Washington did? Why did Horace Mann, the father of the common school movement, lobby so hard for the education of the multitude, whereas Alexander Hamilton not only rejected the multitude but was more candidly a monarchist in a land that he knew outright rejected such elitist sentiment? Why did John Dewey, considered by many to be the most prominent educator of the twentieth century, seem so certain that the immigrant child's ethnic roots would disappear as a penny thrown down a wishing well, while Jane Addams, a progressive reformer and social worker, was convinced the ethnics would not go away or be dissolved into a melting pot? What caused Charles Eliot and James Conant, both Harvard University presidents, to emphasize different education programs for bright and below-average students? And what motivated William Harris, U.S. Commissioner of Education at the turn of the twentieth century, and E. D. Hirsch from the University of Virginia, one hundred years later, to advocate the same curriculum for *all* students?[31]

If you put their thoughts and behavior in context with the times, you begin to appreciate that smart and capable people are not perfect and are influenced by events of the day. They may put their ideas into words and their words may have an effect. But when all is said and done, they are not gods—only supposed models for people like you and me to analyze and reanalyze in history books and in books that have political, social, and economic messages. As humans, we are all affected by our own prejudices and life experiences, which are filtered by historical accident and contemporary experiences.

Keeping in mind historical context, as well as the assumptions and biases of all authors, we can explain the motives and behaviors of our leaders and thinkers—the people who have shaped our history. Of course, our explanations can range from a poignant analysis and masterwork to bawdy and sometimes loose associations, and countless names which whiz past the reader. Allow me a few quick explanations of the likes of Jefferson, Mann, Dewey, and the others just mentioned.

As a Southerner, as previously noted, Thomas Jefferson was haunted by states' rights and knowledge that the Southern economy depended on slaves, whereas Washington was above the fray and did not need the Southern vote to be president. Horace Mann and John Dewey were old-fashioned Protestants who were concerned with the rising tides of immigration and the need for schools to assimilate these children in order to maintain the social order. Jane Addams lived in the ethnic neighborhoods of Chicago and ran a settlement house to assist their social, economic, and education needs, while at the same time she came to understand how the rich and powerful maintained systems of social stratification. Charles Eliot and James Conant were comfortable in elitist circles and had high tea with too many old-line Brahmins and craved their donations and support. Harris and Hirsch are conservative thinkers writing one hundred years apart, both maintaining that core academic subjects, as a liberal arts education, are indispensable for all students, regardless of class, if democracy is to be preserved.

Now all these sentiments, from Jefferson who was the best-known Virginian, to Hirsch who is the least known, have something to do with class and education, and what distinctions in schools and colleges and what teaching assumptions should be made for rich children and lower- and working-class children. Education is neutral. Both Alfred Whitehead in the *Aims of Education* (1929) and Dewey in *Democracy and Education* (1916) made the same point: education can be used to maintain the status quo or to transform people; it can be used as a vehicle for stifling imagination and limiting mobility and opportunity, or it can encourage imagination and enhance mobility and opportunity.

What we have is some sort of a balancing act that goes back to the debates of Jefferson's liberalism and Hamilton's conservatism—to what extent the ordinary American will be given the chance to succeed in school and society. These philosophical differences reflect to what extent modern-day Brahmins and patricians in our country fear the multitude (Hamilton's sentiments), and thus put restraints on and check their mobility and opportunities—and what kind of economic system they devise. We must recognize that, since the colonial period, Latin schools and private tutoring—the gateway to Harvard and Yale—were for rich children, whereas common schools, meager in outlook, were for children of common stock. We must also recognize that the rich make the laws in America and elsewhere; therefore, the tax system, banking laws, and financial markets will favor the rich. (For example, investments and dividends are taxed at a much lower rate than labor; trusts are devised for rich children at birth so they have a financial advantage at the starting gate.)

The poor live without a social contract—at least a contract that Locke, Rousseau, or Jefferson would have written or welcomed. The poor have no government that represents them; they are constrained, checked, and choked by policymakers, the arm of law, and their own miseducation and misfortunes. It is the same system that led to philosopher-kings of Athens and the Caesars and senators of Rome, the aristocratic tenants of the ancient world, bolstered by a slave system, which gave birth to the nobility class and feudal system of Old Europe which our Founding Fathers feared and tried to prevent from spreading in the New World. Periodically, political leaders in America seem to represent the common people, but they come and go, and it is Congress (a Roman and Republic institution that favors the rich and powerful and weakens the democratic ideal of one person, one vote) that continues to make the laws of the land.

Given a little less pessimism and provocateurism, America is the land of opportunity and Americans are the lucky ones. Nonetheless, I am still reminded of the spirit of Michael Harrington and more recently Barbara Ehrenreich, David Shipler, and Louis Uchitelle, who seek to alert a complacent nation to the millions of "invisible," "forgotten," and "disposable" Americans caught in the cycle of poverty—debt, divorce, abuse, malnourishment, unemployment, or underemployment—unable to break into the middle class and share in the wealth of the nation.[32] The issues are rooted in the philosophical differences between Jefferson and Hamilton, the education differences between Harris and Eliot, and the economic differences between Galbraith and Friedman. They are issues that divide Americans and have consumed America, since Shays's Rebellion in 1786 when the ruling authorities were defied by the debtor class over taxes and decided to favor the merchants, bankers, and plantation owners with a tax break.

The Promised Land

The argument can be made that some of my thoughts border on or descend from *soft Marxist* theory, that is, the capitalist class exploits the working class. That argument would contradict my own belief that because America never had a feudal system, as in Europe, the common people could dream the impossible and do what the European lower and working class could not dream nor do. U.S. capitalism and democracy could expand hand-in-hand, which was nearly impossible in Europe. In the New World, there is a three-way correlation between capitalism, economic growth, and social advancement. The Marxist argument would take us down the wrong road and lead to polemics and ignore a larger point that all nations need to revisit their history and resolve political and social issues that haunt them.

Political and social zeal, as well as religious zeal, come in all shades and hues, and involve all kinds of people. Just keep in mind our history: The ideas of the Enlightenment, when transported across the ocean, prevailed over theocracy. Thank the heavens that a group of middle-aged rebels were willing to put their lives on the line, and thank Jefferson who said the right words at the right time and provided the framework that gave us the natural right to establish the rights of people and helped separate the church and state. Of course, the English aristocrats and conservatives did not see it the same way. Harping on the vulgarity and clumsiness of their former colonialists, one English novelist some fifty years ago summed up the American revolutionists as "malcontented" children and Americans in general as "cowards" who were "almost all the descendants of wretches who deserted their legitimate monarchs for fear of military service."[33]

The doctrine of natural rights of man, "the right of life, liberty, and the pursuit of happiness," the idea that "all men are created equal," a belief in "a government of the people and by the people," the equal right to own land, the right to assemble, to protest and express opinions, the devotion to education and self-improvement for plain people—all these principles that we take for granted today did not come easily and required an uphill battle of ideas and for the minds of people. Liberty and freedom are not given to a country, but it is a result of hard-won struggles, a belief in the rights of all people, especially the protection of minority rights. It is not easy to transcend religion in a deeply religious country as ours, and to allow secular laws to prevail. Nor is it easy to overcome the power of the rich, and allow the people to govern, whereby the rich ultimately have to answer to the people. We are the lucky ones. Over the course of two hundred and fifty years, this nation has grown from a small cluster of colonies, with a ragtag collection of people and a makeshift army, to a free, mighty, and wealthy nation—the most influential one in the history of humankind and on the present world stage.[34] How was this possible? Does it boil down to accident, luck, or design?

I cannot give you a precise answer—why we are the chosen ones, or the lucky ones. The answer, to some extent, comes from the heart, from the feelings and emotions of plain people, immigrant people, and working people who inhabit our landscape and who know they are free—free from the yoke of oppression—and therefore strive, innovate, and invent. Despite that we are a nation of many nations, with different customs and folklore, we all speak the same language as free men and breathe the same free air. The answer also comes from all the people around the world who clamor to come to our shores to escape their nations' rulers, tyrants, and oligarchies, to find that pot of gold or golden ring that can only be found in the New World.

James Weaver, a Populist philosopher at the turn of the twentieth century, identified with the Founding Fathers of 1776 and put it this way: "Throughout all history we have had ample evidence that the new world is the theater upon which the great struggle for the rights of man is to be made."[35] Or, could the answer simply be what Otto von Bismarck, the Prussian chancellor, once muttered? "God has special providence for fools, drunks, and the United States of America."[36]

The United States has been blessed, indeed, although probably not in the way meant by Bismarck. De Tocqueville, perhaps the most influential visitor and profound observer of America, put it in more realistic terms in 1835: Whereas a "permanent inequality of condition prevailed" in the old world, where the social conditions tended "to promote the despotism" of the monarchs and ruling class on the masses, the "principle of democracy" prevailed in the United States.[37] Some one hundred and seventy years later, another foreign gentleman, this time an immigrant from the far-off land of India, Dinesh D'Souza (someone much more conservative but just as idealistic as Weaver and de Tocqueville) commented: "America is a new kind of society that produces a new kind of human being. The human being—confident, self-reliant, tolerant, generous, future oriented—is a vast improvement over the wretched, fatalistic, and intolerant human being that traditional societies have always produced and . . . produce now."[38]

Then there is the recent book by French writer Bernard Levy who traveled across America and inserted Tocqueville in the title to move his book up the ladder in sales.[39] Proclaiming to observe and listen to the eyes and ears of America, its ordinary people from small towns and big cities, he characterizes the nation as a land of paradox. America is magnificent and mad; greedy and modest; capable of facing the future but obsessed by its past; existentialist yet devoid of direction; libertine yet conventional; held together by strong bonds and minimal ones; run by power elites but built by people of all classes.

As with most French men, Levy has the tendency to exaggerate and flatter and rely on the superficial. He says that America will endure. "No matter how many dysfunctions [and] driftings there may be . . . no mater how fragmented the political and social space may be, despite [its] nihilist hypertrophy of petty antiquarian memory; despite this hyperbesity . . . of the great social bodies that form the invisible edifice of the country . . . I can't manage to convince myself of the collapse, heralded in Europe, of the American model." In short, the Frenchman reaffirms that America will retain its place and force in the global village we inhabit. And, if you are fascinated by or embrace Levy's thinking, but need to be guided by religious truth, then allow me to add: God is watching us from a distance.

Pushing Ahead

We Americans are a "nation on the make." Our democracy has unleashed the energies of all its people, and with this new energy comes the dissolution of a stratified society. According to Walter McDougall we are "con artists" and "cowboys" and "dreamers" and "inventors," not because we are a different breed of species or better or worse than other nations, but because Americans have enjoyed immense opportunity to pursue their ambitions and dreams.[40] On the positive side, these distinctions have helped Americans to have faith in themselves—to win the West, to innovate, to expand and make it big—not being fixed by Old World church or state hierarchies and social or class distinctions that hold people in place and constrain their innovative spirit and energies, as in most parts of the world.

As a new culture and society, the humblest and poorest have been able to lift up their heads and face the future with confidence; we have increasingly relied on education as an integral part of this process of becoming. On the negative side, this forceful, driving, and imaginative American characteristic has led to political excesses and abuses—nearly wiping out whole civilizations and extracting land from other people and places in order to further and/or protect our "interests." It has also produced some ghastly business ethics—based on greed and creative corruption—highlighted by the Gilded Age, the Wall Street collapse in the 1930s, and the dot-com bust and ethics of "Enronism" in post-2000.

Although some observers might criticize the American character, and comment about our flaws and failures, McDougall (and others) maintain that the formation of the "United States is the central event of the past 400 years." Imagine some ship flying the Dutch, English, or French flag in the year 1600 and then being transported to the present. The difference would astound them. From a primitive and vacant land, we have become "the mightiest, richest, most dynamic civilization in history," exceeding the achievements of not only the European world but also the entire world.[41] We are the most revolutionary country, a society that is constantly changing and reforming and revitalizing itself. To paraphrase Joseph Perkins, a famous orator of Harvard in 1797, we are "the Athens [and Rome] of our age," and until recently "the admiration of the world."[42]

And so, as we define our white, Anglo-Protestant legacy, we have the Enlightenment on one side with its faith in progress, science, and education, as well as democracy with its cherished values of freedom, liberty, equality, and faith in the individual. On the other side, we have materialism, consumerism, and excess—and education that has been "softened" into entertainment, hustle that has turned into hucksterism and opportunity that is currently being diverted into oligarchism. We have liberals and conservatives, each with their own interpretation of what is right and wrong with schools and society. Somehow it seems to go back to the *-isms* of the past and present—between the philosophy and differences of Hamilton and Jefferson, Social Darwinism and Social Democracy, and patrician and egalitarian thought. Perhaps it goes back to how we distinguish ourselves from the Old World. Perhaps it goes back to my original sentence in this chapter—simply, how we perceive *truth*.

GEOGRAPHY AND "SMART" THINKING

On a global, much more theoretical level, growth and prosperity among cultures and civilizations can be explained by environment, or by the limits of geographical isolation. Given a make-believe world in which every individual has identical genetic potential, there would still be large differences in education, skills, and related occupations and productivity among people because of demographic differences that over centuries shape human behavior and attitudes.

For Thomas Sowell, the conservative economist, nothing so much conflicts with desire for equality as geography; it is the physical setting—reflected by large bodies of water, deserts, mountains, forests, etc.—in which civilizations, nations, races, and ethnic groups have evolved and in turn produced different cultures. Put simply, the people of the Himalayas have not had equal opportunity to acquire seafaring skills, and the Eskimos did not have equal opportunity to learn how to farm or grow oranges. Too often the influence of geography is assessed in terms of natural resources that directly influence national wealth. But geography also influences cultural differences and cognitive thinking, by either expanding or limiting the universe of ideas and inventions available to different people.[43]

When geography isolates people, say by mountains, a desert, or a small island, the people have limited contact with the outside world and, subsequently, their technological and innovative advancement is limited. While the rest of the world trades skills, ideas, and values from a larger cultural pool, isolated people are limited by their own resources and what knowledge they have developed by themselves. Very few advances come from isolated cultures, and those that do are usually modified and improved by people that have learned to assimilate and adopt new ideas from other cultures. Until 9/11, we have had the advantage of geographical isolation and protection. This isolation did not hinder our progress because of the large influx of immigrants from around the world who not only brought their meager possessions to our shores but also their ideas, values, and aspirations.

England, France, Portugal, Spain, and the Netherlands were tiny countries, compared to China and India, but the Europeans traveled the navigable waterways of their continent as well as the Atlantic. They came in contact with many countries and civilizations, including South America, Africa, Egypt, Turkey, India, China, Japan, etc.—and thus gained from their knowledge. But the older civilizations did not draw from the Europeans or from each other and eventually those great civilizations (which were once more advanced, but isolated) were overtaken and conquered by the smaller countries that had expanded their knowledge base.

Once Japan broke from its isolation, it became one of today's economic powers, and a comparable process is now shaping China and India. Similarly, the rise of the United States—in particular our skills, technology, innovations, and economic advances—is based on the history of immigrants, people coming from all parts of the world, melting together, and exchanging knowledge and ideas. It is this constant flow of different people from different parts of the globe that helps create an American entrepreneurial spirit and sense of innovation and creativity not enjoyed in more static, less dynamic countries. The first generation of immigrants may not score high on standardized reading tests, because of language differences, but their intellectual resources, hard work, and sweat have spearheaded much of our industrial machinery and muscle in the twentieth century and much of our high-tech/information in the twenty-first century.

Reaffirming the Best and Brightest

Charles Murray introduces a different twist to the record of human history and why Western nations have advanced more rapidly than other
civilizations. Murray was coauthor of *The Bell Curve* in 1994, which relied
on statistical data to make a case for innate and inherited intelligence as
the crucial factor for success in society and the reason why different racial
and ethnic groups think differently (some are more verbal, mathematical,
or abstract). In his new book ten years later, he ranks geniuses throughout
the ages (the last three thousand years). He identifies 4,002 influential scientists and artists, using a method which he claims allows him to rank
individuals from numerous fields and different cultures.[44]

Murray concludes that Western culture has contributed most to the arts
and sciences. What the human condition is today and what human species have accomplished is largely due to people who hail from Western
Europe in a half-dozen centuries. Sure to fire up the critics, as he did with
his earlier book, he makes it clear that white males have been more creative and innovative than minorities and women. Whereas many people
consider science and religion to be in opposition, he argues that cultures
girded by Christianity have been more productive than cultures bolstered
by other religions.

Among the top-ranked, most creative, innovative, and influential people, according to Murray, are Galileo, Darwin, and Einstein in sciences
and Aristotle, Plato, and Confucius in philosophy. Michelangelo is the
greatest artist and Shakespeare is the greatest writer. Murray marvels that
his conclusions coincide with current opinion. Bombast and pompous
thinking come easy to Murray. He asserts the people must be right
because his research gives them (not him) *face validity*. Murray cares little
about opinion, or whether history or philosophy agrees with his conclusions, because his analysis is based on *quantifiable* methods and the opinions of others are based on *qualitative* thought. By the thunderous force of
his ego, he dismisses his critics in advance as reflecting political correct-
ness, trendy relativism, and postmodernist or antiestablishment beliefs.
On the other hand, Murray claims he has science and research procedures
on his side, and any other position is bogus.

Allow me a short aside. If one was a betting man and had been asked
to choose in the medieval period which part of the world would dominate
the others in knowledge and the arts for much of the coming millenniums, one would most likely have put their money on the Islam world—
not Western Europe. The leading scientists, mathematicians, and
intellectuals came from this part of the world, and it was the Islamic
world that created the first global market, linking Europe with Asia
through trade. How Europe and America rose to preeminence after the

Middle Ages is for many historians and philosophers a puzzle. Some say it had something to do with the birth of the Renaissance; others refer to the Enlightenment and Age of Reason. William McNeill, professor of history at the University of Chicago, credits Europe's ascent to its warlike prowess, navigational skills, and resistance to disease.[45]

Rodney Stark, a Catholic historian, argues the rise of the West is linked to the spread of Christianity, with its emphasis on preserving manuscripts and embracing the intellect and reason in advancing the faith. Whereas other religions looked to the past for spiritual guidance, Christianity looked to the future in the coming of the Messiah and thus was more progressive.[46] In Thomistic Roman Catholic theology, faith and reason are complimentary and support each other.

The suggestion that Christianity is built on reason and is based on a progressive interpretation of the scriptures and/or open to competing views is considered a fairy tale by secularists. But Murray also associates the West's rise to global dominance with Christianity, as well as its people having a respect for science, technology, and invention. For the last five or six centuries, the West has cornered the market in knowledge and the arts because of its intellect and open mind and because its thoughts have had a relation to reality—not faith or Zen—and rejected a rigid ideologue. He also argued (as others have) that Christian doctrine allied itself to Greek and Roman art and philosophy. But it is hard not to sense Murray's patrician and elitist background, as his interpretation of the world order is linked to Social Darwinism: Certain people are smarter than others and thus will rise to the top of the ladder and certain societies are more adaptive than others and thus will grow and prosper more than others, while their counterparts falter or decline.

And now for the bad news! Murray warns that the West has peaked. It has lost its vitality and benchmark for history's highest achievers. A champion of excellence, he asserts: "In another few hundred years," we will be explaining why "some completely different part of the world became the locus of great human accomplishment." Sadly, I don't think we will have to wait that long—not if the international test scores in science and math achievement that compare U.S. students to their industrialized counterparts in Europe and Asia are any barometer of the future, and not if the fact that China and India each graduate four to one more scientists and engineers than the United States is an indicator of tomorrow's innovation and invention.

The new wave of scientific and technological knowledge will come from Asia, given existing education and economic trends, coupled with many stories in news magazines such as the *Economist* or *Business Week* and in newspapers such as the *Financial Times* and *New York Times*. There is a shift in brain power from the East to the West, commonly called "brain drain," as foreign students leave, or decline to attend, first-rate U.S. institutions of higher learning and follow the lure of economic opportunity, slowing down in the West and routed back to the East.

Not only has the number of foreign students' enrollments in U.S. colleges and universities dropped since 9/11, down from 583,000 to 565,000, fewer students are opting to come to the United States, even after being accepted. In the meantime, between 2003 and 2004, the number of students from China and India enrolled in Australian universities increased from 13,050 to 47,900. Similarly, the number of students from China and India (the largest source of U.S. foreign students, totaling 25 percent of all foreign students in 2004–2005) has declined because of improved economies and opportunities in these two countries. To be candid, we are losing our competitive edge, as most of these students were enrolled in science, math, and technological fields and then remained in the United States.

The next book on the "best and brightest" is bound to profile an increasing number of scientists, engineers, and knowledge producers from the non-Western world, with hundreds of hard to pronounce names from China and India, and even from Japan, South Korea, and Thailand. Unless some idiosyncratic quirk occurs, America and its European cousins will lose inventive and innovative ground to the East, based on the world's increased production of scientists and engineers now coming from Asia.

The more graduate students in science and engineering we attract from Asia, the larger our pool of human capital that may wind up in Silicon Valley, North Carolina's golden triangle, and other high-tech and innovative centers. "Brain workers" migrate to "brain working" centers. What the United States needs to do is to maintain the flow of "brain drain" from other countries by creating an immigration policy that slashes the influx of unskilled immigrants and rewards human capital with a point-system modeled after Canada and Australia. Given the rapid increase in globalization, brain-based jobs are highly mobile. U.S. immigration policies must attract innovative and technological talent, not repel it by making it difficult to obtain student visas or science/engineering job visas. In making immigration laws, the U.S. Congress tends to cater to big business' demand for cheap labor to fill the ranks of agribusiness, hotel and restaurant industries, and sweatshop manufacturing, while short-changing high-tech, high-wage industries and ignoring the economic advantages of human capital.[47]

New knowledge in the United States doubles about every fifteen or twenty years. In many third-world countries the mule and horse is the main mode of transportation, and the local economy is mainly picking berries, dragging banana trees to market, or having children clean out goat intestines that can be turned into leather. This is the real China,

India, Myanmar (formerly Burma), Pakistan, and the African conti-nent[48]—the rural hinterland—possibly representative of two-thirds of the world, which American students and teachers cannot fathom. This is not to deny these countries don't have a corporate mentality and a class of people that remind us of both old-fashioned industrialists and a new brand of technocrats who are versed in computer software, media, and other high-tech and electronic ventures.

What is less clear is the extent to which this new economic growth and human capital trickles down to the masses who live in poverty, both in the countryside, far away from the "new economy" which deals with the exchange of knowledge and ideas, and in urban squalor, where old and new knowledge, ideas, and values collide: East meets West and high tech meets low tech, causing a great cultural rift and the makings of revolu-tion. Here we envision old catchphrases that divide people into "winners" and "losers," societies of widening disparities, much worse than the United States because of government corruption and a lack of fair laws. We call it the gap between "rich" and "poor." Asians and Africans call it "light" and "darkness." Call it what you want. Extreme disparities and huge inequities hinder mobility around the world.

For two thousand years, before the invention of railroads, trucks, and airplanes, water was the key for traveling and exploring. Up to the 1850s, it was faster and cheaper to travel by water from San Francisco to China than overland to Chicago. The Europeans, since the Viking era, under-stood that geographical isolation could be overcome by the sea or ocean, and, given their capitalistic and conquering zeal and attitudes of superior-ity, they went out and traded with, and also colonized, other peoples and other cultures. Subsequently, they made industrial and technological advances by adopting and modifying the ideas of other civilizations.

Anyone familiar with New York City, Chicago, or Los Angeles under-stands these cities house people from a vast assortment of countries with different knowledge, ideas, and values. The old patrician class has always disrespected and discriminated against these people, but the quest for economic opportunity and the dynamic factors that drove great numbers of these people to migrate to America have managed to overcome some of the patrician forces, customs, and laws that have tried to stifle newcomers landing in these cities. Far from "celebrating" their particular identities, most urban dwellers have contact with different people and become more "hip," "sophisticated," or "cosmopolitan" than their nonurban counter-parts. Even kids who come from the backwaters of the world, say from the rice paddies of Vietnam or the mountains of Montenegro, quickly become enculturated into the American environment, especially if they settle in large cities and they step out of their parents' cultural and historical isola-tion. The computer and cell phone may increase our ability to communicate with people from around the world, but there is still a limitation on exposure to new thoughts without actual contact with different people.

Our thinking in America is shaped not only by our home environment and community but also by diverse people we come in contact with, who reshape and expand our thinking and imagination. Those who come in contact with people from around the world assimilate more information than those who remain trapped in urban ghettos, rural villages, mountains, or islands. To be sure, you can live in most parts of Nebraska and Wyoming, safe from people who have funny-sounding names, different customs, and strange folklore, but you are not going to have the same opportunity to expand your thinking and creative juices. If, on the other hand, you live your life in a melting pot area, you will more likely be tolerant, pursue novel ideas, and resist large-scale bureaucracy, production lines, and routine jobs. The point is that human creativity is the ultimate economic resource and link to national wealth. The chances are, also, that the creative mind will raise productivity, earn more money, and enjoy his or her job compared to a close-minded individual who is insulated from different people with different ideas and different ways of thinking—and works on an assembly line and performs routine tasks.

A Change in Meritocracy

The phrase "postindustrial society," coined by Harvard's Daniel Bell, describes the scientific-technological societies evolving in developed countries in the second half of the twentieth century. The singular feature of this society is the importance of scientific and technical knowledge as the source of production, innovation, and policy formulation. Emerging from the older economic systems in both advanced capitalistic and socialistic countries is a knowledge society based on the preeminence of professionals and managers. In the United States during the 1950s and 1960s, Bell notes, "this group outpaced . . . all others in the rate of growth, which was . . . seven times more than the overall rate for workers."[49] In the 1990s, computer and high-tech sectors outpaced the entire economy, reflected by a soaring NASDAQ market whose bubble burst in 2000. Nonetheless, the stratification structure of this new society produces a highly trained, knowledge-based elite, which is supported by a large scientific and technical staff and which has become the economic engine for the new century. Moreover, it is the only part of society that has successfully competed with patrician society, at least up to the point where the "blue bloods" have taken notice of who is being admitted into Harvard and who is working on Wall Street.

The basis of achievement in the postindustrial society is education. Merit and differentials in status, power, and income are awarded to highly educated and trained experts with credentials; they are seen as the decision makers who will inherit the power structure in business, government, and even politics.[50] Achievement and mobility are also related to entrepreneurship and risk taking: what Ben Franklin would call hard work and Merrill Lynch or *Forbes* magazine might call "making money the old-fashioned way." Paul Fussell, a University of Pennsylvania sociologist, labeled these postindustrial "knowledge workers" as the "X class." C. Wright Mills said the middle-class person was "always somebody's man," whereas the X person is nobody's. X people are highly independent, educated, and achievement oriented; "retirement being a concept meaningful only to hired personnel or wage slaves who despise their work."[51]

This trend toward a meritocracy of the intellectual elite has aggravated inequalities. The majority of people in a democratic society accept this form of inequality, because it is based on individual talent and achievement—not inherited privilege or rank—and because this form of meritocracy is designed, at least in theory, to benefit the common good. Because of socioeconomic deprivation and limited education, poor and minority groups are unable to compete successfully in a society based on educational credentials and educational achievement. Without the appropriate certificates, they are not needed by the economy; not necessarily exploited, but underpaid for their services; not necessarily discriminated against, but not in demand.

An achievement-oriented society based on academic credentials and standardized tests (which compare individuals in relation to a group score, say on IQ, achievement, or aptitude) condemns many people who cannot compete on an intellectual or cognitive level to the low end of the stratification structure. It is the classic problem: the rich (who have more resources for a better education) get richer and the poor get poorer—and gaps between the "haves" and "have nots" have dramatically increased in the last decade. Put in more precise terms, for the last twenty or twenty-five years, the top one-fifth of the population (on the income pyramid) has been improving its prospects while the remaining 80 percent has lagged behind.[52] With the Bush administration, it is the top 10 percent that has glommed almost all of the economic growth because of increased globalization, Wall Street greed and corruption, and free-market economic policies, which create unstable conditions for working- and middle-class people. Surprisingly, no one has rebelled. The majority have not imposed higher taxes on the wealthy; in fact, the opposite has occurred, partially because conservative forces since the Nixon administration have dominated the White House and Congress.

In education terms, however, what counts today is how the government spends money on intellectual capital—federal support of schools, college scholarships, retraining of labor, etc. Human capital (educated and credentialed professionals and business people) is the key for creating economic capital. Should Hamilton's mob be educated, and to what extent? In the final analysis, human capital (Jefferson's position) is more important than economic capital (Hamilton's position) if democracy is to survive and if the country is going to continue to prosper. The irony is, however, inequality is exacerbated by the rise of human capital, that is by an increase of knowledge workers. Inequality is greater in cities such as New York, Boston, and Los Angeles because knowledge workers easily find work in these cities and earn considerably more than people who engage in routine tasks, or low-tech and low-end jobs.[53] But the other side of the coin is that they contribute more to society and therefore deserve to be paid more.

Americans now produce fewer and fewer products; however, we produce intellectual property (i.e., pharmaceutical research, computer chips, software, etc.) which has dramatically increased the nation's innovative, information and high-tech economy. This type of intellectual capital has led to millions of new jobs, the most important reason for focusing on human capital. Bill Gates, who blends Jefferson's politics with Hamilton's economics, is critical of the nation for rationing education on wealthy and suburban children at the expense of low-income and urban children. He has personally committed $1.2 billion for high school reform that would ensure that all students receive a college prep curriculum.[54]

Will the efforts of Bill Gates and other reformers help achieve a more meritorious society? People are human, complicated by a host of flaws including greed and arrogance. If those who advance come to believe they have achieved economic success on their own merits, they may come to believe they are entitled to what they get—and the hell with stupid, slow, or lazy people. According to Michael Young, the English scholar, those who rise in a meritorious society can become smug, just as smug, if I may add, as people who were born on the more fortunate side of the economic divide and used their parents' economic resources and social connections to rise up the ladder of success.[55] The newcomers to wealth, the academic elite, may actually come to believe they have morality and justice on their side.

A new form of arrogance can develop by the creation of meritocracy, by the same people who once believed in and exemplified the political theories of Jeffersonian democracy and the stories of Horatio Alger. If true merit becomes associated with *heredity* or innate ability, as it often is construed, as opposed to the notion of *opportunity*, than meritocracy becomes less of a virtue and more of a propaganda tool for patricians and conservatives to wave and use against the populace who have fewer opportunities because of their social and economic status.

In a society that prizes merit and achievement, the reward structure is linked to a person's natural ability. In *The Rise of Meritocracy*, Young warned that such a society would put most of its resources in programs and schools that favored the academic elite,[56] thus pushing the gifted and talented to the top and the less gifted and talented behind. Even worse, the process would continue over generations because of assertive and class-based mating and the component of heredity, which people in a democracy prefer not to discuss because of its racial implications.[57] Both bright and slow students and adults will continue to compete in school and society, partially fortified by class distinctions (environment) and heredity. Barring drastic government policies, the search for merit and achievement will move capable people to the top and drive the less capable to the bottom. Although some say this is the most ideal society, as it gives everyone the chance to rise to the top, it has serious implications for average and dull people, and with people who have fewer opportunities because of class. If left unchecked or unregulated, it leads to increasing inequality, and ultimately where one group feels they belong to another species—very high or very low.

Trying to figure out the interactions of environment and heredity is a hopeless policy issue, rather the crux of the problem is to deal with the disadvantages of a limited environment because of class factors that twist and deform the spirit and lead to the plight of the next generation. We need to find a balance, some entitlement or safety net, that protects the lower classes and that children and parents of various abilities and talents can accept. The issue can be exemplified in reverse—the recent period which de-emphasized programs for the talented and gifted, due to pressure to create heterogeneous classrooms with a wide range of academic abilities, and in the passage of affirmative action legislation.

There is no set of recommendations that can please the entire American populace. Perhaps someone in a little cabaret in South Texas (a Johnny Cash jingo) or a coffee shop in Hoboken, New Jersey (a Philip Roth location) or a church in Yoknapatawpha County (William Faulkner's fictional but real place) can figure out a solution, as our leaders and statesmen cannot come to a consensus, and instead regularly engage in negative nabobs of negativism. All we can hope for is some balance—some sense of fairness in the search for talent and in the reward system that comprises our society, and some sense of fairness in the distribution of wealth.

RELATIONSHIP OF EDUCATION TO INCOME

Education and income are related in a number of ways. Philosophically, the relationship can be interpreted in conservative and liberal terms. Although both groups tend to blame the other group for America's current economic problems, both groups argue the moral high ground, believe in America's greatness, and rely on their own prominent disciples and theories as they engage in public intellectual combat. Each have their own view of education and equality, and education and economic outcomes.

The Conservative View

Conservatives hold that most social and educational inequalities are not created by some central authority or institutional process (such as schooling or the workplace), but arise out of the individual's innate or acquired skills, capabilities, and other resources. In a society based on unrestricted equality, where the government does not interfere, the individual with greater skills and capabilities will be at an advantage. There will be room for those who excel to climb to the top, but there will also be the possibility that others will not do well in school or will lose their jobs and drop a level or two in social stratification.

In this view, education is conceived as a process involving the acquisition of skills and the inculcation of better work habits in order to increase the individual's productivity. Because income is related to productivity, the more education an individual has, the higher will be his or her income. Education also serves as a screening device to sort individuals into different jobs—the more highly educated individuals will obtain the better jobs and incomes. If we try to intervene and handicap one group or provide special privileges or entitlement for another group, we only cause false benchmarks, social ills, and maladjustment; society suffers in terms of lack of efficiency and productivity.

A certain amount of inequalities will exist in society because not everyone has equal innate abilities or formal education. The explanation is as follows:

1. There are marked differences in individual abilities; those who are more capable will achieve higher levels of education and thus better jobs. Stratification, based on individual merit and performance, will develop. Even in a society where there is inherited wealth, there will still be room at the top for those who are capable.
2. In hiring, it is often difficult for employers to identify potential good employees, but they have observed the qualities that make present workers more productive on the job. Although the correlation between schooling and productivity is not perfect, competitive firms can offer individuals who have done well in school and have completed more years of schooling the better jobs.
3. The more educated get the better jobs because they have been made

more productive by the schools. In a modern, technological society, additional years of schooling constitute a signal of this greater productivity.

4. As long as there is an excess number of applicants for a job, the employer has to use some criterion to decide whom to hire or promote. In some societies, it may be the applicant's race or ethnic group; in U.S. society, it is largely the amount and quality of education. The more educated are not seen as necessarily the most productive; rather, education is a convenient criterion that most people would regard as fair and logical for hiring workers or professionals in a knowledge-based society.

The Liberal View

Various scholars representing the political Left have argued that the conservative view is incomplete and inadequate. Although education often leads to better jobs and higher incomes, it offers no guarantee of either. On some jobs, productivity has very little to do with education; other factors—such as personality, drive, common sense, and experience—are far more relevant than diplomas or degrees. Most important, with the passage of time there is a tendency for many people to be in jobs that utilize less education than they have (service industries, manual labor, the civil service); furthermore, in some jobs, educational advancement or longevity can catapult people out of employment as they can be replaced by others who are just as capable but have less education or experience, or have the same education but are much younger, and therefore command lower wages.

A number of liberals argue that schools have not promoted education nor social or economic mobility but have discriminated against and limited the life chances of the poor, as well as racial and ethnic minorities, by tracking and sorting them into second-rate programs. They contend that members of these groups have always had a hard time in the schools.[58] In the early 1900s, it was the southeastern European immigrants who were most likely to receive failing marks, to repeat grades, and to drop out of school; today, it is poor and working-class students, and black and Hispanic students, who are more likely to do so than white, middle-class, or Asian students.

Not only have the schools failed to recognize the legitimacy of cultures and classes different from the predominant middle class, but through reliance on intelligence tests, achievement tests, and vocational counseling they have also limited the education opportunity of most immigrant and minority groups. Liberals ignore the evidence provided by the numerous working-class ethnics who have risen to the top, and minimize the fact that other social indicators, such as family structure and environmental deprivation, also impact on school achievement. Instead, they argue inequalities exist for the following reasons:

1. The educational system reflects the social and economic system. Schools cannot be reformed until society is reformed; moreover, the schools can only do so much, and it is the larger society that has more impact on student outcomes in terms of producing social capital (family structure and support, peer group influence, and community influence).
2. The relationship among students, teachers, and administrators duplicates the hierarchical division of labor and discriminatory practices of society. Students are graded and ranked, tracked, and sorted by class, thus mirroring society. High academic standards foster a subtle masking of inequality, because middle- and upper-class students are better able to compete in this type of environment.
3. If people are trained to be subordinate and kept sufficiently fragmented in spirit and hope, their aspirations and motivation will be limited and they will remain frozen in their social and economic status.
4. The school's influence is limited in achieving equality of economic outcomes; the only way to achieve equality is through enlightened socialism, income redistribution, and affirmative action. In this connection, affirmation action should be based on class (or income) and not race, which frequently helps middle-class minorities and ignores impoverished groups, the majority of whom are white.

A Synthesis View

The heavy lifting and moralistic strain in our history has been performed by believers of the principles of liberty, justice, and equality. Both ends of the political spectrum claim their speakers and heroes in this arena, and both groups frequently send Americans into their political trenches with accusations and counteraccusations, which make for great television ratings among the viewing audience. The best and most influential political leaders have had the courage to exercise power, disregard partisan consequences, and make demands of their fellow citizens. How we interpret inequality and what our leaders do about our national failings depends on whether we wish to emulate Jefferson or Hamilton, or in more recent times whether we wish to emulate Roosevelt and Johnson or Reagan and the Bush presidents. Speeches and scholarly footnotes, elaborate models, and statistical data cannot hide the fact we are a polarized nation, half of us rallying around the voices of conservative commentators like William

Buckley, Patrick Buchanan, and Ann Coulter and others extolling the liberal virtues of Bill Moyer, Robert Reich, and Maureen Dowd. The situation becomes a little tacky, sort of desperate, when a president (such as the current one) has to invite partisan television and radio talk show hosts to the Oval Office in order to spread the word and to rally and cement voters (in this case, the conservative base).

In simple economic terms, the debate centers on whether government should take a backseat or manage the economy, whether a free market should prevail or whether we should redefine or tinker with market forces, and whether affluence accrues only to the smartest and strongest or spreads to the masses. Because educational impact on economic outcomes is limited (no more than 10 to 17 percent of the variance, the maximum 20 percent, according to social scientists),[59] the question arises whether we wish to tax the rich more than we do and thus redistribute wealth. No matter how we try to weave webs of words, there is no way that schooling as a policy can equalize economic outcomes, not when someone starts life on third base and someone else consistently gets up to bat last or is not allowed to get up to bat at all.

In a four-year study that analyzed the U.S. census figures and more than one hundred high schools, Christopher Jencks of Harvard University asserted that years of schooling and IQ combined, along with socioeconomic status, explained only 25 percent of the existing difference in income. He argued that "luck," or the unaccounted variance, accounted for about 50 percent.[60] Although his data is nearly thirty-five years old, the idea of luck is an interesting and often overlooked variable to consider. In a follow-up study, Jencks and his colleagues reported that family background accounted for 35 percent of the variation in income and educational attainment accounted for 20 percent, but, as family background is highly correlated with educational achievement, the amount of education is not much related to income after taking into account family background. He concluded that past compensatory education efforts, and other school reform measures, have been "relatively ineffective. . . . Thus, if we want to equalize income, the most effective strategy is probably to redistribute income."[61]

Susan Mayer, a student of Christopher Jencks, and Paul Peterson from Harvard have updated the Jencks studies. They conclude from the study, *Earning and Learning*, that cognitive test scores increase wages among adults by 10 to 20 percent. Each additional year of schooling beyond high school increases wages 2 to 4 percent, net of the effect of aptitude or intelligence.[62] Most of the variation in occupational status and wages has little to do with education and is not measured by conventional tests. Employees seek "reliable, creative, confident, honest," and socially skilled persons, but social scientists have devoted little time and effort measuring the effects of these characteristics. "One cannot tell if schools" or other institutions (family, churches, media, etc.) "do a better job of fostering these attributes."[63] (See chapter 6.)

One might even argue that in the case of extreme high-income brackets, the standard model of occupational earnings do not apply. Such variables as legacy, getting your child into Harvard or Yale and the subsequent career advantages it offers, your parents' business, social connections, nepotism, and family trust (earmarked only for rich children) apply in a way that do not correlate the same way as SAT scores on educational levels; they merely lead to and cement a superrich class, the top 1 percent[64] and reveal merit and achievement alone cannot neutralize or match inherited factors. All this new wealth, created by rising inequality in America, has very little to do with going to school or being extremely smart and ambitious.

When a CEO's decisions cause a company's stock to decline 25 percent and he receives a golden parachute worth $50 or $100 million, where is the merit or achievement? When a baseball player earns $22 million (or 44 times the average salary for a professional baseball player) and bats .265, pretty close to Alex Rodriguez's pay and performance, show me where is the merit? When a lawyer working at a top firm bags a big client (with millions of dollars in billing hours) because of family connections or a phone call by dad, and the lawyer receives a $1 million bonus at the end of the year, there is no merit; it has more to do with starting rich or superrich and squeezing the competition (or your own colleagues).

With more share of the income going to the rich and superrich, the rest of the pie is reduced in size and amount for the remaining people. This not only creates resentment among lower-income groups, including gifted and talented people, it has the makings of a class war. At the very least, extreme differences in income and/or wealth create indifferences among the lower base, those at the bottom. It creates a self-fulfilling prophecy which in a bizarre way supports Alexander Hamilton's view of the masses and Herbert Spencer's view of survival; but more to the point, it eventually affects national productivity and growth.

In simple political terms, Americans need to wake up and put aside their cultural and faith-based differences, and deal with economic reality—that most of the earnings and wealth are being gobbled up by a small percentage of wealthy Americans and that there is a surprising lack of change in the overall picture of economic inequality. Education alone cannot equalize wealth or income. While policymakers debate the trade-offs inherent in tax policies that might diminish or increase inequality, and might impede or promote economic growth, the common people must take a realistic, commonsense view and vote for political statesmen who are willing to impose corporate responsibility and support the economic bottom 80 to 90 percent of Americans who I define as the "struggling class."

The Call for Educational Excellence and Equity

Since the mid-1980s national attention has turned to the need for higher academic standards: tougher subjects, more homework, rigorous testing, and stiffer high school graduation and college admission requirements. The educational dimensions of and reasons for this new movement were amply documented in a number of policy reports released between 1983 and 2006. Many of them (including the most famous of these reports, *A Nation at Risk, Goals 2000,* and *No Child Left Behind*) were written and distributed by the federal government, and all called for reforms to improve the quality of education in the United States. The background data to these reports are depressing and indirectly illustrate the effects of a two-tier system of education, based on class and caste (or race), and compounded by two hundred and fifty years of history. Here is the nation's "report card"—and it is failing.

1. Schools and colleges have shifted away from requiring students to take what had been the standard academic core curriculum for graduation thirty years ago: foreign language, mathematics, science, English, and history. Elective courses and remedial courses have replaced many standard academic courses in high school and college.
2. Grade inflation is on the rise, and students are required to complete less homework (26 percent of twelfth-grade high school students completed less than one hour of homework a night and 13 percent claim they have no homework).[65]
3. Although National Assessment of Educational Progress (NAEP) math proficiency improved for all age groups between 1973 and 1999, with nine-year-olds making the greatest gains, among twelfth-grade students only 61 percent were capable of performing at grade level and only 8.4 percent were capable of advanced work such as calculus or statistics.[66]
4. Most distressing is the NAEP achievement gap in reading and math between white and black students: 35 points among nine-year-olds in reading and 31 points among seventeen-year-olds; 28 points among nine-year-olds in math and 32 points among seventeen-year-olds.[67] These trends have persisted since the NAEP data was first collected in 1973, despite billions of dollars annually spent on compensatory and remedial programs.
5. By the twelfth grade, the NAEP gap between minorities and whites

is depressing, especially in math and science. Differences in proficiency between black and white students are more than double in reading, 4.5 times greater in math, and 6 times greater in science. The Hispanic-white gap is slightly narrower: 1.5 times in reading, 3 times greater in math, and 4 times greater in science. The minority-white gap remains constant in all social class levels or measured by parent's education.[68]

6. Between 1992 and 2003 reading and math proficiency scores remained flat for fourth and eighth graders. In 2003, only 22 percent of fourth-grade lower-income students were at or above proficient in reading and mathematics. By the eighth grade 19 percent of these students were at or above proficient in reading and mathematics.[69]

7. Average achievement scores on the Scholastic Aptitude Test (SAT) demonstrate a virtually unbroken decline from 1963 to 1994. Average verbal scores fell over 40 points (466 to 423), and mathematics scores dropped 13 points (492 to 479). In the next five years (1995–2000) there was an increase of 58 points total (verbal and math combined), mainly because the mean scores were adjusted downward in 1995, thus masking the continual decline.

8. For white students, compared to black students, the verbal score was 96 points higher in 1987 and 92 points higher in 1997. In math, they were 103 points higher than black students in both SAT tests. The Hispanic-white gap was about 60 points different in reading and 50 points different in math for both years.[70] All these differences in achievement scores (NAEP and SAT) cannot be fully explained by social class, and depending on somebody's politics the inferences cover a wide and controversial spectrum.

9. International comparisons of student achievement, beginning in the 1970s, reveal that on nineteen academic tests U.S. students were never first or second and, in comparison with other industrialized nations, were last seven times. (The data will be discussed in chapter 6.) By 2003, international test comparisons in math and science were so bleak that the data began comparing U.S. scores with all countries, including those from the third world, thus masking the performance of American students compared to their industrial counterparts. Not surprisingly, U.S. math and science scores were reported above average.[71]

10. Some 23 to 25 million U.S. adults are functionally illiterate by the simplest tests of everyday reading and writing. Moreover, about 13 percent of all seventeen-year-olds in the United States are considered functionally illiterate, and this illiteracy rate jumps to 35 percent among minority youth. The percentage of adults age twenty-

five or older who reported reading any literature (novel, short story, poem, play, newsmagazine article) in the past year declined from 1982 to 2002, from 50 to 47 percent. It dropped to 40 percent among those with a high school diploma and 19 percent for those with less than a high school diploma.[72]

11. The high school dropout rate among sixteen- to twenty-four-year-olds is 11 percent, but for blacks and Hispanics it increases to 13 and 26 percent, respectively, and in some large cities like New York and Chicago it borders on 33 to 40 percent.[73]

12. Business and military leaders complain that they are required to spend millions of dollars annually on costly remedial education and training programs in the basic skills, or the "Three Rs." Between 1975 and 2000 remedial mathematics courses in four-year colleges increased by 75 percent and constituted one-fourth of all mathematics courses taught in these institutions. As many as 24 percent of college students have taken a remedial reading course, and 16 percent have taken three or more remedial courses. As many as 25 percent of the recruits in the armed forces cannot read at the ninth-grade level.[74]

13. All these sordid figures pile up and stare at us, despite the fact that our student-teacher ratios were 16.5:1 in 2000, which put us seventh lowest in the world (whereas such countries as Japan and Korea have higher student-teacher ratios—18:1 and 28:1, respectively), and that our pupil expenditures for education K–12 were the second highest in the world (about $500 less than first-ranked Switzerland).[75]

Racial and Class Implications

How we interpret these trends largely depends on our social lens and political motives, what side of the ideological aisle we sit on, and to what extent and how we balance issues related to excellence, equality, and equity. It also depends on whether we want to focus on class or caste. For example, we can talk about the theme of *cultural inversion*, a concept introduced by black social scientists such as John Ogbu or John McWhorter.[76] Their thesis is that poor academic achievement among blacks has more to do with their own negative attitudes than the effects of prejudice or poor schools; their negativism is rooted in slave history and segregation, but dramatically worsened by a "cult of separation," which makes blacks think that whatever whites do, they should do the opposite; by the "cult of anti-intellectualism," which holds that academic excellence is a white thing, and by the "cult of victimization," whereby they adapt and act out labels or stereotypes of the majority population foisted on black youth—"dumb," "lazy," "delinquent," etc.

This negativism is worsened by quotas and racial preferences, which tell blacks they do not have to be as competent as whites to get admitted to college or to get a job. On the other hand, this negativism is also supported by prejudicial attitudes of teachers and their low expectations of minority students, compounded by years of unequal schooling and institutional racism. Roland Fryer, a black Harvard economist, adds a few novel notions to the mix. He looked at ninety thousand minority students from grades seven to twelve and concluded that acting white and getting good grades is a problem in integrated schools but not in all-black schools or private schools. He concludes that black and Hispanic students with good grades end up with fewer friends at integrated public schools, but it is more a *class* issue than a racial problem. In any society where inequality exists, members of the disadvantaged group have torn loyalties— wanting to excel in the larger society but maintaining kinship and remaining loyal to one's own subgroup.[77]

It's an important idea—particularly now, when race and class vie for the reformer's eye and seem to be competing for popularity in the reform literature—to turn to class. To be sure, there is a history of unequal schooling related to class which dates back to colonial America in terms of who dropped out of school and returned to the farm or became an apprentice in a craft or labor-related position (common student) and who graduated from the Latin School in Boston or a private school in Charleston and went on to Harvard or Yale (upper-class student). Two hundred and fifty years later, as we begin the twenty-first century, class issues persist at Harvard and Yale, with no more than 3 to 4 percent of the student body representing lower- and working-class white students.

You might recall, in fact, that President Roosevelt's "New Deal" and President Johnson's "Great Society" used a poverty index or economic need in lieu of race to determine how additional resources would be allocated. The concepts of welfare rights, affirmative action, entitlements, and reparations have only been tied to race since the late 1960s, coinciding with the civil rights movement although it is justified by two hundred and fifty years of race relations. The civil rights industry deals with helping the victims of past racial discrimination and ignores poor whites who make up nearly 70 percent of the poverty class, as well as working-class and ethnic whites who are unable to afford good suburban schooling or a private college education. Moreover, the entitlement industry can win money and special treatment in many institutions of society without ever having to show progress with poverty, because poverty is not the issue in the civil rights movement or with affirmative action. What we need to do is to return to the poverty index and funnel resources and services based on need or *class*, not for a particular racial/ethnic group or *caste*. It's a matter of focusing on all low-performing, low-income American students, not just minority students.

A Nation of Many Nations

Most of the immigrants today who yearn to breathe free and prosper do not come from Europe; rather they hail from "nonwestern" lands. In fact, about 90 percent of today's immigrants come from Asia, Africa, and Latin America. The noise is no longer from horseshows, from ethnic European clubs and taverns, or from vendors who speak Italian, Greek, or Yiddish. The folklore and language is very different, mainly from Hispanic and Asian cultures, with new music, new foods, new flavors, new customs. Much of the population growth and economic growth in the larger cities have to do with immigrant groups, not second- or third-generation Americans.

The nation's newest immigrants—Mexican, Korean, Indian, and Chinese immigrants—come from lost worlds and have different customs and beliefs than those old ethnics—the Irish, Italian, Greek, and Puerto Rican—who came to our shores generations ago. Members of the new wave of immigrants are permitted to retreat into the images of their lost worlds, to cling to their traditions and culture, but they must learn to decide what works (and what doesn't) and what is relevant (and irrelevant) to their current needs. They must make adjustments to function today on streets such as Clark and Devon in Chicago and Delancey and Essex in New York City, and eventually on "Main Street" in suburban America. All these roads intersect, and they forge a new type of American, who leaves behind the lords and ladies, the landed aristocracy, the pretentious life they could never aspire or achieve in the Old World, as well as the border warfare, political strife, and hunger that was once their world.

The mutations that develop represent the immigrants' accommodations to their new cities, their new homeland, to "Pax Americana,"—the "new Athens" and "new Rome." They may continue with their Indian or Chinese food and celebrate in September for the Hindu New Year and in mid-January or February for the Chinese New Year, but their children will attend American schools and watch American television (now considered the first education system, suggesting that children spend more time watching television than attending school) and eventually exchange curry dishes or oxtail dishes for Big Macs and a bucket of the Colonel's fried chicken and celebrate the "strange" American holidays of Christmas and New Years, and even Fourth of July and Thanksgiving.

Given all the criticism leveled by cultural pluralists and neo-Marxists in general, America has been constructed to absorb any group or any thing that comes along. The "Founding Fathers" who built this nation, despite all the liberal bashing that they were white, Eurocentric, male, and some even slaveholders, gave their descendents something very special, peculiar, and seemingly implausible, if history were to gauge the success of the experiment. They built a sort of perpetual, ever-increasing, rich, multiethnic, multireligious stew. They provided a massive dose of super-strength vitamins, to move people from a sense of uniqueness to a sense of belonging, from a harsh to a compassionate breed of Americans. This is why this nation has been able to grow and prosper more than any other civilization. It is a remarkable story, but there is another side to it—one about which Americans need to be reminded.

As a nation, we all need to learn the lessons of the global village, about people with different customs, folklore, and languages, or else we will decline as a civilization. Our decline will have little to do with the loss of Christian values, faith, and ideals; rather, it will have more to do with the inability of the Western world to fuse with the Asian, African, and Latin American world; the inability of whites to understand, respect, and appreciate people of color. Living in an isolated town in Wyoming or Nebraska, where the deer and antelope still roam, a throwback to the American pioneer, doesn't work and breeds intolerance and disrespect for the people of color of the world. The esoteric abstraction of upper-class "Yankees" living in small secluded villages and towns—still hanging on to the old ways—is a covert, dangerous sentiment, the last flurry of American isolation and hypocrisy. These old families and communities need to open their doors to the world; their children cannot hold back the non-Western and ethnic storm, the mixed blood swirling at their gates and fences.

There are many forks in the road to assimilation, and the themes of melting pot, mosaic, stew, and tossed salad to describe American society are as varied as its people. The word or concept is not as crucial as some of us would like to think. Much of it depends on the upward mobility of minority groups, immigrant groups, and poor whites, which in turn reflects whether a particular group becomes homogenized or accepted as Americans or holds on to its separate identity. If, however, the group perceives itself as "oppressed" or "victimized" by the system, with common historic grievances toward the larger society, then the American concepts of equality, opportunity, and mobility need to be reformulated. If the themes of oppression and victimization, or class warfare dominate, there is no satisfying that particular group. On the other hand, more and more Americans are beginning to say that race, religion, ethnicity, and class should not be descriptions for categorizing people in any form or shape. We are reminded of Martin Luther King's dream that children "should be judged by the content of their character," not by caste or class. It would be nice if some day we could achieve this goal. Part of the problem boils down to money—where it comes from, how it gets distributed, and whether there is real mobility among American castes and classes.

NOTES

1. Williston Walker, *A History of the Congregational Churches in the United States* (New York: Christian Literature Co., 1900), 163.

2. Notice the word "crusade" could have been used, but I chose not to use it because of its religious and political connotations.

3. Daniel L. Dreisbach, "Origins and Dangers of the 'Wall of Separation' between Church and State," *Imprimis*, October 2006, 1–7.

4. Edmund L. Andrews, "Fearing that a Gap Will Become a Chasm," *New York Times*, March 2, 2004.

5. Floyd Morris, "If Home Prices Plunge . . . ," *New York Times*, December 24, 2004; Lee Walczak and Richard S. Dunham, "Safety Net," *Business Week*, May 16, 2005, 15–30, ff.

6. Jacob S. Hacker, *The Great Risk Shift: The Assault on American Jobs, Families, Health Care and Retirement and How You Can Fight Back* (New York: Oxford University Press, 2006).

7. Barbara Ehrenreich, *Nickel and Dimed* (New York: Metropolitan Books, 2001); David K. Shipler, *The Working Poor: Invisible in America* (New York: Vintage Books, 2004); and Louis Uchitelle, *The Disposable American: Layoff and Its Consequences* (New York: Knopf, 2006).

8. Michael Harrington, *The Other America* (Baltimore: Penguin Books, 1963).

9. "Citizens for Tax Justice from IRS Data," *New York Times*, April 15, 2006.

10. Michelle Kennedy, *Without a Net: Middle Class and Homeless in America* (New York: Viking, 2005).

11. Writing this chapter in late 2005, Hewlett Packard announced it will lay off 19,000 to 50,000 employees and reduce pensions by approximately one-third. The U.S. auto industry is expected to lay off approximately 60,000 employees and reduce pensions and health benefits (see chapter 5). The airline industry has laid off another 50,000 workers.

12. There are approximately 12 to 15 million illegal immigrants in the country.

13. The largest employer in the United States is Wal-Mart. Its average wage is $7.50/hour.

14. "Citizens for Tax Justice from IRS Data."

15. Amanda M. Stuart, *Consuelo and Alva Vanderbilt* (New York: HarperCollins, 2006); Consuelo Vanderbilt, *The Glitter of Gold* (New York: Harper, 1952).

16. John M. Perkins, *Confessions of an Economic Hit Man* (New York: HarperCollins, 2005). See also chapter 7.

17. See John Kenneth Galbraith, *The New Industrial State* (Boston: Houghton Mifflin, 1985).

18. William C. Symonds. "Leaving Harvard Greener," *Business Week*, January 24, 2005, 44.

19. Mary Beth Marklein, "Flag is Raised on Admissions," *USA Today*, October 25, 2006.

20. Elizabeth F. Farrell, "Public Colleges Tame Costs of Tuition," *Chronicle of Higher Education*, September 28, 2005, 1, A46; Alan Finder, "Aid Lets Small Colleges Ask, Why Pay for Ivy League Retail?" *New York Times*, January 11, 2006.

21. Mary Beth Marklein, "College Aid Is Up, but Tuitions Are Too," *USA Today*, October 25, 2006.

22. Farrell, "Public Colleges Tame Costs of Tuition"; Joshua Wyner, "Educational Equity and the Transfer Student, *Chronicle of Higher Education*, February 10, 2006, B6–B7.

23. *Barrons Profiles of American Colleges* (Hauppauge, NY: Barron's Educational Series, 2004).

24. Erin Strout, "Community Colleges Struggle When It Comes to Soliciting Private Donations," *Chronicle of Higher Education*, February 10, 2006, A25.

25. Joe Nocera, "The University of Raising Money," *New York Times*, October 21, 2006.

26. Strout, "Community Colleges Struggle When It Comes to Soliciting Private Donations," 26.

27. Allan C. Ornstein and Francis P. Hunkins, *Curriculum: Foundations, Principles and Issues*, 4th ed. (Boston: Allyn and Bacon, 2004).

28. Brian Barry, *Why Social Justice Matters* (Malden, MA: Polity Press, 2004), 74.

29. See Steve Forbes, "The Great Economic Debate in the 20th Century," *Imprimis*, March 2006, 1–7; Peter Hartcher, *Bubble Man* (New York: Norton, 2006). Many liberal economists, including Hartcher, would argue that Friedman, Forbes, and Greenspan do not have all the answers, and Greenspan's mistakes as Federal Reserve Chair contributed to the stock market collapse of 2000.

30. John Kenneth Galbraith, *Money: Whence It Came, Where It Went* (Boston: Houghton Mifflin, 1975).

31. Most readers will not recognize these names. They are not to worry. Here I am speaking to the invisible university, a group of professors in my field of study that often speak to each other in print.

32. Harrington, *The Other America* (Baltimore: Penguin, 1961); Ehrenreich, *Nickel and Dimed*; Shipler, *The Working Poor*; and Uchitelle, *The Disposable American*.

33. Quote by Evelyn Waugh, cited in Geoffrey Wheatcroft, "Smiley's Anti-American People," *New York Times*, January 11, 2004.

34. See Paul Cartledge, *Alexander the Great* (New York: Overlook Press, 2004); Philip Matyszak, *Chronicle of the Roman Republic* (London: Thames and Hudson, 2003). Both authors would argue that Hellenistic Greece and the Roman Empire were more influential in history than the United States.

35. James B. Weaver, *A Call to Action* (Des Moines, IA: Printing Co., 1892), 445.

36. Otto von Bismarck, cited in Allan C. Ornstein, *Teaching and Schooling in America: Pre and Post September 11* (Boston: Allyn and Bacon, 2003), 239.

37. Alexis de Tocqueville, *Democracy in America*, vol. 3 (New York: Knopf, 1945), originally published in 1835), 89.

38. Dinesh D'Souza, *What's So Great about America* (Washington, DC: Regnery, 2002).

39. Bernard H. Levy, *American Vertigo: Traveling America in the Footsteps of Tocqueville* (New York: Random House, 2006).

40. Walter A. McDougall, *Freedom Just around the Corner* (New York: HarperCollins, 2004).

41. McDougall, *Freedom Just around the Corner*. Also see John Ferling, *A Leap in the Dark: The Struggle to Create the American Republic* (New York: Oxford University Press, 2003); David A. Price, *Love and Hate in Jamestown* (New York: Knopf, 2003).

42. Joseph Perkins, *An Oration Upon Genius, Pronounced at Harvard University*, Harvard University, July 19, 1797.

43. Thomas Sowell, *Conquests and Cultures: An International History* (New York: Basic, 1998); Sowell, "Race, Culture and Equality," *Forbes*, October 5, 1998, 144–49.

44. Charles Murray, *Human Accomplishment: The Pursuit of Excellence in the Arts and Sciences* (New York: HarperCollins, 2004).

45. William H. McNeill, *The Rise of the West* (Chicago: University of Chicago Press, 1963).

46. Rodney Stark, *The Victory of Reason: How Christianity Led to Freedom, Capitalism, and Western Success* (New York: Random House, 2006).

47. See Kennedy, *Without a Net*.

48. By Gucharan Das, *India Unbound* (New York: Knopf, 2001); Ma Jian, *Red Dust: A Path through China* (New York: Pantheon, 2001); Peter Maass, "Emroz Khan is Having a Bad Day," *New York Times Magazine*, October 21, 2001, 48–51.

49. Daniel Bell, *The Coming of Post-Industrial Society* (New York: Basic, 1973), 108.

50. C. Wright Mills, *The Power Elite* (New York: Oxford University Press, 1956); Thomas J. Peters and Robert H. Waterman, *In Search of Excellence* (New York: Warner, 1993). Also see Eduardo Porter, "How Long Can Workers Tread Water?" *New York Times*, July 14, 2005.

51. Paul Fussell, *Class: A Guide through the American Status System* (New York: Summit, 1983).

52. John Kenneth Galbraith, "Economic Delusion, Political Disaster," *New York Times*, March 11, 2001; Isabel V. Sawhill, "Still the Land of Opportunity," *Public Interest* (Spring 1999): 3–12; "What the Tax Cuts Mean for Different Families," *New York Times*, February 9, 2001.

53. Peter Drucker, *Post-Capitalist Society* (New York: Harper, 1995); Richard Florida, *The Rise of the Creative Class* (New York: Perseus, 2002).

54. Greg Toppo, "Groups Call for Comprehensive Reform for U.S. High Schools," *USA Today*, February 28, 2004.

55. Michael Young, *The Rise of the Meritocracy, 1870–2033* (London: Thames and Hudson, 1958); Young, "Down with Meritocracy!" *Guardian*, June 29, 2001.

56. Young, *The Rise of the Meritocracy*.

57. John W. Gardner, *Excellence: Can We Be Equal Too?* (New York: Harper & Row, 1961).

58. In this group, I would classify Ivan Berg, David Cohen, Colin Greer, Henry Levin, Joel Spring, and Paul Violas.

59. Otis Duncan, et al., *Socioeconomic Background and Achievement* (New York: Seminar Press, 1972); Richard B. Freeman, *The Over-Educated American* (New York:

Academic Press, 1976); Isabel Sawhill, *Getting Ahead: Economic and Social Mobility in America* (Washington, DC: Urban Institute, 1998).

60. Christopher Jencks, *Inequality: A Reassessment of the Effect of Family and Schooling in America* (New York: Basic, 1972).

61. Christopher Jencks, et al., *Who Gets Ahead? The Determinants of Economic Success in America* (New York: Basic, 1979), 311.

62. Susan E. Mayer and Paul E. Peterson, *Earning and Learning* (Washington, DC: Brookings Institute, 1999).

63. Mayer and Peterson, *Earning and Learning*, 11.

64. Eric Konigsberg, "The New Class War: The Haves vs. the Have Mores," *New York Times*, November 19, 2006.

65. *The Condition of Education, 2001* (Washington, DC: U.S. Government Printing Office, 2001), 42, indicator 22.

66. *The Condition of Education, 2001*, 24, indicator 12: *Digest of Education Statistics 2000*, 140, table 123.

67. *The Condition of Education, 2001*, 122–23, appendix I, indicators 11–12.

68. *The Condition of Education, 2001*, 22–25, indicator 13; *Reaching the Top: A Report of the National Task Force on Minority Achievement* (New York: College Board, 1999), 7, 9.

69. *The Condition of Education, 2005* (Washington, DC: U.S. Government Printing Office, 2005), 142, table 14-2.

70. *Digest of Education Statistics 1998* (Washington, DC: Government Printing Office, 1998), 146, table 131.

71. *The Condition of Education 2005*, 45–47, indicators 11–13.

72. *The Condition of Education, 2005*, 49, indicator 15.

73. *The Condition of Education, 2001*, 43, indicator 23; "Few Minorities Get Best High School Diplomas," *New York Times*, November 30, 2005; "School Finance Case Plays Out in Court," *New York Times*, October 10, 2006.

74. *The Condition of Education, 2001*, 49, indicator 28.

75. *Digest of Education Statistics 2000*, 469, table 412; *The Condition of Education, 2001*, 65, indicator 38; 178, appendix I, indicator 57. Also see Gerald K. LeTendre, "The Problem of Japan: Qualitative Studies and International Educational Comparisons," *Educational Researcher* 28 (1999): 38–48. Also see Fred Lundenburg and Allan C. Ornstein, *Educational Administration: Concepts and Practices*, 4th ed. (Belmont, CA: Wadsworth, 2004).

76. John N. Ogbu, *Minority Education and Caste* (New York: Academic Press, 1978); John H. McWhorter, *Losing the Race* (New York: Simon & Schuster, 2000).

77. Roland Fryer, "Acting White," *Education Next* (Winter 2006): 52–59.

4

✛

What Is Equality?

No country has taken the idea of equality more seriously than the United States. Politically, the idea is rooted in the Declaration of Independence and the Constitution. We have fought two wars over the definition of equality: the American Revolution and the Civil War. The origins of American public schools are also dominated by the concept of equal opportunity and the notion of universal and free education. Jefferson understood that the full development of talent among all classes could be developed in the New World, and especially among the common class. "Geniuses will be raked from the rubbish," he wrote.[1] He added that the common people of America had the opportunity for thinking and discussing social and political problems closed to them in the Old World.

THE ROLE OF EDUCATION

Horace Mann understood it, too, and argued that education was the chief avenue where "humble and ambitious youth" could expect to rise.[2] The rise of the "common school" was spearheaded by Mann in the 1820s. He envisioned the schools as "the great equalizer of the condition of men—the balance wheel of the social machinery."[3] Mann also saw the schools serving a social need, that is, to assimilate the immigrants into the American culture. He skillfully rallied public support for the common school by appealing to various segments of the population. To enlist the business community, Mann sought to demonstrate that "education has a market value" with a yield similar to "common bullion." The "aim of industry . . . and wealth of the country" would be augmented "in proportion to the diffusion of knowledge."[4] Workers would be more diligent and more productive. Mann also established a stewardship theory, aimed at the upper class, that the public good would be enhanced by public education. Schools for all children would create a stable society in which people would obey the laws and add to the nation's political and economic well-being. To the workers and farmers, Mann asserted that the common school would be a means of social mobility for their children. To the Protestant community, he argued that the common school would assimilate ethnic and religious groups, promote a common culture, and help immigrant children learn English and the customs and laws of the land.[5] He was convinced that the common school was crucial for the American system of equality and opportunity, for a sense of community to be shared by all Americans, and for the promotion of a national identity.

Although the pattern for establishing common schools varied among the states, and the quality of education varied as well, the foundation of the American public school was being forged through this system. The schools were common in the sense that they housed youngsters of all socioeconomic and religious backgrounds, from age six to fourteen or fifteen, and were jointly owned, cared for, and used by the local community. Because a variety of subjects was taught to children of all ages, teachers had to plan as many as ten to fifteen different lessons a day. Teachers also had to try to keep their schoolrooms warm in the winter—a responsibility shared by the older boys, who cut and fetched wood—and cool in the summer. Schoolhouses were often in need of considerable repair, and teachers were paid miserably low salaries.

The immigrants and workers saw the schools as a social vehicle for upward mobility, to help their children realize the American dream. Equality of opportunity in this context would not lead to equality of outcomes; this concept did not attempt a classless society. As Stanford professor David Tyack wrote, "For the most part, working men did not seek to pull down the rich"; rather they sought equality of "opportunity for their children, an equal chance at the main chance."[6] Equality of opportunity in the nineteenth and early twentieth centuries meant an equal start for all children, but the assumption was that some would go farther than others. Differences in backgrounds and abilities, as well as motivation and personality, would create differences in outcomes among individuals, but the school would assure that children born into any class would have the opportunity to achieve status as persons born into other classes. Implicit in the view was that the "schools represented the means of achieving the goal . . . of equal chances of success" relative to all children in all strata.[7]

Historical Perspective

In retrospect, the schools did not fully achieve this goal, because school achievement and economic outcomes are highly related to social class and family background.[8] Had the schools not existed, however, social mobility would have been further reduced. The failure of the common school to provide social mobility raises the question of the role of the school in achieving equality—and the question of just what the school can and cannot do to affect cognitive and economic outcomes. Can schooling overcome the effects of class? Such factors as family conditions, peer groups, and community surroundings—all components of class—influence learning. Just what should the school be expected to accomplish in the few hours each day it has with students who spend more than three-fourths of their time with their family, friends, and community?

Class is a matter of culture—what educators now call "social capital," the kind of family and community resources available to children.[9] The difference in capital leads to a system of inequality in terms of how students perform in schools and what kinds of jobs they eventually obtain. The question of fairness or equity is how we interpret this inequality. Do middle-class children simply "outcompete" their poor and working-class counterparts in school and therefore land better jobs (a conservative perspective) or is it discrimination and exploitation that ensures the latter group performs poorly in school and their parents, who clean up offices or hotels or work on assembly plants, earn significantly less than their bosses (a liberal perspective). As middle- and upper-class parents jockey for the best schools for their children and hire private tutors and worry about their children's SAT scores, how are less fortunate students supposed to overcome money, power, privilege, and political connections? How is education expected to overcome a system of inequality that leads to the rich to pressure the government to reduce their taxes while it cuts services for the poor, and provides them with second-rate schools, second-rate healthcare, and second-rate jobs?

The notion of differences in class and differences in heredity have remained in the background in American thought, an idea rooted in the Old World to help explain the success of the noble class—and later used by conservative-thinking Americans to explain the rise of the plantation, merchant, and banking class in colonial America, and later the capitalist class in the late nineteenth century during the Gilded Age. By the 1880s, Herbert Spencer, an English philosopher, maintained that the poor were "unfit" and should be eliminated through competition and the survival of the fittest. At the turn of the century, English author H. G. Wells linked peasant immigration to the country as the downfall of America. "I believe that if things go on as they are going, the great mass of them will remain a very low lower class," and the U.S. population "will remain largely illiterate industrial peasants."[10] Today, the debate is couched in terms like "human capital," "brain race," and "illegal immigration." Many Americans contend we are attracting low-wage, low-educated tomato and cabbage pickers, hotel workers, and landscapers while discouraging the foreign-educated students, scientists, and engineers on which the American economy depends. (See chapter 7.)

Ellwood Cubberley, a former school superintendent and professor of education at Stanford University, and one of the most influential education voices at the turn of the twentieth century, feared the arrival of immigrants from southern and eastern Europe. He argued they were slow-witted and stupid compared to the Anglo-Teutonic stock of immigrants. The new immigrants were "illiterate, docile, lacking in self-reliance and initiative, and not possessing the Anglo-Teutonic conceptions of law, order, and government." Their numbers would "dilute tremendously our national stock and corrupt our civil life." The role of the school was not only to "amalgamate" them, but also to prepare them for vocational pursuits as "common wage concerns."[11] The new immigrant and working-class children had little need for an academic curriculum, according to Cubberley, as they were lacking in mental ability and character; in fact, he insisted the common man demanded vocational training for their children. It was foolhardy to saturate these immigrant and working-class children "with a mass of knowledge that can have little application for their lives."[12]

From the 1950s through the 1990s, conservative psychologists, such as William Shockley, Arthur Jensen, and Richard Herrnstein, placed heavy emphasis on heredity as the main factor for intelligence—and the reason why the poor remained poor from one generation to the next. Although the arguments were written in educational terms, the implications were political and implied class warfare, and, most disturbing, it resulted in a stereotype for explaining mental inferiority among the lower class, especially blacks, thereby explaining the need for vocational programs and putting blacks on the defensive.

Educational Opportunity

The modern view of educational equality, which emerged also in the 1950s, goes much further than the old view. In light of this, James Coleman, when he was professor of education at Johns Hopkins University, outlined five views of inequality of educational opportunity, paralleling liberal philosophy: (1) inequality defined by the same curriculum for all children, with the intent that school facilities be equal; (2) inequality defined in terms of social or racial composition of the schools; (3) inequality defined in terms of such intangible characteristics as teacher morale and teacher expectations of students; (4) inequality based on school consequences or outcomes for students with equal backgrounds and abilities;

and (5) inequality based on school consequences for students with unequal backgrounds and abilities.[13]

The first two definitions deal with race and social class; the next definition deals with concepts that are hard to define and hard to change; the fourth definition deals with school finances and expenditures. The fifth definition is an extreme and revisionist interpretation: Equality is reached only when the outcomes of schooling are similar for all students—those who are lower class and minority as well as majority and middle class.

When inequality is defined in terms of equal outcomes (both cognitive and economic), we start comparing racial, ethnic, and religious groups. In a heterogeneous society like ours, this results in some hotly debated issues, including how much to invest in human capital, how to determine the cost effectiveness of social and educational programs, who should be taxed and how much, to what extent we are to handicap our brightest and most talented minds (the swift racers) to enable those who are slow to catch up, and whether affirmative action policies lead to reverse discrimination.[14] Indeed, we cannot treat these issues lightly, because they affect most of us in one way or another and lead to questions over which wars have been fought.

In a more homogeneous society, such as Japan, South Korea, Norway, or Germany, the discussion of race, ethnicity, or religion would not deserve special attention nor require judicial measures. Although it is doubtful if increased spending in big-city schools (where poor and minority students are concentrated) would dramatically effect educational outcomes, poor and minority students still deserve equal education spending—better-paid teachers, small class sizes, high-tech resources, new textbooks, and clean bathrooms—as in affluent suburbs where expenditures often are twice or more the amount of adjacent cities. Students deserve equality of expenditures simply on the basis that schools are public institutions, not private. In a democracy, citizens and their children are entitled to similar treatment, especially because intellectual capital is a national concern, not designed for the benefit of one class or group of students nor the exclusion of another group.

There is no question that other factors arise that prevent equal school spending that are not simply symptoms of racism or class prejudice. They deal with notion of values and the rights of people: The preservation of neighborhood schools, concern about big government and state-imposed policies directed at the local level, fear of increased taxation and why someone should have to pay for someone else's child's education, and the inability of politicians to curtail well-to-do parents from supporting their own neighborhood schools and property values. The question is how much education equality should society strive for? We can have greater equality by lowering standards or by pulling down bright students. We can have more equality by handicapping bright students (as in affirmative action) or by providing an enormous amount of additional resources for slow-performing students (as in compensatory funding). But eventually we come to a slippery slope and ask: How much money? Who is to pay for it?

In his classic text on excellence and equality, John Gardner points out that, in a democracy, the differences among groups cannot be dwelled on and we go out of the way to ignore them. He describes the dilemma: "Extreme equalitarianism . . . which ignores differences in native capacity and achievement, has not served democracy well. Carried far enough, it means . . . the end of that striving for excellence which has produced mankind's greatest achievements." Gardner also asserts that "no democracy can give itself over to emphasize extreme individual performance and retain its democratic principles—or extreme equalitarianism and retain its vitality." Our society should seek to develop "all potentialities at all levels. It takes more than an educated elite to run a complex, technological society."[15] Every modern society, as well as every ancient society, has learned this hard lesson, some only after tremendous bloodshed and loss of life.

Every efficient and innovative society has also learned to recognize and reward various abilities, talents, and creative endeavors. In school, and other aspects of American society, the chief instrument for identifying ability and talent is a standardized test. It is not surprising, according to Gardner, that such tests are the object of criticism and hostility, because they encourage the sorting and selecting of students into special tracks and programs. The fact is, "the tests are designed to do an unpopular job."[16] They are designed to measure what a person knows or how well a person can perform particular tasks; the data can be used to compare people and make decisions—such as who gets into what college and who gets selected for various jobs. Tests are also used for applying standards to determine quality—and who gets ahead in schools and society. Although, in our society unlike most other societies, we are given multiple chances to succeed, Gardner is still concerned that the search for talent and the importance of education in our high-tech and knowledge-based society will lead to increasing inequality among educated and uneducated individuals.

The issues that Gardner (and test specialists) raise will not go away, at least not in our democratic and heterogeneous society; they directly affect the social fabric of the country and have echoed loudly since the War on Poverty and the civil rights movement. They lead to heated arguments in the media, often where frank discussion is curtailed; the worst culprits are college campus newspapers and forums—ironically a terrible place for academic freedom if the messenger moves too far to the political

Right.[17] While Gardner talks about the difference between excellence and equality, and the need to achieve some balance in a democratic society, we can also distinguish between *equality* and *equity*. These twin concepts were originally introduced by Herbert Gans, of Columbia University, in *More Equality* (1973) and by Frederick Mosteller and Daniel Moynihan, both from Harvard University, in *Equality of Educational Opportunity* (1972). The powerful and troubling analysis of equality and equity persist, best analyzed today by Nathan Glazer and Christopher Jencks— Harvard professors and sociologists who have spent a lifetime studying inequality as it relates to race and class.

Equality has to do with similarity in opportunity or results, but equity (or fairness) deals with a person's or group's effort and the reward (or outcomes) for that effort. Inequality occurs when a person or group works harder but achieves little reward or, in reverse, when a person or group works less and receives most of the rewards. Inequity involves lack of opportunity, whereby the laws and/or social institutions discriminate against certain people or groups based on a perceived characteristic; henceforth, those people will be disadvantaged in society. To be sure, the design of society—equal opportunity or unequal opportunity—determines what happens to people in education, jobs, health care, housing, etc., and how income and wealth will be distributed among people.

Here we are not attempting to achieve equal results, which ignores the concept of effort or ability and assumes that everyone is entitled to equal rewards, regardless of effort or ability. Such an assumption has more to do with affirmative action and quotas. With equity, we are seeking some sort of *fairness*, what Harvard professor John Rawls would refer to as a *just* society. We want to avoid a stacked deck, the existence of inequality and inequity—no matter what their effort or ability some people will always be discriminated against. The potential effects are more than just economic; the outcomes have social, political, and emotional consequences, resulting in feelings of inferiority, anger, self-hatred, and hatred of others, producing pathological and delinquent behavior (in terms of crime, delinquency, and drugs), and detrimentally affects the productivity and vitality of that nation. If a person cannot find viable work, if the deck is always stacked against a person, the argument can be made: Why go to school? Why try to find a job? The system is unfair and unjust; it is easier to drop out.

When we talk about equal opportunity, eventually the question arises as to whether everyone should have the right to go to college. If everyone has the right to a high school education, why not college? But the pool of abilities and talent varies, and there are many children whose academic limitations cannot be traced to poverty or deprivation. Children who come from upper-class homes have the advantage of special tutoring, and have parents who have the ability to move to a successful school district—

where schools are cleaner and more modern, where teachers are better paid and generally have more education and experience, and the school climate is more conducive to learning.[18] But others who are less fortunate start out on a less than equal footing and continue to experience family, school, peer group, and community handicaps that only increase their disadvantages—and thus are often doomed to disappointment.

Despite ability or talent, children who come from advantaged homes have parents with political and social connections that help get their children into Ivy League colleges and high-paying jobs. Competition for good jobs requires that you get into the *right* university, not just a university. Some 35 percent of undergraduates at Princeton are "from nonsectarian private schools [rich kids]: over 20 times their 1.7 percent in the school population."[19] You don't have to be a rocket scientist to get into Harvard or Yale or to work on Wall Street, and many people who accumulate the usual clutch of mansions, fancy cars, and millionaire baubles possess lesser abilities and are "C" students. Ironically, the business world is depressingly full of millionaires who equate their net worth with brains, full of wealthy boys and girls born on third base who think they hold the major league record for triples.

We would like to believe in the image of a person who rose from nothing and who owed nothing to parentage. This is part of the American dream and the notion of the self-made person (usually a man); and there is just enough possibility and truth in these stories, a testimony to American democracy. But the humblest and poorest rarely rise to the top. Statistically the odds do not coincide with popular literature or folklore. For every poor or working-class person that becomes a captain of industry or a super athlete, hundreds of thousands are doomed to live out their life in the same quintile they started, or slightly move, an inch or two higher. Given a highly competitive society, life is not a bowl of cherries or a rose garden and sometimes there is more rain than sunshine. All you have to do is listen to the songs of Muddy Waters, A. P. Carter, and Johnny Cash—and you hear a prickle or sad story about the human condition and reality of life.

THE WINNING OF THE WEST

The Western movement can also be viewed as one of the numerous migrations of Europeans to sparse, somewhat uncivilized lands. Behind this "European invasion" is the assumption that the land was free for military veterans, and to be sold cheap to farmers and speculators who would develop it. There was no need to buy the land from the American Indians; it was purchased from the French and now belonged to the U.S.

government, so the theory went. The idea was to claim the land and occupy it. One historian, Walter Webb, put it this way: "the frontier movement [was] the invasion of land assumed to be vacant as distinguished from an invasion of an occupied or civilized country, an advance against nature rather than against men."[20]

The West was a huge parcel of land, more than one million square miles (stretching from the Gulf of Mexico to Canada from Appalachia to the northwest Pacific coast), more than six times the size of the original thirteen colonies. "Inherent in the American concept of [the] frontier [was] the idea of a body of free land which [could] be had for the taking."[21] The movement was so rapid and extensive that Merle Curti, the liberal historian from the University of Wisconsin, maintains that it actually "drained the population from [Eastern] seaboard regions."[22] It was a rich landscape, ripe for growth and development, compared to the Old World, which was cramped geographically and constrained by heredity and privilege. For John Gordon, a historian and conservative columnist at *American Heritage* magazine, the growth of the American economy was tied to the boundless resources of the West and the opportunities provided to people, which allowed multiple personalities—the Fords (manufacturing), Morgans (finance), Rockefellers (oil), Vanderbilts (railroad and shipping), and Carnegies (steel)—to come alive and thrive.[23] Indeed, we have always paid special attention to the wealthy and powerful among us; there is a certain fascination we have with them, perhaps because of our capitalistic instincts, perhaps because of our dreams. What is surprising, however, is that despite our limited historical perspective we remember the names of these captains of industry and, usually, consider them as folk heroes or patriots who helped build America.

Now the rich were not motivated to go west; they were comfortable in their eastern surroundings and did not want to face the rugged terrain and the hardship of travel. Starting over was for the sod-buster farmer, rugged miner, adventurer, trapper, hunter, immigrant, and cowboy—the person willing to roll up his or her sleeves and go to work. The Western movement can be viewed as the edge of the Western world, the place where the shambles of European liberalism might have one last chance to succeed. It was kind of a class war, where the peasant and "bourgeoisie" class of the Old Order could live without the stratification and privileges associated with the monarchy and nobility of the ruling class. In stratified societies of Europe, in the classrooms of Eton and Exeter, the amount of education received by a child largely depended on his or her class. In the run-down parts of European society and among the masses, talent, merit, and hard work rarely made a difference. The individual was kept down by his or her class, and society paid dearly for instilling the doctrine of heredity and privilege.

The history of education in the United States, and especially in the West, was a long and hard campaign to break from the European system of education, and to reward merit, talent, and effort. One hundred years later, in the second half of the twentieth century, this great fight to democraticize American education was to be called "equal educational opportunity," which had its roots in Jefferson's system of education for his state of Virginia. Jefferson's education plan subdivided the counties of Virginia into wards, each of which would have a free elementary school to teach reading, writing, arithmetic, and history. He rejected the reading of religious materials, including the Bible, because elementary schoolchildren by reason of their immaturity were unable to fully understand the spiritual implications. He did put great faith in moral education when children could fully reason, describing it as education for "good conscience, good health, occupation, and freedom in all just pursuits."[24]

These four characteristics of Jefferson's moral education would become part of the famous Seven Cardinal Principles of Secondary Education, presented in 1918 by the National Education Association (NEA), which could be summed up in twentieth-century "educationese" as ethical character, good health and physical fitness, vocational education, and civic education. For Jefferson, who epitomized the Age of Enlightenment, *education* (a blending of knowledge and reason) and *morality* would foster a free society; these two ingredients would provide citizens with the understanding and virtue to fulfill the obligations and duties of free people.

Also provided for in Jefferson's proposal was the establishment of twenty grammar schools at the secondary level, for which gifted students who could not afford to pay tuition would be provided scholarships. There, the students would study Latin, Greek, English, geography, and higher mathematics. Upon completing grammar school, half the scholarship students would be assigned positions as elementary (or ward) school teachers. The ten scholarship students of highest achievement would attend William and Mary College. These youth would become the leaders and statesmen promoting the interests of the Republic. Jefferson's plan promoted the idea of school as a selective agency to identify bright students for continuing education, as well as the future idea of equality of opportunity for economically less fortunate students.

Jefferson forcefully expressed his view in "A Bill for the More General Diffusion of Knowledge": "Those persons who nurture [their] endowed with genius and virtue should be rendered [or educated] . . . to guard the sacred deposit of the rights and liberties and their fellow citizens . . . without regard to wealth, birth, or other accidental condition . . . whom nature hath fitly formed and disposed to become useful instruments for the public, it is better that such should be sought for and educated at this common expense of all."[25] In the final analysis, Jefferson had the greatest faith in educating the common citizen for promoting democracy, more than the need for the talented to attend college, for it was "the people [who] are the ultimate guardians of their own liberty."[26]

The Democratic Forces of the West

Both Thomas Jefferson and Andrew Jackson had immense faith in the common man, and it was Jeffersonian democracy followed by Jacksonian democracy that flourished in the West. When Jefferson spoke of the American people, he meant the American farmer, who was to be the backbone of American democracy. Jackson meant the frontier people, including farmers, plain people, and those with the "vulgar whims" of the lower class.[27] He rejected the status of class and the view of democracy as led by gentlemen and landed gentry, which Alexander Hamilton, Aaron Burr, James Monroe, and John Quincy Adams all favored. Based on hindsight, Jefferson and Jackson took the most favorable and egalitarian position—recognizing all the classes and hoping plain people and lower-class people would become educated through the schools and gain the proper faith, morality, and knowledge to self-govern—as the nation broke from its European traditions and forged westward in the territory Jefferson had purchased from the French in 1803. In terms of size, resources, and price, it was the best real estate bargain in U.S. history.

American historians would even argue that, if the English colonists had been limited or hemmed in along the coast, American social and political development would have followed the class consciousness and lack of social/economic mobility followed by European countries.[28] It was lawyers who made the laws, who, by background and education, were conservative, patrician, and generally accepted traditional European laws of nature (latter to be called Social Darwinism) and property rights. But these lawyers were forced to translate many of their patrician ideas into the reality of the New World—an American West that had an abundance of land to settle, a mysterious wilderness, vast natural resources, and primitive conditions being populated not by the wealthy but the frontier people and agrarian people who believed in equality and rejected the aristocracy. It was here, in the new and untamed world, where the principles of the French Revolution and European liberalism could flourish. It was in the "wild" West, with its natural streams and rivers, wolves, and bears, that the theories of ancient Greek democracy had the best chance to be translated into practice.

It was the fluidity of life in the West, the hard work, the independence, the new opportunities, the forces of nature, the steady growth of prosperity, and the belief in the rights of the individual, that led to an egalitarianism, to an ideal later implied by the American dream. This sense of equality could never be achieved in the eastern cities, much less in

Europe, where class prejudice, elitism, and etiquette of the more cultured and upper class ruled. In the slums of U.S. cities, it was not unusual for entire immigrant and lower-class families to live in one small room (ten by twelve feet), in buildings without water or heat, with minimal light and ventilation. Disease, alcohol, and crime characterized the city slum—far different from the open landscapes, fresh air, and log cabin homes (averaging 1,000 to 1,500 square feet) on the frontier. While the West was romanticized for its rich resources and vast land, popularized by folklore, ballads of the West, and stories of Buffalo Bill and Wild Bill Hickok, the East was seen as controlled by greedy industrialists and bankers, where products were produced at the expense of labor—producing a new class of "have nots" called factory workers, and later union workers.

It was in the West where the common man had the most opportunity to prosper and realize the American dream. Horace Greeley, the reporter for the *New York Tribune*, put it in simple terms: "Go West, young man." For Greeley and other liberal thinkers, the West was the place where reform was possible, where people could start a new life, and where there was the potential to elevate the common person to vast heights. One hundred years later, President Ronald Reagan would tell the American people that the American West had shaped his character (in fact, the Secret Service nicknamed him "Rawhide"), just as Bush was convinced that Texas had shaped his outlook on life. In "bang-bang, shoot-up" style, Bush declared war on Iraq without fully understanding its consequences and told the world in cowboy slang: "You are either for us or against us." Even worse, Americans who have captured the flavor of the West, partially because of all the John Wayne and Clint Eastwood movies, eventually looked forward to watching the war on television in the same way they looked forward to watching the Super Bowl, NASCAR races, or the World Series.

It was here in the West "where the common school flourished, where there was faith in the common person and a common destiny."[29] The common one-room schoolhouse "eventually led to one of America's most lasting sentimentalized pictures—the 'Little Red Schoolhouse' . . . in almost every community." It had problems and critics, but it symbolized the pioneers' spirit and desire to provide free education for their children. "It was a manifestation of the belief held by most of the frontier leaders that a school was necessary to raise the level of American civilization."[30]

This small school, meager in outlook and thwarted by inadequate funding and insufficient teachers, nevertheless fit with the conditions of the American frontier—of expansion and equality. It was a "blab school," according to Abe Lincoln, but it was the kind of school in which the common person's children—even those born in log cabins—could begin their "readin'," "writin'," and "cipherin',"[31] and could advance to limitless achievements. It was a school local citizens could use as a polling place, a center for Grange activities, a site for dances, and a location for community activities; it was a school controlled and supported by the local community.

The traditions built around the common school in the West—the idea of neighborhood schools, local control of schools, and government support of schools—took a firm hold on the hearts and minds of Americans. America's confidence in the common school helped fashion public schools later in the nineteenth century; it also influenced our present system of universal education.

Hypothesizing about the Past

Allow me the opportunity to push the envelope, to stretch historical interpretation to another level. Much of Jefferson's ideas about politics, education, and equality were rooted in the Enlightenment, and particularly the writings of John Locke, the English philosopher, and Jean-Jacques Rousseau, the French philosopher and educator. It was Locke and Rousseau who popularized the idea of a "social contract"—that is, government is supposed to represent the people, especially the common people, and the people are supposed to elect their government. This being the case, theoretically, government is supposed to protect the people against the aristocratic class and big-business class. But it is questionable if the poor, much less the common man in the United States, ever had a social contract— possibly for brief periods, with Thomas Jefferson and Andrew Jackson and later with Abe Lincoln and Franklin Roosevelt.

Although Jefferson and Roosevelt were from the upper crust, or patrician class, Jackson and Lincoln were from common stock and came out of the prairie. The favored classes differed in intellectual equipment, custom, and attitudes from the plain people, and it was values of the favored patrician class that largely shaped the intellectual thought of the nation in the decades prior to and after Jackson's and Lincoln's election and that voters resented. A democracy led by gentlemen always represented a wing of American political thought, which is a main reason why we have a *republic* form of government based on Roman thinking and not a pure *democratic* system based on the Greek model.

Jackson and Lincoln represent everything the property class and capitalist class feared or resented—the rise of the common man and in Lincoln's words "a government of the people, by the people, and for the people." It is only when the people truly have power, when the government they elect represents the interests of the people and not the interests of big business, that education and other social institutions can play a factor in bolstering economic opportunity and fostering mobility among the common people. If the people lack a social contract, or if the contract has been broken or bastardized, then education and other social and health-care programs play a minor role in the pursuit of opportunity and equality. The abilities and talents of the common people cannot be fully nurtured.

Jackson and Lincoln were part of the strife and adventure of the frontier, but Jefferson also understood the romantic wilderness and the destiny of the people who tilled the soil, hunted in the forests, and constructed homes and roads away from the cities. Rousseau, Jefferson's most important intellectual influence, would have been at home on the frontier. The soil, the forests, the rivers and mountains, and the wilderness were his kind of landscape, his natural environment where the individual could develop and flourish. The frontier was the antithesis of urban life, which Rousseau disparaged and felt would eventually corrupt man and limit the child's natural growth. Jefferson also had great faith in agrarian democracy and believed cities were overcrowded, filthy, and corrupted by the search for profits among merchants and patricians. As a southerner, where land was plentiful, he felt that, in the free air of the country, small farmers could flourish and work with country gentlemen to create a stable society.

Plato influenced Lincoln's views about the need for a strong central government, while at the same time encouraging democracy. But the ancient Greek philosopher believed that equality would promote despotism of the masses. He felt that common people needed to be restrained and guided by philosopher-kings with the help of intellectuals, but that the state was to exist to serve man—a marked departure for that period in which man existed to serve the state. Like Jefferson, Plato believed that through education citizens would gain appropriate knowledge and morality to function in Athenian democracy. The difference is that Jefferson and Lincoln had more faith in the common man, whereas Plato put more faith in an oligarchy and intellectual elite. To be sure, Jefferson and Lincoln had read the ideas of John Locke and Jean-Jacques Rousseau and thus could refine the notion of democracy. Plato did not have that benefit.

How would these three giant philosophers react to the passing of the frontier, and transitional generations benefiting from education? There was a major difference between Plato's republicanism, Rousseau's romanticism, and Jefferson's enlightenment. Plato was at home in the big city-state of Athens, with its inventory of manuscripts and artistic objects and the buzz of people in the marketplaces. He would have flourished in the big cities of Boston, Philadelphia, and New York.

Rousseau would have preferred the old West, seeing it as a "beautiful prison," cut off from the rest of the world, and he certainly would have appreciated Henry David Thoreau's *Walden*, Ernest Thompson's *On*

Golden Pond, and Thomas Hart Benton's water-colored landscapes. Jefferson was comfortable in the big cities of America and Europe (in fact, he lived parts of his life in Paris and enjoyed its "gentler" social life); he was also at home in small, rural communities, the hard path: where people quarried the earth, cleared trees, built their own homes, plowed and grazed the soil, and hunted elk and moose.

Rousseau would have appreciated Thoreau's words: "I went to live deliberately, to front only the essential factors of life, and to see if I could not learn what I had to teach, and not, when I came to die, discover that I had not lived." Rousseau would have cheered the rustic, outdoor, communal life of the American Indians and Eskimos who hunted and lived off the land and water. He would have accepted and lived the life of a Quaker, Friend, or Mennonite, farming the land, cutting trees, framing and erecting their own cabins—and forsaking the evil ways of city life. Rousseau, today, would be at home in Woodstock, New York, as well as Woodstock, Illinois, seeing and enjoying nature, whereby, as Thoreau put it, you could "in a summer day [sit] in the sunny doorway from sunrise to noon, rapt in revery."

Thoreau, like Rousseau, had a way with words. But if we consider that most Americans no longer have time to pick blackberries or mushrooms, much of what both nature lovers have to say is, at best, cute, a little idealistic, and perhaps has an edge in the way they describe how others live, particularly urban dwellers. Then, I think of my ride on the Long Island Expressway, heading west, into Manhattan, and what I call "the road to hell."[32] Maybe the log cabin doesn't look so off-kilter, and the hunters, fishermen, and farmers may know something about life that I haven't learned to appreciate. (Perhaps this is the reason why I drown myself in the music of Johnny Cash and Willie Nelson, where there are visions of old farmers and cowboys, dusty roads, and coal-driven trains along the prairie.)

Jefferson, much more than Rousseau and Plato, would have accepted the passing of the frontier, where the sons and daughter first went to common schools and then to colleges and universities to become doctors, lawyers, and accountants. Life was not easy on the frontier; there was exposure to ungrateful and cruel winters, possible hunger, sickness, and death. Thus, Jefferson would have cheered the rise of today's new generation, performing medical miracles, fighting over legal words and phrases and representing clients, sitting behind desks and clicking computers and shuffling papers, and becoming somewhat "flabby" and affluent by age thirty.

Jefferson would have seen all this as progress, although he would have understood what had been lost; he was too educated and too cosmopolitan not to understand the authenticity of the hard life—on the plains, by the rivers, in the wilderness, on the hills and mountains. Rousseau would have despaired, seeing men and women removed from nature and the physical life; he would have flatly rejected the notion of golf and tennis, games originally for the nobility class and now for a "soft" generation of people. Rousseau would have experienced a broken heart had he lived long enough to endure American progress and American culture by the mid–twentieth century. However, he would have saluted the writings of Theodore Dreiser (*An American Tragedy*), F. Scott Fitzgerald (*Peace of Soul, This Side of Paradise, The Great Gatsby*), Sinclair Lewis (*Babbitt, Elmer Gantry, It Can't Happen Here, Main Street*) and John Dos Passos (*U.S.A., Manhattan Transfer, Three Soldiers*), all of whom denounced America's commercialism and conformity, its materialism and "meritocracy," its urban blight and degenerate lifestyle, its class struggle and inequality among the classes.

Rousseau would have rejected the new Americans, somewhat comfortable and distant from the land, speaking idle chit-chat, drinking "designer" coffee, and measuring their lives and status by the number of toilets in their houses. He would have chastised all the people who now have "gentler" lives and deaths than their ancestors, and who have grown soft, corrupt, and vulgar. Rousseau would have called for SWAT teams to swoop down on all the robber barons, CEOs, and dot-com wizards who move around money and produce nothing and make nothing—the "few who wind up with the savings of many," to repeat one of the Eugene Debs's better ditties.

As Plato was an advocate of a strong nation-state, his greatest concern today would be media images, mass propaganda, opinion polls—and American politics—or how the press treats liberal and conservative government officials. Plato was always at war against opinion makers, especially the Sophists or intellectuals, who used polemics and opinion to formulate policy rather than the truth. Because Plato was cultivated and lived in the city, I suspect that, so long as his philosopher-kings (today's statesmen and leaders) had the opportunity to craft policy, he would accept the mobility of the offspring of the common folk (his workers and soldiers) and feel at home with yuppies and guppies (graying yuppies) now driving around in BMWs, talking about the differences between Merlot and Cabernet, while nibbling on their chocolate-covered strawberries and chatting about the latest exhibit at Soho or the meaning of life at some cocktail party. Plato, I believe, would have toasted the "riches" of the upper class, and viewed their status as, in J. P. Morgan's words, "the reward of toil and virtue." Rousseau would have died a thousand deaths with the J. P. Morgans, WorldComs, and Enrons fleecing the public and robbing the retirement pensions of the laboring class or average worker.

The Voice of Rousseau

If there is anyone among the egalitarian voices—Plato, Locke, Rousseau, Jefferson, Jackson, and Lincoln—who frustrated and occasionally infuriated, as often as he fascinated, his readers, the honors must fall to Jean-Jacques Rousseau. Although the academic world knows and respects Rousseau's ideas, he would never end up in a beach bag at the Hamptons or Nantucket, nor would his biography be placed on someone's coffee table, as might Shakespeare or Dante in good-mannered or upper-class society. But there can be no doubt that Rousseau is the most interesting among the "gang of six"—a classic underachiever who wound up over-achieving, like the three Cs: Churchill (the foreign minister), Cash (the singer), and the Colonel (the founder of Kentucky Fried Chicken). He is a rags-to-riches kind of guy, sort of a Cinderella story, the type of person that Alexander Hamilton would consider a threat to the world order of big business and banking.

Rousseau was an unschooled teenage runaway, a rebellious working-class kid, socially awkward (an early version of the movie star James Dean), suffering from dyslexia, considered a proven failure at one bureaucratic job after another, and somewhat "nuts" and fit for an asylum, as judged in his world. He floundered into his forties; not until his fifties (at an age when most of his contemporaries were already dead and buried) did his writings seep into discussions at the taverns and coffeehouses of Paris, London, and Vienna. Rousseau, after all, was swimming upstream, trying to escape the iron grip of the aristocracy. He was considered by the vast majority to be outlandish and radical. Recall he was writing about a state of nature and the natural rights of man that never existed, about a political system that had never existed even in ancient Greece (as most of its populace were not citizens). Political and social equality, the will and sovereignty of the people (not the lords or barons or priests), and inalienable rights and equality of citizenship were meaningless ideas up to that point in time.

John Locke was the only person who had touched on these ideas, about one hundred years prior, in his *Two Treatises of Government*, which appeared in 1689, followed the next year by *An Essay Concerning Human Understanding*. Rousseau basically stands alone, however, as he ranted and pushed his ideas of a social contract between government and its people and in describing the roots of modern democracy. His novel, *Emile*, which attacked authoritarian schooling and an exclusively verbal education, became the starting point of child-centered and progressive education (which is somewhat ironical as he was never married but fathered five children and then placed them in orphanages).[33] In some ways, he is the mouse that roared; few people took him seriously in the beginning. At the end, however, he set free the political and social winds that turned tyranny and inequality upside down—and helped turn America into a newfangled, free country.

In the final analysis, Rousseau would have enjoyed living in the 1960s, the rise of the New Left and social movement against big business and big government, war, racism, and inequality. He would have attached himself to the social writings of Jack Kerouac and Allen Ginsberg and to the romantic and "nonfiction" novels of Truman Capote, Norman Mailer, and Tom Wolfe, who sent raw narratives and atypically punctuated writings to *Esquire* and *Harpers* until the editors eventually understood it and saw their genius. Like Rousseau who was considered an awkward writer by his contemporaries, this was the band of writers that would not write straight prose, that were considered at first arbitrary and wild, and later innovative and stylish. They startled their readers but later became trendsetters and "literary rock stars," as Rousseau had become a political voice and celebrity in his era. All of them were originally considered a little "cooky" and "nuts" by their contemporaries, but they slowly emerged from the underground as Quixotic characters and voices of social and political change.

Shades of Blue and Gray and Black and White

Our Civil War pitted fathers against sons, brothers against brothers, blacks against whites, and northerners against southerners. Next to the Napoleonic Wars, it was the bloodiest war in the 1800s. It didn't start out that way, though. At the beginning, "fans" from both the North and the South went out to the Virginia countryside with picnic lunches to watch the spectacle of Bull Run, and ended up fleeing from the onrushing carnage, as did the Union troops. It took only a few weeks for the country to get the message, as stated by Secretary of War Edwin Stanton: "Champagne and Oysters on the Potomac" no longer is the day.[34]

David Eicher, a military historian, reminds us that more than 620,000 Americans died during the Civil War—more than eleven Vietnams. At Antietam, in one day, there were 26,190 casualties, the bloodiest and longest day in America.[35] Merle Curti puts it this way: "Of the 2,500,000 soldiers involved, one in four were killed in action or died of wounds or disease." (Actually more died from disease than by fighting.) Its toll was enormous, equal to the number of American soldiers and sailors lost in *all the wars America has fought*—including the American Revolution, the War of 1812, the Indian Wars, the Mexican and Spanish American Wars, and the two World Wars.[36] In terms of percentage of population at that time, 31 million in 1865, no other country in modern time lost as many soldiers vis-à-vis the total population until World War II, when modern machinery and human madness combined to create a larger catastrophe and waste of human life in Germany (5 million dead) and Russia (30 million dead).

America was ripped apart by the Civil War, first over the issue of federal and state rights, then over slavery. It still has emotional resonance, almost one hundred and fifty years later, not only in terms of black-white relations, but also as it relates to many school and social issues, such as desegregation, federal and state funding, affirmative action, voting patterns and rights, the election of presidents and the selection of Supreme Court judges, and the formation of white-rights groups and black-rights groups—all doing battle over states' rights, civil rights, and equality.

Almost one hundred and fifty years later, the question still haunts us: What is equality? What is America all about? How do we ensure that all groups get a piece of the pie and that it be distributed in a fair manner? When I grew up, it was really simple—the prevailing philosophy was based on equality of opportunity. Individual merit and test scores counted, and no one received extra points or consideration for being "slow," "disabled," or "language deficient," or mentally or emotionally challenged. Educational policy statements focused on academically bright students during this period, and tests were used as a benchmark for sorting out capable from less capable students. Scholarships were primarily based on merit; only a few were given for sports or financial reasons. Education was reflected in our national priorities, with emphasis on science and math as well as high academic standards. That's how the country defeated Hitler and his master race, how we won the atomic bomb race against the Germans, and how we eventually won the Cold War and preserved our way of life.

But it is all over now. Milton Berle and Ed Sullivan are gone, Branch Rickey and Jackie Robinson are historical memories, and "father no longer knows best." Gone are the placid, tranquil Eisenhower years—when there were two separate societies, one black, one white, and when in the South there were separate toilets, separate counters, and separate schools. What we have today are cultural wars, an extension of shades of blue and gray, black and white, and now blue and red. Sixty years ago, as the Cold War began to heat up and McCarthyism burst forth on the political horizon and war-torn world, conservative thought captured the imagination of the American people and put liberal thought on the junk heap of American life, as communists were seen lurking on every corner, in schools and colleges, in the movie industry, on television, and in the press.

Ten to fifteen years later, the United States was in the first phase of a conservative backlash, as the Kennedy and Johnson era came to the forefront and impacted on the American mind. The culture wars were gathering momentum as the political Left captured the headlines but splintered over issues involving patriotism and the war in Vietnam, civil rights and black power, and later feminism. Reacting to the Carter years in which Americans seemed to have lost their national faith and purpose, the Reagan era saw a revival of free-market ideology, religious fervor, and superpatriotism—and some wild-eyed ideas about the Soviet Union as the "evil empire," space lasers and star wars, and Armageddon beginning in the Middle East. The Left continued to splinter as Reagan possessed a gift of gab and forged his conservative ideas on the American landscape. The situation was not much different than Bush's tax policies that favor the rich, coupled with his religious and ideological zeal, antiterrorist dictums (which replaced Reagan's anticommunist chatter). In the post 9/11 era, the political Left has completely unraveled, feeling not under a dark cloud as they did during the McCarthy and Reagan years, but under the yoke or hammer, as the cultural wars have decimated their political base and robbed them of votes. The 2006 elections might be considered the first crack in the conservative control of the nation, a crack which has a tendency to widen unless promptly sealed up.

The clash of ideas between the Left and Right persists today. The Old Left (which I'm part of) is still uncomfortable with political or social ideas that drift from class. The Right still struggles with the reordering of God-given identities and categories of people, or what may be considered as social hierarchies (which stem from the shape-shifting ideas of the old Tories, Federalists, and Protestant establishment). Meanwhile the Center, or majority populace, has trouble readdressing the wrongs of history and providing more than equal opportunity (affirmative action, quotas, reparations, etc.) for minorities or other groups defining themselves as a political minority or oppressed class. It also resists identity politics, which tends to balkanize the country into various groups (ethnic, racial, religious, gender, sexual orientation, handicapped, aged, etc.) seeking various entitlements and preferences.

All of these ideas boil down to conceptions of *equality* and become sort of realpolitik, a clash between the political Left and Right, with the Center making the difference in which direction the political winds will blow— what today would be labeled part of the cultural wars influencing the character of the nation. It is sort of whether you believe that the last shall be first and the dispossessed and despised shall inherit the earth, a theological and hopeful reflection that stirs the heart and soul, or whether you believe that the strong shall survive and the weak shall perish, a social Darwinism perspective of society. In political and economic terms, it comes down to who is running the country and benefiting most from its wealth. Should there be a government by and for the people and should various people organize into pressure groups for purpose of political power and a piece of the economic opportunity? Or should the rich folks and corporate world, the old titans of business and the Protestant establishment, run the country as a free-market exchange and for their speculative endeavors?

If we look in the looking glass, then it boils down to what kind of society we are. What kind of Congress and president should we elect? Do we want a social welfare state, with safety nets and progressive taxes? Or do we want a corporate-run state, where individual responsibility determines our values and there is little sense of community? Do we expect people to fend for themselves, a combination of old Social Darwinism and modern Orwellian logic? Or are we willing to provide minimum levels and decent services and benefits, including education, health care, unemployment insurance, and Social Security, so that low-income and moderate-income Americans, as well as retirees, can live in a dignified way and share in at least a small portion of American fortune? These are questions that determine the fiber of our society and who we really are and what kind of place our children and grandchildren will inherit. In the end, these political and economic questions lead to moral issues raised two hundred years ago by Immanuel Kant, as well as issues concerning social justice raised more recently by John Rawls. These are issues that should not be issues—not in a decent, compassionate, and progressive society.

Today, given the context of the times, some of us would argue for equal results (not equal opportunity), group rights (not individual rights), and even reparations (not saving or investing). Others, including most of my old friends from the schoolyard, along with their children, would still advocate equality of opportunity, where individual performance counts and produces differences in outcomes. The commitment to provide a fair chance for everyone to develop their talents remains central to the national creed for the vast majority of Americans; it has deep political roots, and, according to Isabel Sawhill, is what distinguishes us from the history and philosophy of Europe. Virtually no one favors equal distribution of income, for it would discourage hard work, savings, investment, and risk taking. Some form of inequality, based on abilities and talent, is the price we pay for a dynamic economy and the right of each individual to retain the benefits of his or her own labor.[37] The idea, for Sawhill, a Brookings Institute liberal economist, is not to address the symptoms or results of inequality, but to address the causes of inequality.

SOCIAL MOBILITY AND SOCIAL STRUCTURE

Social scientists study social mobility in order to ascertain the relative openness or fluidity of a social structure. They are interested in the difficulties different persons or groups experience in acquiring the goods and services that are valued in the culture and may be acquired through unequal contributions.

In *ascriptive* societies, the stratification system is closed to individual mobility because status and prestige are determined at birth. One's education, occupational status, income, and lifestyle cannot be changed. In an *open-class* society, although people start with different advantages, opportunities are available for them to change their initial positions. The life chances of a welfare recipient's child born in the slums differ considerably from those of a banker's child born in the suburbs, but in an achievement-orientated society the former can still achieve as much as or more than the latter.

The emphasis on vertical social mobility in the American social structure is one of the more striking features of our class system. Kurt Mayer, in a classic sociology text, maintains that the United States puts emphasis on social mobility, more than any other nation in modern times: "Americans have firmly proclaimed the idea of equality and freedom of achievement and have acclaimed the large numbers of individuals who have risen from humble origins to positions of prominence and affluence." Indeed, the belief in opportunity is so strongly entrenched in the culture that most Americans feel not only that each individual has the "right to succeed but that it is his duty to do so."[38] Thus, we look with disapproval upon those who make little or no attempt to better themselves—or who become "welfare junkies."

There is historical evidence of considerable social mobility in the United States. Studies of *intergenerational mobility*—the occupational career patterns of individuals in terms of their mobility between jobs and occupations during their lifetimes—reveal that a very large proportion of American men have worked in different communities, different occupations, and different jobs. Nonetheless, there are certain limits to the variety of such experiences; most notably, occupational mobility is confined primarily to either side of a dividing line between manual and nonmanual occupations and between nontechnical/nonprofessional and technical/professional jobs; little permanent mobility takes place across this basic blue-white collar line.[39] Increasingly, little mobility is taking place across any class line.

Once we were called a classless society. Class, today, is blurred by dress and credit card debt (permitting people to buy more than they can afford). Most Americans charge and borrow. As a nation, we owe approximately $750 billion in revolving plastic debt, a six-fold increase from twenty years ago.[40] In 2005, the personal savings rate fell below zero for the first time since the Depression,[41] an indication of the nation's growing debt, which is approaching $10 trillion. In the meantime, the White House response is "Don't worry, be happy, keep spending"—and the hell with the next generation. Americans are willing to pay high interest rates and live in debt without a thought to its implications. Under the guise of "democratizing credit" and making things more accessible to moderate-earning Americans, the credit card industry is sealing the fate of the bottom half and possibly two-thirds of Americans; they will remain buried in their lower income quartiles or classes and not have the capacity to get out of debt.

Measures of Inequality

Given the fact that we all have a different gene pool, and grew up in a different environment and our family heritages are varied, we should expect and accept some inequality. However, the major reason for economic inequality has less to do with ability or talent, and more to do with our roots. For some of us, our ancestors were slaves with no ability to accumulate and pass on wealth. Others are descendants of peasants and refugees who came to America with little more than their shirts on their back and a few suitcases of clothing and family trinkets. On the other side of the divide are descendants of wealthy parents and grandparents who have provided their children with investment trust funds and stocks, as well as fine art, a family business, and large homes, including beach homes on the Cape or in the Hamptons.

Most of us are the children of parents who can be classified between rich and poor, with a mom and/or dad who managed to earn a living as a laborer, factory worker, or government bureaucrat. We grew up in apartments or row houses in the cities, and others grew up in steel towns and mining towns, small suburban and rural towns. Our parents did not earn enough to accumulate wealth; rather they provided us with love, hope, and motivation to go to school to work hard. As students, we grew up with our own dreams, and our aptitudes and performance was measured in school and predicted from early grades. More than two-thirds of us graduated from high school, and we would expect less imbalance and less stratification than what presently exists.

There are many ways of quantifying inequality. One of the accepted ways among economists is to use the *Gini* indices, which are based on grouping Americans into quintiles or fifths. The *Gini* index reports inequality by referring to a single number, with one as complete inequality. (A few households have all the income and wealth, and the others have nothing.) In this vein, zero is considered to be total equality, a perfect socialist state.[42] The *Gini* idea is simple to follow, but because it deals with an average there is noise in the data.

Based on the 1998 "Survey of Consumer Finances," Douglas Clement, from the Federal Reserve of Minneapolis, reports the *Gini* index for *wealth* (net worth of households) to be .803 and for *income* (revenue from all sources) to be .553. In simple, comparative terms, the wealthiest 1 percent of households held 1,335 times more wealth than, and 73 times the income of, the bottom 40 percent. For *earnings* (wages and salaries), the *Gini* index was .611, which translated into a top 1 percent receiving 158 times more than the bottom 40 percent.

In terms of quintiles, the top fifth (or 20%) had an average *wealth* of $1.2 million, whereas the bottom fifth average was negative $4,100.[43] (They owed money.) For *income*, the top fifth averaged $159,100, while the bottom fifth made $6,400. For *earnings*, the top 20 percent earned $127,500, while the bottom 20 percent lost $300. Actually, 23 percent of American households had zero earnings—no wages or salaries—and .24 percent has negative earnings.

As for the top 1 percent, in 1998 they owned 35 percent of the total wealth, received 17.5 percent of the total income, and received 15.3 percent of the total earnings. Whereas earnings are more unequally distributed than income, the situation is reversed for the richest in both respects—that is, inequality is greater for income than earnings. But the greatest inequality is tied to wealth, reflecting the fact that wealth is passed on from generation to generation so that the wealth gap increases over time. In simple terms, it means that the rich get richer and the rest of us, the bottom 80 to 90 percent, get poorer relative to the rich. It also suggests there is less mobility than we realize if we compare Americans over more than one generation. First-generation college-educated people, including gifted and talented people, may earn good money but haven't built up much wealth. It often takes more than one generation to create wealth, thus suggesting that heredity, privilege, and rank is more pervasive than most of us might realize.

Income quintiles (among the poorest, middle-class, and upper-class groups) have hardened. In simple terms, people at the bottom remain at the bottom, and the people at the top remain at the top, with little movement between quintiles. Moreover, between 1979 and 2000 the gaps between poor, middle, and rich increased. The after-tax income of the richest 1 percent climbed 201 percent. Among the middle fifth it increased 15 percent, and among the bottom fifth it increased 9 percent. The process involves simple economics: The very rich find ways, both legal and illegal, to shelter their income and taxes. In addition, the superrich, since 1970, have become big winners in the growth of the American economy and the global marketplace, compounded by a soaring stock market (in which most of these people knew when to sell because of inside information) and real estate market; new high-tech businesses; huge salaries and bonuses to CEOs, sports figures, and movie stars; and tax cuts for the wealthy under the Reagan and Bush administrations.

Still another way to show the gap in income and wealth is to compare the bottom 90 percent of the population with the top .01 percent, that is, those whose 2005 income was $117,000 or less and those who earned $1.6 million or more. From 1950 to 1970, for every additional dollar earned by the lower 90 percent, those in the top 0.1 percent earned $162. From 1990 to 2002, for every extra dollar earned by the lower 90 percent, these top taxpayers earned an additional $18,000.[44] The outcome is frightening; the average annual wage increased about $10,000 in twelve years, but the top earners or 0.1 percenters saw their income increase on average about $18 million. This figure is skewed because the top 400 taxpayers include the top .01 percent, whose annual income averaged $87 million in 2005.[45] In short, the nation is experiencing growing inequality; not since the late 1920s, just before the Great Depression, has it approached this level. Even then, it was not as bad. The major factors saving us are our safety nets, which conservative thinkers now want to whittle away. Most important, if you're not fight'n mad about the facts and figures I've just cast into your brain, then you might as well disappear in the breeze or slip into oblivion and watch the nation splinter.

So long as people are able to keep their bellies full and attend to their basic needs, they are more likely to tolerate these differences in income and wealth. So long as the system is perceived as fair, most Americans feel the superrich are entitled to their bundles. (Actually, there is a false belief that the system is fair when in reality it is unfair.) It comes pretty close to Orwellian logic or *doublethink*: Forget facts that are inconvenient or "draw it back from oblivion for just as long as it is needed, to deny the existence of the reality which it denies."[46] Here I have conflicting conceptions of what is morally right or good for the majority of people, and what should be done to restrict or regulate the smart and swift. It has very little to do with a game well played, as the very rich do not play by the same rules as the common people do. They have a host of advantages and clout, of which the average person is unaware. Sadly, most people play by the rules and get nowhere; they are barely treading water and staying afloat—trying not to accumulate too much debt and go under. This is not a great testimony for the world's largest democracy, which once professed there was gold in the streets to be found for those who were willing to work hard and play by the rules.

A JUST SOCIETY

Harvard philosophy professor John Rawls examines the notion of equality and inequality in what he calls a "just and fair society," one which is grounded in liberal and democratic principles of political rights. He provides four reasons for a society to regulate economic and social equality, and to limit inequality.

1. In the absence of special circumstances (such as war, disease, economic depression), it is wrong for the least advantaged group(s) to suffer personal *hardship*, not to mention hunger and treatable illness. In a fair society, *basic needs* for everyone should not go unfilled, while "less urgent ones of others are satisfied."
2. Political equality is essential to prevent one part of society from dominating the other. One group should not have the ability to pur-

sue its political or economic interests at the expense of another group, or to exact a legal system that ensures its continued dominant position in the political system or economy, or to make "many peoples' lives less good than they might otherwise be."

3. Equality of opportunity is essential so as not to "encourage those of lower status to be viewed by themselves or by others as *inferior*." Such an arrangement fosters arrogance, exploitation, and evil.

4. A just society must avoid the conditions of *monopoly*, not only because it reduces equality but also because it leads to inefficiency and permits the dominance of a wealthy few at the expense of the remaining populace.[47]

These four elements help comprise what Rawls calls "democratic equality," and they should exist if society is to be just and fair, if there is to be "social cooperation between free and equal citizens," and if there is to be consideration for the common public good. In short, in a just society, "everyone as a citizen should gain from its policies."[48] Moreover, I would add that the gains should not be overly lopsided in favor of the rich, such that the least advantaged groups get minimal benefits and there is increasing inequality. No point on the economic curve should exist where the gap is too wide to overcome by education and/or hard work, thereby curtailing mobility. Just where this point lies on the curve, and how to regulate this point, is debatable and makes for liberal and conservative labels. In my world, the entertainment and sports industries, along with the corporate elite, are leaving middle- and upper-middle-class Americans behind—eventually leading to political and tax-code backlash, and the sooner the better.

Here I would add two other reasons for enhancing equality and reducing inequality. First, there must be *equality of opportunity*, whereby the least advantaged groups feel they have some chance to succeed; otherwise, they will grow frustrated and cynical and retreat from the larger society, forming a subculture of their own and rejecting the values of the larger society, possibly engaging in criminal and deviant behavior and affecting everyone in the larger society except the very wealthy, who can insulate themselves or create buffers.

Second, for people to be committed to society they must lead a decent life, a minimum level that meets their basic needs. Everyone in a democratic (and humane) society is owed at least this much; moreover, it is politically prudent to diminish the potential for civil strife and violence. The concept of minimum level is vague because guidelines and definitions fluctuate, depending on the political and moral views of those in power. Nonetheless, there is practical interest to prevent social unrest.

The policies of a democratic (and humane) society must try to maximize the prospects of the least fortunate and avoid a culture of poverty, passed from one generation to the next, that in turn will sap the health and vitality of society. Developing a social and economic minimum level must include, today, *educational opportunity* for the most disadvantaged populace. In this way, ability and talent can be nurtured and not lost at the expense of the individual and society. John Goodlad, former professor of education at the University of Washington, reminds us that "millions have fallen far short of their potential by the simple fact of their birth."[49] These millions serve as a reminder that we are not the nation we think we are. We still have a ways to go in terms of humanity, opportunity, and prosperity for all.

Social cooperation and commitment, or a *common good*, whereby those in political power work with leaders of social institutions to formulate prudent public policy, must exist. If, however, self-interest or ignorance dictates policy, if the robber barons are not curtailed, if Ayn Rand's idea that business excess and greed are good for growth and productivity overrides the basic checks and balances first proposed by John Kenneth Galbraith; or if Milton Friedman's unregulated capitalism overshadows Rawls's conception of justice and fairness, then by inference the common good will be shoved to second place. Here I am reminded of the graphic words of Jay Gould, the ultimate capitalist and robber baron. Bragging he could break any strike, he said in 1886, "I can hire one half of the working class to kill the other half." In 2006, 140 years later, I read that several Wall Street CEOs received $25 and $50 million annual bonuses, a form of lunacy that one Chicago economist, David Autor, blamed on globalization and expanding profits, while former AIG CEO Hank Greenberg warned against penalizing success, as defender of the free-market system.

You would hope that we have come a long way from the robber baron days of the nineteenth century. These were the days when business tycoons amassed fortunes by trampling competition, exploiting workers, and fleecing the public. All you need is to be reminded that big business, in the spirit of Gould, is today ready and willing to hire illegal immigrants at $7 or $8 an hour and replace American laborers that expect $20 or $25 an hour for the same work. What does $20 an hour mean? Considering an eight-hour day, five-day work week, and fifty-week wage, that amounts to $40,000—less than today's average American annual wage. Also consider that nearly all the major multinational companies in America are outsourcing jobs for approximately one-third to one-fourth the American wage. Sadly, the American workforce has become a disposable workforce, under the guise of competition, efficiency, and supply-demand curves.

The fact that our intellectual capital is also being drained by outsourcing scientific and technological jobs and by development of new manufacturing sites abroad doesn't seem to concern the power brokers and money movers of the American political and economic system. No one seems concerned that future generations will have trouble finding decent, middle-class jobs. The free marketers continue to tell us that globalization and unrestricted trade policies are good for the nation. Good for whom? The unemployed accountant and airplane ticket reservationists who saw their jobs outsourced to a worker in India? The small business person who manufactured furniture or worked in the garment center and had to close shop because of cheap Chinese imports? It may be good for the consumer now, but in the long run the U.S. consumer will become unemployed or underemployed because of global markets.

Where I stand politically, I see little difference in the outcome caused by the tactics of Gould and the titans of nineteenth-century industry and the tactics of Kenneth Lay (Enron) and twenty-first century Wall Street CEOs and investment bankers, who move money around the world with a click of a mouse and have little or no concern about the average 9 to 5 working stiff, someone can earn 500 to 1,000 times more than the average workers in their companies, another form of lunacy. You might argue that American labor must learn to trim costs and that outsourcing and global trade is inevitable. That is all well and good, but the only people in our country benefiting from these new trends are the wealthy, who invest capital, and not their labor. Whatever increased productivity or profits is gained by hiring illegal immigrants, outsourcing jobs, or developing new plants abroad is not shared by the vast majority of American people or the American workforce.

Power, Privilege, and Elite Institutions

The Ivy League colleges were built on the premise of educating the children of the elite class, originally when young men graduated from the Latin School in New England colonies and into the mid-twentieth century when they gradated from private academies like Groton, Choate, and Exeter, which were modern "knockoffs" of the old Latin School. Presidents Franklin Roosevelt, John Kennedy, and both Bush presidents were graduates of these private academies and moved easily to Harvard and Yale, despite their "so-so" academic achievement.

Up to the 1930s, most people who applied to Harvard and Yale, and other places like Princeton and Dartmouth, were admitted because people who were not from the proper social class did not bother applying, as they knew better than to waste their time. The history of admission into these elite colleges is the history of the conflict between merit and privilege. The voices of reform began to conflict with the voice of tradition over what kind of applicants to accept and to what extent should class, alumni status, and social connections trump academic ability and scholarship. According to Jerome Karabel, a sociologist from Berkeley, it was not until the Jews began to apply—students who prized scholarships, academic achievement, and high test scores—that the Ivy League colleges faced a dilemma.[50]

Slowly and grudgingly, the Ivy League colleges modified their anti-Semitic policies and allowed a small number of Jews into their institutions, although the number was restricted. Embodied by the spirit of the American dream, so characteristic of all immigrant groups, these striving Jews were merely seeking bits and pieces of the opportunity that their parents had been denied in Europe. For readers who fail to grasp the historical and contextual meaning, the story is played out in *Chariots of Fire*. Although the movie takes place at Cambridge University in England, all the reader needs to understand is that Harvard, Yale, Princeton, etc. are forged on the basis of Oxford and Cambridge universities.

Despite the shocked reaction of the Protestant establishment, the genie had been released from the bottle by aspiring Jews and once freed it paved the way for other high-achieving immigrant groups to apply; and, later, minority groups wanted the American dream. In a way, the admissions process at Harvard and Yale, among other Ivy League colleges, provided a valuable preview of the coming civil rights movement that was to soon explode, where the democratic forces of fairness, equality, and equity were pitted against the traditional forces of protection and privilege. (You can say that this battle has been waged since Jefferson crossed swords with Hamilton, or as far back as the Greeks who tried to forge their theories of democracy in the town squares of Athens and Delphi.)

Given the beginning of the Cold War in the late 1940s and early 1950s, and the need to produce scientists and engineers to defend against Soviet expansion, the faculties at Ivy League colleges slowly began to stress academics. At the same time, James Conant was president of Harvard. He was a man of his times, the most influential educator of the midcentury, and when he spoke the educational establishment listened. Conant urged that American schools and colleges add academic rigor to the curriculum, upgrade teacher training, test and measure students' achievement, and devote more resources for the education of the top academic 20 percent, especially the gifted and talented students.[51] The Boston Brahmin's idea of "The Harvard Man" was much more progressive than "The Yale Man," as perceived by Yale's president Alfred Griswold, who, in 1950, reassured the Protestant establishment and Yale alumni that the future graduate would not be a "beetle-browed, highly specialized intellectual, but a well-rounded man."[52]

The conflict between both forces persists today by nuance, by putting as much emphasis or more on "character" than academics. Academic merit is but one of many criteria used to judge applicants along with social skills, leadership skills, and creative/artistic skills. All these set of skills, along with alumni linkage, is designed to allow sufficient flexibility to preserve the status quo and power of these institutions, to ensure that "well rounded" students are sought and accepted. The balance between academic *mediocrity* and *merit* permitted children of the rich and powerful to be admitted because of hereditary privilege. This is the way it was, and this is the way it is, despite the rise of a new educated class, men and women of high academic caliber who were unable to go to Harvard or Yale, or even the likes of Princeton and Dartmouth, and had to "settle" for the University of Michigan, University of Wisconsin, or University of Illinois—all top-notch colleges, but not part of the cultural and financial elite, not part of the Protestant and corporate establishment.

If the upper class seizes the benefits of an education (say by spending in schools twice as much money on their children as low-income children and by ensuring their children are admitted to Harvard or Yale), and seizes the gains of national productivity, as they have in past decades, we have a situation where the advantaged group "ruthlessly exploits its position to ensure the dominance of its class." Surprisingly, these are the words of David Brooks, the *New York Times* columnist and the liberal's favorite conservative. Members of the upper class are more likely to inter-marry, which "is really a ceaseless effort to refortify class and solidarity and magnify social isolation," and thus perpetuate their dominant posi-tion. Given his conservative views, Brooks surprisingly and whimsically urges "uneducated workers of the world [to] unite. . . . You have nothing to lose but your chains." He concludes: "I don't agree with everything in Karl's manifesto, because I don't believe in incessant struggle, but I have to admit, he makes some good points."[53] Brooks has a sense of humor, but he is making a serious point. For the last three decades, the winds of big business have been whipsawing and blowing strong, from coast to coast and through the heartland, financially breaking the lives of many ordinary people, creating a rising scourge of debt, decline, and despair among working- and middle-class America, and leaving everyone behind except the high-end and wealthy elite. To be sure, this is not the America I grew up envisioning and believing in. For the sake of my children and their children, I hope this is not the America I know when I take my last breath and make peace with the Almighty.

A Final Comment

The nation was conceived by the principles of political liberalism and democratic philosophy: certain natural rights, egalitarian values based on fairness (Rawls's term), excellence and equality (Gardner's terms), and equity or opportunity (Rawls, Gardner, and Barry).[54] Capitalism would be encouraged to expand, but there would be no feudal class, no peasant class, no serfs perpetually indentured to the nobility class. There would be genuine social reform in which people engaged in different occupa-tions would come nearer in speaking the same language and having the same opportunities and rights, the same spirit and soul, than anywhere else in the world. That is, for me, the American invention, or what others might refer to as the "American character."

A basic tenet satisfying the principles of democracy is to curtail a reward system based on inherited privilege and power, so that we don't consistently have the same "winners" and "losers" from one generation to the next. This idea is not based on Athenian democracy as some might believe, but rather rooted more in the ideas of John Locke and Jean-Jacques Rousseau, who in turn influenced the liberal wing of our Founding Fathers such as Thomas Paine and Thomas Jefferson. It is the same ideas expounded more recently by political scientists and philosophers such as Brian Barry, John Gardner, and John Rawls (the latter two who recently died). As in a sporting event, the winners should deserve to win, noting that chance and luck are factors and can enter into the final outcome. In a fair society, rewards are distributed on the basis of ability, talent, and creativity, and ways are provided to encourage those who have such native endowments to seek education and training to fulfill their potential.

The concept of *meritocracy*, a relatively new idea which coincides with the coming of the knowledge society and information age in the 1950s and 1960s, is based on rewarding the deserving, as long as their abilities and talents are put to good use—to benefit the larger society and contribute to the good and prosperity of others. Differences in rewards are accepted so long as those people with special endowments serve the common good and do not use them against society or an individual, say in robbing a bank or an individual. While there is an expectation that a variety of abilities and talents will be recognized and rewarded, it makes no sense to encourage or reward esoteric abilities and talents, such as standing on one's head for an hour or repeating the names and addresses of all the people under the letter A or B listed in the local telephone book.

Most people in a democracy accept there will be a difference in rewards for individuals who use their talents for the general good. There is a legitimate expectation that deserving people will share in greater power, honors, and income, so long as agreed-upon rules are followed. There is also an expectation that society will establish appropriate institutions such as schools and colleges to nurture those differences in abilities and talents, but it must also provide opportunity for other people who are not as smart or talented. Otherwise, the discrepancies between high-achieving and low-achieving people will become too large and threaten the principles of democracy. At all costs we need to provide safety nets, second chances, and multiple chances for those less able to reach their full potential. We also need to recognize different forms of excellence. If we remain blind sighted to different kinds of abilities and talent, then the principles of democratic equality will be lost under the guise of a restricted form of meritocracy. Not everyone can be a scientist or musician; some of us will be plumbers and truck drivers. Not everyone will get "As," and we need to ensure that opportunity is provided for the least advantaged groups so that society doesn't lose a critical mass of people because of background, or differences in wealth and status.

The more the distribution of rewards is based on inherited wealth and power, the more inefficient and less innovative society is; in the end, it will become stagnant and corrupt, and possibly decay. Whatever general wealth that exists within a society, the existing inequalities should be considered for the purpose of its redistribution, so as to benefit less privileged groups, to the point that they feel they have some chance to succeed through education and hard work. Real opportunity must exist: Everyone cannot hit home runs, but everyone should get up to bat in a democratic society. What's worse is when some people never get up to bat at all. What's almost as bad is that throughout life someone has always batted last. Eventually, the sandlot ballplayer who always bats last gets the message and drops out. It's no different in school and society. It comes down to what kind of society we want. Do we want one where there is a distinct cleavage, one group always hitting doubles, triples, and home runs and another group striking out, or not even getting up to bat, living a half-life, passing time away and doing very little for themselves and society? The situation I describe leads to a large economic underbelly, class antagonism, and eventual decline. If this sounds like reality, then we might as well cede the twenty-first century to China and India. We might as well crawl into our caves and do nothing, with a tiny group hoarding the money and engaging in excess (big houses, big boats, and lavish entertainment) and the masses living day-to-day, on the edge, in debt, cogs in the machinery of big government and corporate America.

To what extent wealth should be redistributed depends on the people in the power and their moral fiber and values, their belief in equality and inequality. There will never be full agreement on this issue, and that is what makes liberals and conservatives debate across the aisles. Rawls and Gardner would argue that laws and social institutions should be developed that do not lead to unfair advantages for some at the expense of others. Everyone should be working for the common good, rather than their own interests. In this connection, social and economic inequalities are acceptable so long as they benefit the larger society, including the least fortunate.[55]

Here, I disagree with Rawls and Gardner, although I have some reservation as Rawls is considered by most informed readers to be the number-one American philosopher of the last half of the twentieth century and Gardner, founder of Common Cause, is considered one of the most enlightened public servants. When you criticize an icon or hero there is potential to get your nose punched in by some young twerp or curmudgeon-like critic who gets bent out of shape by what you say—or thinks he or she can do better. That is part of the risk you run as an author, especially in academia, as most professors are born critics and are liberal like Rawls and Gardner.

The point is, benefits are rarely proportioned equally among advantaged and disadvantaged groups, so that the unequal distribution of the economic pie will not have the same benefit for those who are on the lower end of the totem pole. Similarly, it becomes a nightmare to try to agree that someone's success benefits the less well off. It might be easy to determine how a physician or judge benefits society, but it would not be easy to show how baseball players or rock stars earning $20 million a year benefit society or less fortunate groups. When all is said and done, most people act on self-interest. The only fair method of curtailing greed and materialism is to establish laws that restrain powerful people and wealthy people who inherit large sums of money or annually earn tens of millions. The need is to redistribute wealth so that those with natural abilities, talent, or strength do not run away with most of the gold. The goal is to achieve compassion and charity, to be fair and just, to appeal to the better angels of our instincts.

The question is, when is enough enough? How much money does someone have to earn before he or she says I earn enough? A 2 percent tax increase, from 33 to 35 percent, of the richest 5 percent would raise $17 billion of revenue over five years.[56] A tax increase to 50 percent on the same group of people would raise approximately $150 to $175 billion, enough to bolster programs like Social Security and Medicare. If we started to phase out government subsidies for special interest groups (i.e., farm subsidies cost the tax payer $20 billion per year) and funnel it to the least advantaged groups in terms of food, housing, health, and education, then inequalities would be further diminished. But "government programs, once created, become virtually immortal," and no government official wants to incur the bad publicity of taking something from anyone who regularly votes.[57]

If we are forced to rely on the wisdom and goodwill of politicians, who are often influenced by big business and special interest groups, then the working and middle class (even the midly affluent) become unknowing victims and duped by the people they trusted. In some ways, then, we are forced to reread the ideas behind a *social contract*, the principles that this country was founded on. Here I am talking about the theories of Locke and Rousseau, bolstered by Thomas Hobbes's *Leviathan* (1652) and Immanuel Kant's moral doctrines. Once more it comes down to Jefferson's thoughts on freedom and liberty and about the rights of people. Some readers might say I'm putting too much stock in one person, that Washington, Lincoln, or Franklin Roosevelt are presidents that no one in American history rivals. So be it! We all have our own gods and idols, heroes, and superstars that we worship or praise. Where I stand on the political fence, Jefferson was the first to put these important political and social ideas on paper, and in the right way.

Conservatives seem to prefer now to tax less and spend more. They are also forced to preserve unneeded programs, earmarks, and subsidies and allow interest payments to grow and expand the federal debt. Deficit spending is bound to influence the standard of living of our children and grandchildren by limiting essential services and/or raising prices for those who need it the most and cannot afford it. Reduction of social, health, and education spending only increases inequality because the rich are still able to pay for services they want. Moreover, the fight for essential human services will most likely be tilted in favor of the aging baby boomers at the expense of school spending, because they represent the largest and most consistent block of voters.

Education as a social category or variable cannot alone reduce inequality or uplift the masses. To put it in reverse: Only if inequalities of income and wealth are kept within a limited range can education be used as an equalizer. To achieve greater equality and to assist the unfortunate, we need to increase taxes for the wealthy (top 10 percent); improve tax compliance; shut down tax loopholes and offshore companies that avoid taxes; regularly audit the tax returns of the wealthy (with annual incomes of more than $500,000 and/or assets of more than $5 million); and limit estate trusts, which save taxes from generation to generation and allow the transfer of wealth. The need is to ensure a wealth transfer tax at every generation, especially after the $5 million level. (This level only effects the top 0.1 percent of taxpayers, but such a law would sharply reduce runaway inequality or the makings of a financial oligarchy.) If we don't address these issues first, and put restraints on money mogels, then we are spinning our wheels in debating educational equality or opportunity or the correlation between education and mobility, and whether the American dream still exists for the majority of Americans, despite what they hope or believe.

Because these measures are not being implemented, we are witnessing a rise of a new aristocratic class, based on wealth and power, far worse than the European model our Founding Fathers sought to curtail. What we need are a set of political, economic, and moral principles that are based on our history, philosophy, and literature. I would start with the Hebrews and the *Talmud* and the Greeks, with the "liberties of the ancients" during the time of Pericles, and work my way up to the great books and great minds of humankind. Locke, Rousseau, and Jefferson would be high on my recommended list, along with Kant and the current readings of Rawls and Gardner. Of course, anyone with a half wit would know that I would favor these voices of reason.

NOTES

1. Thomas Jefferson, *Notes on the State of Virginia, 1782* (Chapel Hill: University of North Carolina, 1955), 14.

2. Maris Vinovskis, "Horace Mann on the Economic Productivity of Education, *New England Quarterly* (April 1970), 550–71.

3. Lawrence A. Cremin, *The Republic and the School: Horace Mann and the Education of Free Man*, rev. ed. (New York: Teachers College Press, Columbia University, 1957), 39.

4. V. T. Thayer and Martin Levit, *The Role of the School in American Society*, 2nd ed. (New York: Dodd, Mead, 1966), 6.

5. Cremin, *The Republic and the School*; Jonathon Merserlie, *Horace Mann: A Biography* (New York: Knopf, 1972).

6. David B. Tyack, *Turning Points in American Educational History* (Waltham, MA: Blaisdell, 1967), 114.

7. See Henry M. Levin, "Equal Educational Opportunity and the Distribution of Educational Expenditures," in *Rethinking Educational Equality*, ed. A. Kopan and H. J. Walberg (Berkely, CA: McCutchan, 1974), 30. Also see Marvin Lazerson, *The Education Gospel: The Economic Power of Schooling* (Cambridge, MA: Harvard University Press, 2004).

8. George Burtless, ed., *Does Money Matter: The Effect of School Resources on Student Achievement and Adult Success* (Washington, DC: Brookings Institute, 1996); Christopher Jencks, *Rethinking Social Policy* (Cambridge, MA: Harvard University Press, 1992).

9. Social capital is distinguished from human capital, as the latter involves an economic component dealing with growth and productivity.

10. H. G. Wells, *The Future of America* (New York: Harper & Bros., 1906), 142–43.

11. Ellwood P. Cubberley, *Changing Conceptions of Education* (Boston: Houghton Mifflin, 1909), 15.

12. Ellwood P. Cubberley, "Does the Present Trend toward Vocational Education Threaten Liberal Culture?" *School Review* (September 1911): 461.

13. James S. Coleman, "The Concept of Equality of Educational Opportunity," *Harvard Educational Review* (Winter 1968), 7–22.

14. Nathan Glazer, "The Affirmative Action Stalemate," *Public Interest* (Winter 1988), 99–114; Allan C. Ornstein, "Are Quotas Here to Stay?" *National Review* (April 26, 1974), 480–81, 495; and William G. Tierney, "The Parameters of Affirmative Action," *Review of Educational Research* (Summer 1997), 165–96.

15. John Gardner, *Excellence: Can We Be Equal and Excellent Too?* (New York: Harper & Row, 1961), 17–18, 83, 90.

16. Gardner, *Excellence*, 62.

17. Diana Jean Schemo, "Ad Intended to Stir Up Campuses More than Succeeds in Its Mission," *New York Times*, March 21, 2001; David Horowitz, "Racial McCarthyism," *Wall Street Journal*, March 20, 2001.

18. Fred Lundenburg and Allan C. Ornstein, *Educational Administration: Concepts and Practices* (Belmont, CA: Wadsword, 2004); Gary Orfield, "Polity and Equity," in *Unequal Schools, Unequal Chances*, ed. F. Reimers (Cambridge, MA: Harvard University Press, 2000), 401–26.

19. Brian Barry, *Why Social Justice Matters* (Malden, MA: Polity Press, 2005), 67.

20. Walter P. Webb, *The Great Frontier* (Boston: Houghton Mifflin, 1952), 2.

21. Walter P. Webb, *The Great Frontier*, 3.

22. Merle Curti, et al., *History of American Civilization* (New York: Harper & Bros., 1953), 148.

23. John Steele Gordan, *An Empire of Wealth: The Epic History of American Economic Power* (New York: Harper Collins, 2004).

24. Thomas Jefferson, "Notes on the State of Virginia," in *Crusade against Ignorance: Thomas Jefferson on Education*, ed. G. Lee (New York: Teachers College Press, 1961), 95.

25. Thomas Jefferson, "A Bill for the More General Diffusion of Knowledge," in *The Writings of Thomas Jefferson*, ed. P. L. Ford, 220–21 (New York: Putnam, 1893).

26. Jefferson, "Notes on the State of Virginia," 96.

27. Merle Curti, *The Growth of American Thought*, 2nd ed. (New York: Harper & Bros. 1951); Vernon Parrington, *The Colonial Mind: 1620–1800* (New York: Harcourt, Brace, 1927). Also see H. W. Brands, *Andrew Jackson: His Life and Times* (New York: Anchor, 2006).

28. Charles A. Beard and Mary R. Beard, *The American Spirit* (New York: Macmillan, 1942); Fredrick Jackson Turner, *The Frontier in American History*, rev. ed. (New York: Henry Holt, 1950). Originally published in 1893.

29. Allan C. Ornstein and Francis P. Hunkins, *Curriculum: Foundation, Principles, and Issues*, 4th ed. (Boston: Allyn and Bacon, 2004), 71–72.

30. James H. Hughes, *Education in America*, 3rd ed. (New York: Harper & Row, 1970), 233.

31. Carl Sandburg, *Abraham Lincoln: The Prairie Years* (New York: Harcourt, Brace, 1926), 19.

32. The perfect question is: Why travel to hell? I guess it has something to do with my soul mate. Actually, my preference is to pedal down some obscure highway where I can hear frogs and crickets and give my readers a dutiful description of weather changes, landscape, traffic conditions, and the people I meet along the way. Indeed, I cannot think of America as a single place—so much is so different and contradictory—and there is so much to see.

33. Leo Damrosch, *Jean-Jacques Rousseau: Restless Genius* (Boston: Houghton Mifflin, 2005).

34. Jay Wink, "A Narrative of Hell," *New York Times Book Review* (September 16, 2001), 23.

35. David J. Eicher, *The Longest Night: A Military History of the Civil War* (New York: Simon & Schuster, 2001).

36. Merle Curti et al., *A History of American Civilization* (New York: Harper Bros., 1953), 323. I would add Korea and Vietnam to the list.

37. Isabel Sawhill, "Still the Land of Opportunity?" *Public Interest* (Spring 1999), 4.

38. Kurt B. Mayer, *Class and Society* (New York: Random House, 1955), 69.

39. Otis D. Duncan, "The Trend of Occupational Mobility in the United States," *American Social Review* (August 1965), 491–99; Seymour M. Lipset, "Social Mobility and Equal Opportunity," *Public Interest* (Fall 1972): 90–108.

40. Federal Reserve Report, cited in "When the Joneses Are Wearing Jeans: Spotting Signs of Status," *New York Times,* May 29, 2005.

41. Paul Krugman, "Debt and Denial," *New York Times,* February 13, 2006.

42. Douglas Cleinent, "Beyond 'Rich' and 'Poor'," *The Region* (June 2003), 12–16.

43. In 2007 dollars, that would translate to about $1.6 million, assuming 3.5 percent increases in the CPI for the previous ten years. Actually, 7 percent of Americans were millionaires in 2005. The average is an inflated figure because it includes people with tens and hundreds of millions, that is the top one-half. A more accurate figure would be the midpoint or median of the top and bottom quintiles.

44. Geraldine Fabrikant, "Old Nantucket Warily Meets the New," *New York Times,* June 5, 2005.

45. "The Wealthiest Benefit More from the Recent Tax Cuts," *New York Times,* June 5, 2005.

46. George Orwell, *Nineteen Eighty-Four* (London: Secker and Warbug, 1951), 220.

47. John Rawls, *Justice as Fairness: A Restatement* (Cambridge, MA: Harvard University Press, 2001), 130–31. (The italics are framed by this author for emphasis, not by Rawls.)

48. John Rawls, *Justice as Fairness,* 133.

49. John I. Goodlad, *What Schools Are For* (Bloomington, IN: Phi Delta Kappa Educational Foundation, 1979), 22.

50. Jerome Karabel, *The Chosen: The Hidden History of Admission and Exclusion at Harvard, Yale, and Princeton* (Boston: Houghton Mifflin, 2005).

51. See James B. Conant, *The American High School Today* (New York: McGraw-Hill, 1959).

52. David Brooks, "Getting In," *New York Times Book Review,* November 6, 2005.

53. David Brooks, "Karl's New Manifesto," *New York Times,* May 29, 2005.

54. Barry, *Why Social Justice Matters;* Gardner, *Excellence;* and Rawls, *Justice as Fairness.*

55. John Rawls, *A Theory of Justice* (Cambridge, MA: Harvard University Press, 1971); John Gardner, *In Common Cause* (New York: Norton, 1974).

56. Robert J. Samuelson, "A Deficit of Seriousness," *Newsweek,* May 16, 2005.

57. Samuelson, "A Deficit of Seriousness."

5

✛

Education, Mobility, and the American Dream

G iven my advancing age, and the fact that time changes a person's thinking, in some sort of sneaky, wrenching way, I now realize my *education* heroes are not William McGuffey but Horace Mann; not Charles Eliot but William Harris; not John Dewey but Jane Addams.[1] These people I mention were influential educators and social reformers for their period and had an everlasting effect on schools and society, yet most of you may not know who I'm talking about because these names do not appear on the *New York Times* best selling lists, on MTV, nor do they get regularly listed on Amazon.com.

Suffice it to say that educators and social workers are not considered famous or sexy—and thus not worth too much time or space in the media. They don't help sell products such as underwear (Michael Jordan), guns (Charlton Heston), or drugs (Dorothy Hamill), nor do they help sell tickets to stadiums or movie theaters. They are considered a cost item, not a money-making component, and therefore they are underpaid and not respected nor appreciated by the public. In a world driven by money and materialism, by type-A powermongers with power ties and crimson suspenders and the gift of arrogance and greed, these dedicated professionals are going to rank low in status because of their earning power—or lack of it. These educators and social workers do not have bottomless expense accounts and all-knowing attitudes, nor do they fly around in corporate jets. They are nothing more than average, the garden variety you would find on Main Street, U.S.A.

CONSERVATIVE AND LIBERAL THOUGHTS
CONCERNING CLASS

I realize I should go beyond the education and social world as I distinguish between the "good guys" and "bad guys," as I interpret the world of *equality* and *equity*. Allow me, then, to take you backward into a time tunnel. We will start with colonial America and in warp speed arrive in the twentieth century, say in two or three minutes of reading, depending on how well your brain cells work. My first antihero is Joseph Morgan, the self-proclaimed spokesman of the Lord who in 1732 argued that the poor should be "content with their station" and that the rich had a "miserable life . . . full of Fear and Care . . . whereas a man that have but food and Raiment with honest labour, is free from the fears and cares." My hero of this time period is the Quaker preacher John Woolman, who declared in 1754 the Christian virtue of "a just distribution of man's worldly goods, that excessive richest and abject poverty led to endless ills" in society.

One hundred years later, my antihero is Frances Bowen, the conservative Harvard philosopher, who in 1859 declared great wealth as a moral right "following from Christianity and humanity." He recognized and accepted "the aggregation of immense wealth at one end of the scale, and the increasing amount of hopeless poverty at the other," so long as the wealthy did not "cease to bring this interval between themselves and the poor by personal exercises of sympathy, . . . common brotherhood . . . and [giving] largely to public charities." For the same period my hero is labor leader Thomas Skidmore of New York, who in 1829 maintained that education alone was bound to prove ineffective "in redressing the economic grievance of the working class," and that the system of production and distribution had to be addressed, otherwise the "American worker would be in the same desperate condition that darkened the existence of his fellow worker in England" and the rest of Europe.

At the turn of the twentieth century, the conservative antihero is E. L. Godkin, editor of the *Nation*, who maintained in 1896 that he knew of "no more mischievous person than man who, in free America, seeks to spread . . . the idea that they [the workers] are wronged and kept down by somebody; that somebody is to blame because they are not better lodged, better dressed, better educated." The liberal counterpart is Charles Francis Adams, a descendent of John Adams, who expressed in 1916 general disdain toward the new wealthy class and giants of industry who he felt defined national destiny in terms of laissez-faire economics and self-interest and believed the duty of government was to encourage expansion and protect big business. "Not one I have ever known would I care to meet again, either in the world or the next; nor is one of them associated in my mind with the ideas of humor, thought or humanity."

I have dredged up these people from the skeletons of American intellectual thought, knowing full well these names are not household names, or superstars or super athletes—and thus not worth much time or space for the average reader, blogger, or computer surfer. But, for those of us who appreciate the fine touches of history and social thought, their influence was felt in their period, and they help show a consistent thread in the struggle for equality and equity.

From my list of antiheroes, it is safe to say I'm not a blue-blood or Yankee fan, more like a Johnny Cash fan whose words describe the common man. I am especially not fond of Charles Darwin, although many of my colleagues treat him as a scientific rock star, sitting in some hall of fame, not in Cleveland but at the Westminster Abbey, with Galileo, Bacon, and Newton, and other gods in the pantheon of science. And, if allowed to make a giant leap, perhaps unfounded to those who sing the praise of Adam Smith (a conservative economist who maintained that capitalism succeeds in a free-market system and provides spontaneous webs of cooperation and economic growth), Social Darwinism discourages the development of people's talent. Survival of the fittest infers that certain segments of society are not capable of being fully educated, to reflect, problem solve, or engage in creative thought, and thus they should work with their hands.

For those readers who are more apt to believe in the hereditarian conception of IQ, in predetermined progress, natural selection, and/or evolutionary sociology and economics (in simple terms, the smartest rise to the top), Darwin provides an English-honored, aristocratic explanation for history, human causation, and design of all life. He is, to his fans, the greatest English thinker since Newton, fitting into both Victorian colonialization and U.S. Gilded-Age capitalism, setting forth a doctrine of the strong celebrating the rightness of their power and status over the weak. The doctrine is antithetical to all the urban people brought up on the wrong side of the tracks playing hoops or listening to hip-hop and all the folk people in rural America, playing their fiddles, banjos, and guitars on the porch and singing from the darkest hollows, "Don't forget me. I was someone. I mattered!" For Darwin, and his fans, these lower-end people don't count; they are either invisible or to be exploited in some form by those on top of the economic ladder. For the fans of Social Darwinism, the free marketers and blue bloods who belong to old-line snob institutions—prep schools, Ivy League colleges, private golf clubs, and Episcopalian churches—the idea is to shut down or limit old-time socialists who breathe hellfire and damnation on those who subscribe to capitalism and competition, and to ensure that everyone knows their place in the pecking order of wealth and power.

The Rich and Poor

As far as places etched in time, I have lived among the business and Brahman classes of Yankeeville for more than thirty years, first in Winnetka, Illinois, and now Manhasset, New York, where my antihero class now walks the streets, feels comfortable and content, and believes in Camelot. Nevertheless, I would rather talk about ordinary people and the songs of Johnny Cash, the man in black who would not change colors until things got better for the plebian class or ordinary person. Let me say it in a different way with the hope you see the light, so you can see life in the way Johnny saw it and the way Darwin (and the money class) could never see it because of their aristocratic lens, which filtered through their historical distrust and disdain toward the immigrant, lower, and minority classes. The rich emphasize shrewdness and strength to explain their own rise to the top and why the poor and labor class remain in their station for life. Moreover, the people at the bottom tend to adopt the language of their "oppressor," call themselves ignorant, and adapt fatalistic and self-depreciative attitudes. It is what Frantz Fanon, the French-Algerian psychologist, would call the "psychology of the oppressed."[2]

The titans of the Gilded Age were self-made men, and literacy, culture, and education were not part of their self-making. But the rise of obscure and ordinary men (and women) to great wealth is becoming a caricature of the past. Today, education counts even less in the "new law of the jungle," highlighted by corporate greed and get-rich schemes for milking the public. In an age of declining influence of meritocracy, from a social standpoint it is family wealth and power that now provides much more opportunity to accumulate good fortune. The vast majority, despite increased education,[3] are condemned at birth to become part of the new "struggling" working- and middle-class people who were once called the "toiling class" in the Old World, "common folk" during the Jacksonian period of democracy, and the "silent majority" in the mid-twentieth century.

It is Cash, not Darwin nor Dewey, who provided a voice for the downtrodden, for all the lost souls and lost causes that might have found a place long ago;[4] but have no place in the American dream today. The American dream today is slowly evaporating due to new tax laws and estate trust rules that favor the rich (and help perpetuate wealth), and still other taxes that set lower rates on investments and assets and higher rates on work and labor. Despite increased education levels among Americans, there are more struggling Americans than ever before because the gap between the top 10 percent (especially the top 5 percent and 1 percent) and the remaining populace has increased dramatically in the last twenty-five years or so, which conventional economists have ignored. This trend should become increasingly apparent as we read the following pages of this chapter.

Cash and Darwin came from totally different backgrounds and time periods. Yet their conclusions are somewhat similar: The strong survive and get ahead, and it has little to do with schooling. In light of postmodern America's obsession with education, it is remarkable how reluctant we are to admit that education has become less important in defining jobs, income, and especially wealth. Although it would be hard for the reader to render me as some sort of Republican, I am not comfortable with Old Left or New Left -*isms*; and I do believe that such a philosophy extracts the liberalism out of liberal arts and turns individuals into "idealots" or, even worse, a mob. My ideas are more contextual, rooted in the ideas of the Social Democrats (apt terminology for describing Princeton's economist Paul Krugman and University of California at Berkeley's economist Robert Reich, also the former Secretary of Labor during the Clinton administration). That said, the current trends reflect the makings of a dynasty or financial oligarchy, in which income gaps between the top 10 percent and the remaining population are growing.

But undoing centuries-old values of the American business class and upper class is a losing proposition. It was F. Scott Fitzgerald who some seventy-five years ago was able to capture the leisurely and extravagant life of the upper class in stories such as *This Side of Paradise*, *Flappers and Philosophers*, and *The Great Gatsby*: "The rich are different from you and I." Lower-class and working-class youth knew it, feeling rejected by their middle-class and upper-class peers, and formed their own subculture, reminiscent of the movies *Grease* starring John Travolta and *Rebel Without a Cause* starring James Dean. The hippie poet of the post-1960s and 1970s Allen Ginsberg understood and noted in his book *Howl* that money was the driving force in American culture.

Greed and self-interest are good in Ayn Rand's world in *The Fountainhead* (1943), as well as in Dinesh D'Souza's world in *The Virtues of Prosperity* (2000), where capitalism and corporations are designed to maximize profits. Capitalism is where self-interest and competition meet—and become a self-regulating mechanism—so that government regulations are supposedly unnecessary. In a free economy, according to a younger Alan Greenspan, government may step in "only after . . . fraud, . . . crime . . . or damage to the consumer,"[5] which basically puts the average person at the mercy of big business and assumes people in power are naturally ethical. (Really?) Joseph Othmer, an old-time business executive and author of *The Futurist* (2006), presents a view from the inside of corporate

America, viewing capitalists as nothing more than "arrogant," reckless, and "unapologetic" criminals who think they "run the country" and are the "masters of the universe." They defy rules and ethics, charge dinners with fictional clients, keep two sets of books, and sell their stocks while telling shareholders it's a bargain. "They do it, all in the name of capitalism . . . and for America."[6]

The New Titans and the New Workers

In a nineteenth-century system based on survival of the fittest and a twentieth-century system based on free markets, and in both cases no government intervention, the strong survive and the weak and poor are "unfit"—destined to decline and to remain in the deep hollows, invisible and without a political or economic voice. Indeed, there are no minimal safety nets designed for the slow runners and the uneducated in a corporate and business world. The American economy, rooted in the ways of railroad magnates like Vanderbilt, trading tycoons like Gould, oil barons like Rockefeller, and mass manufacturers like Ford, has been positioned first to exploit the vast landscape and then its workers. Safety nets, if any existed, were and still are for CEOs and other executives; they know when to jump ship and sell their stock because they control or have inside information. They are provided with golden parachutes, amounting to tens of millions of dollars, sometimes hundreds of millions, while workers often watch their stocks and pensions tumble during an economic downslide.

Case in point: Wallace Mallone received a $135 million parachute, after only fifteen months as Wachovia's vice chairman. James Kilts, who ran Gillette for four years, received $175 million when the company was sold to Proctor and Gamble. Philip Parcell became eligible for a $113 million payout when he left Morgan Stanley.[7] Company losses do not seem to matter. Pfizer's CEO Henry McKinnell received a $200 million lump sum, in addition to his $6.5 million a year pension, despite the fact that the company lost $137 billion or 43 percent in value since he became the chief in 2001.[8] EMC's chief executive received a 112 percent increase in compensation from 2004 to 2005, but the company had a negative return of 8 percent. The Gap's CEO took home 125 percent more in 2005 than the previous year, but the company experienced a 17 percent loss. Home Depot's CEO Robert Nordelli was paid $245 million for his five years (2001–2005), during the same time when the company's stock declined 12 percent while the stock price of its principal competitor, Lowe's, soared 173 percent. After fourteen months of dismal company performance, Disney sent Michael Ovitz on his way with $140 million of stockholders' money, despite charges by Disney's CEO Michael Eisner that Ovitz had a "character problem" and was "too devious, too untrustworthy . . . and only out for himself." Franklin Raines, Fannie May's CEO, was allowed to keep $90 million in bonuses generated by accounting tricks that allowed him to meet bonus targets, while his company had to restate $10.6 billion in losses in 2005. His company paid $400 million in fines, a slap on the wrist.[9] These are the same corporate leaders, along with their conservative base, that have held a needed increase in the minimum wage hostage for more than a decade under the pretense that doing so is the best way for corporate America to compete in the global economy.

Then there is the surreal world of hedge fund managers. The average take-home pay for the top-paid twenty-five managers was $365 million in 2005, sometimes with only single digit returns. The top two earners were James Simons of the Renaissance fund and T-Boone Pickens, Jr. of BP Capital fund, each earning $1.5 and $1.4 billion.[10] A significant, often overlooked factor of hedge funds is that they are private investment pools of wealthy individuals and institutions, thus lightly regulated and rarely checked or audited. The point is, they slip under the public radar gun and Security Exchange Commission scrutiny. Managers and their favorite clients do well while widows, retirees, endowments, and museums have barely broken even in recent years.

When it comes to retirement in 2004, the average retirement package for a Fortune 500 company's chief executives exceeded $1 million per year in terms of pension pay and perks, with some companies such as Exxon, Pfizer, SBC Communications, United Airlines, and United Health dishing out more than $5 million *per year* for retirement of executives.[11] Compare the $1 million annual CEO figure to the private pension for average Americans, amounting to less than $5,000 per year, and the multiplier is 200; the $5 million pay-out figure equates to 1,000 times. These outrageous figures are dismissed by consultants for big corporations: A retirement plan replaces income; it does not create wealth, so we are told. The fact is, if you take into consideration life expectancy of the various CEOs, these pensions amount to annuities worth approximately $100 million, and they are not linked to performance measures or company stock earnings.

Often members of a compensation committee are former chief executives who identify with other executives and have a tough time saying no to salary increases of fellow executives. Furthermore, CEOs benefit from one another's pay increases because compensation packages are often compared or based on surveys of what their peers are earning. It's like an "old boy" network, each person taking care of and benefiting from the salary demands of their fellow club members.

Although outside consultant firms assure the public that CEO salaries and pensions are competitive and in line with what other CEOs earn, they fail to reveal the lucrative relationships with the same company execu-

tives they are evaluating to determine executive pay and other compensation matters such as bonuses, stock options, etc. One example among
many firms is Hewitt Associates, which earned $2.8 billion in 2005 for
consulting and investment advice and wore two hats with companies like
Boeing, Morgan Stanley, Nortel, Procter & Gamble, Toro, and Verizon.
They were hired by corporate boards to provide advice on paying corporate executives, the same people who hired them for other consulting services. This is the closest thing to corporate incest, although the consulting
firms claim they are offering a broad range of services and can manage
the potential conflict of interests.[12] This might be great for public consumption, but it is hard for a stockholder to swallow who is counting on
the company's performance and profit for his or her retirement and
watching the stock go down while the CEO's compensation goes up and
up each year. I would like to think that the day of reckoning is coming,
that pouring money into the pockets of CEOs without justification is coming to an end. Either the courts will intervene or shareholders will take
the initiative.

Despite whatever spin someone puts on CEO pensions and payout
plans, it becomes tragic when we consider GM's 2006 announcement that,
after losing sales for two decades to its Asian rivals, it had offered buyouts to its 113,000 factory workers. This is on top of its 2005 announcement that it would eliminate 30,000 factory jobs and close down twelve
plants throughout the Midwest through 2008. (Ford made a similar
announcement; it would eliminate 30,000 jobs to keep competitive. Delphi
Corporation, GM's auto supplier, proposed cutting one-third of its 33,000
employees and reducing wages from $27 an hour to $12.50.) Buyouts for
GM ranged from $35,000 to $140,000 for those who had ten to twenty-six
years on the job and were willing to surrender health-care coverage.[13] Pick
a number from $35,000 to $140,000 for someone who had been working
for twenty to thirty years, and now compare it with someone who
received $135 to $200 million for working fifteen months (Mallone) to five
years (McKinnell) as a CEO.

Do the math any way you want. Use any model you think is appropriate, and ask how do we respond to the issues of equity and fairness or
the simple fact that no one, except perhaps McDonald's or Wal-Mart at $7
or $8 an hour, will hire a "washed-up" thirty-year veteran GM worker. I
don't think we have to worry about people like Mallone, Kilts, and
McKinnell, but we do have to worry that their payout plans create huge
inequality which in turn affects the standard of living of *all* Americans
(because of their purchasing power which drives up prices for the rest of
us). The point is, the growing rise of increased income at the top leaves
less and less for the majority of Americans to share.

In the midst of working Americans losing jobs, pensions, and health plans as corporations reorganize or declare bankruptcy, huge executive pay and pensions lead the average American to conclude that business funnels money from workers to the rich, and thus the rich get richer. If executives are making lots of money, it has to come from someone's pocket. To be sure, a 2005 Roper poll concluded that 72 percent of the public believes there is widespread wrongdoing in the business world. But the public feels helpless. In a 2005 Harris poll, 90 percent of respondents maintained that big business either highly influences or runs big government.[14] The chief executive of Delphi, the auto parts company and former subsidiary of GM, put it bluntly: "Society has come to believe that the term 'crooked CEO' is redundant."[15]

Teddy Roosevelt was following public opinion when he broke up the monopolies at the turn of the twentieth century. One hundred years later, it's time to clamp down on business wrongdoing, better regulate big business, and require that shareholders approve executive pay and executive parachutes. We also need to put sufficient pressure on external auditors and public attorneys, who we expect to guarantee public trust and ethical corporate behavior, to do their job. The only institution that can enforce these ideas is government, but it is deemed by the public as inefficient and incapable. I would add that government is unwilling to do it, because business interests and lobbyists are in bed with politicians. What hurts the American workers most is not the dishonesty or crookedness of big business, but the silence of the victims and bystanders who are capable of going to the ballot box and voting for reform, instead wink at betrayal or say "losing is a way of life."

Left Behind Americans

Overall, AARP reports that only 46 percent of American workers, part-time or full-time combined, participate in any kind of retirement plan. The dismal fact is that the average 401(k) plan contained only $39,600 as of 2005. Saving for retirement is not enough. The lesson is, make sure you have marketable skills into your sixties and seventies. Today, 23 percent of all people in the sixty-five- to seventy-four-year-old bracket holds jobs, compared with 16 percent just two decades ago, according to the Labor Department. A 2005 Putnam Investment study found that the number of workers in the sixty-five- to seventy-four group grew three times the rate as the overall workforce in 2004 and that 10 million previously retired people were forced back to work in order to make ends meet.[16]

This is not a pretty picture of retirement, an increasing number of older Americans with empty pockets, forced back to work to maintain a minimum, decent standard of living. In fact, as the increase in the minimum age for eligibility to collect Social Security is phased in, from sixty-five to sixty-seven years, and as life spans continue to lengthen, an increasing number of older people will be forced to work. This trend will be acceler-ated by a growing number of Americans sixty-five and older, which is expected to double by 2030 and reach 70 million.[17]

This new group of retirees can be combined with their close counter-parts, people in their forties, fifties, and early sixties who have been laid off (or displaced) by companies that have moved (to other states or coun-tries), shrank, closed, or went bankrupt. The result is tens of millions of "graying" Americans who cannot find jobs or wind up with replacement jobs at $10 to $15 per hour, about half their original earnings. Education and retraining are considered the great panacea for these people, but their wage loss is real and, multiplied by the millions of the laid off, it is stag-gering. Nearly every politician and educator is sold on retraining and retooling displaced workers, but few people are willing to admit that the labor market has changed and retraining is not going to help much.[18]

For every job opening between 2002 and 2004, when the economy rebounded and was growing, there were 2.6 displaced job seekers. As much as 55 percent of the hiring for displaced workers in the Midwest was at $13.25 an hour or less, amounting to no more than $27,000 a year. These figures do not consider the sad fact that, nationwide, one-third of all laid-off workers, after two years of looking, are still not working. According to the Labor Department, 73 percent of laid-off workers earn less or have no job at all.[19] The fact is, displaced workers in their forties or fifties have to compete for new jobs as if they are again newcomers to the workforce. Despite pretty resumes or job counseling, if companies are not hiring mechanics or accountants, or are hiring relatively few, the supply-demand curve will reflect upon job opportunities and wages.

The outcome is that lay-offs have become an acceptable trend, part of the new economy. Displaced workers, along with those close to retire-ment who were forced to retire, as well as retired people whose pensions have been sliced up because of company losses, form a new category of older "invisible" and left-behind Americans, nothing more than a new statistic for sociologists and economics to analyze for the purpose of some report. This new social-economic category makes up part of the strug-gling American populace, those who may be labeled the "new poor," or just above the threshold of poverty, people in the winter years who have "no fun in the sun."

Simply put, there is nothing romantic or exotic about being poor or near poor, imprisoned in small rooms and tired surroundings, when most of your life has passed you by. Living under the spell of poverty, or inches above it, in your declining years has the same flavor whether you are liv-ing in the northwestern rim of a mountain-top town or some small rural town in Texas or Tennessee, or renting a hole-in-the-wall in the southern Keys of Florida. You might get used to it, but it's not the life most people bargained for, nor what I would wish for you or any American; it is certainly not a memory to celebrate or toast at your son's or daughter's wedding day or your dad's or mom's silver anniversary. There is nothing good about being poor and old, or living near the edge of poverty, unless perhaps you are some artist or gypsy living in the south of France or some far-off community or mountaintop wary of outsiders and in centuries of isolation.

It is not supposed to happen this way, but this is how life in America is shaping up. If the money spent for one month fighting in Iraq could be used for people to simply improve their lives, say for Social Security retirement benefits, the future I'm painting would have a much happier resolution. Considering four years of fighting, if the money ($450 billion as of 2005) were used for social and health benefits for those born between 1946 and 1964, then the baby boom generation would experience boom, golden years and not doom, tarnished years as I'm predicting for tens of millions or at least half the 70 million Americans sixty-five and older within the next three decades.

Imbalances of Big Business

From the age of Gould, Rockefeller, and Vanderbilt right down to present-day CEOs such as Dennis Kozlowski (Tyco), Ken Lay (Enron), and Bernard Ebbers (WorldCom), Social Darwinism,[20] as interpreted by conservative thinkers, provides the materialistic conviction and macho image of individuals bleeding and plundering their companies of hundreds of millions of dollars in salaries, perks, and parties while the pay of smart, educated, and articulate teachers today averages $47,000 (2003–2004 school year) and the average blue-collar worker in 2005 earned $16.47 per hour or $34,000 a year.[21]

More than 72 percent of the workforce saw their real wages (adjusted for inflation) slide since 1979, despite a 40 percent increase in productivity in the last twenty-five years. On the other hand, in 2001 the average CEO from the Fortune 500 companies earned 425 times more than the average worker; in 1979, it was forty times.[22] Indeed, there is a serious fog in values and ethics when we begin to describe the differences between the American business class and educator class, between the capitalistic class and shrinking middle class, between those who absorb the lion's share of corporate value with inflated executive pay and working people who have seen their stocks tied to pensions and retiree benefits dwindle in value.

While teachers may earn $1,000 extra for merit, if their school district has devised a merit plan, it is not uncommon for chief executives to earn merit bonuses that exceed $5 to $10 million. In simple terms, that amounts to 5,000 to 10,000 times what a teacher might earn for good performance. Sounds absurd? Well, then, there is the "wicki-licious" annual bonus of

$53.4 million in 2006 to Lloyd Blankfein, Goldman Sachs's CEO. The disconnect between executive pay and performance is fuzzy. It's one thing to reward executives when stocks go up, but there is a growing trend to reward them with extra pay when stocks drop, as in the case with Blockbuster, Eastman Kodak, Eli Lilly, Home Depot, Merck, Pfizer, etc., in 2004 and 2005.

Among the twenty-five companies with the most outrageous records of compensating CEOs for poor performance, the average pay in 2005 was $16.7 million. The stocks for these companies declined an average of 14 percent, while the companies' overall average income fell 25 percent, all in the name of corporate compensation.[23] The "big fat" paycheck is supposed to be tied to profits in the form of bonuses and stock options. But this motivates executives to make decisions that yield short-term results (such as trimming jobs or outsourcing them, at the expense of American workers, or reducing capital improvements and research budgets) and long-term disasters.[24] Even worse, there is the temptation to falsify profits and commit accounting fraud, as in the recent case of AIG, Enron, Fannie Mae, Qwest, Tyco, United Health, and WorldCom.

John Bogle, who has been a Wall Street insider for fifty years, as the founder and chief executive of the Vanguard fund, abhors what he views as "rampant cheating" among his peers—not only among stockbrokers and fund managers (who by nature are "greedy-pigs"), but also among bankers, lawyers, and accountants who are supposed to protect the public. In his book, *The Battle for the Soul of Capitalism*, he points out that more than sixty major corporations (whose stock market value totaled more than $3 trillion) had to restate their earnings during a recent two-year period (2003–2004).[25] It had nothing to do with reflection or redemption, or a sudden flash of honesty; rather they were under pressure from Eliot Spitzer, then the New York State attorney general and William Donaldson, the chairman of the Securities and Exchange Commission. Spitzer eventually ran and won the governorship of the state and was overwhelmingly supported by Wall Street—in its desire to rid itself of the prosecutor. Donaldson eventually was forced to step down, under pressure from the Bush administration and business interests who viewed him as too zealous. The idea for Wall Street and the money movers was to eliminate Spitzer and Donaldson, so they could go back to rigging the system in favor of the ruthless pursuit of profit.

In this connection, in 2005, eight out of the ten of the largest financial institutions—such as Citibank, Merrill Lynch, and Morgan Stanley—had to give back a portion of their profits in penalties amounting to $1.4 billion because of conflicts of interests and misleading the public in investing in shaky companies (companies they knew were going "south" such as Enron and WorldCom). Actually, $1.4 billion is a "drop in the bucket" for those eight companies, compared to AIG Insurance having to pay $1.6

billion to settle charges involving a wide range of regulatory issues, including but not limited to bid rigging, refusal to pay claims, accounting fraud, and creating shell companies to hide insurance losses. Although AIG's CEO was forced to resign, he was allowed to keep control of two spin-off companies that own a total of $22 billion in AIG stock.[26] (I said billion, not million.)

In simple terms, a lot of pain and suffering among middle-class Americans whose retirement packages are tied to the market has come from business wrongdoing (i.e., $2.1 billion loss in pension money to Enron's 5,600 employees). Given the low barometer of business ethics in America, no one should be startled that more than 75 percent of college students admit they have cheated on tests—all in the spirit of getting ahead and succeeding. Now, we all eventually learn that the world is unfair, and that it is "a rich man's world," as the musical group ABBA claims. But these kinds of settlements, amounting to "slaps on the wrist" with banks, brokerage and investment companies, and insurance companies, bring American democracy and its related dream of small people getting ahead to a grinding halt, if not into dangerously reverse gear. There may still be legitimate ways of getting ahead in America, and the American psyche needs to know there is still a chance, but it's becoming more painful and more difficult for the common person to beat the odds with this kind of corporate corruption.

Hope I'm not traveling down a lonesome road, attacking the love of the nation, that is the American dream. I'm doing what I have to do, trying to preserve it—attacking stock pickers and Wall Street millionaires, all hunched over their computer screens—moving money while the rest of us toil for peanuts, as most of the common people have for centuries. Remembering my roots and looking for a reason, I'm bewildered by what is happening to America but I still love this country. Looking for a sign from a poet, philosopher or media-host king, it's up to free-market pundits to set Americans free from Wall Street plunderers, junk-stock dealers, and banking/investment stars from Greenwich, Connecticut, and Kenilworth, Illinois.

CHANGING AMERICAN SOCIETY

David Riesman's *The Lonely Crowd* appeared fifty years ago. Its central thesis coincided with the most important change shaping American culture during this period: moving from a society governed by the imperative of production and savings to a society governed by technology and consumption (which in turn led to the rise of the Motorolas, Hewlett-Packards, and IBMs of the world and shopping centers and regional malls around the country). The character of the middle class was shifting and

Riesman conceptualized and described its change and new habits—from *inner-directed* people who as children formed behaviors and goals (influenced by adult authority) that would guide them in later life to *other-directed* people, that is, children (even adults) sensitized to expectations and preferences of others (peers and mass media).[27]

The book was expected to sell a few thousand copies in college social science courses, but wound up selling over 1.5 million copies by 1995—making Harvard professor Riesman the best-selling sociologist in U.S. history.[28] The ideas helped explain a new generation of middle-aged men and women like Willy Loman, Mrs. Robinson, and Beth Jarrid, caught in the web of conformity and conspicuous consumption.[29]

The first three hundred and fifty years of American society were inner directed. The commercial and industrial revolutions ushered in discovery, innovation, change—and a new dynamism characterized by the landing of the pilgrims, America's Declaration of Independence (and the American Revolution), nineteenth-century westward expansion, Darwinist thinking, and early twentieth-century capitalistic and colonial expansion. Experimentation and progress (including American pragmatism and progressive thought) became important patterns of conduct and behavior. Within this shift came an *inner-directed society*, characterized by increased personal mobility, population shifts, growth and expansion, accumulation of wealth (but not necessarily its display), exploration, and invention. Tradition gave way to individual initiative; the strong survived and even conquered the weak or more traditional societies; in fact, this is one explanation for Manifest Destiny and the near annihilation of Native Americans, as well as our "Big Stick" policy in Latin America.

The prevailing values of inner-directed society also highlighted Puritan morality, work ethic, individualism, achievement and merit, savings, and future orientation, with the nuclear family and other adults (teachers, police officers, clergymen, etc.) knowing best and influencing the behavior of children and youth. On a sour note, however, minorities were "invisible," out of sight, segregated—on the other side of the urban tracks or buried in blighted, rural towns; women knew their place, subservient to men and aspiring to become typists or teachers (until they married), and gays and lesbians were in closets—also locked out of sight. Betty Friedan's *The Feminine Mystique* (1963) had not yet appeared or challenged all the unfulfilled and alienated wives who read *Ladies Home Journal* and *Popular Gardens*.

Finally, other-directedness is the emergent character of American society, evolving since the post–World War II period. It is the product of a social and cultural climate that has come to support and encourage teamwork, group integration and gregariousness, organizational behavior, and homogenized suburbs—and to disparage the individualism and independence of inner-directed virtues. The other-directed psyche aspires to fit and belong to the group—whether it is "Big Blue," the local PTA, or golf club—to be accepted by peers and coworkers. Conformity is extracted from peers, as well as the mass media and popular culture. (In the "Pepsi generation," "Gap world," and Calvin Klein ads, everyone looks and acts the same.) Conspicuous consumption and display of wealth are important to other directed persons. The idea is to own a big car, big boat, and big house. If you have it, then flaunt it.

In the other-directed society, parents and other adults have less influence over children than they did in the inner-directed society, and adult knowledge is diminished relative to children's knowledge. First television, and now the Internet, provide young people with access to information that in the past was mainly limited to adults; the information barrier between children and adults is increasingly shattered, at least made porous, and in some cases the children know more about certain subjects than adults—a hard fact for many adults to digest.

Education, leisure services, and entertainment come together with increased consumption of words and images from the new mass media and flow of communications. Increasingly, relations with the larger society and with various subcultures are mediated by emerging ideas—resulting in rapid synthesizing of new fads and trends. The individual is atomized and depersonalized by large and/or loud groups, often confused and confounded by the bombardment of new images and ideas from the mass media and popular culture. Writers for the last fifty years have described this shift in culture in terms of the "organization man," "future shock," the "greening of America," and the "postmodern world."

The Organization Man, described in William Whyte's best-selling book of corporate America and suburban culture, was a cousin or off-shoot to Riesman's book.[30] Published three years after *The Lonely Crowd*, both books described the "successful" business and corporate model, of people keeping their nose clean, following orders, and conforming to company rules and group norms. These business people were not risk takers, innovators, or explorers—characteristic of inner-directed society. They sought a "good job" at IBM, AT&T, or G.E.; they relied on a combination of hard work, merit, and social skills, and followed the expectations and preferences of their bosses. Climbing the totem pole of success, they eventually became imprisoned by their comfortable surroundings and alienated by suburban life and the demands of the corporate culture. Many eventually became burnt out, like Willy Loman in *Death of a Salesman*.

Fifty years ago, the Willy Lomans of America lasted into their fifties and sixties before losing their jobs. Today, there is little loyalty between corporate America and working Americans, and the new Willy Lomans are learning early in their life that their jobs can be outsourced or their company can either lay off thousands of workers, reorganize or go bankrupt to save wages and reduce pensions, and seek other concessions at the expense of the workforce. It seems safe to say that Frank Lorenzo, some twenty-five years ago, showed the way, by first taking Eastern Airlines and then Continental Airlines bankrupt—laying off thousands of workers and replacing them with new pilots and flight attendants for half the old union salaries.

It is hard for Americans to accept that the wealth and long-term productivity of the nation is slowly evaporating. If you are looking for a new corporate spin, then reorganization and bankruptcy is not a tactic, rather a last resort by businesses to keep afloat and to compete in a global economy. Big business continuously reinforces the idea that the day of labor receiving $50 to $65 an hour in overall compensation (which provides workers with full pensions, sick leave, and health benefits) makes no sense today in a world where Americans are competing with China and India, and now Eastern Europe. There is just not enough growth in the economy to support a worker for thirty years with all the benefits we have come to expect, and then be retired for another twenty or thirty years and live "the good life." We are waking up, sadly, to a new reality. More of us will be singing the blues or the work songs and railroad songs of Johnny Cash. Most Americans have already accepted the new American economy with a shrug, while the executives of companies continue to take fat paychecks home and golden parachutes at retirement.

Globalization may result in some benefits for consumers on a short-term basis; however, it costs U.S. manufacturing slippage and factory jobs on a long-term basis. But the challenge of globalization does not affect most aspects of the service industry, especially the low-end part such as hotels, restaurants, retail, and the social and health industries. Here we need to raise the wages for this sector of the economy, as these workers are usually paid minimum wage, or near-minimum wages, with little or no benefits. In fact, many of the same economic trends that impact on the poor, such as a decline in safety nets (pensions, health care, sick leave, unemployment benefits, etc.) are now hurting the middle class. It's a whole new world of struggling middle-class families trying to make ends meet. There is a whole new group of Willy Lomans, younger and more vulnerable than originally described by Arthur Miller, being beaten up and disposed by big business in the middle of their working years.

It used to be that, if you went to school and worked hard, you would be almost assured to be in the middle class and have some kind of decent retirement. Well, all bets are off now; the rules have changed today and the status and life chances of the middle class are in jeopardy. Without the fear of being labeled unpatriotic or defeatist, it's time for Americans to wake up to reality, the tick-tock of the clock. We are now losing our economic power and productivity, to the extent that many young, aspiring college graduates will not get the kind of jobs and wages they originally expected. Prepare for the future; start learning Mandarin or Hindi.

Post Sputnik Schooling: Talent, Testing, and Tracking

The basis of achievement and economic driving force in the postindustrial meritocracy is education, whereas in the aristocratic society of the Old World it was inherited wealth. Merit and differentials in status, power, and income are awarded to highly educated and trained experts with credentials; they are seen as the decision makers and leaders who will inherit the power structure in business, government, science, and politics (just as the coming of the bourgeoisie society in nineteenth-century Europe shifted income and wealth through business and the professions).[31] Thus the term "best and brightest," used to describe the Kennedy advisors, later described the intellectual elite and power elite of the new technological and information society that we still hear so much about and in which we live.

The traditional view of meritocracy holds that most inequalities are not created by some central authority or discriminatory policy but arise out of the individual's innate or acquired skills, capabilities, education, and other resources. In a society based on unrestricted equality, where the government does not interfere, the individual with greater skills, capabilities, and/or education will be at an advantage. In some ways, however, the post–World War II period, bolstered by the Cold War and the need to beat the Soviets, led to a search for talent and ability, spearheaded by conservative or Essentialist educators such as University of Illinois historian Arthur Bestor, Harvard president James Conant, and Admiral Hyman Rickover. The political and social landscape produced a trend toward meritocracy of the intellectual elite and briefly aggravated inequalities from the mid-1940s to the 1980s, coinciding with the Cold War.

For example, Richard Herrnstein did not bother to check the social or cultural pulse before offering his blunt, often incendiary opinion that, as a society succeeds in equalizing opportunity, differences in outcome will emerge between groups based on IQ scores and talent. The more equal opportunity there is, the more it drives "the heritability component higher, making [it] progressively more important." Increasingly, new legislation will be introduced to solve problems "whose roots are both biological and social,"[32] but it is far more cogent to say that the problem is social. It's one thing to talk about smart or intelligent *individuals,* but it is totally different to talk about differentials in smartness or intelligence among *groups.* Herrnstein did not explicitly "slip into error . . . and explicitly draw the second conclusion,"[33] but the hint of biological factors as opposed to environmental factors was enough to draw intense criticism among his academic peers, especially from the political Left.

John Gardner, as you recall from chapter 4, was concerned about balancing excellence and equality. He was also worried about a sorting-out process based on ability and pointed out that "social hazards existed in rigorous selection" based on intelligence. He felt that the sorting-out process, both in schools and society, was one of the "most delicate and difficult" processes we face as a democratic nation. It translates into: Who goes to college? Who is going to manage society? Who is going to earn more money? In a stratified society—based on a corrupt or tyrannical government, a religious order, or inherited aristocracy—there is no dilemma, for everyone knows their place. Given our democratic principles, we are easily able to distinguish "excellence and mediocrity in athletics but refuse to be similarly precise about difference in intelligence."[34] However, Gardner and others like Bestor, Conant, and Rickover were unable to judge the declining influence of education and the growing financial oligarchy based on inherited wealth. This trend first became noticeable in the 1990s, given that the great wealth produced by an expanding gross domestic product was gobbled up by the richest Americans, particularly in outrageous salaries and stock options of CEOs and super salaries of modern gladiators and rock stars. (Education requirement: none.)

In an expanding economy, the search for talent is relentless and those with grades and desirable skills who attend the best colleges can expect to earn the most money—creating inequality based on merit, which coincides with the role of education. Of course, those born to privilege and wealth always have had a better chance for a good education; thus the playing field for the lower strata has never been equal. A class war has always existed, but since the days of Thomas Jefferson it has been hoped that those who are talented and without money would find the way to go on to college. Here one might argue that Jefferson was merely arguing on behalf of an intellectual elite, not necessarily an egalitarian society. But most of us who believe in the American dream are willing to accept elitism based on intellectual pursuits and merit, as opposed to elitism based on inherited wealth and privilege. However, merit, which we thought had replaced heredity privilege, and which was once the driving force behind American growth and prosperity, is becoming a diminishing asset in the great transformation taking shape as the rich now get richer and the rest of us get less.[35]

By reducing the importance of merit, we invariably reduce mobility and move the nation toward an aristocracy based on wealth; moreover, we wind up stifling invention and economic productivity, turning the nation of innovators and strivers into inheritors and idlers, re-creating a political and economic system we thought we left behind in 1776. If all this sounds melodramatic, hypothetical, or like liberal rubbish, then the forces of rank and social stratification have infected your brain cells and outweigh the forces of common sense and common good. You have been duped and have become a casualty in the culture wars. Unless you rank in the top tenth percentile of earnings, income, or wealth, you have picked the wrong side, but there is still time to find redemption or just change sides in the next election.

The problem is that we do not all begin equally at the starting gate, as evidenced by the large number of school children entitled to Title I funds and free lunch, and others who barely get by and don't expect to achieve beyond their blue-collar status. Not only do schools have little measurable effect on students' test scores and future earnings, what accounts for the assumed relationship between education and occupation and income are a number of underlying variables related to education such as family structure, inherited intelligence, peer group, and socioeconomic class.

Regardless of our so-called egalitarian views, those who start at the lower-income brackets have less social capital than those who start in the middle or higher income categories; moreover, those with less social capital come to school with few cognitive skills, and the gap worsens as the students are passed from one grade level to the next. Furthermore, parents with more social capital are able to move into high-performing school districts, provide private tutoring for their children, and work the system through university alumni associations, professional networks, and social contracts—thus assisting their children's careers and ensuring the advantage of class. In a recent interview, former Harvard president Lawrence Summers, who is better known for his politically incorrect statements about female scientists, warned that "for the first time probably in the history of our country, the gap in life prospects between the children of the fortunate and the children of the less fortunate is rising."[36]

Summers's concern is still a major reversal from the Harvard president of one hundred years ago, Charles Eliot, who believed in a stratified society and a curriculum that destined working-class and immigrant children into a vocational track and upper class, Anglo-Saxon children into a college track. Nonetheless, in *Left Back*, Diane Ravitch, a conservative education historian, considered Eliot as a liberal reformer intent on expanding public education at the turn of the twentieth century. I guess what it all boils down to might be called "historical slant" and laced between words and sentences are the thoughts and biases of any author, including myself as well as Ms. Ravitch. Of course, my slant, I believe, coincides with those who have big hands and big hearts, those who understand the blues and travel dusty roads and know the skin of Johnny Cash and Merle Haggard (another one of my heroes)—and never heard of Ravitch.

It can be argued that stratification based on meritocracy in its own way is unjust as any of the historic forms of aristocratic privilege. Of course, those who believe in democracy or in the capitalistic system see no problem with a society based on merit; it certainly beats the notion of hereditary privilege and power. But if some citizens have more goods than others it has been accomplished by either the loss of freedom or economic hardship for those who have fewer goods. This is a zero-sum analysis: The more someone's income and earnings exceed the average, the less other people have in the distribution of money. That makes good sense if you believe that smart and gutsy people are entitled to the fruits of their labor. In a moral society, however, there must be some point where even free marketers give back an increasing portion or at least a flat percentage of their earnings to the larger society in order to help pay for human services required for a decent standard of living for the common people. Here the interests of the common good must exceed the interests of the individual if society is to prosper.

Because of social and economic deprivation, and resulting cognitive deficits, members of lower-class and minority groups start school at a disadvantage in terms of basic skills and are unable to compete successfully in a society based on educational credentials. Given a pessimistic interpretation of the American education system, that is the durability of a two-tier system of schooling, a class war in schools has been fought since the days of the Great Awakening in New England. At that time, the study of the classics seemed a useless luxury for lowly and ordinary people, but in order to get accepted into college during the colonial and postcolonial period an applicant had to be well versed in Latin and the classics. It wasn't until the turn of the twentieth century that Harvard eliminated its Latin requirement for applicants, in the midst of vocal criticism among many of its alumni, sought of a last breath for the sentiments of elitism.

Class war is still apparent, today, on the playing fields of Dalton (in New York) and Eaton (in Massachusetts), as well as in the school yards in Harlem and Roxbury. Without appropriate credentials, people are not needed by the economy; they may not be exploited as many liberals contend, but they are underpaid for their services, not necessarily discriminated against, but not in demand. An achievement-based society, based on tests and academic credentials, freezes most lower-class groups (who start the race with major handicaps) in the lower-end of the stratification structure.

Equal Opportunity

It is not surprising that those who find it difficult to compete within this system will condemn the selection procedures and seek other remedies and social policies. The rejection of measurements that register the consequences of poverty or deprivation has political and social implications and reinforces the belief that certain groups are superior or inferior, or to put it in more generic terms: "We made it. Why can't they?"; "We didn't have much money when we started out, but we worked hard. Why can't they?"; "Our ancestors were discriminated against when they came to this country. They lived in segregated neighborhoods, too. But they didn't become crack addicted, give birth to illegitimate children, or wind up in prison." Whereas this kind of logic was once considered acceptable, in an age prior to multiculturalism and pluralism, these stale pieties today result in close political and cultural scrutiny and criticism from the Left.

In a postmodern era, where groupthink abounds, generalizations about any minority group, including the disabled, overweight, and even elderly is forbidden. Sorry, those who know heartbreak and have to get picked up off the ground, and those who have been drowning since they were ten or eleven, don't necessarily count nor are considered a protected class.

For most educators, the phrase "equal opportunity" conceives school as a process involving the acquisition of skills and the inculcation of better work habits in order to increase the individual's productivity. As income is related to productivity, the more education an individual has, the higher will be his income. Education also serves as a screening device to sort out individuals into different jobs; the more talented and highly educated individuals will obtain the better jobs. The resulting stratification, based on merit or performance, is acceptable to most of us in a democratic society. The democratic system breaks down, however, when inherited wealth becomes entrenched and passed to future generations, which the conservative *Wall Street Journal* calls "lasting legacies" and "dynasty trusts"—permitting huge sums of money to be passed from one generation to the next while avoiding taxes.[37] The system also loses its health and vitality when the gap between the wealthy and unwealthy (with similar amounts of education) increasingly become lopsided. Hence, the relationship between education and income diminishes—and class, rank, and privilege increasingly outweigh talent, ability, and performance.

In a modern democratic society, additional years of schooling are supposed to constitute a signal of greater skills and productivity—and higher income. This is true so long as salaries continue to outpace the cost to satisfy basic needs such as food, health, housing, education, and transportation, and the government is able to impose checks and restraints on the free-market system and some form of redistribution of wealth to provide education, social, and health services. In a highly progressive society, health care and college education are free or at a minimal cost. In an aging society, more government regulation is to be expected. Now it is doubtful if people who write for *National Review* or *Economist* would accept such a view, as it would put a damper on free-market capitalism, lead to more audits and enforcement of the law, and commandeer the financial resources of the rich and superrich. It might lead to more prosecutions, fines, and prison sentences for the titan class; at the least, it would spoil their holidays at the Hamptons and French Riviera and it would curtail their "antiquing" for furniture for their offices.

Conservative and Liberal Educators

Regardless of our political stripes, most of us admit that old-fashioned populists and liberals have their own blizzard of polemics and are often motivated by concern for the downtrodden. We know that liberal views vastly outnumber conservative views on college campuses. It is much easier in academia to be politically correct than politically incorrect, as well as politically Left than politically Right. Based on my experience, I have a strong hunch that liberal authors get assigned five or six times more than conservative thinkers in the arts, humanities, and social sciences. How can it be that the smartest or most relevant educators are from the political Left? Or is it that many professors have their own liberal biases, and just prefer not to discuss the conservative viewpoint? What is this thing we call balance or neutrality? Which college professors, in a rare instance of academic freedom triumphing over politics, never bother to check the cultural pulse related to gender, race, or ethnicity before offering their opinions? You can probably count the number on your toes. Now, who are your heroes? Who among us reading this book wishes to discuss their academic champions? Professors (and teachers) are not considered handsome, cool, or charismatic. Biographies of them are basically nonexistent, compared to our obsession with sports figures, actors, generals, CEOs, and politicians.

SUPPLY AND DEMAND—AND
THE AMERICAN DREAM

The changing American economy is beyond official measurement. For example, workers are counted as employed if they hold any job, whether they work ten hours or fifty hours a week, temporary or permanent, earn $8 an hour or $80 an hour, so long as they get a 1099 IRS Form at the end of the year. Nearly 10 million American workers earned the minimum wage in 2003, another 15 million workers earned less than $8 an hour,[38] and still another 6.4 million workers were employed part time but wanted to and could not find full-time employment. The three groups, when counted and added to the official employment rate, total more than 40 million workers (or about 30 percent of the workforce that files a tax return); the groups' net effect is to disguise or reduce the unemployment rate—that is, people actually out of work—by about 8.5 million (varying annually).[39]

From 1993 to 2006, the unemployment rate dropped, and it hit a five-year low in 2006, but compensation for semi- and unskilled American workers remained substantially the same, as most new jobs were low-end, in sales and service.[40] (It was in the high-end job sectors that salaries increased beyond inflationary rates.) Even worse, official unemployment statistics do not count people who have given up after their unemployment benefits expire or who are forced into early retirement because of job displacement or reduction in a particular corporation or economic sector.[41] These "invisible," uncounted workers (forced retirees) total another 8 to 12 million workers, depending on the survey we read, whether they are corporate or union sponsored. Assuming 10 million as an average, if we add it to the 40 million, the number is now 50 million workers (or about 37 percent of U.S. taxpayers).

Current official economic statistics reflect a healthy job market and mask the fact that millions of people, not classified as poor or unemployed, do not make a decent living and are not part of the American dream; it is also doubtful if their children have adequate nutrition for learning and proper dental care (pain inhibits learning). If we consider that the poverty index is based on artificial and politically driven definitions, and only considers the minimum costs for the barest necessities for health care, food, rent, utilities, and transportation, and does not make adjustments for regional differences, many more Americans (and their children) are struggling and many more students than just those entitled for free lunch or Title I programs are economically deprived and educationally handicapped at the starting gate.

In short, when these 50 million "invisible" Americans, who are just getting by day-to-day are added to the number of poor Americans, some 35 to 37 million, the result is not only shameful given the overall wealth of the nation, but it also fosters a separate and unequal class of Americans that we tend to overlook because they are not storming the Bastille or burning down cities. Although the data are not precise, and the 50 million figure is only an estimate, we can assume there are many more poor Americans than the official count.

The Changing Market Place

Ordinary people, today, have to work two or more jobs and spouses need two incomes to keep up with a 1967 standard of living, an era portrayed by David Riesman's *The Lonely Crowd*, William Whyte's *Organization Man*, and TV's popular show *Ozzie and Harriet*. Back then, it took a sociologist (like Riesman) or psychologist (like Dr. Spock) to tell people what they were feeling. Now commentators like Lou Dobbs, Brian Williams, and Paula Zahn report to Americans how they feel, how they struggle to make ends meet, and, even worse, how our jobs are being exported abroad (85 percent of our retail purchases is now manufactured overseas), which in turn compounds the imbalance of trade (cheap overseas labor markets entering as goods on the U.S. market). Moreover, the outsourcing of jobs is now affecting middle-class and white-collar employment as such jobs increasingly include the engines of the knowledge, technological, and digital economy.

For example, IBM announced in 2005 it would shift 114,000 high-paying, high-tech jobs (paying $75,000 or more) to India at salaries of about one-fifth of those in the United States and Western Europe. Hewlett-Packard stated the same year it would lay off nineteen thousand to twenty-five thousand employees earning between $50,000 and $125,000, representing a savings of $605 billion per year and build a new assembly plant in India. The next year Dell announced it would double the size of its software workforce in India to 20,000; it is also expected to shift tens of thousands of additional jobs once it set up a new manufacturing site in the country. Similar announcements have been made by Cisco, Intel, and Microsoft, the engines of the technological future, which plan to double and triple their workforces in India.[42] Cisco and Intel each plan to invest more than $1.1 billion in India, and Microsoft will invest $1.7 billion.[43] Boeing, G.E., GM, and Motorola are right behind these high-tech companies, opening up new factories outside the United States, in the Asian rim to save money. Even our old enemy Vietnam is on the radar screen for billion-dollar investments by high-tech firms such as Intel and Hewlett-Packard. The ripple effect of these investments in terms of future science, research, and technological jobs is estimated to create four times more the number of initial jobs. In other words, jobs create other jobs, and science and technology jobs have a fourfold impact in a growing economy—and the impact continues to multiply so long as there is a healthy growth pattern.

The fact is that nations are no longer able to isolate themselves and pursue policies that are incompatible with an increasing global market. The types of jobs and services that generate economic wealth for nations are more mobile than ever, based more on a broadband and Internet connection than geography, and policies that shackle international business hinder economic growth. With globalization, the average U.S. worker is exposed to much more competition and job insecurity. As the world becomes more globally interconnected, jobs became more mobile. Hence, the jobs at home that become more plentiful are for less educated, displaced, or part-time workers—mostly low-paying jobs such as "hamburger helper" or Wal-Mart hostess (also called a "greeter"), which on the scale of one to ten (ten being the best) is a one or two. This is the future for our children and grandchildren unless we do something about it now.

What jobs are left for the schools and colleges to prepare their students? The fact is that to maintain our standard of living, the American working- and middle-class populace now works more than six hundred hours in a year than their thirteen industrialized counterparts, and we are the only industrialized nation whose worker hours have increased since 1980. Married women are not only forced into the job market to help supplement their husbands' income, but also a growing number of spouses are purposely working different shifts in order to save the cost of child care. American society is much different today than fifty years ago when a one-income household could identify and support the American working- and middle-class household. The economy still works for the rich, but it is becoming increasingly more difficult for the average worker or common person, and it is rapidly expanding to include the middle- and upper-middle-class populace.

During the age of meritocracy, that is coinciding with Sputnik and the Cold War period, education was considered the be-end, end-all panacea for improving social mobility. Most of us still operate under these assumptions, not realizing that market conditions have changed. The economy is no longer expanding at the same postwar rates and college graduates have flooded the marketplace and are no longer in great demand. The outsourcing of professional and service jobs are common-place, compounded by the theft of intellectual property by Asian manu-facturers, especially the Chinese who consistently engage in piracy and "reverse engineering." The latter concept implies taking a known product and working backward to copy it and pay foreign, especially American, patent holders zero. For example, it is estimated that 90 percent of the software used in China is unlicensed. Pirated copies of Windows cost 10 yen or $1.25; a legitimate copy costs 6,000 yen or $750. A drop of 10 per-cent in software piracy would reduce the U.S. trade deficit by approxi-mately $65 billion and lead to an extra 1.8 million jobs in the information industry.[44] What this means is that American science, innovation, and entrepreneurship, the last economic sector we still dominate and the key to our future economic growth, is at stake.

Salaries of college graduates remained high during the period of meri-tocracy, highlighted by the fact that college graduates were in short sup-ply so that the ratio of professional and managerial jobs was in greater demand than the supply of graduates. For example, in 1950 as many as 2.3 million students were enrolled in degree-granting institutions; 186,000 bachelor degrees and 26,000 master degrees were awarded. By 1998, there were some 14.6 million students enrolled in higher education institutions with 1.2 million bachelors and 430,000 masters awarded.[45] In 1952, 7.9 per-cent of the workforce had college degrees, and there "were [some] 2.33 college-level jobs available" per college graduate. In 1969, 12.6 percent of the workforce had college degrees, and the ratio of college-level jobs to applicants was 1:9. By 1974, "the college-graduate share of the workforce had risen to 15.5 percent, reducing the ratio of jobs to workers to 1:6."[46] At the beginning of the twenty-first century, supply-demand was upside down. More than 30 percent of the twenty-one to twenty-five age cohort had four or more years of college and jobs for college graduates was -1 job per 5 to 10 applicants, depending on the job and region of the country, creating significant unemployment, underemployment, and part-time employment for those starting their careers. Teaching as a second career is big business in many schools of education; preservice student counts are up as college graduates find themselves underemployed and unem-ployed, and switching to education.

Allow me to put the situation in some folksy language. When I graduated from college, John Kennedy was president. That may seem like the
Dark Ages for some of you—before plastic money, moon landings, and
cell phones—but only 11 percent of any age cohort held a bachelor's
degree. The postwar economy was booming, and there was no such thing
as an unemployed or underemployed college graduate. Economists say
that, between 1961 and 1970, the starting salary advantage of college graduates over wage earnings was 17 percent (in 1961) to a high of 24 percent
in 1970. By 1974, it had plummeted to 10 percent, and it continued to
hover below that figure until the mid–1980s.[47] America was in the midst
of a recession. Today, we call it an "economic slow-down," a "dot-com
bust," or a "soft landing," and except for Wall Street the starting salary
advantage of college graduates (adjusted for inflation) has declined. Welcome to the underemployed and "wonderful world" of college-educated
waiters, taxicab drivers, and flight attendants! Rather than having a shortage of skills and training, millions of American workers, including college
graduates, have more skills and training than jobs require. Wake up to the
world of a shrinking middle class, a world where education counts much
less than it did in the age of meritocracy, when I graduated college. To
put the situation in terms that college graduates will understand, once we
consider inflation the income of a typical household headed by a college
graduate was lower in 2005 than 2000.[48]

Mounting Debt and Declining Mobility

What do all of these facts and figures mean? These trends hint that
Americans are overeducated relative to job opportunities and that education is no longer the great panacea or guarantee for the good life in
America. Market factors other than education weigh in and influence job
opportunities and economic outcomes. Even worse, ordinary students
have had to borrow their way to a bachelor's and a graduate degree. As
many as two-thirds of college graduates are in debt. The median debt was
$19,300 for a person graduating from college and $45,000 from graduate
school in 2003–2004.[49] More than 50 percent of these debt loans are considered unmanageable. With short-term loans and plastic interest rates
between 9.5 and 18 percent, the cumulative effect is that merely keeping
one's head above water, rather than getting ahead, has become top priority for Americans between twenty-one and thirty-four. Moreover, many
of the so-called good jobs for college graduates are found in the big cities,
where rents are the highest and young college graduates have to devote
nearly half of their take-home pay for rent. Pursuing the American dream
today, taking a shot at middle-class bliss, is not a "slam dunk" and

requires serious capital up front or a safety net provided by parents; then, there is no guarantee the investment will get you where you expect to go.

As Harvard Law's professor Elizabeth Warren puts it in her book, *The Two Income Trap*, the next generation is starting its economic race fifty yards behind the starting line.[50] Once you have accumulated debt, "the debt takes on a life of its own" and for years continues to take a bite out of your paycheck. Indeed, the middle class is not only shrinking, but it is also struggling. The good news is that, if you are willing to teach in the inner city, you might find a teacher education program that pays for a portion or all of your tuition. And you can always risk your life and join the military and have Uncle Sam pay for your college education. No wonder then that the rank-and-file teacher force and military force is comprised of the lower class and working class trying to get ahead and realize some segment of the economic pie, an American dream that is evaporating for an increasing percentage of ordinary Americans.

Of course, there is just enough truth left in the idea of the American dream, of the self-made man (woman), to keep the masses sedated and believing in the system. Interclass mobility is frozen more than we think, less fluid than the old American dream of "rags to riches" might suggest. As many as 85 percent of American families remain in the same class or move up or down one quintile three decades later. Putting the stats in a different way, some 61 percent of families in the lowest quintile in 1967 were in the same bottom level in 2002. In reverse, 59 percent of families in the highest fifth in income during the same thirty-five-year period remained at the same level.[51]

Statistically, first generation immigrants have the best chance for upward mobility. Although they no longer arrive with "rags," they usually start at the lowest or next lowest point on the totem pole—and thus have more chance for improvement (a simple regression to the mean) than the average American. Through sweat and hard work, they are able to succeed in one generation, more than "American Americans" who have been embedded in the social system. The reason is that immigrants are rarely burdened by the culture of poverty, which inflicts great social and psychological damage over generations; they are a self-selective group, highly motivated by the fact that they have uprooted themselves and come to a new land to start a new life. That said, American immigrants, as a group, have greater zeal, and thus education has greater impact for them than their American counterparts who know how to work the "freebee" system and/or have various safety nets (mom and dad). If we exclude the immigrant population from our calculations, interclass mobility is either frozen or limited to one quintile upwards (or downwards) for the vast majority—80 to 90 percent—of American families, or what I call our "struggling class" and "broken dreams."

To get into finger pointing about heredity or environment, or about the influence of education on economic outcomes, reflects our misconceptions about the nature of intelligence, talent, and merit. You can be very intelligent and talented in all sorts of ways but be handicapped by class (and race) or you can be relatively stupid and over your head on your job but be saved by the rank and privilege of class; CEOs, generals, and politicians are the best examples, especially if the rise to the top had something to do with family connections or family fortunes. Some of us refer to the latter as part of the "Peter Principle." I call it the "Idiot Principle" after John Hoover's book, *How to Work for an Idiot*. His contention is that idiots roam all levels of the workplace. Despite their education, they cause organizational waste and chaos and have a tendency to chew up and eliminate talented people.[52] Most of us are forced to work for idiots for portions of our careers. Just listen to workers (of most professions) in the cafeteria or lounge describe their supervisors; they tend to complain much more than they compliment their boss. The bad news is a worker's relationship with his or her boss is nearly equal in importance with a spouse's relationship when it comes to mental health and psychological well-being. The data suggest that approximately 50 percent of all workers have a shaky, if not downright terrible, relationship with their boss. It is the chief reason for quitting a job or taking early retirement.[53]

Money and Morality

"Money, money money. Always sunny. In a rich man's world." These are the words of ABBA, four retired rock stars of the 1970s from Sweden who summed up life in a capitalist world. Several years ago these four rock stars turned down $1 billion to reassemble as a group and perform one hundred rock concerts around the world. One billion dollars split four ways means that each ABBA singer would have ranked within the super-rich of the world. ABBA had no price, which is unusual in a world driven by money, and because the overwhelming majority of us do have a price. It is worth noting that the issue here is not morality; rather it deals with ethics, which overlap at one point with morality. The difference between ethics and morality is a philosophical quibble and depends on which sources you read and how you personally view the world. Right now, most of us would agree that there is a moral vacuum in our schools, workplace, and society, although conservative and liberal thought would differ over the causes and solutions.

Given the competitive nature of our society, there is a tendency to cheat—to wink at dishonesty—and to get ahead and win at all costs. Given high-stake testing and the nature of grading in schools, which eventually affects who gets tracked into what program and who gets accepted into what college, there is a tendency among students to cheat. According to Nel Nodding, the retired Stanford professor of education, "many students deny that cheating is wrong" and teachers fail "to protect students who are committed to fair competition."[54] A recent study at Duke University indicates that about 75 percent of college students acknowledge some academic dishonesty. Why? Typical responses are: "There are times when you need a little help." "Just about everyone is doing it." "You need to do it to keep the playing field even."[55]

We can blame the school system, and argue that it fosters an emphasis on test scores and grades, which leads to winning at all costs. We can also blame parents for creating pressure to succeed, starting before their children enter school, when they begin lap reading and introduce their children to alphabet games in order to create supersmart toddlers on the road to Harvard or Yale. We can blame the capitalist system, which fosters competition, dishonesty, and various fraudulent schemes to create an illusion of profits. Or we can blame society—the brutal law of survival of the smartest and most cunning.

The bottom line is that cheating reflects moral laxity, and competition reflects the desire to win—where our heroes and stars compete and cheat—and the rest of us wink and nod. Athletes take drugs to enhance their performance because the result is higher salaries and more endorsements for more money. Politicians lie and are often caught with their fingers in the cookie jar or hiding stuffed shoe boxes in their closets and safe deposit boxes. Judges are bought and decisions are often based on politics and not the law. Legislators are often influenced more by lobbyists who represent big business, and not by the people who elected them. The clergy steals children's innocence one moment, creating fear and guilt for the rest of those children's lives, and preach the gospel the next moment. Money managers are paid in full for investing retirees' pension plans but the retirees are not always paid in full.[56] CEOs invent new accounting tricks to disguise losses and receive bonuses, then proceed to cheat their employees and the general public out of billions of dollars while they become millions of dollars richer.

The goal should be to work for the common public good so all of us can improve our quality of life, rather than to focus only on "money, money, money," at the expense or exploitation of those who run a slower race or are not as shrewd or capable. What we have evolving in American society, starting with preschools and continuing into the workplace, is a small group of people able to get an edge, play the system, and "screw" the other person in order to win the race.

Once upon a time, not long ago, when there was no plastic money, heart transplants, or satellite systems, when *Ozzie and Harriet* and the *Andy Griffith Show* dominated television airwaves, when children showed respect for adult authority, cheating was a "no-no" and there was a moral code that guided behavior. Given the modern world we live in, the Internet and instant communication, fast foods and fast cars, along with sex, drugs, and MTV, the youth of America have little connection with the traditional values of society—what some kids might label as the "stone age" and what intellectuals writing about morality might refer to as the "pre-post modern age," "pre-Prozac era," or what Riesman dubbed as the *inner-directed* society. We live in an age where materialism, conspicuous consumption, and greed are king. This is an era where deviancy is considered normal or cutting edge—evidenced by new art and music, new models or heroes to emulate: Ludacris, Terrell Owens, Rod Strickland, Eminem, Madonna, Howard Stern, Cher, and Snoop Dogg—what traditional folks might say is a little perverse, or at least stretching the boundaries of decency.

Let us remember why our Founding Fathers risked their lives and signed the Declaration of Independence, namely for the natural rights of the people. But equality of political rights will not substitute for the decline in equal opportunity and equity in sharing the nation's wealth. Our ethics of wealth should be simple: America should be where the son or daughter of a laborer can rise to governor, Supreme Court judge, or president, and the son or grandson, daughter or granddaughter, of a millionaire can descend to the working class.

That kind of mobility is accepted in American folklore. But on a more realistic level, we now live in a society where our moral compass has been stretched and sidelined by money making, and the small businessman has been trounced by big business. It all leads to an increased struggling class. The muckrakers of the early twentieth century wrote about titans of industry and banking, and how they decided to skip over the laws of the land to get rich. They described the law-breaking machinations of the Gilded Age, where the idea was to outsmart and outswindle the competition before they did it to you, and to raid the public treasury before someone else cut a deal with a politician and ran off with loot.

Not much has changed today; in fact, now we live in a narcissistic, postmodern Gilded Age. If you want to shoot point-blank at our corporate society, we can say that the Enron's are "bustin' out all over"; corporate excesses and abuses run amok; regulatory commissions are asleep at the wheel; politicians are bought and bribed by big business; and people seem only concerned about investing in Wall Street, and not Main Street. Silence in the face of these offenses implies consent. Free marketers are still tooting their theories. Wall Street buccaneers are still running wild, selling this stock or that stock. Scholars and money managers alike are now writing books on how to invest and become the next millionaire. The simplest advice, according to one expert, is to limit all the daily, unnecessary extravagances that drain your resources. Skipping Starbucks and compounding the savings should save you $500,000 by retirement—what David Bach calls the "latte factor."[57] Then, there is corporate America, in the other corner, encouraging you to spend and live happily, or as Citigroup ads exhort "live richly."

Whereas the populist agitation of the late nineteenth century and muckraker reform movement of the early twentieth century was about the money class sucking the blood and sweat out of the agrarian and labor classes, now it can be said that the Ken Lays and Jeffrey Skillings (Enron), Bernard Ebbers (World Com), Franklin Raines (Fannie Mae), and Jack Grubmans (Salomon Smith Barney) of the world have sucked the heart and soul out of the average person who had his retirement or pension money, his job, or child's college tuition tied to some stock or mutual fund that went south or even disappeared from the charts. It's the heyday of the Gilded Age, all over again, but with more downside as the general public (more than 50 percent of Americans) is involved in Wall Street investing.

Worsening Gaps between the Superrich and Nonrich

I guess the lessons about class differences, and about money and morality, are not the kind of lessons Americans want to learn. It's more comforting to our morale and spirit to believe in the American dream, as well as to deny that this nation is becoming a financial oligarchy. The time has come to get real; the vast majority of Americans, about 90 percent of us, have become big economic losers in the last twenty (to twenty-five) years, at the same period when college enrollment rates of high school graduates increased from 50.4 percent to 62.4 percent and college enrollments (colleges and universities) increased from 8 million to 15 million students,[58] implying that education means less today in trying to achieve the American dream.

In short, we have allowed the government to ignore income gaps between the superrich and ordinary Americans, and by remaining indifferent we are witnessing the slow and steady decline in the standard of living of the vast majority of Americans. Failure to understand that the recent past and present have seared the American dream in terms of class, opportunity, and mobility could consign us to a terrible future. Our standard of living is likely to worsen, as income gaps widen between the superrich and the rest of America, thus driving up the cost for basic items related to health, housing, transportation, education, etc., and reducing the future quality of life among the vast majority of Americans. Hence, there is no good reason why a trip to the baseball park, to see the American "pastime," should cost a family of four sitting in the grandstands, three hundred feet from home plate, eating some burgers and cokes, buying two programs and one baseball hat, and parking one car, 40 to 50 percent of the weekly take-home pay of the average working person (making $40,000 to $45,000 a year). Another factor may be in play. Fear of a tax that goes after the rich doesn't sit well with our history or sense of fair play. Americans don't seem to have problems with superrich people who are self-made, even when they can pass their wealth to their next generation. We seem to be okay with people like Rockefeller, Kennedy, and Bush, and don't think about what "side" deals were made and who was hurt to amass such fortunes. We merely refer to their descendants as part of the "lucky sperm club," not recognizing inherited wealth under capitalism is not much different than the Old World and its aristocracy, exactly what our Founding Fathers despised and revolted against. By default we have allowed the superrich to pass huge estates to their descendants against the interest of the vast majority of Americans. Meanwhile, the U.S. government, unlike those of other industrialized nations, did very little in the past twenty to twenty-five years to improve the status of its working- and middle-class populace. Productivity is up, but wealth is also funneled upwards; very little drips downward.

Now if I've made you feel uncomfortable or second-best, if I have put a dent or damper on your idea of the American dream, and how the rich may have amassed their fortunes, then I beg your indulgence. Unfortunately, questionable corporate malpractice and fraud continue apace, and auditors and prosecutors know what trails to follow but fail to hold executives accountable for trouble that surfaces on their watch. Lawmakers need to get a grip on reality and do what is right by representing the people—and not the corporations. There is opportunity to devise progressive tax systems and income-sharing systems, to reduce the rewards of inherited wealth and unfair chances of life—to help level the playing field at the starting gate and to provide multiple chances to succeed.

The Declining Influence of Education

Most educators and parents would like to think that education counts, and the big winners of the booming economy are college graduates who have agreeable personalities and middle-class values. But the winners are few and far between, not more than 10 percent, as I have earlier reported, or not more than 5 percent, according to Paul Krugman. In fact, he maintains that even this top group (one out of twenty) has seen its real income increase less than 1 percent a year between the late 1970s and 2004. But the real income of the top 1 percent has nearly doubled, and the richest .01 percent—people with incomes of more than $5 million a year—has increased five-fold.[59]

The point is that schools cannot equalize the social and cultural advantages that exist between classes. But Americans also have the vote and ability to effect a peaceful change in the government and tax system that would reduce inequality, especially among the top 1 or 5 percent of American households, where it is most lopsided. However, as much as 40 to 45 percent of qualified voters seem unable to find the voting booths during presidential elections, suggesting that our own indifference is slowly changing our land to a foreign country—a metaphoric equivalent to our vanishing democracy and the middle class that is the backbone of our democracy.

In a period where meritocracy is waning, or defined in vague and different ways that reflect not an objective criterion but a point of view, or when grade inflation makes it impossible to distinguish between A, B, and C students, the value of an education is further reduced. Equality between occupations is nearly impossible in a society based on supply and demand, division of labor, and other free-market conditions. But when inherited wealth allows the same people, even incompetent people, to get most of the rewards, then to multiply their wealth because assets and investments are taxed at a lower rate than income, which ordinary people earn through their work, then the system becomes increasingly skewed. Not only is upward mobility hampered, but also the vitality and growth of society is at stake. It is the same system of wealth that allowed George Bush to become president, considered by some liberal critics to be the most ignorant and incompetent president America has had.[60]

I do not like dividing the United States into the capitalist class and working class, or the superrich and nonrich, because of the label that comes with this ideology. I am not one of the fans of Eugene Debs, the railroad unionist from Terre Haute, Indiana, and the twentieth-century architect of American socialism, and therefore I am not advocating a boxing match with rival fighters (government versus business; the common folks versus the rich; red versus blue voters) in opposite corners. I'm appealing for the rights of small people to be heard and appreciated as in the tradition of Jefferson, FDR, JFK, and LBJ. We just seem unable to make an issue out of growing inequality, or the decimation of the middle class, fearing that it sounds un-American or like class warfare. It is puzzling why the rich should not be asked to bear their full share of government burdens, especially now with the government in deep debt.

Sadly, most of us fail to grasp that we are approaching a surreal sense of dislocation and fundamental shift in our democratic idealism. There is a "point of view," and the phrase here implies either a work of fiction or a serious point in our history. We are at the crossroads as to whether this nation—envisioned by its Founding Fathers as the new Athens and a country dearest to the Enlightenment—has lost or is about to lose its reason and humanism. Have we really become a foreign country in our own land? Are we a lost time, a lost generation, a lost people—strangers in our own land? Are we too blind-sighted or just too plain indifferent to recognize or admit that corporate practices, built on arrogance and greed, compounded by a tax system devised by and for the rich, keep down all the people who cannot successfully compete or run a swift race in second place, or worse? Are we not undercutting the value of education and ignoring our working- and middle-class values of hard work? I leave you with the twin questions: What is the value of an education and what is happening to the middle class when a teacher can barely afford a bungalow, and some captain of industry, entertainer, or sports figure lives a more luxurious life than the land barons of the aristocratic Old World that we had hoped to eliminate in the New World?

A Final Comment

In a break with normal academic practice, I have spent some time chatting with you, or what Lawrence Summers once called "plain talk." My voice has been quite personal, but I have avoided the trivia such as my favorite ice cream or chewing gum flavor. I have tried to focus on the big picture, the ebb and flow of macroeconomic/education events and trends, rather than crowd the pages with facts and figures as to resemble a sports-bar screen full of obscure sports stats or a CNN business report accompanied by a continuous scroll of NASDAQ stock prices. Having gone out of my way to avoid tiny pieces of information, I have touched on an important theme, the big picture stuff involving class, inequality, and education.

Right now, the mobility ladder is missing several steps; it needs major repair, and I doubt whether teachers or schools, or accountants and lawyers, can fix the ladder while our society is manipulated by a few powerful, rich people. We are at the moment in society when knowledgeable people and groups that comprise our leadership in business and government must hold up their bargain with American society for the common good. One of the obstacles to the full development of a democracy, noted by Thomas Jefferson and Horace Mann—the sparks behind free and universal education—is that we have not learned to make the most of bright and talented students who begin life in an impoverished or modest working situation. Then, there is my untidy subjective thought. Having once embraced the pervasive utopian American dream, I now have doubts and believe it is dwindling for most of our children and grandchildren.

Here at the end, I have memories of *Moby Dick*, which I read when I was a much younger man. The images have been transformed over time. I now feel an unsettling glimpse of Melville's whale circling around us, slowly gaining momentum, in the deep bottomless water. "Our fate awaits us . . . and there is no escaping it," like Ahab's destiny. Now look toward the horizon, while you still can, and see the fault lines and cracks rippling on the water surface. (The metaphors here are the economic faults and social cracks of society.) Beyond the horizon is the declining sun—the long, cold night—and the whale is still circling and coming closer. We can hear and feel the unending anxieties of those who, if we continue to undercut and devaluate them, will, alas become nothing but statistics.

NOTES

1. McGuffey is best known for the McGuffey readers, content consisting of procapitalistic stories and profiles of American heroes. Horace Mann is considered the father of the common school movement and most influential educator of the eighteenth century. Charles Eliot was the president of Harvard University and advocate of school tracking and a stratified form of schooling. William Harris was the U.S. Commissioner of Education at the turn of the twentieth century and believed in a uniform curriculum for all students. John Dewey is considered the father of progressive education and most influential educator of the twentieth century. Jane Addams was a social worker who was a friend of Dewey and could be dubbed a "social democrat," although the term did not exist until the 1920s.

2. Frantz Fanon, *The Wretched of the Earth* (New York: Grove Press, 1963).

3. In 1910 only 13.5 percent of persons age 25 and older had a high school diploma or higher compared to 83.4 percent in 2000. See *Educational Digest 1971* (Washington, DC: U.S. Government Printing Office, 1972), table 11, page 9; *Education Digest 2000* (Washington, DC: U.S. Government Printing Office, 2001), table 8, page 17.

4. Elsewhere I have argued that Dewey was the most influential educator of the twentieth century.

5. "When Greed Was a Virtue and Regulation the Enemy," *New York Times*, July 21, 2002, section 4, page 14.

6. James P. Othmer, "Masters of the Universe, Unite!" *New York Times*, May 26, 2006.

7. Eric Dash, "$135 Million Parachute for Banker," *New York Times*, January 31, 2006, 15; Claudia H. Deutsch, "Take Your Best Shot," *New York Times*, December 9, 2005.

8. Gretchen Morgenson, "Fund Manager, It's Time to Pick a Side," *New York Times*, March 26, 2006; Morgenson, "A Lump of Coal Might Suffice," *New York Times*, December 24, 2006.

9. Ian Ayres and John J. Donohue, "The Knicks Boldly Go Where Companies Have Not," *New York Times*, July 2, 2006; Gretchen Morgenson, "Are Enrons Bustin' Out All Over?" *New York Times*, May 28, 2006.

10. Jenny Anderson, "Atop Hedge Funds, Richest of the Rich Get Even More So," *New York Times*, May 26, 2006.

11. Eric Dash, "The New Executive Bonanza: Retirement," *New York Times*, April 3, 2005.

12. Gretchen Morgenson, "Outside Advice on Boss's Pay May Not Be So Independent," *New York Times*, April 10, 2006.

13. Micheline Maynard, "GM Will Offer Buyouts to All Its Union Workers," *New York Times*, March 23, 2006; Mark A. Stein, "GM Offers Pay for Its Workers to Go Away," *New York Times*, March 25, 2006. Also see "Delphi Proposes New Contract to Auto Workers Union," *New York Times*, March 25, 2006.

14. Deutsch, "Take Your Best Shot."

15. Deutsch, "Take Your Best Shot," 14.

16. Anna Bernasek, "The Golden Years: Travels, Hobbies, A New Job, Too," *New York Times*, January 29, 2006.

17. Joseph P. Fried, "Life, and Work, After Retirement," *New York Times*, March 19, 2006.

18. Louis Uchitelle, *The Disposable American: Layoffs and Their Consequences* (New York: Knopf, 2006).

19. Louis Uchitelle, "Retraining, But for What?" *New York Times*, March 26, 2006.

20. Darwin conceived human nature as plastic, capable of adapting to the environment and improving it. The philosophical and economic interpretation of Darwin by conservative thinkers advocated the growth of full individuality. The smart person would adjust to changing needs and conditions, rising above the competition and crushing the little fellow. In a highly competitive social/economic system, students in school are groomed to succeed; moreover, they are sorted and tracked into programs based on their competitive nature and abilities. Some students are earmarked to go to Harvard and others fall to the wayside and drop out of school or graduate as functional illiterates. The "sorting machine," what some people might refer to as an aspect of Social Darwinism, merely perpetuates prior class distinctions because from the start advantaged children have greater chances of going to Harvard and disadvantaged children have greater chances of failing in school.

21. "Nightly Business Report," April 23, 2004; "The Labor Picture," *New York Times*, March 11, 2006. Also see Jack Rasmus, *The War at Home: The Corporate Offensive in America from Reagan to Bush* (San Ramon, CA: Kyklos Productions, 2005).

22. Claudia H. Deutsch, "My Big Fat CEO Paycheck," *New York Times*, April 3, 2005; Joseph Nocera, "Disclosure Won't Tame CEO Pay," *New York Times*, January 14, 2006.

23. Gretchen Morgenson, "The Best and Worst in Executive Pay," *New York Times*, September 17, 2006.

24. Claudia H. Deutsch, "My Big Fat CEO Payment," *New York Times*, April 3, 2005.

25. John Bogle, *The Battle for the Soul of Capitalism* (New Haven, CT: Yale University Press, 2005).

26. Jenny Anderson, "AIG is Expected to Offer $1.6 Billion to Settle with Regulators," *New York Times*, February 6, 2006.

27. David Riesman (with Nathan Glazer and Ruel Denny), *The Lonely Crowd* (Garden City, NY: Doubleday, 1953).

28. Todd Gitlin, "How Our Crowd Got Lonely," *New York Times Book Review*, January 9, 2000.

29. The references are to the movies: *Death of a Salesman, The Graduate,* and *Ordinary People.*

30. William Whyte, *The Organization Man* (New York: Simon & Schuster, 1956).

31. C. Wright Mills, *The Power Elite* (New York: Oxford University Press, 1956); Max Weber, *Economy and Society* (New York: Bedminster Press, 1968).

32. Richard J. Herrnstein, *IQ with Meritocracy* (Boston: Little, Brown, 1971), 45, 53.

33. Herrnstein, *IQ with Meritocracy,* 54.

34. John W. Gardner, *Excellence: Can We Be Equal and Excellent Too?* rev. ed. (New York: Norton, 1984), 82, 85.

35. See the discussion about merit in chapter 3, particularly the contributions of Daniel Bell, John Gardner, and Michael Young.

36. Lawrence Summers, "Plain Talk from Larry Summers," *Business Week,* November 8, 2004, 73.

37. Rachel E. Silverman, "Looser Trust Laws Lure $100 Billion," *Wall Street Journal,* February 16, 2005.

38. Assuming a forty-hour work week, this amounts to $16,640 per year, which was below the poverty line ($18,850) for a family of four in 2004. See *Federal Register,* February 13, 2004, 7336–38.

39. "How Many People Are Unemployed in the U.S.?" *Pacific Views,* December 29, 2003. Originally published in the *Los Angeles Times.* Also see Rasmus, *The War at Home.*

40. The number one American employer is Wal-Mart. The average salary for full-time employees is about $7.50 an hour. One-third are part-time employees—limited to less than twenty-eight hours of work per week—and are not eligible for benefits. The rapid turnover—70 percent of employees leave within the first year—is due to a lack of recognition and inadequate pay. www.pbs.org/itvs/sorewars/stores3.html.

41. As many as 48 percent of retirees were forced into early retirement. Of this group, 38 percent were for health reasons, 16 percent for job elimination, 10 percent for a buyout, and 7 percent for problems in the work environment. As many as 43 percent of retirees feel they are in a precarious position, and another 25 percent have serious concerns about their standard of living worsening. www.asec.org/rcs_key.htm.

42. "Dell Announces Plan to Double India Work Force," *New York Times,* March 21, 2006; Saritha Rai, "Dell to Double India Work Force," *New York Times,* March 21, 2006.

43. Saritha Rai, "Microsoft Joins Industry Trend of Investing Heavily in India," *New York Times,* December 8, 2005.

44. David Lague, "China Begins Efforts to Curb Piracy of Computer Software," *New York Times,* May 30, 2006.

45. *Digest of Education Statistics 2000* (Washington, DC: U.S. Government Printing Office, 2001), tables 172–73, pages 201–2.

46. Richard B. Freeman, *The Over-Educated American* (New York: Academic Press, 1976), 18.

47. Richard B. Freeman and J. Herbert Holloman, "Declining Value of College

Going," *Change* (September 1975), table 1, page 25; George L. Perry and James Tobin, *Economic Events, Ideas and Policies* (Washington, DC: Brookings Institution, 2000).

48. Paul Krugman, "Winning Over Discontent," *New York Times*, September 8, 2006.

49. "Lou Dobbs Report," May 11, 2004; Brandan I. Koerner, "Generation Debt: The New Economics of Young," *Village Voice* (March 17–23, 2004), 1–8.

50. Elizabeth Warren and Amelia Warren Tyagi, *The Two Income Trap* (New York: Basic, 2003).

51. See Paul Krugman, "Democracy at Risk," *New York Times*, January 23, 2004; Krugman, "Jobs, Jobs, Jobs," *New York Times*, February 10, 2004; Krugman, "Promises, Promises," *New York Times*, March 9, 2004; and *The State of Working America 2002–2003*.

52. John Hoover, *How to Work for an Idiot: Survive and Thrive . . . Without Killing Your Boss* (New York: Career Press, 2004).

53. Willow Lawson, "Matter of your Universe," *Psychology Today* (November/December 2005), 17–18.

54. Nel Noddings, *The Challenge to Care in Schools* (New York: Teachers College Press, Columbia University, 1992), 101.

55. Glen C. Altschinler, "Battling the Cheats," *New York Times Education Life* (January 7, 2001), 15.

56. For example, in the years between 1999 and 2003 pension professionals who ran United's pension plan received $125 million in fees but the plan lost $10.2 billion. Because of the government's pension insurance, the retirees will only lose $3.4 billion. Uncle Sam will foot the rest of the bill—meaning the U.S. taxpayer, you and me. See Mary W. Walsh, "How Wall Street Wrecked United's Pension, *New York Times*, July 31, 2005.

57. David Bach, *The Automatic Millionaire* (New York: Broadway, 2004).

58. *Digest of Education Statistics 2000*, tables 163, 170, 171–72; pages 180–81, 192, 200–1.

59. Krugman, "Winning Over Discontent."

60. The theme of ignorance and incompetence is frequently raised by TV commentators such as Lou Dobbs and Chris Mathews and by *New York Times* op.-ed columnists such as Maureen Dowd and Frank Rich.

6

✝

The Golden Years Are Over

Stop the presses! Within just a few years we've had one scandal after another involving world-class accounting firms, blue-chip corporations, and mutual funds (which own 60 percent of the corporations), and guru CEOs. The outcome is always the same: The money makers move money around and few people outside Wall Street understand or know about the shuffling and side deals under the table. The rap sheets of the scoundrels are similar. The all-pervasive philosophy is the same: "Greed is good." The losers are the same: the public. In fact, the rollercoaster of boom and bust, the frenzy to buy followed by a panic or crash, is a trend that any good historian knows from the days of Washington to Bush: 1792, 1837, 1873, 1893, 1930s, 1980s, and 2000–2001. The world of Wall Street, banking, and finance have been riddled with arrogance, materialism, corruption, and criminality since the rise of big business in America, with one difference. Back then, whether we are talking about 1792, the Depression years, or the Reagan years, relatively few people were investors. As of 2000, just before the tech and Internet bubble bust and stream of corporate scandals, more than half the population invested in the market in some way. That is a dramatic difference from, say, 1960, when 10 percent invested in stocks.[1]

The scandals of 2000 have been bumped off the front pages; the damage has already been done to small investors who lost savings, pensions, and retirement funds—many whose lives were radically changed when retirement plans, mortgages and homes, and college plans and dreams were intertwined directly and indirectly with Wall Street in a way never experienced before. The investors' losses were in the trillions, although estimated to be $7 million by Alan Greenspan who was Federal Reserve chair when the bubble burst;[2] and fines imposed by the Security Exchange Commission, under the chairmanship of William Donaldson, on the major Wall Street firms and banks totaled $5.3 billion.³ Not a very good recovery for the investors! The popular hostility toward Big Business and Big Banking has receded, even in the teeth of the most stunning Wall Street frauds since the crash of 1929 and the Gilded Age of 1873 and 1893.

The problem is that history has a way of repeating itself. There is a tendency for Americans to engage in political and social neglect, divorce themselves from civic participation, and accept the power of corporations and the unequal sharing of American wealth. Ralph Nader, who some like myself consider in his aging years to be more like "Don Quixote," argues that the power of corporations and their lack of social responsibility leads to civic indifference. The failure of citizens to act and vote threatens our democratic way of life and everything that matters to us.⁴ The refusal of the Attorney General, Security Exchange Commission, Federal Reserve Bank, and Federal Trade Commission to seriously clean house means that the experts we pay and depend on to safeguard and protect the common people from the corrupt people have failed; consequently, lives are continuously being destroyed and others are being yanked backwards and out of the middle class.

On one level, most people are easily misled with a string of economic statistics by experts in their naive belief that professionals with pinstriped suits and the gift of gab can be trusted. The average person is impressed and willing to listen to people with all-knowing corporate titles.⁵ On still another level, there is a significant percentage of Wall Street and Big Business buccaneers who tend to cheat and defraud the public because of their inherent motivation or obligation to pursue profit without regard to costs incurred by others. Old restraints ranging from unions, churches, communities, and government and civic agencies have been rendered impotent over the last fifty years or more.

According to David Callahan, the founder of Demos, a small, liberal public policy organization, America has lost its moral compass. There is much more cheating, lying, and stealing from corporate boardrooms to university exam rooms, from law firms that overbill to electronic piracy—a basic unraveling of the nation's old values. According to Callahan, the political right has defined values in a narrow way—around family, sex and abortion, crime and drugs, and faith and personal responsibility—in home, school, and community. They have ignored the decline of business ethics and corporate social responsibility—and winked at the rise of materialism, conspicuous consumption, and greed; bigger houses and bigger cars; cutthroat competition and the general fleecing of the public.⁶

The dilemma facing corporations, and the need to protect the public through government regulation and civic participation of the public, is best delineated by the contradictory conventional wisdom and words of Peter Drucker, the ninety-five-year-old preeminent business and management consultant who died in 2005. He wrote in the 1970s: "If the managers of our major institutions, and especially of business, do not take responsibility for the common good, no one else can or will." More recently, during the boom years of the last rollercoaster ride, just prior to 2000, Drucker said: "If you find an executive who wants to take on social responsibility fire him."[7] Drucker maintains that his last comment was taken out of context in an interview with Joel Bahan, in his recent book *The Corporation*, and that the intent of the author was to make a political point by turning an icon into a straw man. The other possibility is that Drucker was "losing it," given his advanced age. Although some readers may never have heard of Drucker, there exists a critical mass of Wall Street money makers and investment bankers that have been manipulating the markets, and sucking blood and money out of the public, way before modern business consultants have wrangled over and characterized the American corporate business world. The manipulation and machination of American big-business leaders go back to the reconstruction years after the Civil War, commonly called the Gilded Age.

THE GILDED AGE

The Civil War and its aftermath (the next fifty-plus years) shifted the national wealth from the old patrician class and "planting aristocracy of the South" to the capitalists, industrialists, entrepreneurs, and investment bankers of the North and Northeast.[8] The era was characterized by large-scale corruption, graft, and greed—whereby alliances were forged between politicians and the new capitalist class. According to Henry Perkinson, a retired professor from New York University, politicians at all levels (local, state, and federal) got "rich by selling jobs, contracts, franchises—whatever they had in their power"[9]—to the highest bidders. Entrepreneurs and business people competed with each other in bribing politicians, and the price for political favors continued to spiral. As other historians put it, "Politics . . . became one of the great businesses of the nation," and those in power sought gain "like any other enterprise in a competitive society."[10]

The "best people," the old-money class of America, sat on the sidelines in dismay and saw the country being run by a group of political and business thugs. In the words of the editor of the *Nation*, E. L. Godkin, a gang of political "spoilsmen" were in cahoots with the "new rich" or business opportunists who lacked the "restraints of culture, pride . . . class or rank."[11] Fraudulent government and banking practices became synonymous with the financing of railroads, canals, bridges, roads, utilities, and sewer systems. Bribes, payoffs, profits, and investment opportunities went directly to politicians who in turn sold patronage and jobs to workers and officeholders, and special favors and subsidies to industrialists and big-business leaders. Such bribes and scandals determined whether or not, and how, business would be regulated, taxed, and/or protected in terms of tariffs and which business titans could squash the competition and get away with it.[12] At all levels of government, jobs were considered as part of a spoils system that "the victorious party expected to distribute as patronage to party stalwarts" and loyal jobseekers.[13] The titans of industry, the Wall Street swindlers, the interlocking corporations and trusts, and the land and railway developers were in bed with politicians.

The Triumph of Big Business

Conceivably, the great figures in manufacturing, banking, railways, land development, mining, oil, steel, and other exploiters of natural resources were nothing more than manipulators of the marketplace who "seized the moment" or "got there first" and thus accumulated immense wealth, power, and fame. It might also be argued by the defenders of the faith that the great fortunes of the Rockefellers, Vanderbilts, Carnegies, Mellons, etc. were based on their strength and natural intelligence, and that the rise of so many obscure, uneducated, and uncultivated men to wealth was evidence of the great opportunities of America, the American dream (rags to riches), and the cult of success. The achievement of great fortunes might also have had something to do with the doctrine of Social Darwinism (the smartest and the strongest, certain in their own convictions, will shape the landscape and acquire its wealth); what Herbert Spencer called economic laissez faire; what some preachers such as Henry Ward Beecher, Daniel Gregory, and William Lawrence considered part of the divine order, or that God had determined the success and failure of his children[14]; or simply what the muckrakers later referred to as the "law of the jungle."

Listen to what Andrew Carnegie had to say in 1889 in defending the theory of the elite, delighting in the self-made man and industrial giant: "While the law may be sometimes hard for the individual, it is best for the race, because it insures the survival of the fittest in every department." He bluntly continued, "We accept and welcome . . . great inequality of environment, the concentration of business [and wealth] in the hands of a few and the law of competition . . . as being not only beneficial, but essential for the future progress of the race." Based on "the law of competition . . . human society loses homogeneity and classes are formed." But the "socialist" who seeks to overturn present conditions is "attacking the foundation upon which civilization itself rests."[15] In other words, any person or group trying to (1) regulate business practices, (2) limit huge conglomerates, (3) protect investors or shareholders, or (4) introduce a progressive tax policy (to pay for human services such as health, education, or welfare) would be considered anticapitalist and anti-American. The "Americanization" of the continent, its economic growth and productivity, included the ruthless subjection of the land and immigrant and nonwhite people, and all the mess and industrial slough wrought by mines, railroads, factories, and energy systems.

Carnegie cast the wealthy into the stewardship role of American opportunity by advocating that the "millionaire [must become] a trustee for the poor." The person "who dies rich dies disgraced." It is the millionaire's duty to the poor to bring his "superior wisdom, experience, and ability to administer, doing for them better than they would or could do for themselves." The idea is to support public institutions (such as schools and libraries) "which will improve the general condition of the people; in this manner returning [his] surplus wealth to the mass [of the people] in the forms best calculated to do them lasting good."[16]

Now read William Graham Sumner, the sociologist from Yale and a disciple of Herbert Spencer: "The social order is fixed by laws of nature," and all economic contests are "struggles of interests for larger shares in the produce of industry." Any social legislation designed to help trade unions or cure poverty is to "mar the operation of the social laws."[17] Taken to its logical conclusion, Sumner's seemingly innocent dictum leads to three possible worlds: (1) Charles Dickens's *Tale of Two Cities*, with *revolution*, the storming of the Bastille and the overthrow of the nobility class (including the titans and captains of industry); (2) Victor Hugo's *Les Misérables*, with *no escape*, "look down, look down. . . . This is your future"; or (3) the bizarre world of *Blade Runner*, with its *grotesque* sights and sounds, somewhat freakish or surreal, where the strong survive and weak become easy pickings for buzzards and bloodhounds.

Sumner warned repeatedly against governmental interference with the social and economic order. The more competitive the society, he argued, the greater the innovation and progress of the society. "It may shock you to hear me say, but when you get over the shock, it will do you good to think of it: a drunk in the gutter is just what he ought to be," Sumner told the Historical Society of Brooklyn in 1883. "Nature is working away at him to get him out of the way."[18] For the Yale professor, great wealth was an inducement for business efficiency and social progress. "In no sense whatever does a man who accumulates a fortune by legitimate industry exploit his employees; or make his capital 'out of' anybody else," he declared. "The wealth he wins would not be but for him [and] it is a necessary condition of many forms of social advance."[19] The wealthy did not owe anything to the common person, for the captains of industry had made their money based on their own talents and hard work. For Sumner, the common people had only excuses and selfish reasons to hold back a superior person's force and drive of genius and productivity—all to the detriment of individual performance and social efficiency.

Sumner and his contemporaries failed to recognize that large amounts of wealth are created by the labor of others and by receiving money from the masses in terms of products or services rendered. As greater fortunes are made by a few people, and as the economy grows, the gap between the rich and poor widens. The outcome is a dominant-subordinate class relationship—a split within society that eventually tests the fiber of society. This may not be so evident in the United States, because of the "cult of success" and belief that the humble can rise to the top. Given the knowledge that the average person cannot easily rise (which Carnegie admitted to be a flaw in the social and economic system in his description of "the gospel of wealth"), even when talent and abilities are considered, this leads to a feeling of frustration, and hostility bubbling within the system. It becomes compounded and more glaring when variables such as race, ethnicity, or gender are used to show differences in wealth and income and this is what happened, beginning in the 1960s, when the civil rights and feminist movements descended on the American landscape. In a global economy, a more recent trend, the gap between entrepreneurial elites and average workers widen because the market expands, permitting more profits, but the distribution of gains remain unequal.

The good society recognizes there are differences in talent and abilities and makes adjustments in a wise and fair way; it also builds safeguards into the system to prevent the abuse of power and wealth. However, Sumner (and others) believed in the "law of nature" and "law of competition," as well as the notion of individualism, evolution, and struggles of interests among people or groups for larger shares of wealth without any type of social legislation or government interference. The conservative defense envisioned any concession or balancing act as a form of paternalism or socialism—even worse as corrupting the morality of the family, church, and country. It envisioned any form of government regulation or increase in government powers over business as inefficient, disruptive, and disastrous—as a boom to socialism.

One hundred years later, Steve Forbes, who is the chief editor of *Forbes* magazine, warned that "misguided government policies . . . dried up the flow of capital . . . and [caused] free-market failure" during the Great Depression of the 1930s and massive inflation of the late 1990s. "In the real world, therefore, free markets operate rationally and efficiently in a way that government regulators simply can't."[20] In his classic text *Free to Choose*, Milton Friedman argued that government intervention breeds conflict and inefficiency, and free markets breed cooperation and efficiency. At the end of the day, according to Friedman, political freedom and economic freedom go hand-in-hand; it is essential for political freedom to "recognize in the law each individual's natural right to property [and] that they have control over, and that they can dispose of."[21] By rejecting government intervention, both Forbes and Friedman evidence contempt for political and social reform and merely perpetuate the Hamiltonian view that the best government serves those who own property. At the very least, a weak or unresponsive government permits almost limitless reward for those who have the right skills and connections, and get lucky, without having to share their gains with the rest of the community; it boils down to a few elites leaving everyone else behind.

G. Stanley Hall and E. L. Thorndike, the two most influential psychologists at the turn of the twentieth century, also supported the cult of individual success and the notions that the inequality resulting from competition and differences in talent and abilities reflected heredity and that the outcomes and differences in human behavior were rooted in human nature or the gene pool; no one was responsible for this inequality, and there was no reason to penalize intelligent or superior people for their success.[22] This type of relationship—superior and inferior, smart and dumb—is what some might innocently call a "sorting out process" or "tracking system" in school, whereas others would label it as discriminatory and as potential social dynamite. This conflict becomes increasingly evident when the economic gap between the upper and lower echelons are extremely widened, and if the lower base comprises an overabundance of people who feel trapped or discriminated against.

For Hall and Thorndike, the main criterion for success or fortune was inherited intelligence. The captains of industry had forged their own success and accumulated fortunes because of their unique abilities. Their psychological theories not only fit into the business explanation of wealth, but also the religious explanation of stewardship and charity, including all those who used God and his infinite wisdom to support the business buccaneers and property interests of the wealthy class. Once more listen to the voice of Steve Forbes: "The real virtue of capitalism is that it guarantees that as we develop our talents, we're contributing to the public good. . . . The U.S. is both the most commercial nation and most philanthropic nation in human history."[23] And now listen again to the renowned and conservative Milton Friedman, "Our first task: Stop the growth of government. The second task is to shrink government spending and make government smaller." The idea is to make "people responsible for themselves and for their own care."[24] I guess this all makes sense if you believe in Social Darwinism or if you are on the top of the totem pole of success—so the hell with the less fortunate, the sickly, and the disenfranchised. The whole idea of limiting government fails to consider the compact in America that everyone should do better, not just highly talented or privileged people by birth, not just those with entrepreneurial spirit or the temperament to win.

Engendering the American Dream

So long as people believe in the golden ring, that there is real opportunity, then the multitude will remain sedate. And there is just enough truth in this generalization to keep people believing in the American dream without realizing the dream is disappearing for the vast majority of the populace. Statistically, today, most people are locked into their economic station, commonly referred to as quintiles (fifths) in the current population surveys published by the U.S. Census Bureau. For example, 61.5 percent of families who were in the lowest quintile in 1969 were in the same income bracket twenty years later. Of the families that did move to another income level, 85 percent moved up or down one level.[25]

It was also argued during the Gilded Age that westward expansion, social and economic progress, exploitation and harnessing of natural resources, the splendors of industrial capitalism, and corporate growth explained the American character. Rugged individualism, hard work, thrift, and the itch for speculation helped grow the country and created an ethos for profit and wealth. The concept was idealized and sentimentalized by the Horatio Alger stories, firmly rooted in Ben Franklin's *Poor Richard's Almanac* and Abe Lincoln's biography—how the pioneer boy became president.

Two opposing views surfaced. America has always had a certain amount of elasticity, uncommon in other parts of the world, that allowed you to achieve the big dream so long as you were a person as big as the dream. It has allowed people like Lou Gehrig, George Gershwin, Andy Warhol, Michael Jackson, and Ruth Bader Ginsburg to achieve what they could not achieve in any other country, and this is what has always distinguished America from other countries. To be sure, the pictures at Ellis Island tell a tale of people clamoring to come to America, some weeping for joy as they passed into the New York Harbor and saw the Statue of Liberty beckoning them—the huddled masses yearning to be free. The American dream is built on the aspirations and achievements of these immigrants, risking life and limb to come to our shores. There is no better way to judge this country, or any country, then by the numbers of people trying to get into it, as opposed to other parts of the world where people are desperately trying to exit their countries.

But there is a flip side, a little less glowing and a little more critical description of America. The conservative intellectual and money class identified their values with the common good, the doctrine of Social Darwinism and evolution that ascribed to the superiority of certain ethnic stocks and the Christian notion that God in his infinite wisdom had willed the control of property and wealth to a select group. Those who stood outside the ranks of the privileged few accepted one or more of these notions—so that the rich and robber barons did not have to mount a defense to preserve the status quo. Hence, the American attitude toward individuals achieving great wealth, even at the expense of working people, is relatively benign compared to other industrialized countries. Labor tried to present another view, but it failed because conservative critics were successful in associating its leaders with the ideas of radicalism, collectivism, socialism, and communism. And which good person is going to rock the boat if they live in a big house with sunny rooms, a perfectly manicured lawn, and big trees in the backyard?

Although Carnegie donated vast sums of money to public institutions, and thus made a case for the theory of accumulating wealth and for the moral character of wealthy people, Sumner and other evolutionary theorists, as well as most of the benefactors of the Gilded Age, did not care about the common people, nor public institutions, much less their competitors, investors, or stockholders as evidenced by all the scandals, kickbacks, bribes, and overgenerous salaries for themselves. It was this species of big business and corporate malfeasance that infuriated the Populist reformers more than one hundred years ago, and now infuriates the public today and has produced front-page exposés—the loss of trillions of dollars in the stock market from millions of average people. It's as if very little has changed in America, despite what laws or government regulation is supposed to exist to protect the public. In short, the theories of Darwin and Spencer, supported by Sumner, prevailed—that is the triumph of materialism and money over morality and fairness and salesmanship and corruption over stewardship and honesty. In short, the arrogance of greed, self-interest, and competition, characterized by the economic theories of Adam Smith, then the nineteenth century industrialists, and now the free-marketers, have devoured the common people and working people for centuries.

The Ideal Industrial Model

Henry Ford's first two automobile companies went bust. His third try was the Ford Motor Company. He wasn't much different from other captains of industry, except that he had the audacity to pay his workers $5 a day in 1914, double the pay of the average factory worker. His rivals were horrified and concerned that the policy would spoil workers and lead to socialism. However, Ford argued that the $5-day rate was a winning strategy; it "started [his] business, for on that day we first created a lot of customers." Ford's reasoning became a new philosophy known as "Fordism."[26] The high wages would motivate his workers, which in turn would lead to greater production and profits, while allowing his own employees to increase their spending and afford an automobile and thus lead to more production and profits. The concept became the pillar of twentieth-century American industrialism and unionism. His biggest problem was to build cars fast enough to satisfy demand. Auto production jumped from 82,000 cars in 1913 to 189,000 cars in 1914 to 585,000 cars in 1916 to two million in 1923.[27] The American assembly line and American industrial model were born that year (1914) and were in full gear by 1920.

What was so reassuring about Fordism was that the philosophy suggested a self-reinforcing growth cycle. Only if workers and the middle class did well could the nation as a whole prosper, and the entire workforce would share in American prosperity. As the country grew richer so did the American working and middle class, thus reinforcing the virtuous concept that democracy and capitalism went hand-in-hand—and what was good for Ford (and later GM) was good for the country.

But it is no longer 1914. The ninety-year cycle has ended. The Model-T is a bygone era. Henry Ford is but a memory, and his once proud and powerful company is sick and staggering. Along with GM, it is struggling to stay alive and stem the tide of bankruptcy. Both giants have been replaced by the Toyota model, and Ford is seeking help from Toyota on ways to improve efficiency. Globalization and foreign competition have put the two giants of American industry into a downward and cost-cutting cycle. Although international finance, along with technology and innovation, has helped many high-paying professionals and upper-class Americans get richer, American factories are closing, jobs are disappearing (others are being outsourced), wages are depressed, and thousands of local economies are sick and small cities and towns are hurting. Supporters of globalization and free trade are fooling themselves if they think they need only to better explain so-called benefits to workers.

In the midst of increased globalism and competition from abroad, the social contract that once existed in many industries between employers and employees has all but disappeared as salaries, pensions, and health benefits have been trimmed. Despite broad economic growth, about 3 percent per year between 2002 and 2006, the average hourly wage of the American workforce more or less remained at the same level. In fact, for the last thirty years the hourly wages of workers in America have remained flat after inflation.

Making matters worse, not only has the social contract between American capitalism and American workers disappeared, replaced by low-paying jobs, but there is growing acceptance among liberal economists such as Jared Bernstein and Jeffrey Sachs that America no longer needs an equitable distribution to have a growth economy. Paying decent wages, providing adequate safety nets, and limiting outrageous executive salaries is now behind us, part of yesterday, negotiated away by big business under the threat of bankruptcy and by CEOs who gobble up remaining profits, regardless of whether their companies make or lose money.

Despite our enlightened social conscience and social policies, the status of the American workforce rose with Fordism but is now reversing and coming close to what it was like at the turn of the twentieth century. The strides made by unions after the Great Depression, from the 1940s to the 1960s, have been superseded by the Wal-Mart model: low wages, few benefits, and high turnover. It not only destroys competition and puts people out of work, it helps destroy the American standard of living. Actually, the nation's decline began with the steel strike of 1959, when the U.S. steel industry began to flounder because of foreign competition and was forced to take back many of the previous gains given to steel workers. A once proud industry began its decline. Small towns that were robust and prosperous went bust as steel mills around the country closed in the late 1960s, similar to what is now happening to the U.S. auto industry and what previously happened to the lumber, paper, and printing industries, clothing and textile industries.

The American workforce has lost its place in the sun, along with its industrial model. It was good while it lasted, and we were the envy of the rest of the world. They were good days. But now it is coming to an end. We need to understand that America as a nation is moving into the slow lane. Our last cutting-edge industries—semiconductors, telecommunications, computer software, nanotechnology, and Internet services—are slowly being moved to the Asian rim where talented technical specialists are cheaper and in abundance. Similarly, U.S. science and technology companies are being challenged by the technological, industrial, and entrepreneurial growth of Asian countries and even parts of Eastern Europe. It's happening all around us.

The best advice: If your job can be digitized, it is only time before it becomes moveable to the other side of the world. Technology permits companies to rapidly grow and become larger. China, India, and a few other Asian countries such as Japan, South Korea, and Singapore in short time will be the center of action; this is where new products and new ideas will derive from, the center of the future global workplace. If you think I'm talking about some far-off place or a fantasy world, then you need to read Thomas Friedman's best-selling book *The World Is Flat*. He warns that the economic playing field has been leveled by computers, broadband and cellular networks, and the Internet. Global trends indicate continuous growth in investments and jobs in China, India, and other Asian countries and the slow demise of American workers who are unable to compete in a global economy[28] and, if I may add, the slow transfer of trillions of dollars of wealth from the United States to the Asian rim countries.

But Americans have never been ones to lay back and let history take its course. Since coming to the Promised Land in 1624, Americans have ventured into the wilderness to seek their fortunes and have navigated through storms to protect their freedoms. Since the turn of the twentieth century, we have came to the aid of our allies to ward off despots and totalitarianism. We are now facing one more external threat that will eventually become part of history, which we must confront as a nation. The economic crisis we now face will become a generational journey, one we will face for the remaining century, as we try to transform ourselves and cope with the coming storm. This crisis will not be solved by rallies in the streets (a liberal response) or by paying executives more money (a conservative response). It will be resolved by painful changes involving a shared moral foundation and a sense of justice, adopting new policies that protect American workers from corporate America and from foreign competition, providing progressive taxes and regulating markets, and marching to the ballot boxes in record numbers in order to elect people willing to make these kinds of changes.

Visions and Divisions of Reform

But the naysayers and critics have to admit there were some "good old days," when Ford and GM were models of corporate responsibility and there seemed to be a social contract between employers and employees. I guess that period coincides with the production of the Model T up to the 1950s or 1960s, except for the years of the Great Depression. Do you remember your mom or dad, or maybe your grandma or granddad, telling you about growing up in some small town in America? Do you remember those old days—the moss-laden landscape of yesterday, with the white picket fence, the Sunday mass and church choir, the Boy Scouts, the school hop, and a family of four with a mom and a dad?

Those old days lasted right up to when "Mr. Rogers" taught us about charming neighborhoods in small, simple rural and suburban towns, further reinforced by *Dick and Jane* readers and *Reader's Digest*. No one seemed to challenge the social and economic order, except perhaps a few angry populists from places that no one had ever heard of or could locate on a state map, and a few radical anarchists who spoke about human misery and workers' rights. However, all these ideas were foreign to those who supported or belonged to the church choir and Boy Scouts of America. And yet, today, any policy or campaign to achieve economic well-being for average Americans must rest on strong moral and religious foundations, consistent with compassion for common people and concern for the common good, a social ethos you would expect to find in small towns. People have a choice, according to news reporter and author Louis Uchitelle: to again become a community of people who are willing to help one another and share in the prosperity of the nation or act as a collection of individuals, each one concerned with his or her own well-being and self-interests.[29]

There is a point on the economic scale of self-interest that goes beyond individual well-being, self-actualization, and personal success. That point, although we may disagree because of social and economic theories, is destructive to society as a whole and is a formula for mass unemployment and underemployment, the elimination of social programs and services for the working- and middle-class populace, and even increased poverty, starvation, and human misery. The self-interest principles of Adam Smith, coupled with the ideas of Ayn Rand and modern capitalists that greed and ruthless pursuit of profit leads to improved productivity, and the ideas of Milton Friedman and Steve Forbes that markets left unregulated for speculative investments lead to well-being and prosperity, are all vehicles for human folly. Given a dose of reality, or more accurately acknowledging my own interpretation of present events, these ideas lead to massive inequality, lack of opportunity and mobility, and the selfish rise of a tiny collection of individuals (say 1 percent) at the expense of the masses in America.

Democracy cannot exist for long, according to John Rawls's theory of justice, unless we place ceilings on individual performance (and pay) and floors for which no individual, regardless of their abilities, can fall. There must be some kind of end points or limits we cannot break through, and some kind of balance or tipping point between excellence and equality. (See chapter 4.) Conservative prophets have convinced the lower and working classes who vote that regulation of markets (as well as increased taxation on the "fruits of labor") are tied to liberalism; moreover, they have dismissed liberal arguments as irrelevant—as "chloroform in print."

Disregard all liberal and conservative agendas for the moment, and forget about Democratic and Republican platforms. If we refuse to make changes in the social and economic system and recommit to community responsibility and the common good, then as Thomas Kochan, professor of management at MIT warns, "future historians will look back and chastise us for standing idly by during some of the darkest days in American history.[30] If we fail to revamp the economic system in the United States, fail to allow for ethical, fair, and just policies to interplay with, or more precisely to curtail, personal self-interest, materialism, and greed, then we are heading for social and economic disaster. We need to remember the past, go back to the source of an America that was formed by a compact with its people, the longing for the spirit of 1776. In the thinking of John Kenneth Galbraith, government must interject progressive and ethical standards to curtail corporate monopolies and malpractice, to ensure decent work for the common person, and provide adequate social services. Critics respond that this is the road to a social welfare state, and voters have heard this type of talk since the Reagan administration, from the likes of Milton Friedman, the former University of Chicago economist, and Arthur Laffer, the former Pepperdine University economist and intellectual guiding light behind "trickle down" economics.

For those of us who still believe in Cinderella stories, or remember the management principles of Peter Drucker, first appearing in the 1940s and 1950s, which fused business leadership and management with morality, corporations need only to smooth out the edges to get things right for employees, customers, suppliers, and stockholders. This argument flooded the book market in the early 1980s, when American manufacturing was first threatened by German and Japanese production, with books like William Ouchi's *Theory Z* and Thomas Peters and Robert Waterman's *In Search of Excellence.*

No true-blooded American could find fault with those rosy books and descriptions of the best-run American companies; it was almost like "chicken soup," something that mom would recommend when you were sick. In the wake of the AIG, Enron, Qwest, Tyco, and WorldCom scandals, however, where the CEOs were involved in fraudulent practices, a new round of books have appeared which focus on the leadership style of executives. The focus on morality and ethics is part of the new advice, a return to the principles of Peter Drucker. For example, Daniel Yankelovich, a management consultant, leaves it up to each executive to promote enlightened self-interest. By taking into consideration all stakeholders— workers, customers, stockholders, etc.—the companies will make more money because workers will work harder, customers will be loyal, and stockholders will experience greater profits.[31] In Ben Cohen and Mal Warwick's *Values-Driven Business,* the authors (Ben Cohen is a founder of Ben and Jerry's ice cream) outline a "triple bottom line" to judge companies: its profit and how it treats people and the planet.[32] Similarly, Starbucks CEO Howard Schultz claims his company's success has more to do about corporate relationships with its employees and customers than selling coffee. In short, companies acting good will do good.

The latest round of books fail to consider that much more needs to be done to curb the self-interest of executives and managers before it translates into greed and curb greed before it leads to fraudulent practices. Hence, regulation, audits, and strict internal and external controls are needed to check and balance corporate behavior; otherwise, we have the rehash of the movie *Wall Street,* in which Michael Douglas's character made famous the phrase "greed is good" and business is depicted as promoting selfishness and criminal behaviors.

Criticism of Corporate Industrialism

From a liberal or radical perspective, the robber barons and great titans of industry were plunderers who made their money through "gentlemen's agreements" with crooked and corrupt politicians, and even judges who aided and abetted them, and who also relied on backdoor, fraudulent, and unscrupulous practices to make huge sums of money. Behind every great fortune of the period is a long list of crimes and corruption. Although not in the spirit of American capitalism nor the American dream, the behavior and character of the period strongly suggests that the great wealth of the Rockefellers, Vanderbilts, Carnegies, and Mellons, and other robber barons such as the Drews, Fisks, Goulds, Lodges, and Morgans, was based in part on economic exploitation, illegal monetary enterprises, and the looting of the public domain. Such an interpretation of corporate America is not only highly subjective, but it can also be vilified by conservatives as ludicrous and unpatriotic. Carried to the endpoint, they would claim, it could limit all future innovators and risk takers like Michael Dell, Bill Gates, and Steve Jobs. People born in America with talent and guts have the right to develop them to the fullest, and this is what fuels our economic engine and separates us from the rest of the world.

Certainly I'm not trying to curtail or counterbalance great man theories or great minds. The triumphs of American innovation rest on the freedom to think and develop new knowledge and concepts. Nevertheless, these robber barons were hustlers and opportunists, living their life as if they were in Dodge City or Tombstone, with guns drawn, shooting down workers, crushing their rivals, bribing government officials, and fleecing the public. On a miniature scale, today, what happened in New Orleans after Katrina was a repeat performance, with contractors from all over the country swooping down and vying for a piece of the action, paying off local and federal officials, grabbing huge contracts, and defrauding taxpayers out of an estimated \$1 billion, while most of the people in New Orleans were hurting. This is what the titans of industry did one hundred and twenty-five years ago, as they built America. The difference is that they made history and socially benefited the nation although they were more unethical and corrupt; in fact, the higher we go up the corporate chain, the greater the opportunity to take advantage of the system and the more intricate the potential web of intrigue, deceit, and corruption we usually find.

Michael Corleone, in *The Godfather*, understood human behavior and combined money and bribes, government and church corruption, and violence (just like some of the titans) to crush his competition and achieve his ends. The titans of industry also hired "hit men" to curtail labor and social unrest and to maintain their own economic well-being. Don't ever think they were innocent and made their money the old-fashioned, honest way, as purported by Ben Franklin quaint ditties and the Horatio Alger stories. There might not have been mutual funds, hedge funds, and tax shelters available—"tough guys" and "Wall Street Kings" with arrogance and a sales speech, engaged in creative accounting and fraudulent and criminal practices. But wake up! The golden age of stock indices and stock investments, along with hostile acquisitions, mergers, and monopolies, had its historical inspiration from the Gilded Age.

Despite the corrupting effects of materialism and greed, political and economic reform were slow to develop, so the robber barons, the pirates of industry and society, had to make few concessions. The reformers' stories went unheeded. Nevertheless, Henry Keenan, in *The Money Makers*, depicted the "blighting effects" of big money on legal, moral, and decent human values. Joaquin Miller, in *The Destruction of Gotham*, described the "tips" and "trickery" of corporate leaders and money makers on Wall Street. Frank Norris in *The Octopus and The Pit* told how small businesses were driven out of business by unscrupulous and fraudulent practices of big businesses. Upton Sinclair's *The Jungle* described the horrible working conditions and food-borne disease threats of the meatpacking industry. Many of the problems exist today and, were *The Jungle* written today, the name Jurgis Rudkins would have to be replaced by Jose Rodriguez. Very little else would need to be changed.

Henry Adams, in his autobiography, was to damn "caesarians in business" and did not hesitate to express his disdain of the "big financial class" and "new money class." Regardless of their millions, he felt their lives lacked refinement, culture, and class; moreover, they were driven by crass materialism, ruthlessness, and inhumanity. If he were alive today, he would be saddened by how little these populist authors and books have taught us. They represent only the tip of the iceberg; they describe a callous America, driven by materialism and greed, in which the almighty dollar triumphs over justice and the common good. The authors were critical of capitalism and cried out for social reforms and social justice.

Notwithstanding all the donations and support of colleges and universities, hospitals, museums, and libraries, the robber barons made their millions through unregulated markets and unrestrained competition, chicanery and back-door dealings with politicians, and human exploration. They were so Machiavellian in their schemes and calculations that the various robber barons would often outbribe, outfox, and outswindle each other, as they bought, consolidated, and "cornered" gold markets, bank notes, and stocks, as well as railroads, water rights, and energy and oil companies. Jay Gould was probably the most devious of the lot; he would short the stock of his own railroad company, thus devaluing it, and wiping out a host of poor saps. Then, he would buy back the stock at half-price or even lower and in a few days make a small fortune.[33]

Today, there are literally hundreds, possibly thousands, of Jay Gould types, engaged in stock swindles and manipulative trading, improper and bloated fees, illegal payments and favored treatment of large clients, backdating of stock options for top executives, hostile takeovers and hiding losses, and cooking books in order to run up stocks, sell them, and leave the ignorant public holding on to devalued stock. A small percentage of the Gould types today are caught and forced to settle lawsuits brought by investors and regulators. The regulators and auditors often wink, and the members of the public often shrug their shoulders not knowing what to do, even when they get ripped off and see their investments and pensions shrinking. Without strict government regulation, the "little guy"—John Doakes or John Q. Public—is always a potential victim and at the mercy of the "big guy." Just think of what happens to the small business person and average worker on Main Street when Wal-Mart (the number-one U.S. employer) moves into town.

A "Modest" Proposal

Given the traditional and optimistic faith in the American way, the notion of the American dream and the self-made man, it is hard to accept the idea that it is almost impossible to make huge fortunes without bending or breaking the law. It would be nice, sort of mythical and surreal, if all the remaining trust money of big business's descendents—the captains of industrial America and the barons of Wall Street—could be returned to the public today as reparations for the looting of the public domain, the destruction of the nation's natural resources, and the exploitative effects they had on the factory workers, tradesmen, and small farmers who built America and kept the system running. These are the working people, plain people, and common people that the Reverend Jonathan Harrison dubbed as the "lower strata" in his defense of "the more fortunate classes" and "the value of acquisition." It is the same people John Hay depicted in *The Breadwinners* as the "labor class," who he chastised as "violent" and "lawless."[34] These are the same people today who play by the rules and after ten or twenty years on the job get escorted out five minutes before the day ends—or, in other cases, before they know it with the click of a button, watch their jobs evaporate and outsourced to Beijing or Bangalore.

The problem is that the so-called lower strata and labor class—the multitude—are relatively docile; they believe in the American dream and the folk belief that the rainbow is reachable for anyone, that it is just around the corner, and with luck they can reach it. They foolishly accept the fact that the law is often twisted and bent by corporate America and the capitalist class (or those in power) in their pursuit of profits. Average Americans naively accept the view that each new boom cycle brings higher peaks and a bigger wealth gap within the system. They fail to take political and social measures to curtail public looting and to make things fairer for them, and to change the economic system which divides people into dominant and subordinate classes, relationships, and roles. They fail to appreciate that the political ideology controlling the seats of power in Washington, D.C., can make a difference in terms of reducing inequality and strengthening safety nets and social programs.

The reformers' philosophy is not necessarily Marxist, as some conservatives would have us believe; rather most of their lofty ideals and passion came out of the populist movement, straight from the heartland. They appraised the money class—the corporations, trusts, and titans of big business—"as sucking money out of the agrarian class [and consumer] since the end of the Civil War." It was evidenced by the liberal Republican platform of 1872, which sought to eliminate the "roguery and plunder, born of the multiplied temptations which the [post] war [era] furnished, and stealthily crept into the management of public affairs." The party proposed radical reform, to rid government of the "scalawags and thieves" and to "emancipate [the nation] from the rule of great corporations and monopolies."[35]

It was Walt Whitman, among the reformers, who in *Democratic Vistas* (1871), expressed deep concern over the prevailing materialism, consumption, and superficiality of the period. Appealing for a nobler race of men and women who would develop the full potentialities of democratic society, he poured out his scorn on the "corruption, bribery, falsehood . . . and scoundrelism . . . of respectable and nonrespectable" government officials and business leaders. "In business . . . the one sole object is, by any means, pecuniary gain." In the fable, "the magician's serpent ate up all the other serpents; and money-making is our magician's serpent, remaining today sole master of the field."

Although America has had great success in uplifting the common people and creating a solid middle class, the backbone of democracy, the question is: What has changed since 1872, in the last one hundred and thirty-five years? Money is still king, materialism today outweighs moral decency, and corporate corruption continues to bite the common people. The law of the jungle and the principles of history have been stuck at the same juncture: The small fish gets eaten up by the medium-sized fish, and the medium fish gets eaten by the big fish. The Gilded Age doesn't provide lessons for us in the here and now. It just highlights that with American capitalism—then and now—rogues, scalawags, and thieves may not always run the system but they milk and exploit it. Look around today. It's probably too strong to say the country was built by "rogues." But the same kind of people now manipulating Wall Street, running hedge funds, bribing politicians, cooking the books, and getting rich at the expense of the public did so yesterday (since the post–Civil War years); they are no better and maybe worse than the old robber barons as they have stolen more money and inflicted more damage on the public because globalization ensures greater income scales that are not spread evenly and more people own stock than in the past. To be sure, we are living in the midst of a new Gilded Age.

Of course, if you are an unyielding *conservative*, and your heroes are Alexander Hamilton and Ronald Reagan, then you would find fault with my *liberal* perspective of the turbulent Gilded Age and the rising scourge of titans. As for the thieves I have just picked apart, you would consider them good guys, not robbers or looters. You might even argue they made money the old-fashioned way, by brains and guts and not by exploiting workers and competitors; by innovating, building, and possessing an entrepreneurial spirit and not by bribing government officials, ripping off customers, and fleecing the public; by believing in God and giving back to the community and not by believing in the all-mighty buck and plundering communities. If this is where the reader stands on the cultural divide, then we are so far apart on substantive matters that one of us might view the other as the "mad hatter" or some "rat-tat" person puffed up with hot air. I know: Either me or my critics need to post a white flag and surrender to the voice of reason. In a post-Enron era, I believe that my eyes and ears are open to the rhythm of life and what I say is more on the mark than off the mark, despite the temptation of my critics to demonize my slant and style. But here I'm not trying to convert conservatives or free marketers; rather, I'm appealing to the people in the middle who vote and determine the fate of the nation and hopefully reflect on the widening wealth gap.

U.S.A. TODAY

The United States is a country where teenagers have credit cards and spend $150 on sneakers, where well-heeled men spend $25 on a Cuban cigar and women spend $1,000 on a Gucci handbag, and still others spend $10,000 on a Piaget watch. This is the nation where the superrich can spend more money on one meal in an upscale restaurant than what hundreds of millions of third-world laborers earn for the year. Such people in third-world countries work hard and have no time for polemics or protests, but they can be easily led by a person or movement that promises a better future—or that promises to bring down the "big bully" on the block. Despite America's idealism and sense of self, "as the home of the brave and home of the free," we need to look inward and see how much of the world perceives us. As in life, there is always another explanation for analyzing events.

Some of you who are more optimistic about American history might say the anger of the world directed toward us, especially the Muslim world, is linked to their own countries' inability to develop economies that prepare its people for the modern world; they are venting their own frustration and misery and religious beliefs on the Western world. But America's story has its own biblical (or crusading) mission, starting with the Pilgrims who landed on Plymouth Rock right up to Bush's "Pax Americana" strategy for bringing democratic capitalism to the Middle East and for appeasing the Christian Right and saving souls. I do not wish to get into the meaning of the American saga as it relates to Christianity, but God did not give us any mission to expand beyond the oceans. We need to understand the dangers of believing that God (or any *-ism*) guides our hand, or that the empty pockets of people at home or abroad have something to do with the clash of intelligence or the clash of civilizations, or even God's will. Geographical isolation and natural resources, historical accident and luck, and personal interpretations and political agendas are prime factors to consider in what has happened to America and the rest of the global village.

Bundles of Money

Granted there are different gauges of inequality and diverse sources of expert opinion to determine inequality. But how much inequality is permissible in a country that boasts it is guided by democratic and moral principles? Should the highest 1 percent own 35 percent of all the nation's wealth while the bottom 50 percent own 2 percent? Should the same top 1 percent receive 57 percent of the growth in income from 1990 to 2004 while the bottom 90 percent receive 2 percent?[36] Like it or not, this is how the social/economic pyramid is shaped in this country. On an individual basis, should someone such as Sylvester Stallone or Tom Cruise earn $15 to $20 million a movie or should someone who hits a golf ball three hundred yards down a fairway or hits a baseball four hundred feet in the stands on a regular basis earn $25 to $50 million a year (with advertising and endorsements), while 35 to 50 million Americans live in squalor (depending on how we measure or define poverty) and another 225 million or more just get by in what I call the "struggling class."?[37] Ayn Rand, Milton Friedman, and Dinesh D'Souza would welcome such a world, based on the doctrines of capitalism and individual achievement, and without apologies. That's a hard pill to swallow, if we consider morality, fairness, and what's good for society.

Should a CEO or boss earn two or three hundred times more than his or her workers? And what about workers in China, India, or Indonesia? Should Eddie Bauer's CEO, Nike's CEO, or Polo's CEO, who employ third-world workers, earn five thousand times more? Should Master Card's Robert Selander have received 287,341 shares of stock for free on the day the company went public, worth $13 million two weeks later, while each of the company's 4,400 employees received one hundred shares, worth $4,700 for each employee. Is one person's value to a company worth 2,766 times more than the average worker in the same company? These monetary conditions lead to immense disparities and are symptomatic of the problem of inequality facing the nation.

The Rich Get Richer

In 2005 executive pay increased 27 percent from the prior year, $11.3 million, based on a survey of two hundred selected companies within the Fortune 500. That may be a pittance to Bill Gates or Warren Buffett, but the average worker earned $43,506 in 2005, an increase of 2.9 percent from the previous year.[38] The same year twelve CEOs earned over $100 million.

William McQuire of United Health topped the list and earned $1.6 billion, largely due to stock options he cashed.[39] These kinds of disparities create a new group of "haves" and "have nots" within the same companies. Moreover, the runaway salaries of executives have little to do with performance, and the people minding the store (corporate boards) don't seem to care. (See chapter 5.)

Then there is Kevin Phillip's new book, *Wealth and Democracy*. He describes the dramatic increases in salaries and bonuses among the top ten CEOs in the United States. These captains of industry were paid an average of $3.5 million in 1981 and $154 million in 2000, including stock options, bonuses, and other benefits—an increase of 4,300 percent in twenty years, compared to wages, which slightly more than doubled. Eric Dash of the *New York Times* is a little more conservative. He reports the average CEO compensation in the past twenty-five years has only increased 600 percent, but he adjusts for inflation.[40] Either way we are talking about fat paychecks for gilded executives, not to mention the fact that no one seems able or willing to stop these huge compensation packages. Updating Phillip's and Dash's figures, and at the risk of repelling readers, Michael Eisner of Disney earned $577 million in 1997, largely from stock options, Steve Jobs of Apple took home $775 million in 2000, and Lee Raymond of ExxonMobil received more than $400 million in 2006 after receiving $140 million the previous year. (See also chapter 5.) These figures do not include future stock options and pensions, which in Raymond's case totaled $98.5 million, estimated to be $144,500 a day.[41]

What to make of these astonishing trends? At what point is too much more than enough? At what juncture is the pay divide between the new "haves" and "have nots" considered too wide, perhaps dangerous? There is no rational reasoning for such CEO compensation, and the silence is deafening. Some economists, along with people who are true believers in the American system, claim that these executives (along with movie stars, pop singers, and athletes) operate in a free-market system and their compensation reflects the demand for their services or their celebrity, plain and simple. But with so many people owning stocks and mutual funds (nearly 150 million people), and so many people paying $250 to $500 to sit in a box seat at a basketball game or rock concert (for Madonna it could cost up to $3,500), the free market is not as free as some think it is. Someone, some group, needs to say enough is enough. Simply what needs to be done is to get rid of the hard-line free-marketers and conservatives and elect politicians who respect the common people and can prevent such a concentration of wealth by revising tax codes, limiting the amount of inheritance, eliminating off-shore tax loopholes, and prosecuting CEOs who bend the law and accountants who lie and cheat for their clients.[42]

Now consider the Bush tax cuts on dividends and capital gains. Should Americans, whose annual incomes of $1 million or more, comprising one-tenth of 1 percent of all taxpayers, receive 43 percent of all the savings on investment taxes, as they did in 2003?[43] The top 2 percent of taxpayers, those earning more than $200,000, received more than 70 percent of the tax savings from this new tax law on investment income. Analyzed in slightly different terms, taxpayers who made between $1 million and $10 million received $59,200 in tax savings and those that earned more than $10 million received $522,000 in tax savings. At the other end of the income divide, those earning less than $50,000 (70 percent of all taxpayers) saved an average of $10 more than the previous year, a total of $435 in total tax cuts; those earning between $50,000 and $100,000 (20 percent) saved $1,588 in total tax cuts.[44] In short, for the 90 percent of all taxpayers who made less than $100,000, only 14 percent benefited in dividend tax reductions and 5 percent benefited from capital gains reductions. I guess it's a wonderful world if you are rich and can convince the politicians that your investments will create new jobs and grow the economy, or that government intervention is to blame for stagflation, recession, or any economic woe.

The irony is that supporters of the tax cuts for the rich argue in perverse logic that the savings did not go far enough because the more money the wealthy class has to invest the more jobs will be produced. Stephen Entin, president of a Washington-based institute on taxation, asserts that the tax rate on investment income should be zero.[45] Now anyone concerned with how the United States is to pay for a war, fund Social Security or Medicare, and/or reduce deficits would conclude that the tax cuts for the superrich are outrageous—and in the long run may have negative effects on the economy. Furthermore, the Congressional Research Service, a branch of Congress that examines social and economic issues, concludes that much of the reduced taxes on investment income is funneled outside the United States,[46] creating jobs for non-Americans while making the few wealthier even wealthier.

Lessons to Learn

The acquisition of wealth, since the age of Rockefeller, Morgan, and Vanderbilt, has always been the chief index of American civilization. In fact, it goes back to Christian duty to accept the worldly lot of the poor. According to Rev. Joseph Morgan, in 1732, the poor are meant to be poor; and there is no reason to complain. Likewise, "the accumulation of wealth is a public good."[47] It has been common to emphasize how capitalistic titans made immense fortunes through shrewdness, strength, and exploitation of others. In religious terms, "God in his wisdom and mercy turns our Wickedness to public Benefits."[48] True believers and conservative pundits today would rather not mention that bribes, scandals, fraud, and land stealing have always been part of big business since the post–Civil

War period and Gilded Age.[49] Why should it be different now, with an army of well-paid, Ivy League–educated lawyers and accountants to protect CEOs from the arm of the law, from the public, and from their employees?

For any economist to argue that these new robber barons are worth what they get paid, because of their achievement or because they keep the engines of capitalism running, is outrageous. Just consider the greed, scams, market riggings, and fraudulent practices used by today's CEOs to hoodwink the public into thinking their companies are productive, long enough for these executives to cash in their stock options while their employees are encouraged to buy more stock and members of the public are robbed of their pensions.[50] To say that such lopsided compensation doesn't matter because there is huge mobility among the working class ignores the growing concentration of wealth among the descendents of the superrich, much more than the robber barons of the Golden Age ever dreamed of or passed on to their children and great-grandchildren. One reason is that the superrich hire lawyers and accountants to evade personal income tax and hereditary taxes, achieved mainly through special deductions and trusts.

So what does all this mean to the average person who believes in the American way—American capitalism, social mobility, and equal opportunity? Democracy is faltering, and they don't recognize it. We either reaffirm our traditional beliefs in democracy, with economic checks and balances to prevent the rise of a nobility class, or watch its slow demise in front of our eyes. *Demise* may be too apocalyptic. If so, then call it something else—*plutocracy, nobility, the superrich*, or some other name. As a nation, we either reduce the concentration of wealth or our children and grandchildren will be faced with greater inequality and struggle the rest of their lives. A couple of "pep talks" by the president of the United States or a ten-step recipe book by some mutual fund manager or Wall Street broker at Borders or Barnes and Noble or on television on how to become the next millionaire is not the answer. The answer lies with stiff ethics and laws to guide our schools, churches, and workplace. If we continue to remain silent on cheating and corrupt practices in the these crucial institutions, then a few think-tank experts at Brookings Institution or Rand Corporation soon may very likely be reporting the next book about America: *Upside Down Democracy, Plutocracy and Policy*, or *The New Law of the Jungle*.

On another level, we all seem to be caught up in a social disease afflicting most of us who live in what Harvard professor David Riesman, in the *Lonely Crowd*, called the "other-directed" society (see chapter 5), what Alain de Botton, the British author, a half-century later calls "status anxiety," or what I will simply call "keeping up with the Joneses." You can now forgive yourself if you wish to brag about your South Hampton or

Cape Cod beach house, your son's Harvard degree, or your daughters 3.5-carat engagement ring. Most of us are all caught up in conspicuous consumption, materialism, and ambition, and the more we rise up the status pole the more we want to talk about our successes and receive our neighbor's esteem. De Botton analyzes Western history and makes the case that first Christianity, and later Marxism, elevated the moral status of the poor and working class to compensate for their low social rank, while the rich pursued their pleasures under the umbrella of avarice and corruption. But since the Gilded Age, and into the twentieth century, money began to look like a barometer of achievement and character. The rich were not only wealthier, but plain better; they were considered smarter and stronger. Lower status came to be seen as not only regrettable, but also the result of a lack of brain power or laziness. Given the status syndrome that exists, this is a hard pill for some of us to swallow.

Religion, today, is status anxiety's most important antidote. There is nothing like good, old-fashioned religion to expose the vanity of worldly pursuits and materialistic endeavors and to restore a sense of humility and sense of purpose to our lives. Particularly helpful is the new emphasis on morality and faith of Evangelist preachers; in fact, the new faith-based and born-again religious fervor serves as a means to comfort the masses who are struggling economically and live either a "low-brow" or "middle-brow" existence. You don't need a summer house or prestigious college degree to find God. In the end, religious faith serves as the great equalizer—dust to dust—and poor people have the same or better chance, we are taught, to rise to heaven. To be sure, status today is a complex phenomenon, based primarily on class and how we live. Once we introduce religion into the mix, anything goes. But money is not supposed to matter at least according to most evangelist preachers. Faith counts more than a person's social or economic hierarchy—great therapy for the masses who are struggling to pay their bills and one reason why religious fervor is spreading in the midst of abundance.

For the last two thousand years, since Matthew and John preached the Gospel, in the battle for the minds of people—good versus evil, redemption versus Satanism—we have been told the faithful will be rewarded and enter everlasting paradise and the unfaithful will suffer eternal damnation. The Bible tells you so, the church tells you so, the priests say so, and so does Billy Graham (who has retired) and now Franklin Graham (his son), as well as evangelists Jerry Falwell and Pat Robertson. And so, the common people struggle day to day, and shrug off their existence, without revolution or anarchy, waiting for the Promised Land.

Oops, a Different Historical Perspective

The interpretation of American history has changed over centuries. Originally analyzed by American historians and friendly visitors like Alex de Tocqueville as the cradle of democracy, America was rooted in the Founding Father's belief in the God-given or nature-given rights of freedom and liberty. But Edward Gibbon, the English historian (see chapter 1), who knew something about the sword and pistol and the ups and downs of history, dubbed the revolutionists "a race of convicts," who deserved nothing less than hanging. To understand history through the eyes of the other side, in this case the British, helps to remind us that the past (and present) can be viewed from multiple perspectives. To be sure, an American triumph was not inevitable, despite what our history books in the fourth or fifth grade say, and had the French failed to reinforce Washington's makeshift, ragtag army, or had the British generals been a little more bolder and braver, the outcome would have been profoundly different, and the likes of George Washington, Thomas Jefferson, and Alexander Hamilton would have been probably hanged as traitors, rebels, or just plain losers. Ah, we must be the lucky ones, or perhaps God chose us as his chosen people.

On another level, justice does not necessarily reside with those who are morally or politically right, or believe they have God or righteous ideology on their side; rather it usually lies with the winners of war. You can be sure that Washington, Jefferson, and Hamilton would not be considered American heroes or Founding Fathers had the winds of war gone the other way. And, most likely, at least according to one historian, "we would all be Canadians,"[51] with more progressive taxes, some sort of socialized medicine, lower college tuition, and have a greater fondness for ice hockey and snow boarding.

If we place American history into a global perspective, say from 1776 to 2006, we should better understand the changes in the analysis and interpretation of our relations to the rest of the world. There is a bootleg side to our history that we tend to gloss over: our treatment of Africans and our belief in holding them in bondage; our treatment of Native Indians and Mexicans as we moved westward and plundered the people and countryside; and our treatment of Latin Americans and Caribbean people as we imposed the "Big Stick Policy." Coinciding with the theme of the world's greatest nation, we tend to emphasize the noble side of America: welcoming immigrants, fighting to preserve democracy during World War I, fighting against fascism and Nazism during World War II, and then containing Soviet and Chinese communism.

Alongside these crusading and democratic ideals, we have been told by well-respected American historians that the United States has embodied the principles of individual achievement or meritocracy, equality, and capitalism—in sum what liberal historians such as Richard Hofstadter called the "central faith of America" and Arthur Schlesinger Jr. termed the "vital center,"[52] or what some others might call the "whiggish middle." What we really need is another "class traitor," like Franklin Roosevelt, who favors the workers and contains the rich, perhaps has them lose ground as they did in the Roosevelt years.

Disappearing Dollars

Deficit spending cannot go on indefinitely. Our economy is slowly collapsing. The United States borrows $2.1 billion everyday to keep the economy afloat, and the average American household is carrying some $9,000 in credit card debt.[53] We had a $318 billion budget deficit in 2005 (or more than one hundred countries combined); moreover, two-thirds of this deficit is owed to foreign countries, particularly due to our trade deficit, which is now $800 billion a year.[54] Our future prosperity is being mortgaged away in order to pay off our growing trade deficit and national debt, the latter of which has increased more than $2 trillion since 2001.[55]

In fact, since 2001, 73 percent of new government borrowing comes from foreign countries; and 43 percent ($4.8 trillion) of the U.S. national debt comes from abroad. In effect, the United States has been borrowing huge sums of money from other countries so that American consumers can buy the goods these countries make. All told, Japan, China, and Britain alone now hold $1.18 trillion in U.S. treasuries.[56] As we all know, good things eventually come to an end. The time will come when foreign investors will stop buying American treasury notes to lend back to the United States. The dollar will sink and inflation will soar. In the end, the value of a dollar will determine how well Americans live, what they can produce, and what kind of foreign policy they can implement.

Historically, for Milton Friedman, one of the best-known conservative economists, and now Steve Forbes, a less-known conservative economist, there is nothing wrong with huge trade deficits. In fact, the argument is made that the United States has had a trade deficit for more than 80 percent of its existence, and it was deficit borrowing that provided the funds to build our railroads, canals, and other industrial infrastructure. If Friedman and Forbes had a choice between a $1 trillion deficit and a balanced budget, they would opt for the red ink.[57] All that sounds cute and cozy, especially if you believe in the rationality of an unregulated free-market system, that U.S. productivity and technology will continue to create U.S. jobs, and that risk takers, entrepreneurs, and Wall Street investors will do what is best for America and contribute to the public good. If this is the case, as conservative thinkers believe, then there is that much less to worry about. We might even relax and paint pastoral landscapes and people in parks, as the French impressionists did at the turn of the twentieth century.

The trouble is that our own overseas borrowing does not leave us stronger but weaker, and reflects our inability to compete globally, our continuous consumption of cheap foreign goods and dependency on imported oil, and our inability to save money; in fact, Americans tend to convert their home equity into spending money, which in turn creates a false belief that the economy is growing. Even worse, our overseas borrowing is not fostering an economic boom as it did in the past. Considering the size of our economy, Paul Krugman believes that our investment is low by historical benchmarks and we are not only using borrowed money to consume goods and import oil, but also to finance our federal deficits. Americans are now spending more than they are earning. In the end, the house that is built on a shaky foundation will collapse, as two of the three piggies found out.

The average American fails to grasp that American wealth is being redistributed to other countries because of our military overreach, trade policies, and job outsourcing. In addition, we have lost our manufacturing might to the Asian rim countries. What keeps our economic engine running now is our intellectual property—information, technological, and electronic knowledge—and this is slowly being transferred to China and India. This new problem is illustrated by the fact that large U.S. companies in high-tech and knowledge-based industries, the backbone of our human capital, are hiring people from and moving plants to these countries. (See chapter 5.) It is further evidenced by the harsh trend that 90 percent of the world's scientists and engineers will reside in Asia by 2010.[58]

The gravity of the situation, the downward spiral, becomes increasingly evident as consumer prices spike more rapidly than earnings, also manifested in the lives of Americans every day with the loss of jobs overseas, lower wages at home, evaporation of unions, underemployment among college graduates, economic insecurity among older workers, the collapse or reconstructing of major corporations and subsequent loss of health benefits and pensions for employees, and vulnerability to Chinese and Indian entrepreneurs. It is reflected by the creeping and cruel trend of Americans having to work longer hours and holding down two or three jobs to make ends meet. It is also illustrated by middle-class families, with two working spouses, saving less and owing more than a single-income and middle-class family of thirty years ago. The economic situation is serious enough for some economists to argue that America is going broke, highlighted with the publication of recent books such as Kollikoff and Burns's *The Coming Generational Storm* (2004) and Peter Peterson's *Running on Empty* (2004). Basically, their theme is that the next generation is being sold out by the present generation, with its failing military, trade, and financial policies.

Paul Krugman, the Princeton economist, adds a twist to the situation. Class warfare is at an all-time high because of tax policies that favor the rich. He maintains that "working-class families aren't sharing in the economy's growth, and face economic insecurity."[59] There is reason to believe the middle class is disappearing, not only because of tax policies favoring the rich, but also due to the slow erosion of their safety net—health insurance, pensions, and moderate college tuition. As for average Americans, bankruptcy rates have doubled since 2000, especially among the poor and working class, largely due to medical costs and job loss. The real estate boom has protected middle-class homeowners who are taking on more home-equity debt to pay their bills and stay out of bankruptcy. In the meantime, the "credit clock" is ticking for millions of middle-class people relying on paper profits from their homes to keep them afloat.

But the federal government, under the Bush administration, implemented a much tougher, procreditor bankruptcy law that went into effect in 2005 to teach people a lesson. It's a law that makes it harder to go bankrupt and puts your home at risk or only protects portions of your home equity (i.e., $37,000 in New Jersey and $100,000 in New York).[60] Alan Greenspan, the former Federal Reserve chair, refers to the situation as a busted "piggy bank." It's more like the Titanic: people hanging on, but for how long? The new bankruptcy law puts the middle class on notice: Live the American dream, if you can, but if things don't work out, then your lifestyle tanks and your home is at stake.

Some Oldies and Goodies

To repeat an old cliché that goes back to Homer and the ancient Greeks: "change is inevitable." Possibly, we have seen our best days, post–World War II, when we were on top of the world and Europe and Asia were in shambles. There was no nation that could rival us on the moral, military, or economic playing field.

Given the wisdom of the old Greek philosophers, I'm not too sure if it's worth repeating Bob Dylan or Peter, Paul, and Mary, some business gurus like management consultant Peter Drucker or former CEO of G.E. Jack Welch, but the winds of change are blowing right into our faces as we plummet into debt and decline. It's a little lonely when you are on top of the heap, but it is worse when friends and allies abandon us. As Johnny Cash once said, Sunday morning coming down can be awfully lonely, like a disappearing dream—in this case, the American dream. I think more Americans will be living on the wrong side of town, despite the fact that conservative pundits claim we are doing mighty fine on all economic fronts.

Americans are going to have to get used to the fact that extended wars can deplete our economy. (The war in Iraq cost $100 billion in 2005, or about $450 billion since its inception, and has crippled social and health benefits that otherwise could be funded.) There is an abiding belief, at least by the Reagan and Bush administrations, that we will always be rich and productive and always be able to exercise our military power. Both assumptions can be questioned, given dramatic changes in world opinion about our foreign policies and intentions, the splintering of our allies, which puts the military and economic burden on us, and a host of new enemies throughout the world that are jealous of our prosperity and hostile toward our democratic values. Extended warfare is a very risky option, built on the arrogant assumption that we will always be all-powerful and productive. It fails to consider that American corporations are having trouble competing globally and can no longer afford to pay high wages and good benefits to the American workforce. Nor does it consider that military production enhances the wealth of a limited number of companies and people involved in wartime products and does not lead to many other jobs as peacetime products and services do. (Peacetime jobs have the ripple effect of leading to approximately four times more jobs.)

Interjecting a little popular music or some big-business pundits may seem a little silly or surreal, but there is need to lighten the straightforward prose and drive some readers a little wild with some playful prose, regardless of whether they are inclined to vote red or blue, whether they believe in heaven and hell or just middle earth, or whether they are flag-waving, patriotic Yankee men or some highway men or rebels, with beads and a beard searching for peace and rejecting war. Just open up your eyes, regardless of who you are—whether you are young and spirited or old and ugly, part of the crowd or look like a fish out of the water—and see that yesterday is gone. The good old days are fading, like the sun going down. No amount of special pleading or political slogans from the Right or Left can set us free from history, no matter how responsive or unresponsive to it we may be. History has a way of disposing of empires, as the Greeks and Romans and our European allies know firsthand. The decline admits of no innocents and spares no one. Fools go first, despite their convictions or religious beliefs. And that's the way it is—that's the way history has been written for the last twenty-five hundred years or more.

Hopefully, somewhere over the hill, there is a new horizon, a fresh morning dew. If you believe in the miracle of America, then we will prevail and someone like Washington, Jefferson, and Hamilton will step forth and unify the nation (like Washington), instill yeoman confidence and public philosophy (like Jefferson), and restore economic health and vitality (like Hamilton). For this to happen, you need to be a true believer. Or, as Winston Churchill once said when he visited our shores after Pearl Harbor: "We have not journeyed all the way across the oceans, across the mountains, across the prairies, because we are made of sugar candy."

What a neat idea, if I may say so myself: Having George, Tom, and Alex come back from the hinterland to rescue us. I bet you really like the idea. How weird, me too! Listen here, the "All-American Trio" will not come back. They're history! No matter how trite it seems, the power rests with the people. Given the issues at stake, the American people need to take a stand. They need to go to the ballot box and elect leaders who have a reasonable and just plan for the future. The assumption is that 51 percent of the voters are smart enough to be influenced by their pocketbooks, or at least common sense would suggest so. We don't need scholars, whiz kids, or cowboys, as presidents, nor do we need graying middle-aged men flying in jets, dressed in fatigues, landing on battleships for a cameo appearance, and then reading from a script. We need plain politicians who speak the plain truth and who represent the interests of plain folks— the same people who teach our youth, protect our streets, build our bridges, fight our wars, and pay their fair share of taxes.

ECONOMIC BUST WITHIN
AN ECONOMIC BOOM

Paychecks that rose with America's productivity gains in the post–Sputnik and Cold War period, no longer keep up with economic growth or inflation. Economic productivity since the early 1970s has had little impact on the poor and working class who, with their dependents, add up to about 125 to 150 million Americans. In fact, one of the major characteristics of the booming economy in the last forty years has been the increase in working and low-skill employment sectors. More low-skill employment exists in today's "New Economy" than in the past four decades. Between 1965 and 1998, for example, employment in the retail and service sectors, the two lowest-paying sectors, has increased from 30 to 48 percent.[61]

These employment trends may provide more economic participation, especially among recent immigrants who are willing to work for less than American citizens, but they have not reduced poverty. Actually, poverty among full-time workers has climbed upward from 2.2 million in 1973 to 2.8 million in 1998; including dependents, the number adds up to 5 million Americans.[62] More recently, Henry Paulson, the Treasury Secretary under the Bush administration, bragged that 5.2 million jobs were added to the economy between 2003 and 2005,[63] but he failed to tell us that about two-thirds paid less than $35,000 per year and carried no pension or health benefits. Even worse, the Wal-Mart model has kept down wages, hiring more part-timers without benefits. It's one thing for knowledgeable people to distort statistics and mislead the public by holding back information, but it is much worse when we consider that most young workers are now on their own when it comes to basic social and health programs. Moreover, employees know that, with conservatives in power, the people who are supposed to protect labor are on the side of big business, not the working people. In addition, the tax burden on the blue-collar and white-collar worker has increased dramatically during the last two decades in terms of Social Security payroll tax, state income tax, and sales tax—leaving them with less disposable income.[64] The costs of housing, health, transportation, and college tuition have risen much more rapidly than the income of the working and middle class.

If we analyze more recent data, from 1999 to 2004, income (after inflation) for the bottom 80 percent slightly declined, for the next 15 percent it was flat, and it rose for the top 5 percent. In fact, between 2001 and 2004, average wages fell 3.6 percent after inflation, while the economy was growing and home values were soaring. In 2005, the inflation–wage increase ratio was roughly even, and in 2006 wages inched 1.9 percent higher due to low unemployment and low inflation. In other words, the wealthier got wealthier and the lower rungs got poorer, directly weakening America's working and middle class. In addition, the ranks of the poor reached an all-time high in 2004, amounting to 37 million Americans,[65] and we know or should know that the government definition of poverty ($19,200 for a family of four) is politically suspect and economically substandard. Income inequality is a social and economic reality, and is aggravated by the fact that, between 1997 and 2004, the minimum federal wage was frozen at $5.15 per hour and about 25 percent of the American workforce earned less than $7.50 per hour.[66] Income gaps are aggravated not only by major tax cuts for the top 2 percent and premium increases for Medicare (up 13 percent from 2005 to 2006),[67] but also by the recent reduction in federal student loans to help pay for the war in Iraq and cuts in Medicaid and food stamps because the states are financially in crisis.

To add to the mix, there is an ongoing ideological clash as to how to assist the poor and working Americans. Conservatives argue that a growing economy is in the interest of all Americans, regardless of their incomes, and is fostered by reducing taxes for the rich, which in turn stimulates capital investments and job expansion. Liberals respond that, when President Clinton raised taxes in 1993 on prosperous families, the economy boomed, monetary surpluses were at an all-time high, and unemployment and poverty was at an all-time low. When Bush came to office and lowered taxes for the "rich and famous" in 2001 and subsequent years (three cuts in five years), the poverty rates increased most of these years and government deficits replaced surpluses.

Conservatives are quick to point to the wars in Afghanistan and Iraq as the reason for the deficits, while liberals argue that the deficits are also tied to the tax reductions for the wealthiest Americans, amounting to about a half-trillion dollars over five years.[68] (This money could have been used to buy a lot of guns.) It seems like the warring camps cannot agree over simple steps to tighten the budget and spur economic growth in which all of us share, but the logic of shared sacrifices (and shared gains) requires that tax cuts for the rich be allowed to lapse. In fact, I would take it one step further and raise taxes to the pre–Kennedy administration level, bringing it up to 70 percent for those whose annual incomes exceed one million dollars and also tax wealth (profits, dividends, interest, etc.) at much higher rates in order to reduce inequality. Although there is a bill in Congress to raise the minimum wage to $7.25 by 2009, it is tied to a huge reduction in the estate tax and other tax breaks for the rich. In a nutshell, the working person is destined to receive a few crumbs, while the rich and superrich receive the bulk of the pie, millions in reduced taxes. Hopefully a more liberal Congress will modify this legislation and save the tax breaks for small businesses and the average American.

Feed the Workers More Pork

The gross national product (GNP) per person grew some 75 percent from 1973 to 2004, but adjusted for inflation the median hourly wage of male workers rose a farcical two cents from $15.24 to $15.26.[69] Family incomes are up over the last thirty-plus years, no question, and the bottom 80 percent of the American workforce is able to purchase more goods and services, though only because wives have entered the workforce in record numbers and everyone (male and female, young and old) is working longer hours. Americans are working harder and getting nowhere faster. The fact is there are now as many or more job losses, due to downsizing, outsourcing, and corporate mergers and bankruptcies, than there were in the 1970s or 1980s. (Politicians like Treasury Secretary Paulson only talk about gains, not losses.) With job loss, there is usually the subsequent loss of health insurance and pensions,[70] followed by credit card debt and the lowering of standard of living. Were it not for government health insurance at the local, state, and federal levels, as well as Medicaid, the ranks of the uninsured—45.8 million as of 2005[71]—would be close to 100 million.

Medicaid, which provides health insurance for more than 50 million low-income people, is no bargain; in fact, it is financially sick. The states, which provide most of the money, are forced to fund their own budgets and reduce Medicaid spending. It's a matter of limiting benefits for each recipient and deciding which benefit to cut and which people get what. In simple mathematical terms, Medicaid costs increased an average of 13 percent annually between 1999 and 2005, but states' revenues on average grew 6 percent each of those years.[72] The poorer states in the South have cut back as much as 33 percent of their benefits and duration and scope of services.

With regard to health and jobs, most Americans are peddling backwards, and with job loss there is growing insecurity among all workers, effecting not only blue-collar workers but also those who Google at computers, employ headhunters, and read the latest business jargon in *Business Week* and *Money* magazine. All the faceless, remote middle managers and professionals—the people who believe in the system and earned the appropriate educational credentials—are not necessarily being rewarded. A growing number of the unemployed and underemployed are white-collar workers who have been downsized and/or outsourced, according to Barbara Ehrenreich, the Ph.D. journalist and modern critic of capitalism.[73] These people played it by the rules, and received a good college education, with the intention of getting a "piece of the rock" and all types of great job offers, only to find the system is flawed and they now feel vaguely swindled.

The proven formula, get a good education and then get a good job, has fallen flat. It's hard for educators to accept the flattening of the formula, as they are in the business of teaching and learning, but, if you ask the average middle-class working person in transition from a job and now networking, attending job fairs, and scrambling for job interviews, you might get a different view about the benefits of schooling. It's as if we were trying to do away with the middle class. Even Ivy League graduates who are accustomed to the fast track in their career advancements are under the gun, given the new business models that entail cost cutting, job displacement, and corporate movement of high-paying jobs to other countries—commonly referred to as "globalization."

Job insecurity and job displacement, according to Robert Reich, are undermining free trade agreements that promote global stability. Not only has support for free trade declined since the mid-1990s,[74] but job loss is also impacted by our manufacturing decline. Between 1993 and 2005, the United States lost 15 percent of its manufacturing jobs to Asian countries and Mexico. Since 1979, when manufacturing employment peaked, it has declined 25 percent.[75] Technology is also taking its toll. Every time Wal-Mart or Citibank replaces a person with a machine, they're eliminating hundreds of thousands of jobs, both blue and white collar. Of course, it is one thing for a machine to replace Joe Doakes or Jane Doakes, but it becomes emotional when you consider some college kid from India replacing them for one-fourth the cost. We can't stop technology or globalization. These are mega trends, like them or not! Moreover, if you push China or India too far, they will go elsewhere and strike deals. The people who are going to win are the people who say, "This is a fact of life; let's figure out how to adjust or take advantage of these trends." In the meantime, a lot of American blue-collar and white-collar jobs are going to the wayside, which is bound to affect our future economy and standard of living.

To offset job loss and to help create new jobs, government pork has dramatically increased. Pork programs, or "special projects" for local and state jobs with huge price tags, have increased from 4,126 (costing $23 billion) in 1995 to 13,012 (costing $67 billion) in 2005.[76] Ironically, the Republicans who profess to wanting to cut entitlement programs voted to create a whole new one. In 1987, Reagan vetoed a bill because it contained 172 earmarks. In 2005, Bush signed one with more than six thousand earmarks.[77] Most of these programs are characterized by waste, bribes, and bloated budgets, and they amount to tens of billions of dollars flushed down the toilet each year. They soak up and divert money that could be used for real productive jobs, leading to real profits and lower costs for American goods and services. In real dollars, it is estimated that $2 trillion could be saved over the next five years, $232 billion alone in fiscal 2006, if the wasteful duplicative pork programs were cut from the federal budget.[78] Instead, these pork programs lead to economic dead weight, government dependency, fiscal imbalances, and higher taxes—and cause reduced spending on needed health, education, and human services. The programs undermine real economic growth and signal to some extent the decline of stable job growth and wage increases for moderate-income workers that characterized the mid-twentieth century.

It's great for lawmakers to campaign and tell the folks back home how they are pursuing and bringing home new jobs. Pork is the money that goes to someone else's state. It's great to twist the truth. (Mr. Paulson claims the gross domestic product has steadily increased since 2001, and is expected to grow 2 to 3 percent in 2007.[79] But he fails to point out that the only people who benefited by the growth were the top 5 percent of the income and earnings ladder.) Big picture statistics are useful for economists and politicians who wish to bend the truth the way they want, but it doesn't help pay the mortgage or junior's college tuition bill.

Retiring and Rethinking College Saving Plans

The best illustration of just how bad things have become for the majority of Americans is that financial advisors with fancy degrees and three-piece suits are now giving what may sound like crazy advice. Don't save for your children's college education; instead make sure you put away enough money for your own retirement so you can ride around in style during your golden years. The reason is simple. Social Security benefits are forecasted to taper off (deferred payments and/or reduced annual payments) because funds are being exhausted. Private pensions are being slashed as cost-saving devices, and, in other cases, due to bankruptcies, pensions are being defaulted or dramatically reduced. The new guide for planning your future retirement is reflected in Fred Brock's best-seller, *Retire on Less Than You Think*, that is, how to live almost as well on less.[80]

Between 1920 and 1995, the number of companies that eliminated pension plans in conjunction with bankruptcies, which pensions the federal government's Pension Benefit Guaranty Corporation became responsible for (and paid out reduced benefits), averaged eight per year. For the years between 1996 and 2004, the number of defaulted pension plans covered by the feds soared and averaged forty-five per year.[81] In addition, present retiree health benefits and pension plans are sending major reverberations through troubled industries such as the auto, retail, and airline industries. Paring down or getting rid of a pension or health plan for a retiree or a current employee is a great way for a business to save or make money, or to stay afloat and avoid bankruptcy. In the meantime, the conservative and corporate world is dominated by the view that what's good for the rich is good for America. There is no sympathy for complaints about *oversized* executive compensation and pensions while employees are forced to *downsize* their retirement and health-care plans.

Now the bad news about college costs. The tuition at four-year state colleges has increased approximately 8 percent per year in the last five years, from 2000–2001 to 2005–2006. At private four-year colleges, the tuition rose about 6 percent per year during the same period. In 2005–2006, tuition alone averaged $5,490, and tuition, books, and room and board averaged $15,556, at a four-year state college for an in-state resident and $23,239 for an out-of-state resident. At private colleges the average cost was $31,916.[82] Tuition breaks and scholarships provide a disproportionate benefit to families earning $50,000 or more a year; the latest reports show this group received 70 percent of the benefits of federal tuition tax credits.[83] Merit-based aid also tends to favor middle- and upper-class youth, students who would most likely finish college anyway. "We are at a point," according to William Kirwan, chancellor of the University of Maryland, "where a low-income, high ability student is no more likely to attend college than a low-ability, high-income student."[84]

Adjusting for inflation over the last five years, the amount of aid, grants, loans, and work-study arrangements is flat, and students are being forced to rely more on private loans to finance their higher education. But considering that tuition costs have increased more rapidly than inflation rates during these years, the buying power of college aid— scholarships, loans, etc.—has declined, disproportionately hurting students from lower- and working-class backgrounds. In 2005–2006, students took out $17.3 billion in private loans to offset rising tuition costs, 25 percent more than the $13.8 billion the year before and 913 percent more than a decade ago.[85] Although the student loan default rate has declined from 22 percent in 1990 to 4.5 percent in 2003, corresponding with a steady drop in the prime interest rate, the lowest default rate still saw 115,500 borrowers go into default. But the percentage of students forced to take out loans for college has increased from 49 percent in 1992–1993 to 66 percent in 2004–2005,[86] thus indicating the growing cost of college and the decline in federal scholarships and grants, and, if I may add, the shrinking middle class.

More and more students are forced to borrow money and rely on private loans, which have no limits on interest; ironically, those least able to pay, that is low-income students, are charged the highest rates because of their credit history. With interest rates beginning to spike upwards, and new federal laws that took effect in 2005 making it nearly impossible to discharge student loans, moderate- and middle-income youthful borrowers are going to face hard times managing debt, while the wealthiest in our society will start their careers and credit profiles with a clean state. The good news, according to conservatives, is that the loans can be deferred if the borrower is unemployed or encounters other economic hardships. Nonetheless, the burden still rests with the borrower, the deferral period is limited to three years, and the interest mounts. Climbing out of a credit crunch or dark ditch becomes that much harder.

At the top private colleges in 2005, college cost $160,000 for four years; parents can expect in the next twenty years for the bill at private colleges to hit $500,000 (and $250,000 or more at state colleges for out-of-state residents). At that rate, parents need to save approximately $1,000 a month for a child's private college tuition (and $500 a month for state tuition) and, on top of it, earn a whopping 10 percent a year from the time junior is born.[87] Keep in mind that college tuition at private colleges has increased about twice the inflation rate for the last ten years, not to forget that federal and state loans have decreased, while the medium family income ($44,390 in 2004) remained relatively flat, up about $1,000 in the last five years or less than 1/2 percent a year.

The mainstream opinion among financial advisors for new parents is to rethink college savings. It is sort of a Hobbesian choice. If your children don't have enough money to pay for college, let them get part-time work and loans. They're young and will have more energy and time to pay the loans than you when you reach sixty-five. Better they be in debt than you have to skimp in your "golden years." Moreover, the less money your children have for college tuition, the more discounts they will receive from many colleges.

This new "wisdom" may sound immoral or surreal, but it reflects the fact that the middle class is struggling and shrinking. For twenty-five-year-old parents to retire at sixty-five and then live a modest lifestyle, and pay for one child's private college tuition ($500,000) starting in their early forties, the couple needs to save $1,700 a month, assuming a 4.5 percent investment return per year after taxes. After college tuition is paid, the amount of money left for retirement approximates $1.6 million.[88] Assuming a lifespan of twenty years beyond sixty-five that sum suffices today, but it is not impressive once you consider inflation for someone who is twenty-five years old. Given a 3.5 percent inflation rate, $1.6 million forty years from now has a present value of about one-third or $533,000. That's not a hell of a lot of beans or boggles, and it is bound to turn your "golden years"—those twenty years of so-called bliss—to "gold plated" years. God forbid you live longer; then, you might have to become a Keynesian or supply-side believer and rationalize spending as if it were savings. Of course that doesn't work in the real world, only if you are presidents Reagan or Bush, or if you have the genius of Milton Friedman or the wit of Arthur Laffer.

Leaving the Old Folks Behind

Hopefully, Social Security and Medicare will be around, despite the current projection that the flood of baby boomers, some 78 million Americans born between 1946 and 1964, now or soon retiring will cause federal spending on old-age benefits to consume as much as the nation's economy as the entire federal budget does now. The number of retirees is expected to increase from 40 million today to 76 million by 2030, which means that fewer dollars will come in from payroll taxes, and many more dollars will be going out for retirement and medical benefits. Unless taxes are increased or benefits reduced, the Medicare trust is expected to start running a deficit in 2013 and Social Security is expected to go bust by 2044.[89] Looming deficits are projected in tens of trillions, not billions, which will force the government to go into more debt or curtail benefits. Forty years from now, if we journey forward to 2046, it is projected there will be 79 million Americans between the ages of eighty and one hundred,[90] and there will be a much lower ratio (about 50 percent lower) of working people between the ages of twenty-one and sixty-four paying into Social Security and Medicare to support the coming "Age Wave." If that doesn't take away your breath or make you blink, then you are partially brain dead or half asleep.

Remember, the American dream was never guaranteed, neither were your winter years guaranteed to be without frost. In short, the potential problems of retirement, including Social Security and Medicare, dwarf the short-term problems of saving for your child's college education. Your golden years may very likely be blemished or tarnished, despite the taxes you now pay and the expectations of future social benefits.

Most Americans are in denial and are unprepared for their own retirement; actually, they have little savings and are facing potential erosion of their Social Security and cuts of company pensions. And, if you were thinking of inheriting money from your parents when they die, then think again. Many economists originally thought the vast pool of wealth accumulated by the generation born before the second half of the twentieth century would prop up the finances of their offspring. Revised statistics provide a bleaker picture. While hundreds of billions are passed on yearly for their offspring by the superrich, the vast majority of Americans, 86 percent of U.S. households, will not receive any inheritance.[91] This decline in inheritance among the majority populace can be explained by the increase in life expectancy, rise in health-care and nursing-home costs, and the decrease in retirement benefits, especially private pensions. For example, even though most seniors want to keep their homes, 44 percent of homeowners at age seventy will have sold their houses by age eighty-five.[92] Just as grim is the fact that the Federal Reserve reports that, between 1999 and 2006, more than $3 trillion was extracted by homeowners through refinancing and home equity loans.[93] Then there is the growing demand for reverse mortgages among senior citizens, that is the need to turn home equity into monthly income or a line of credit to pay for living costs and basic needs. As debt increases, equity falls, and the lender recoups the debt when the house is sold or the owner dies.[94] A lot of old folks have squeezed out the last bit of equity from their homes, which represents for most their number-one, most profitable investment. Not only is the piggy bank broken, but so is the potential for young folks to inherit assets with value.

For those people who inherit money, only 14 percent of U.S. households, the total annual value of inheritances has more than tripled from $55 billion in 1965 to $190 billion in 2005, but the median inheritance has fallen from $42,200 to $29,200 during the same period. This means that large inheritances are increasingly concentrated in the hands of a tiny percentage of Americans: Two percent of the richest estates were worth $782,000 or more in 2005, whereas the bottom 30 percent were worth less than $2,600 and the next 60 percent were worth $2,600 to $244,600. The median number illustrates a darker picture. The median inheritance for the bottom 90 percent of the 14 percent of the population that received any inheritance was approximately $15,000; for the bottom 95 percent it was $19,000.[95] If you put all the pieces together, the younger folks who have not yet retired will probably be worse off financially than the old folks who have moved closer to the sun and are closely guarding their retirement savings while their children sink into debt. In fact, a critical mass of their children will be in debt as soon as they graduate from college and will have to deal with debt for much of their lives, especially if they do not inherit money. The baby boomers around age fifty-five and over are the last group of Americans that expects, indeed demands, that they be able to retire with dignity.

So here we are at the end of the chapter. If you lay awake tonight and think about the message, and its implications, it's got to hurt and you have got to cry. Perhaps it is best to be abstract and think about the sunny side of the street, how fortunate Americans are compared to others and sing some Evangelist rhythm or some flag-waving song. But just remember that the conservatives you elect will protect upper-class and corporate interests. So long as the masses from parts of the heartland and South remain suspicious of liberals, people like me, and refuse to vote their economic interests, then they should be prepared for more pain and tears—

for the weakening and darkening of America. Or, if you think I'm an overeducated snot, confused about American values or the American dream, then sit back, yawn, and do nothing. If you feel my words make you wince, or my sentences are stuffed with conjecture or jingoism, then go back to your blogs, podcasts, and other video-viewing devices and audio earbuds. Avoid reality and create your own illusions of the world. Ignore the rising inequality consuming America, and the transfer of wealth to a tiny group at the expense of more than 90 percent of the nation's populace. Fill the moral vacuum with blizzards of diversionary details—or think of plays, poems, and cartoons that help you escape the repercussions.

NOTES

1. Steve Fraser, *Every Man a Speculator: A History of Wall Street in American Life* (New York: Simon & Schuster, 2005).
2. See chapter 3.
3. Joseph Nocera, "Donaldson: The Exit," *New York Times*, July 23, 2005.
4. Ralph Nader, *The Good Fight: Declare Your Independence and Close the Democracy Gap* (Washington, DC: Regan Books, 2005).
5. Here I am reminded of Stanley Milgram's "shock machine." While at Yale University, he conducted experiments on influence and obedience. As many as 65 percent of his subjects, who were ordinary residents of New Haven, were willing to follow orders and give what they thought were harmful electric shocks (up to 450 volts) to loudly protesting "victims," simply because some scientific-looking authority commanded them when the victim wrongly answered a question. The victims were actors who did not actually receive the shocks, but the subjects were convinced during the experiment that they were instilling the electric shocks. Milgram's work did not receive attention in most psychology texts because his experiment was considered highly provocative, involving ethical questions about human subjects; nevertheless, the experiment is a gripping example of how and why people follow orders and engage in herd behavior when there is approval of some authority. See Stanley Milgram, *Obedience to Authority* (New York: Harper, 1983).
6. David Callahan, *The Cheating Culture* (Orlando, FL: Harcourt, 2004).
7. Although some readers may never have heard of Drucker, the Wall Street money makers and big bankers who have been manipulating financial markets are well aware of his theories.
8. Charles A. Beard and Mary R. Beard, *The Rise of the American Civilization* (New York: Macmillan, 1942).
9. Henry J. Perkinson, *The Imperfect Panacea: American Failure in Education, 1865–1965* (New York: Random House, 1968).
10. Thomas Cochran and William Miller, *The Age of Enterprise*, rev. ed. (New York: Harper & Row, 1961).

11. E. L. Godkin, cited in Eric Goldman, *Rendezvous with Destiny*, rev. ed. (New York: Vintage, 1916).

12. See William O. Foulke, *Fighting the Spoilsmen* (New York: Putnam, 1919); Cornelius C. Regier, *The Era of the Muckrakers* (Chapel Hill, NC: University of North Carolina Press, 1932); and James B. Weaver, *A Call to Action* (Des Moines, IA: Printing Co., 1940).

13. Perkinson, *The Imperfect Panacea*, 167.

14. The divine and natural order, and the stewardship of great riches, are discussed in detail by Merle Curti, *The Growth of American Thought*, 2nd ed. (New York: Harper & Bros., 1951).

15. Andrew Carnegie, "Wealth," *North American Review* (June 1889), 254–56. Also see Andrew Carnegie, *Triumphant Democracy* (New York: Scribner's 1886).

16. Here the $64,000 question is: What percentage of a person's wealth gets returned to the public and what amount is left to his or her descendants, which could lead to a caste system or oligarchy in future generations?

17. William Graham Sumner, "Reply to a Socialist," in *The Challenge of Facts and Other Essays* (New Haven, CT: Yale University Press, 1914), 55–62.

18. William Graham Sumner, "The Forgotten Man," in *Essays of William Graham Sumner*, ed. Albert G. Keller and Maurice R. Davie, 481 (New Haven, CT: Yale University Press, 1934).

19. William Graham Sumner, *What Classes Owe to Each Other* (New York: Harper & Bros., 1883), 54.

20. Steve Forbes, "The Great Economic Debate of the 20th Century," *Imprimis* (March 2006), 1–2.

21. Milton Friedman and Rose Friedman, *Free to Choose* (Chicago: University of Chicago Press, 1981).

22. Merle Curti, *The Growth of American Thought* (New York: Harper & Bros., 1951); Charles H. Hopkins, *The Rise of the Social Gospel in American Protestantism, 1865–1915* (New Haven, CT: Yale University Press, 1940).

23. Forbes, "The Great Economic Debate," 2.

24. "A Conversation with Milton Friedman," *Imprimis* (July 2006), 4.

25. "Change in Income Inequality for Families: 1947–1998," *The State of Working America 2002–2003* (Washington, DC: U.S. Government Printing Office, 2004). Also see *Current Population Survey* (March 1948; March 1999).

26. David Leonhardt, "The Economics of Henry Ford May be Passé," *New York Times*, April 6, 2006.

27. Steven Watts, *The People's Tycoon* (New York: Knopf, 2005).

28. Thomas Friedman, *The World Is Flat* (New York: Farrar, Straus & Giroux, 2005).

29. Louis Uchitelle, *The Disposable American: Layoffs and Their Consequences* (New York: Knopf, 2006).

30. Thomas A. Kochran, *Restoring the American Dream: A Working Families' Agenda for America* (Cambridge, MA: MIT Press, 2005).

31. Daniel Yankelovich, *Profit with Honor* (New Haven, CT: Yale University Press, 2006).

32. Ben Cohen and Mal Warwick, *Values-Driven Businesses* (San Francisco: Berrett-Koehler, 2006).

33. Edward J. Renehan, *Dark Genius of Wall Street* (New York: Basic, 2005).

34. Jonathan Harrison, *Certain Dangerous Tendencies in American Life* (Boston: 1880); John Hay, *The Breadwinners* (New York: Harper & Bros., 1884).

35. "The Liberal Republicans of 1872," in *A Documentary History of the American People*, ed. Avery Craven, Walter Johnson, and F. Roger Dunn, 452–58 (Boston: Ginn & Co., 1951). Originally published in George W. Julian, *Political Recollections 1840–1872* (Chicago: Jansen, McClurg & Company, 1884), 329–50.

36. Douglas Clement, "Beyond 'Rich' and 'Poor,'" *The Region* (June 2003), 13–16. One percent of the population owned 29 percent of the nation's wealth in 1989 and 35 percent of the nation's wealth in 1998; it is estimated that by 2008 it will approach 40 percent, based on extrapolation. (I understand that projections have an element of uncertainty.) Also see Eric Konigsberg, "The New Class War," *New York Times*, November 19, 2006.

37. The number of poor depends on which report you read. For 2002, according to the U. S. government, the poverty threshold for a family of four was $18,400. For an individual, the amount was $9,2000. The poverty rate among blacks rose to 24 percent, counterbalancing years of progress in the 1990s when the economy was booming. Some economists argue that the government threshold is too low. Given a higher benchmark for defining poverty, $20,000 to $21,000 for a family of four, the poverty rate figure can increase from 35 million to 50 to 60 million. This does not account for millions of low-paying workers who see nothing getting better and who are not considered poor. They used to earn $20 to $25 per hour in a skilled job, but they were recently displaced by a machine or by "outsourcing" to third-world workers—and now earn $10 an hour as a busdriver or handyman with no benefits. I would put all unmarried teachers in the "struggling class," unless they have inherited money, won the lottery, or hit the jackpot at Las Vegas.

38. Eric Dash, "Off to the Races Again, Leaving Many Behind," *New York Times*, April 9, 2006.

39. CNN, "Executive Pay," April 14, 2006.

40. Kevin Phillips, *Wealth and Democracy* (New York: Broadway Books, 2002). Also see Eric Dash, "Compensation Experts Offer Ways to Curb Executive Salaries," *New York Times*, December 30, 2006.

41. Jad Mouawad, "For Leading Exxon to Its Riches, $144,573 a Day," *New York Times*, April 15, 2006.

42. For the three hundred and fifty top CEOs, stock options and insurance policies allow executives to pass on their estate to their heirs free of income tax. See JoAnn Lublin, "Under the Radar," *Wall Street Journal*, April 11, 2002.

43. David Cay Johnston, "Big Gain for Rich Seen in Tax Cuts For Investments," *New York Times*, April 5, 2006.

44. David Cay Johnston, "Big Gain for Rich Seen in Tax Cuts For Investments," *New York Times*, April 5, 2006, C4.

45. Stephen Entin, president of the Institute for Research on the Economics of Taxation, cited in *New York Times*, April 5, 2006.

46. Entin, *New York Times*, April 5, 2006.

47. Joseph Morgan, *The Nature of Riches* (Philadelphia: Dunn, 1732), 14–15.

48. Morgan, *The Nature of Riches*, 21.

49. Allan Nevins, *The Emergence of Modern America: 1865–1878* (New York: Macmillan, 1927); Clifford W. Patton, *The Battle for Municipal Reform: 1875–1900* (Washington, DC: America Council in Public Affairs, 1940).

50. Paul Krugman, "Plutocracy and Politics," *New York Times*, June 14, 2002; Charles E. Morris, "Greed is Good, but Only Later," *New York Times*, June 8, 2002.

51. Barry Gewen, "Forget the Founding Fathers," *New York Times Book Review*, June 5, 2005.

52. Richard Hofstadter, *The American Political Tradition* (New York: Knopf, 1948).

53. Robert Samuelson, "A Deficit of Seriousness," *Newsweek*, May 16, 2005; Elizabeth Warren and Amelia Warren Tyagi, *The Two-Income Trap* (New York: Basic, 2003).

54. Edmund L. Andrews, "Those Wild Budget Swings," *New York Times*, July 16, 2006; Ben Stern, "A Quick Course in the Economics of Confusion," *New York Times*, May 28, 2006.

55. "Don't Know Much about History," *New York Times*, July 3, 2006; "Top 10 Foreign Holders of U.S. Treasuries," *New York Times*, November 4, 2006.

56. David Leonhardt, "A Gamble Bound to Win, Eventually," *New York Times*, November 1, 2006; Floyd Norris, "Off the Charts," *New York Times*, November 4, 2006; Steven R. Weisman, "U.S. Trade Gap Called a Threat to Global Growth," *New York Times*, September 9, 2006.

57. Forbes, "The Great Economic Debate," 1–7.

58. Michael Fix, interview, "On the Money," CNBC, September 24, 2006.

59. Paul Krugman, "Losing Our Country," *New York Times*, June 20, 2005.

60. Ford Fessenden, "My House, Mr. Piggy Bank," *New York Times*, October 2, 2005.

61. "Does a Rising Tide Lift All Boats?" Federal Reserve, Research Report 1271, June 2000, tables 3–4, page 8.

62. "Does a Rising Tide Lift All Boats?" Federal Reserve.

63. Daniel Gross, "When Sweet Statistics Clash with a Sour Mood," *New York Times*, June 4, 2006.

64. "Taxes, Tax Credits, and Poverty Measurement," Federal Reserve, News Release #4572, The Conference Board, June 2000.

65. "Life in the Bottom 80 percent," *New York Times*, September, 1, 2005; Richard J. Newman, "Can America Keep Up?" *U.S. News & World Report*, March 27, 2006, 48–56.

66. Ironically, $7.50 roughly coincides with the average Wal-Mart wage, and, as we know, Wal-Mart is America's number-one employer.

67. Robert Pear, "Premium for Basic Medicare Increasing 13% Next Year," *New York Times*, September 17, 2005.

68. Jason DeParle, "Liberals' Hopes Ebb in Post Storm Debate on Poverty," *New York Times*, October 11, 2005.

69. Robert B. Reich, "An Economy Raised on Pork," *New York Times*, September 3, 2005.

70. Mary W. Walsh, "Whoops! There Goes Another Pension Plan," *New York Times*, September 18, 2005.

71. "Life in the Bottom 80 Percent."

72. Robert Pear, "U.S. Gives Florida a Sweeping Right to Curb Medicaid," *New York Times*, October 20, 2005.

73. Barbara Ehrenreich, *Bait and Switch: The (Futile) Pursuit of the American Dream* (New York: Henry Holt, 2005).

74. Reich, "An Economy Based on Pork."

75. Floyd Norris, "Off the Charts," *New York Times*, October 15, 2005.

76. "Cost of Government, 2005: Wasteful Spending Taxes Its Toll," Citizens against Government Waste, news release, June 6, 2005; Sheryl Gay Stolberg, "What's Wrong with a Healthy Helping of Pork?" *New York Times*, May 28, 2006.

77. "Election 2006 Aftershocks," *Newsweek*, November 20, 2006, 64.

78. "CAGW Release Prime Cuts 2005," Citizens against Government Waste, news release, September 14, 2005; "Top Prime Cuts Recommendations," Citizens Against Government Waste, news release, undated, 2005.

79. Gross, "When Sweet Statistics Clash with a Sour Mood."

80. Fred Block, Retire on Less Than You Think (New York: Henry Holt, 2006).

81. Lynn M. LoPucki, *How Competition for Big Cases Is Corrupting the Bankruptcy Courts* (Ann Arbor: University of Michigan Press, 2005); Walsh, "Whoops! There Goes Another Pension Plan."

82. *Trends in College Pricing 2005* (New York: College Board, 2005).

83. *Trends in Student Aid 2005* (New York: College Board, 2005).

84. William E. Kirwan, chancellor of University of Maryland, cited in Elizabeth Farrell," Public Colleges Tame Costs of Tuition," *Chronicle of Higher Education*, October 28, 2005.

85. Elizabeth F. Farrell, "Public Colleges Tame Costs of Tuition," *Chronicle of Higher Education*, October 19, 2005; *Trends in College Pricing 2005*.

86. Sandra Block, "Private Student Loans Pose Greater Risk," *USA Today*, October 25, 2006; Jonathon D. Glater, "It's Payback Time," *Education Life*, April 23, 2006.

87. Damon Darlen, "Today's Lesson: Rethink College Funds," *New York Times*, September 24, 2005.

88. "To Retire Well or to Educate Well?" *New York Times*, September 24, 2005 (based on projections of TIAA-CREF, one of the nation's largest pension funds).

89. Edmund L. Andrews, "Fearing That a Gap Will Become a Chasm," *New York Times*, March 2004.

90. Marco R. della Cava, "2046: A Boomer Odyssey," *USA Today*, October 28, 2005.

91. Michael D. Hurd and James P. Smith, *Rand Corporation and National Institute on Aging* (Washington, DC: Rand Corporation, 2005).

92. Hurd and Smith, *Rand Corporation and National Institute on Aging*.

93. Damon Darlin, "Mortgage Lesson No. 1: Home Is Not a Piggy Bank," *New York Times*, November 4, 2006.

94. Half of all reverse mortgages have been issued in 2005 and 2006, indicating the surge in baby boomers reaching retirement and surge in hard times. See Jeff D. Opdyke, "Making Your House Pay in Retirement," *Wall Street Journal*, December 27, 2006.

95. Eduardo Porter, "Inherit the Wind, There's Little Else Left," *New York Times*, March 26, 2006.

7

✛

World Inequality

It is a cliché to say American society (or the world) is changing; it is like saying change is inevitable. Nonetheless, change is more swift and complex since 9/11, due to increasing war-torn regions, energy consumption, climatic changes, and proliferation of nuclear club members, as well as a shift in manufacturing prowess to China and Southeast Asia and advances in genetic engineering, robotics, infotechnology, and nanotechnology (the science that constructs infinitesimally tiny devices). We are required more than ever to know the world to make informed choices about problems that impact on our society. As the new century unfolds, we are experiencing the first wave of events that have the potential to dramatically change our society, possibly to turn the world upside down. Hang on tight. This chapter is guaranteed to be bumpy and apocalyptic. Our storytelling begins with the number-one, world-class city—for some modern-day dwellers, the center of the world.

NEW YORK CITY: AN ELECTRIC JOLT

My new home is New York. What a jolt! It is the antithesis of "Yankeeville," where I lived for more than thirty years and where my children went to school and grew up. The flow of immigrants to New York is mind-boggling: forty-three percent of its residents were born outside of the United States, surpassing the previous record from the 1910 census.[1] The city is constantly reinventing itself because of this dynamic flow of people, energy, and ideas. It exemplifies how the superrich and the superpoor, different ethnic and religious groups, and people speaking multiple lists of languages can live side-by-side in harmony.

As a visitor, you quickly come to realize that New York City is a noisy, grimy and dirty, and overpopulated place, and there is too much traffic. Most of the street cart venders and souls in the subway and restaurants do not come from Europe and do not have blonde hair and blue eyes. You witness the flow of thousands of people on the street walking together, crisscrossing paths—a test of tolerance among so many newcomers and diverse people yearning to be free, to escape the old prejudices of the older countries.

New York City is the place where J. Hector St. John de Crèvecoeur's letters (written in 1782, describing America as a land where there is "the mixture of blood which you will find in no other country"), the Statue of Liberty, Ellis Island, and Nathan Glazer and Daniel Moynihan's *Beyond the Melting Pot*[2] fuse in a meaningful way: where the people from the four corners of the world come together, where they grow and prosper, and where they head out to the rest of America. New York City explains America to Americans and to the rest of the world. Visitors from all over the globe go to "the City" to take their pictures and visit museums—not to Bronxville, Greenwich, or Kenilworth, that is, the "Yankeevilles" of America, and not to the heartland of America.

New York City is the world; it is where people learn to live with their differences, with their own identities, and with respect for the identities of others. The city is an agglomeration of people; one hundred and twenty-five languages (according to former mayor Rudy Giuliani) are spoken. New York students do not need a course in multiculturalism. You come to this city, as a visitor, to have your lessons in pluralism and diversity; the people living here accept people of all stripes, sizes, sexual preferences, and colors—no matter how different they are. New York is the place where differences are celebrated, and where very wealthy and very poor people live on top of each other, sometimes separated only by a doorman and high-resolution camera.

Here in New York, you can be who you are no matter how different you are. You can hip-hop on 42nd Street, dancing to the beat of the latest funky Caribbean music, in front of hundreds of tourists; or you can attend the opera at the Met or Lincoln Center and listen to the sounds of Andrea Bocelli or Luciano Pavarotti. You can hawk $10 look-a-like Rolex watches or sell "I Love New York" shirts, three for $10, a block from Tiffany or Gucci, where someone else might spend $100,000 on some luxury item. No one cares! Everyone in New York City can do their thing and reach their potential, whereas, in more provincial parts of the country, you might be labeled, discriminated against, or held back because of your differences (fat, gay, artsy, etc.) or because you're not part of the "old guard" (or you have the wrong last name).

Sometimes resented by Americans because it is the most famous city in the world, New York has the most of almost everything. It is a cultural, entertainment, and intellectual force, and the economic and financial center of the nation. It is the world's art center, publishing center, entertainment center, theater and drama center, media center, sports center, and fashion center. It has more museums, schools, colleges and universities, theaters, restaurants, jewelers, and furriers than any other city in the world. It has many of the tallest buildings (the glass and steel center of the world), the largest transit and underground train system, and the largest fire department and police force (larger than most standing armies of the world), and it attracts more tourists and has more beautiful women than any other city. Next to the Boston-Cambridge area, it has the most international students and, next to downtown Cairo and Istanbul, it has the worst traffic jams. The city has more superrich people per square mile, as well as more poor people concentrated in places like Harlem and Bedford Stuyvesant; there is more inequality in some square blocks than anywhere else in the world, because there are so many superrich people living in New York. The city provides the opportunity for Americans to make oodles of money, and many European and Asian people with bundles of money have come to the New York because of its vitality and international flavor.

New York is the warmest, most diverse, and most powerful city in the world. It is modern Athens and Rome rolled up in one metropolis. American icons and American heroes have all come to the city to be honored or to speak to its people. This is where America's monuments and American people come together to fulfill their slogans and dreams: "Give me your tired and wretched poor," "I have a dream," and others. This is where you find survivors of Auschwitz and former Nazi soldiers, Irish rebels and British royalists, Croatian freedom fighters and Serbian farmers living together on the same block, shopping in the same grocery store—living in a new world amid new nostalgia. I don't believe social science scholarship can fully catch the moment, describe the city, or even film it. You have to experience it, see it, smell it, and become part of the street hustle and bustle to fully grasp it.

Now listen to E. B. White's timeless description in *Here Is New York.* "It's noise, its glitter, its harshness, its tolerance." The city is a contradiction, congested, implausible. "Every facility is inadequate. The hospitals and schools and playgrounds are overcrowded, the highways . . . and bridges are bottlenecks." The city is "uncomfortable, so crowded, so tense." It's hard to get into a restaurant, find an affordable apartment. "Buses are standing room and taxis are not to be found." But the city forms "a rich ethnic stew." It makes up for its inadequacies by "supplying its citizens with . . . the sense of belonging to something unique, cosmopolitan, mighty and unparalleled."[3]

Every imaginable city problem smolders in New York: infrastructure problems, pollution problems, traffic problems, race problems, crime problems, welfare problems, and education problems. But the number or intensity of the problems is not what makes the city so different, as they exist to some lesser extent in smaller big cities from coast to coast, but it is the truce, patience, and lack of bigotry. It is the city life, built on people, streets, and neighborhoods that makes the city different. It is the opportunities "to make it big" in finance and commerce, fashion and food, theater and art, publishing and writing, that draws young blood, like a magnet, from Maine to Mississippi from the heartland to the "Big Apple." Fresh talent and fresh ideas from other parts of the country are constantly injected into the city, making it the most vibrant city in the world. Coming to New York from small town U.S.A., or some rust-belt city, means shooting for the moon, going for the golden ring, breaking away from home, and fulfilling the American dream.

New York is the heart and soul of America; and, since 9/11, it has become the symbol of America rising above a fiery graveyard. It best represents what the American dream is all about. The city is loved by visitors from all parts of the world; it reaches out to them and represents the best place where everyone can live, work, and prosper together. That is what this country is about—why it is so wealthy and why people from all over the world want to emigrate and even assimilate. People don't come to New York or to the United States to hold on to their own identities, or to be near people of their own group; they come for opportunity and a better life than in the place they left behind. Coming to New York means breaking away from the old ways. The children of the new arrivals have no desire to follow their parents' occupations or to speak the old language; they may cling to their people and live in "Little Italy" or "Chinatown" because of trust, business opportunities, and political clout, but, in the end, the American lifestyle shapes their lives and produces a new breed of Italian Americans and Chinese Americans—what I call "assimilated Americans." Despite what cultural pluralists might say about the assimilation process or advocate in its place, America has been assimilating its immigrants for three hundred and fifty years, before it even became a nation and will go on doing so as long as the flow of new arrivals continues.

PERSONAL IMAGES AND INTERPRETATIONS

Where were you that day in September when the world stopped? Certainly every reader can delineate the place, the people, the memory. I was in New York, and I still see the smoking ruins and collapse of the towers, the people who chose to jump out windows knowing full well what it

meant, the firefighters who knew in their minds and hearts the outcome
as they rushed to their deaths.

I think of Lincoln's words at Gettysburg's "cemetery," which were
repeated by several speakers across the country on the anniversary of September 11. I think of phrases such as "four score and seven years ago,"
"the unfinished work," "the final resting place," "all men [and women]
are created equal," and that government should be "of the people, by . . .
and for the people." I think about how I used to repeat by rote these
words when I was in school, and recall how a nation rose from the ashes
and anguish of death and destruction. And so it is "fitting and proper" to
remember the dead and to go on as part of "the living," to finish "the
great task remaining before us," and to "provide a new birth of freedom."

It was the haunting lyrics of Lincoln's message, some 269 words,
reflecting both great suffering and spiritual triumph, the mysticism and
skill in his use of words and images, that made me appreciate the great
struggle that profoundly affected the nation. Lincoln's address enriched
the nation's literature, depicting heroic action, poignant humanity, the
scars of the war, the nation's obligation to its dead, its rebirth, and principles of unity, liberty, and democracy.

As I reflect on President Lincoln—the man who was born in a log cabin,
a simple farmer from the prairie, with one year of formal schooling—I
think of America reborn from all the dead he came to honor at Gettysburg
and at other battlefields and bloodbaths of the Civil War. I think it is "fitting and proper" that we remember and add all the sermons, speeches,
empty coffins, and last good-byes as part of the "new birth," new spirit,
and new hope of the nation.

Then, I think of the Lady in the Harbor, how breathtaking and proud
she looks. I've never seen her look more magnificent than today, and I've
never fully appreciated, until now, how my grandparents might have
felt—and the millions of other immigrants, many who were outcasts and
downtrodden—when she loomed in front of them.

So, Frederic Auguste Bartholdi's gigantic effigy has become the "welcoming lady," her torch held high, touching the rising and setting sun—a
symbol of American principles and freedom and hope to the entire world.
Last week, when I flew home to New York, I gazed out the window as the
jumbo jet made the last turn to descend onto the runway. I never had such
a feeling—a feeling of love and adoration toward the Lady in the Harbor,
beckoning at the entrance to America. For a split second, I thought of
Athena, some twenty-five hundred years ago, mounted on the top of the
Acropolis.

I shall never forget the way she looked, Lady Liberty in the harbor who
welcomed my grandparents nearly one hundred years ago and provided
a safe haven, hope and opportunity, birth and rebirth. She remains to me
the spirit of America, welcoming old people and young people, from all

walks of life, from all four corners of the world, one hundred and seventeen years after her unveiling. She is my favorite lady and she still brings tears and emotions to my senses and soul. She has become anchored to the passions and beliefs of all Americans, and of all the people clamoring to come to America—an image, a thought, a metaphor, an idea, a symbol, navigating adroitly between the past, the present, and the future. But the lady, and what she stands for, is being challenged as the world around her changes. And, as I think about all the great things this country has achieved, there is still the other side of the divide. We cannot bury our heads in the sand and ignore the underdeveloped and developing world, what others call the "third world," gripped by poverty, human misery, and thousands of years of war and governance that squandered much of their wealth.

GLOBAL INEQUALITY AND INSTABILITY

Anyone with an ounce of brain matter understands that the attack on the World Trade Center and the Pentagon was an act of war against the United States and the free world—the worst attack on the United States since Pearl Harbor, and one that actually did more damage. This was a day in our lives that almost everyone can say changed everything. Our world will never be the same. Although terrorists violate all fundamental values of civilized and free society, we need to understand that for people living in the desert, distant mountains, or jungle, whose worldly possessions amount to owning a wood-burning stove, two goats, and a tent and who have never seen a television or computer, two collapsing buildings have no real meaning.

We also need to understand that a nation-state, movement, or organization waging war today without technology is forced to fight on a different level with different rules of engagement. The British soldiers, at the time of the Revolution the best-trained fighting force, invaded the colonies in their red uniforms and shiny boots and marched on the open battlefield, ready to fire on the enemy in a sequenced and prescribed manner, according to the rules of civilized society and gentleman soldiers. The American troops, a ragtag army dressed in tattered and farm-patched clothing, hid behind trees and rocks, and resorted to unusual rules of engagement, including surprise and hit and run, all of which were construed by the British as ungentlemanly and somewhat uncivilized. (See chapter 1.)

I would argue that the world is a paradox, full of misunderstandings and subjective and contextual interpretations of people and nations. Let me explain. While Americans worry about whether the steak they ordered in some restaurant will come out medium rare, or whether they will have time to shop at the next Gucci sale, there are billions of people worried about their next meal and whether the clothes on their backs will suffice for the winter cold. Depending on which countries you include, one-third to half the world, or two to three billion people in the third world, can be radicalized by a political or religious zealot who feeds and clothes them and is intent on using this new force to challenge our way of life or to try to bring us down.

Allow me another comparison. In 1900, a nickel did not make you rich, but it gave you a sense of empowerment. If you were living in New York or Chicago, for five cents, you could buy a beer, a cup of coffee, a hot dog, three donuts, or an ice cream cone. John Rockefeller, the world's first billionaire, tried to improve his image by handing out dimes to children on the streets of Cleveland during his Sunday walks.[4] One hundred years later, in the impoverished third world of Latin America, Africa, Asia, and the Middle East, $1,000 can turn an impoverished teenager or young adult into a human bomb. The larger sum may have something to do with inflation or the reduced value of life among "true believers." But consider that there are some 2 to 3 billion people marginally existing on either $1 or $2 a day, and another 1.5 to 2 billion people earning between $2 and $3.50 a day and the number is growing because of the "population bomb."

How much of a divide between "haves" and "have-nots" can the world tolerate without instability? What role does the United States play? Should it be the world's policeman and moral compass? Based on whose values? Should the American president decide who is qualified to possess nuclear weapons? Why India? Why not Iran? Can our nation afford to remain isolationist, distant, or indifferent? How much of our resources should we share with third-world populations? How much money should the average American be taxed to hopefully gain friends or converts abroad? What can educators do to prepare students, the next generation, for the world of 2050 and beyond in which it is estimated that the world population will reach about 10 billion. Can people living in a tent in the desert or on a mountaintop, distant from modern civilization, be expected to understand why American jets have invaded their sky?

The Changing Global Village

Colonists used the metaphors of a "subject people" in their petitions and "slavery" in their public debates to condemn the British. In their victory, Americans made freedom and liberty fundamental principles,[5] but the Founding Fathers were the offspring of the British and European traditions and permitted subject peoples and slaves to become part of this nation's history. Although the new nation was pluralistic and remarkably diverse with the arrival of European and African people, living among

Native Americans, cultural and racial conflict was also part of its history. Our European ancestors had to adjust to a new social order in which cultural and racial domination had to be curtailed, far different than the Old World Order, which was characterized by class distinctions and lack of social mobility.

The growth of the nation included a collection of the most diverse and motley human beings on a scale never imagined anywhere in the world before the 1600s. Confronted by people from all different parts of the world, the early American colonialists had to rethink and reconceptualize their social and cultural world, their religious beliefs, customs, and language,[6] as well as their view of society and the relationships between education, mobility, and economic opportunity. Hierarchy, elitism, class distinctions, and titles were unacceptable, far different from mother England and Old Europe, because there was a mixing and melting of a diverse people—Europeans, Africans, and Native Americans, and later Latin Americans and Asians. The new nation had to deal with its whiteness and at the same time create a nation that reflected a multicultural, multireligious society. It had to develop a system of education that was free of religious influence and that recognized diversity among the states and local communities. The concept of a ministry of education for a federal system of education was rejected, thus reducing the potential of a political or religious ideology influencing or seizing control of the schools.

The significance of the United States lies in the convergence of people from multiple nations and multiple religions coming together into one national story, one country indivisible, one nation becoming less white. Overall and over time, the nation has favored inclusiveness and not exclusiveness, pluralism and not homogeneity, assimilation and not domination. But critics can also show ways in which there was more misunderstanding than understanding, more mistreatment than fair treatment, more inequality than equality, and more injustice than justice. Thus, there is the clash between conservatives and liberals in interpreting American history and society.

There are many critics who take great pride in holding a mirror in front of us, to show only the cruel side of America. I cannot fathom, and only fear to think of, a world without the United States. Without this land, there would be no asylum for the wretched poor, little hope for the masses from distant places to escape from their oppression and misery, and the world would be possessed by one or more of the great evils— Nazism, Japanese imperialism, Stalinism, and/or Maoism. I would not exist nor my children; my ancestors would most likely be buried in some mass grave at Belostock (the most violent Russian pogrom),[7] and the others at Auschwitz, and most of the civilized world would be "subject people" or puppets of some foreign political order. Sadly, however, many

Americans take our human rights and our blessings for granted. We are ignorant of the history that molded America, lacking the barest concept of the hopes and dreams of millions of early immigrants, many who were illiterate or semi-illiterate peasants and laborers, making the perilous journey, often on unseaworthy and fever-ridden "coffinships"—and the spirit of reform that has guided that American political and social order.

Today, I write from the perspective of a third-generation American, proud and thankful that I am an American. Had Europe been a different place, I might have spoken a different language and had a different set of experiences and relationships. To this extent, I am a citizen of an ideal land because of the cruelty and hatred of other lands that my ancestors were fortunate to escape with three or four bundles on their backs. As uneducated peasants, they never read Plato, Locke, or Rousseau nor the writings of Jefferson and Madison, but they understood that America was the asylum for the oppressed, regardless of their background—what other immigrants from other places also understood, and what foreign observers like de Tocqueville and Lord Bryce eyewitnessed and translated into magical words, and what artists such as Irving Berlin, George Gershwin, and Rogers and Hammerstein have put to music in Broadway hits.

Had my ancestors not understood the story of America, I would have no story to tell, no existence—one out of many millions whose ancestors were reduced to nothingness by plunder and war in Europe. In fact, many of us reading this book would have no existence, had their ancestors not made the long, treacherous journey across the ocean that once took several months. I don't think modern multiculturalists or speakers of immigrants, including Nathan Glazer, Oscar Handlin, Michael Novak, or Ben Wattenberg, could say what I just said with any more appreciation, conviction, or passion toward America and our way of life.[8]

I also write as a global citizen who feels that human beings are 99 percent alike in terms of DNA and human characteristics, a map of eighty thousand genes in every human cell. Yet, it is the 1 percent differences (usually based on race or color) that humans focus on. As a recent resident of New York City, with the greatest percentage of first- and second-generation immigrants than any other American city (more than 75 percent), I am aware of the world's diverse population. In a two- to three-block stretch in parts of Manhattan, Queens, Brooklyn, and the Bronx, some forty to fifty different languages are spoken. You cannot find that type of diversity anywhere in the world; in fact, New York is a microcosm of the world, inhabited by many who have escaped from the third world.

The Shrinking White World

Given the shrinking white world we live in—from 13 percent in 2000, to 9 percent by 2010, and to 5 percent by midcentury—there is need to understand, respect, and get along with people of color. The fertility rate in Southeast Asia is 7.8 children per female; the average fertility rate of whites is 1.7 children per female, which illustrates the reason for the world decline of the white population.[9] This decline is most pronounced in Europe, which had a 2000 white population of 727 million and is projected ("medium rate") by 2050 to be 603 million. This unprecedented drop represents a loss of 17 percent, which has serious social and economic implications. The "low" (and most likely) projection puts Europe's population at 556 million, a loss of 24 percent. If the birthrate remains this low, the European Union will have a shortfall of 20 million workers by 2030 and possibly 40 million by 2050, putting a huge strain on pension plans, health care, and the workforce. No European country today is managing its population. Through births, with rates commonly at 1.2 or 1.3 for most countries,[10] the demographic trends in Europe represent one reason why these nations are willing to take in a large number of Middle Eastern and Asian Moslems and black African immigrants.[11] The problem with this policy is that it results in a surge of uneducated and low-wage earners who depress the overall labor market for European workers (similar to what is happening in our own southern border-states). The growth of Moslem and Arab immigrants in Western Europe is so dramatic that by the end of this century Europe may become Euro-Arabic, a form of Pan-Arabism or Islamic expansion. Given the ultraconservative and extremist segment of the Moslem world, both anti-Western and intent on disrupting Western societies, these population trends are considered alarming by many policymakers in Europe and the United States.

White populations in Western and technological countries continue to shrink and populations of color in poor countries continue to accelerate (the fastest growing in Africa). For example, the Congo population will increase from 49.1 million in 1998 to 160.3 million in 2050 (226 percent change); Ethiopia from 59.7 million to 169.5 million (184 percent change); Ghana from 19.1 million to 51.8 million (170 percent change); and Uganda from 20.6 million to 64.9 million (216 percent change).[12] All the old legacies of "separate" and "unequal" in the United States and "colonization" and "white supremacy" abroad are viewed as self-destructive in nature. Although the health and vitality of America depends on technology and efficiency, they also assume a good political and economic relationship with Africa, Asia, and Latin America—the non-Western world, people of color—as well as people of all races and ethnic groups getting along in our own country.

Although the United States is the only Western country (along with Australia) expected to grow in population in the next several decades, by 2050 the majority (white) populace in the United States will be in the minority and the minority population (blacks, Hispanic Americans, and

Asian Americans) will be the majority.[13] Put in different terms, about 65 percent of the U.S. population growth in the next fifty years will be "minority," particularly Hispanic and Asian, because of immigration trends and fertility rates. In fact, from 2000 on, the Hispanic population will increase twice as fast as the black population because of Hispanic immigration trends (whereas blacks have no comparable immigration pool). Thus, by 2010, there will be more Hispanic students than black students in U.S. schools.[14] Most of this population growth will take place in ten states (with the main shift in California, Texas, Florida, and the New York-New Jersey metropolitan area).

Although the world population is expected to increase at 75 to 80 million a year, we are now aware of a shrinking white world. The world is becoming more urban. As of 2007, there were some 425 cities worldwide that had one million or more residents, compared to one hundred years ago when there was none. Moreover, by 2025, as many as 75 to 80 percent of the world's urban population (projected to be more than 6 billion urban dwellers) will live in mega cities of 25 million or more, in the cities of developing countries such as Beijing, Bombay, Cairo, Calcutta, Dhaka, Jakarta, Lagos, Mexico City, and Sao Paulo[15]—freewheeling places of outrageous contrasts, with wealth (less than 0.5 percent) coexisting with abject poverty (about 90 percent) and the remaining working- and middle-class populations. Even among high-growth countries such as China and India, the vast majority of the populaces have watched fellow citizens, usually land developers or business people with government contacts, gain the benefits of prosperity. In the rural parts of these countries, where still more than 50 to 60 percent of the people live, the overwhelming number struggle for subsistence. Hundreds of millions of Chinese and Indians still survive on less than $1 day; more than half of the Chinese and nearly half of the Indians (mostly women) are illiterate. All those microchip designers and engineers we hear about, although numbering in the millions, represent a small percentage of the population.

HIGH-TECH VERSUS LOW-TECH NATIONS

The cell phones, Internet, and cable TV that we are accustomed to are apparitions to the population of poverty, a world of color that is growing rapidly, and are the gulf where danger resides. Put simply, the low-tech/disconnected world could overwhelm the high-tech/connected world. So long as these poor remain docile, they remain invisible to us, and we remain unaware and unconcerned about billions of people running through heaps of garbage and sleeping in the streets, places where the majority of children drop out of school by the sixth or seventh grade and are called "street children," "beggars," and "no-hopers." Our education system is divorced from this global reality; yet this world (the third world) may weigh down the world we know—what most of us would call the Western world, or industrialized world.

Despite the world increasingly speaking English and drinking Coca-Cola, most of the inhabitants in developing areas of the world are rural immigrants and urban refugees within their own countries, many living in streets, drinking poisonous contaminated water, sip by sip, people adrift and yearning for a better life and a little dignity. These poor and wretched people are the new proletariat—possessed by a growing dislike, jealousy, and even hatred toward Western values. These are the same kinds of people Europeans, and to a much lesser extent Americans, have exploited through colonization and capitalism.

Third-world nations are now trying to pull themselves into the world market by selling their agricultural products, only to come upon the rich nations' insistence on subsidizing their own farmers, creating rock-bottom prices. Poor people, often farmers, are unable to compete on a global basis and continue to struggle on a daily basis. The developed world's (or G-8 nations') annual $320 billion in farm subsides dwarfed its $75 billion in assistance to the undeveloped world. A 1 percent increase in Africa's share of world exports would amount to $70 billion a year, some three times the amount ($25 billion) provided in aid in 2005.[16] This "rigged game" of keeping agribusiness afloat in wealthy nations fuels poverty and is sowing great hostility toward the United States, as it is viewed as the principle architect of the world economic order. (Actually, the United States spent $19 billion in annual subsidies to American farmers, as compared to the more than 60 billion spent by the European Union.) In short, poor nations are unable to expand their agriculture markets, which would shift hundreds of billions of dollars from the rich to poor nations of the world. By rich countries imposing tariffs and eliminating the farm competition of poor countries, they have added to both malnutrition, as well as illegal immigration to Europe and a movement of rural poor to third-world cities—increasing worldwide, urban squalor and sowing the seeds of radicalism and anti-Western movements.

This is an obscure but serious trend: billions of people, about two-thirds of a growing world population, squashed by a new kind of economic imperialism and resenting the United States, representing an inevitable force with a reason to rebel and bring down our way of life—not by invading armies but through social breakdown, health problems and viruses, rebellion from mountains and jungles, as well as overpopulated cities, nuclear terrorism, and/or cyber warfare. Conservatives might argue that our nation has never been so misunderstood by the world, but I would argue that the world knows us much better than we know the world. They would also argue that globalization will eventually lead to a trickle-down economic benefit that over time will help the poor and make production more efficient and less expensive. Such an argument is rooted in the idea of a free-market economy, whereby consumer demand and efficient production win the day for capitalists while benefiting the masses with lower consumer prices.

To be sure, protectionism remains the major threat to global growth among the poorest nations of the world. In 2003, total exports of the fifty poorest nations of the world amounted to $46.3 billion. In contrast, the U.S. trade deficit with China was $202 billion in 2005, and another $70 billion with the European Union. Worldwide the flow of goods and services in 2006 was valued at more than $12 trillion.[17] Lifting trade barriers, especially farm subsidies (tobacco, sugar, cotton, fruits and vegetables, etc.) which are mostly situated in red-voting states holds the most hope for the least developed countries. (Now the trick is to get Republicans to agree.)

Depending on the benchmarks we employ, about seventy-five to one hundred countries are caught in a "poverty trap," a term used by Columbia University's Jeffrey Sachs to describe a combination of poor geography, poor infrastructure, poor health care, and limited educational resources[18] and, if I may add, poor transportation links, a shortage of skilled labor, and nonexistent credit. Moreover "dirty" money and money laundering, as well as the smuggling and trafficking of people and goods, make up half the economies of nations in Africa, the Middle East, and Latin America.[19] About the only thing holding the world's poor populace together is their government, and we are forced to support corrupt leaders and dictators and hope these governments can restrain the extremist part of the population that wants to cripple the West. These impoverished people are to some extent the people we once called barbarians, who brought down Rome. The world has not changed much in the last one thousand years, at least not when it comes to counting powerful people and powerless people, except maybe the scales are more lopsided and there are more poor people in the world willing to sack the place where all roads lead (no longer Rome, now Washington, D.C.).

Is foreign aid the answer? Will money solve the "poverty trap?" Sachs believes that, if rich countries increased their annual foreign-aid budgets between $135 to $195 billion for the next decade, extreme poverty in the world would be eliminated. Conservative critics would argue that Sachs needs a reality check—that political, social, and cultural conditions prevent economic improvement in the foreseeable future. Even if oil or other resources were discovered in these countries, political and business corruption would prevent the vast majority of the populace from receiving benefits. The money would wind up in the hands of a tiny group of families or politicians, nothing more than a mirror of the history of most third-world, poor nations. Sometimes it is European businessmen protecting their investments, sometimes it is home-grown mercenaries or rebels, and sometimes it is government officials or the country's ruling class hatching plots and stealing the riches from the country's oil fields. Typical cases where political corruption, family conflict, or mercenaries steal or squander oil revenues or prevent oil production are countries like Azerbaijan, Kazakhstan, the Congo, Nigeria, Sudan, and Yemen.

Given our wealth and resources, and our belief in the rule of law, how do we prepare our children and their children for this age of uncertainty, for what endures around the world, and for what might be. American students are unaware of the global village and feel they are on top of the heap, but all around us there are ghettos and genocide, starvation and malnourishment, sickly and starving people living amidst rampant political waste, fraud, and corruption, a pending global apocalypse. Do American teenagers who visit Nike and Reebok outlet stores, or who shop at J. Crew and the Gap, understand the thousands of foreign factories, many American, taking advantage of low wages and lax child labor laws in the pursuit of profits?

Do you think that the millions of U.S. teenagers who listen to the repugnant lyrics of Eminem and other hip-hop sounds,[20] coupled with photographs of multiracial sex acts or a sadomasochistic gay culture on VH1 or MTV, can make the leap and listen to the sounds and cries of the poor a world away from them? Do Americans understand that we are no longer the source of "cool," that our movies, music, and art no longer win friends but make enemies? In the past (and even today), Americans have been unable to make the leap to the other side of the tracks, one or two miles away, to understand what sociologists have called the "invisible poor." How are Americans expected to make the global leap to better understand the world around them, when 60 percent of college-age Americans do not know where the United Nations headquarters is located and cannot find Iraq on the map.[21]

The Growing Proletariat

The world's poor are a forgotten people; few people know or care to know their plight. About 40 million third-world people are infected with HIV; 300 to 500 million people are infected with malaria every year; 20 million children in third-world countries die of starvation each year, while another 800 million people suffer daily from malnourishment and hunger; and 50 percent of the world's population lives on no more than two dollars a day.[22] Ironically, in ten years, between 1987 and 1998, poverty (defined by the World Bank) increased 20 percent in Latin America, 40 percent in South Asia, and 50 percent in Africa. In Eastern Europe and Central Asia, it increased more than 1,000 percent. In twenty third-world countries (ten in Africa), the life expectancy is expected to dip below forty years. In Sub-Saharan Africa, children under five die twenty-two times the rate of children in industrialized countries, and also twice the rate of the entire developing world.[23] According to economist and professor Gregory Clark of the University of California, Davis, living standards in almost half of Africa have fallen below hunter-gatherer times and 40 percent below the living standard of eighteenth-century England.[24]

An angry urban proletariat is growing around the world as poor populations—namely, hundreds of millions of rural migrants—flood to grimy, overpopulated urban areas. There, they are assaulted by what is perceived as Western culture: luxury cars, nightclubs, sex and drugs, porno movies, gangs, and prostitution. Their daily existence is plagued by electric blackouts, unsanitary drinking water, overflowing sewage, and an assortment of five killer diseases—tuberculosis, typhoid, malaria, measles, and AIDS—annually killing some 54 million people worldwide.[25] It is not uncommon for more than half of this new proletariat to live on rooftops, street alleys, and the outskirts of the cities by garbage dumps. This is the world, the real world, that Americans do not understand or know, given the paradox of American prosperity.

As America preaches the gospel of freedom and democracy, and romanticizes market globalization, high-tech gadgets, and entrepreneur capitalism, there is a growing post–Cold War proletariat class that infests, digests, and surrounds the cities of the most populated, underdeveloped and developing countries: Afghanistan, Bangladesh, Colombia, Egypt, India, Indonesia, Myanmar (formerly Burma), Pakistan, Laos, and even parts of Brazil, China, and India, and almost all or most of the African countries. Whatever their language, whatever their skin color, religion, or tribal descent, they resent the national government that often rigs elections, if there are any, and that is corrupt and unable to provide basic necessities of life. Because of economic and social conditions, plus political corruption and dictatorship, the value of life is not the same as in Western society.

The result is that many of these people find salvation in revolution and guerilla warfare, and still others in religion that offers eternal hope for a better life, including extreme and fanatical groups that preach U.S. hatred. Many of the nations in the developing worlds are going to unravel, not all at once, but in piecemeal fashion. As we try to assist these countries and buy off their political leaders, it will be the challenge of modernity itself (and with it comes Western culture) that will make so many of these people more bellicose toward the United States.

As for Africa, which houses the world's greatest concentration of poverty (and is beginning to splinter), the only way a citizen is going to rise to a higher existence is to get out. Despite all the rhetoric of American black radicals like W. E. B. DuBois, Marcus Garvey, Richard Wright, and Stokely Carmichael, who idealized Africa and suggested Afro Americans should emigrate to Africa, the idea for blacks is not to return to Africa, but to make the trans-Atlantic voyage to America or Europe. Where all avenues of mobility have failed, because of continuous government corruption, waste, civil war, and disease, Africans hope to go abroad for the education and decent job that Africa has denied them. The passport to social mobility in Africa is to leave and come back with an education and money. However, most blacks fortunate enough to obtain citizenship in England, France, or the United States do not want to return to Africa.[26] Africans will privately admit that theirs is a "Dark Continent"—what the white world knows but refuses to say anymore publicly. It is bound to remain dark for scores of years to come.

Now there is nothing wrong about encouraging African dance groups and art in black schools and communities in the United States, and there is a lot to be said for black children wearing a T-shirt of Kunta Kinte, the hero of *Roots*, or knowing that the word "uhuru" means freedom. But it is counterproductive (uh-oh, here goes another white person giving advice to a black person) to expect Africa to solve the psychological problems that blacks may possess because of American institutional racism. On the other hand, poverty and malnutrition in Africa drive many children into high-risk jobs with meager pay in mines and quarries. Some 49 million children age fourteen and younger worked in sub-Sahara Africa in 2004, 1.3 million more than only four years earlier in 2000.[27] To be sure, child labor is tied to the lack of prosperity. To talk about some sentimental notion of returning to Africa and being made whole or finding prosperity and self-fulfillment (secular or spiritual) rejects common sense and the flow of immigrants from Africa seeking a better life and running from the squalor of a continent where the sun never rises. It flies in the face of African reality, a world described by one African commentator as led by "dictators, murderers, and thieves"[28] and, if I may add, a world ransacked by conflict, corruption, starvation, and a medical/health nightmare.

William Easterly, a former economist with the World Bank and professor at New York University, argues that poverty in Africa has increased despite $2.3 trillion dollars of foreign aid by the West over the last fifty years; it still has not managed to prevent infections and diseases from killing the poor in Africa. For less than $1 dollar in medicines and $4 in bed nets, half of all malaria deaths could be prevented and a simple twenty-five-cent condom could prevent half of HIV infections. Western nations take a scientific and rational approach to planning and developing aid strategies, instead of working with local institutions and recognizing local customs. They measure success by how much money they spend, almost like reviewing a business budget, but fail to consider actual results.[29] They are better at documenting failures and reporting the grim statistics of malnutrition, disease, and death than analyzing and implementing success. Americans are not necessarily ugly or mean-spirited people; we are a most generous people but possess a low global IQ because we have been protected by the oceans for centuries. Well, times have changed; we need to take off our blinders and improve our international intelligence.

The Third World Is Growing

Dealing with global poverty is essential if capitalism is to continue to prosper; otherwise, the growing world poor may tip the scale and its weight may eventually bring down capitalism. At the present, capitalism is basking in its victory over communism, unaware that, as global poverty increases, radical and fanatical elements of third-world countries gain in power and the potential to challenge the existing system.

The people of third-world countries are not burning the American flag or effigies of President Bush, nor are they rioting in the streets on a regular basis. Their anger toward the West and rich nations is loosely articulated, because these people, for the greater part, are working and struggling on a daily basis to exist and do not have time to take part in demonstrations. The third-world people we do see demonstrating on CNN are riveting to the American audience, partially because of their anger toward the United States, partially because of their zeal, and partially because they seem to exist in another world so different from ours. For the most part, the world's poor believe, or are led to believe, that the United States is the cause of their squalor and misery, that their government cannot function efficiently because of U.S. dependence. In their need to lash out at someone, to vent their subsistence existence, they are recruits for various anti-American movements, including totalitarian and religious extremists.

Here in the United States, radical and neo-Marxist critics have hinted about capitalistic exploitation and a growing crisis between dominant and subordinate groups, white and colored people of the world, and the need for human liberation. Eventually, the capital-rich nations of the West will be challenged by "no-hopers"—people who have nothing to lose since life means very little in a society characterized by squalor and misery (for which they believe America is to blame because of the way capitalism exploits). This "no-hopers" concept partially explains why it is easy to recruit guerilla soldiers intent on battling American-sponsored dictatorships who are anticommunist and/or pro-American; it also explains why terrorists are easily recruited from poor rural villages and urban hellholes. In this connection, Iraq serves as a good example; it only breeds more terrorists and insurgents bent on destroying our way of life—not much different than Rome, when it began to engage in military overreach. Of course, we would like to believe we are promoting democracy in Iraq.[30]

The old elite, the wealthy in third-world countries, live a life walled off from the masses who are poor and who have migrated from rural shanty towns to urban squalor, where children die from starvation and disease, a world ripe with catastrophe that has lost much of its meaning to wealthy nations. By 2015, more than fifty cities in developing countries will have populations of 5 to 10 million in which the poor have no land, no business, no machines, no tangible assets to create wealth—only the labor or sweat on their backs to offer, presently at a minimum wage for twelve to fourteen hours of work per day.

It is these places, the rotting cities or urban garbage heaps of the world, where a new proletariat is being created—one in which the present governments are unable to provide basic necessities. While some of these governments have been celebrated in the West and in the United States as pro-American or "democratic," this new and growing proletariat sees their governments as corrupt, elected by ballot-rigging or overrun by military coups, and supported by U.S. dollars, which get diverted to the pockets of the politicians and military at the expense of the inhabitants. The paradox is that, as government authority is weakened or overthrown, the people of the third world are being organized by regional, guerilla, or religious parties at the expense of national, progressive, or secular ones.[31]

The governments in power must contend with, and in some cases to survive work with and actually parrot, extreme religious and left-wing political ideologies. In the meantime, the third-world proletariat grows larger—fostered by increasing poverty, illiteracy, and birthrates; and it is being fueled by anti-American and anti-Western sentiments which are easy to induce because of the growing gap between the rich and poor in the world, between the West and the third world, between modern-day rationalism and medieval irrationalism. For the greater part, the third-world cities are severely dysfunctional places, consisting of crumbling infrastructure, urban decay, drugs, and disease—and getting worse. It is happening slowly enough to avoid public sensitivity and sudden catastrophe, but it is happening in front of our eyes. Anyone who wishes to deal with a dose of reality can read about it in the *New York Times*, the UNESCO reports, sometimes in *Time* or *Newsweek*, or see it live on CNN and Fox news. You are not going to read about it in school textbooks, and very few teachers seem to have interest or time to discuss these problems in class for more than two or three days—simply because the curriculum doesn't allow time for it.

According to the sociologist Hernando de Soto, Marx was right in claiming that capitalism strips workers of their assets, except their labor. They are unable to accumulate capital legally because they don't own property or other tangible assets, such as businesses that create capital and permit people to accumulate wealth. So the market is restricted, mobility is inhibited, and wealth is limited to those who control the property and other tangible assets.[32] The only way for the poor in these countries to accumulate money is to deal in drugs, arms, sex trafficking, or some other black-market product or become a corrupt government bureaucrat and provide some service for a fee.

It staggers the imagination of the American mind, but from Chad to Cambodia, and from Uruguay to Uganda, the situation is similar for the world's poor. Democracy and free trade, the globalization of the world, means, in blunt terms, the West is dominating third-world countries. The reason is that there is no legal avenue for the poor population in third-world countries to acquire assets (or education) and break from their misery and squalor on a scale sufficiently large to reverse worldwide growing poverty. Government officials in these countries are rarely held accountable; the powerful few—landowners, top military echelons, and drug lords—continue to plunder the country and keep the poor in "chains," a metaphor described by Marx and Lenin and subscribed to by today's neo-Marxist commentators. Modern-day smugglers and traffickers fleece and menace governments by trading military equipment, engaging in sex trade, and smuggling heroin or weapons of mass destruction. In short, world corruption and criminal behavior are rampant among the powerful and not so powerful within most developing and undeveloped countries. Greed is not an American invention, but is rather part of the human condition. Adam Smith's theories of profit were read by more than Americans and our English cousins, and a lot more people around the world saw Michael Douglas's movie *Wall Street*, which glorified money and materialism.

But all people want to eat and have a roof over their heads. You need only to visit a third-world country as a tourist and see the entrepreneurial culture. Taxicab drivers are hustling you; vendors are trying to sell you their goods in streets and flea markets, even behind garage doors; women are selling their bodies; and old people and children are begging. Everyone is trying to make a dollar, to keep alive. The vast majority are not trying to rob or fleece the tourist. The people are not lawless, nor are they demonstrating; they are working.

Educators claim that the key to alleviating poverty is through education; sociologists claim that the key is to limit population growth; and business people claim that the key is industry, technology, and free trade. Neo-Marxists (including de Soto) have a different spin, and it has some historical validity to it. They would like to redistribute the property, factories, businesses, and machines to the poor so they can accumulate capital—in short, so they can buy into the capitalistic system, instead of relying only on their labor, which amounts to continuous exploitation. The validity to the argument is that, in the Western world, this is how Australia and Canada were settled. People searched out and were able to acquire land for free by squatting on and settling it. The American government permitted its immigrants to acquire large tracts of farmland for free or for a few dollars, and the English nobility sold ninety-nine-year leases for low rent on many rural estates to the "common folk."

As the third world continues to grow in population, the West, and especially the United States, will become the target for global hostilities. There are too many people wasting away, severely deprived, running from dying villages to cities that don't function and cannot serve their needs. Guerilla warfare, civil strife, and terrorism will become increasingly more commonplace, driven by people who have nothing to offer but the sweat on their backs and little to lose except for a life that has little meaning in a world governed by corruption, famine, drought, and war. There is almost nothing for the world poor to grab on to, to hope for, except some totalitarian or religious idea that provides some kind of promise of a better world or better hereafter. To be sure, the United States cannot police the world, nor does the United States have any fiduciary duty to economically support it. In short, there is no easy answer to this growing tide of world discontent, which is continuously boiling. Similarly, the United Nations lacks the status, flexibility, and powers to serve as a moral authority or react to military challenges. Even worse, their own audits point to mismanagement and fraud in their global operations.

POSTMODERN REALITY

What do we tell American students so they wake up to world reality? How do we explain all the anti-American sentiments seen on cable television? How do our future citizens learn to deal with world anger, millions and billions of people driven by poverty, famine, and backbreaking labor? Even in boomtowns, the poor vent their anger at the West, and it becomes increasingly obvious in the media. Textbooks in American schools are currently censored and sanitized—and rarely reflect the political and economic realities of the world. Given different interpretations of that world, and that historical facts are little more than biases of the political Left or Right, how and what should American teachers do to prepare their students for globalization?

The ice cap is melting, the air we breathe is polluted, our energy resources are being depleted, drinking water is in short supply, sexual slavery and AIDS are a fact of life, the worldwide landscape has been continuously plundered, and third-world big business people and politicians are often corrupt and drain off resources from their nations. Ask yourself how U.S. textbooks and teachers sanitize these issues, or the way they interpret "facts," and then ask what makes for a sound education. How do we prepare the next generation of Americans for what they will inherit? Indeed, the third world is growing in population and surrounding us! We are no longer able to live in a vacuum or on an island; 9/11 shattered our protective layer.

Some of us are buying new cars and larger houses, and others are visiting shopping malls and purchasing the latest cell phones, iPods, and computers. But the apple cart is bound to be turned over by the growing imbalance of world economic scales. We have rogue nations that possess "the bomb" and others that have access to biological and chemical weapons. If you cannot recall the movie *On the Beach* or the television program *The Day After* because of your age, there is always Three-Mile Island and Chernobyl (which is less than twenty years old) to remind you of a serious meltdown and the effects on air, food, and water supply. Global weather patterns know no national boundaries, and concentrated radiation or viruses can affect human populations at home or thousands of miles away.

Given today's era of computers and satellite communication systems, nuclear plants, and a high-tech infrastructure, it is almost impossible to speculate the damage and ripple effect of a major terrorist attack on fragile utility and high-tech sites. Most Americans are unable to imagine the World Trade Center loss in dollars and jobs, its effect on the national economy—somewhere between $250 to $500 billion. In the meantime, the U.S. government is preparing for a potential smallpox or virus attack, and inoculating 500,000 health and medical personnel—the front-line soldiers of this possible war and terrorism. The government is also laying the groundwork to mass-vaccinate the public, a policy abandoned thirty years ago.[33] The problem is, however, no government can prepare its populace for all potential terrorist plots.

The "Population Bomb"

Now for the "population bomb." Paul and Anne Ehrlich several years ago did an excellent job describing and projecting global disaster; the world ecosystem is in jeopardy and is having difficulty supporting the growing world population.[34] The point is that a parade of grim environmental realities makes for a long list, with the loss of large portions of vegetation, top soil, natural resources, and animal life (*Homo sapiens* included) as a real possibility in the twenty-first century. If these threats are acknowledged as real, no educational system hoping to prepare students for the world of tomorrow can ignore the environment (and population explosion) as an important subject.

The good news is that the third world understands that the environment is globally connected; the bad news is that the United States is considered the worst culprit, the biggest user of world resources, warming the Earth with carbons. It refuses to ratify the Kyoto climate change treaty in which 162 nations have agreed to reduce emissions. President Bush's argument is that Kyoto "would wreck our economy . . . and put a lot of [American] people out of work."[35] (In the meantime, a world wildlife leaflet on my desk tells me the United States releases approximately forty thousand pounds of carbon dioxide per person annually; time to turn off the air-conditioner [which releases carbon emissions], open the windows, and breathe the "fresh" air!)

Put in terms of the richest nation vis-à-vis the rest of the world, the United States releases twenty tons per person whereas China and India release less than five tons per person. The problem, however, is that China is growing at a 9 to 10 percent clip and is the world's largest market for many products. India is growing at 7 to 8 percent.[36] Their combined population is over 2.5 billion people, and with their growth comes more power and chemical plants, metals and mining, cars and refrigerants—increasing carbon emissions, elimination of the protective ozone layer, and destructive climate changes. Unless new and improved fossil-emission policies are quickly introduced, projections are that China's emissions by 2030 will surpass the entire industrialized world's, and India's emissions will rise more than 70 percent of the current amount.[37] Beijing and New Delhi are willing to discuss lower targets, but they feel Washington, D.C. must cooperate and even foot some of the bill because the United States is the major culprit and our economy has benefited the most by carbon emissions.

We already feel the pain—hotter summers, more frequent and intense storms, and warmer winters. Weather-related insured losses have already cost the U.S. insurance industry $70 billion extra from 2003 to 2005. The earth has been warming since the turn of the twentieth century, but the rate of warming has risen three times the average since 1970; seas have risen seven inches globally over the last 105 years, and the rate of increase has risen 25 percent faster in the last ten years. Climate models estimate that by 2100 Greenland's ice sheet will have melted and Lower Manhattan will be under water.[38] Several greenhouse scientists have alerted the nation to the pending crisis, but conservatives have successfully linked *green* with liberalism, antibusiness, and antipatriotism. As many of the catastrophic events do not happen for one hundred years, it is hard to persuade American voters to take action and the American people to change habits.

With a paralyzing view of the world, Americans want to do very little in changing their lifestyle and habits to keep the environment safe from ruin. So it may be argued that some rogue nation or individual nut may bring us to the brink of catastrophe, but the United States may bring the world to a slow death. I guess that, so long as you recycle your plastic containers, you get a good feeling and believe you are doing your job for humankind—a typical American rationalization. We can also hope that Captain Kirk will beam us up to a new world—with all our molecules and information in place to start over.

As Captain Kirk is an American invention, we can stretch our imagination and claim the universe will be saved by American ingenuity and know-how. Of course, this opinion is laughable, even farcical, but some of us might claim there is an element of truth: Nuclear energy or the computer will save us. Now this view should not be totally dismissed, as some of us understand quantum physics and quantum computers and, therefore, believe that the universe is manifested in Newtonian mechanics and that energy (kinetic and potential) can be conserved, modified, increased, and transported.[39] The "big bang" theory, Albert Einstein's theory of relativity, Wernher von Braun's work that got Americans to the moon, and "the bomb" are all based on Newtonian principles—as are the computers we use at home, in school, and at work. If you believe in postmodern philosophy, if you are anti-American or anti-Western, or if you are predisposed to techno-exuberance or alternative realities, then you cannot get on board and beam up, because that would be the triumph of science, traditional research, and Western thought.

Ah, some good news to offset the doom and gloom about global warming. Recent population estimates show a decline in birthrates in many nations where poverty and illiteracy are still widespread. This trend appears to be linked to recent educational opportunities of women, the growing awareness of women as to how to gain control of their bodies, and the increased impact of world health organizations, along with women's rights. Many third-world countries are no longer crippled as much by traditional culture and religious doctrine that encourages large families; women from these parts of the globe are beginning to engage in contraceptive and other birth control methods, including the pill, as they gain information from international organizations and satellite television.

In places like Brazil, Egypt, India, and Nigeria, some of the world's most populated developing nations, there has been recent decline in birthrates and revised projections indicate the world's population may tip from 12 billion to below 10 billion by the end of this century. In India alone, by 2010 there is now projected 600 million fewer people than predicted prior to 2000; the fertility rate is now 2.1 which is considered the conventional replacement rate. In Brazil, the fertility rate has dropped from 6.15 in 1950 to 2.27 in 2000;[40] predictions are that the rate will drop to 2.1 within the next ten to fifteen years. In China, government policy still encourages one child per family. But where strong traditional and religious beliefs still prevail, especially in many poor Moslem countries, there is very little hope for population decline or any form of female equality.

Women in one village making a decision to have one or two fewer children is a small factor by itself. Compounded by millions of women, it has significant global implications. Just as women in most parts of the world are pushing for more education and greater rights (the two trends are interrelated), it seems they are becoming more assertive about family planning. There is one single catalyst among all factors. Education is the key—leading to the transformation of a worldwide female population from illiteracy to literacy—and is affecting the thinking and actions of women.

Inequality and Third-World Women

Throughout the world and throughout history, women have been marginalized by society—mainly as a result of cultural and religious traditions that dehumanize them into third-class citizens (or objects)—deprived of education, health, and equal rights in the workplace, church, and marriage. Where there is extreme poverty, lack of education and opportunity, and ultraconservative religious influence, women are often indiscriminately beaten and abused. The war against women is intense. In some Muslim countries, a woman cannot prove that she was raped unless four men testify on her behalf. In India, thousands of wives annually are murdered, maimed, or set ablaze because of the size of their dowries or simple disputes. In what was once Yugoslavia and now Africa, women have been purposely raped as part of warfare tactics. More than 130 million women have been victimized by genital mutilation. And the record goes on and on.[41] Only in the Western world, which accounts for about one-fifth of the world population, do they get a fair shake, at least protected by secular and democratic laws.

In a world where women are held hostage in many third-world countries, there is little chance to speak about peace or prosperity for women. There is need to break the silence—of both shame and blame—and to give women equal rights. Only when women move forward toward equality will the third-world, particularly the Muslim world, increase modernization and the democratic order. One social commentator points to a statistical model of Egypt indicating that, if mothers with no education had at least completed elementary school, poverty would have been reduced by one-third. The U.N. has produced similar findings in other third-world countries where women's education is severely restricted because of tradition or religion.[42]

When women's equality increases a number of trends are evidenced: The moderate political voice is strengthened, poverty is reduced and the middle class expands, the potential for war is reduced, birth rates fall, and the education of children is enhanced. Subsequently, there is political and economic stability and modernization. In contrast, where religious extremism surfaces, as in Afghanistan, Algeria, Bangladesh, Iran, Lebanon, and Palestine, moderate governments frequently fall and economic instability increases. In such places, as well as in northern India, where tribalism and religious custom prevail, "sexual terror [is] waged against its female citizens," in gang rapes over family disputes and the "belief that a raped woman's best recourse is to kill herself" because she is deemed impure. "It doesn't matter," according to Muslim law, if the "act was consensual or forced."[43] Just as Americans often seek the politically correct voice and refrain from criticizing moderate Muslims for remaining neutral or blind to oppressive Muslim customs, the moderate Muslim voice has not dared to challenge the power of the fundamentalist Islamist clergy.

Where a backlash against women surfaces, often uneducated, unemployed, or working-class men seize the public forum and abuse women; in some countries (in northern Africa) they "herd" women, and in other places (in the former Soviet republics, Eastern Europe, and parts of Latin America and Asia) they force them into prostitution.[44] Secular and religious laws can be used for all purposes, both good and evil, so legal or religious scripture cannot be counted on to protect women. Under the guise of natural and divine law, people of many nations have viewed the abuse of and violence toward women as a recreational activity, encouraged the rape of women as an instrument of war, as well as in tribal or personal disputes, conducted medical and biological experiments to advance their "scientific" theories, circumcised them to ensure their chastity and docility, and burned them at the stake as witches.

In militia, rebel, and refugee camps around the world, from Bosnia and Kosovo to Rwanda and Darfur, very little attention is paid to the rights of women in these camps, where they are almost always susceptible to abuse. The horse-riding outlaws known as *janaweed* have been ravaging the countryside and raping women before Rwanda and Darfur caught the attention of the Western media; rape, sexual slavery, and forced prostitution, and the "herding" of women (as if they were cattle), have been used as an instrument of war for thousands of years with thousands of different armies. The problem today is that there are too few women making foreign policy and prosecuting criminals, and, when there is the opportunity, few push for international reform, for laws with teeth, and for more attention to gender balance on war tribunals and in federal or national prosecutors' offices. The women's movements that exist in third-world countries are underfunded and given little political support from government (or religious) authorities.

Given the history of rape and violence toward women living around the world, should abused women today have special asylum claims in the United States? We profess to be a nation in which those who have been persecuted in their own country can be guaranteed a new home. But the issue of U.S. asylum for women highlights the issue of violence and abuse that has been inflicted on women throughout the world since the dawn of civilization.

In totalitarian regimes, as in times of war, women are the object of prey for the state militia and roaming armies. In times of peace, there is abuse and sexual assault on women as a matter of custom, "a systematic form of persecution by those that make life unlivable for members of a hated religion or political movement."[45] In simple terms, there is a relationship between the "weak" and "strong," as there is between poor and rich, throughout this world. In both cases, our sense of morality fails to grasp the issues involved, and we tend to focus on issues of race, ethnicity, religion, and membership of a political group when we deal with questions of immigration and asylum.

And, now, almost all of us talk about gender politics. But for all the Marias and Rosas I know from Guatemala, Haiti, and Colombia who have been in the United States for the last five or six years, seeking a safe haven from countries in which being a female is reason for second-class status, even abuse and torture, I raise the question why their appeals to become American citizens have been delayed. My female counterparts at universities, and the female teachers I have taught, don't seem too concerned about the Marias or Rosas who are seeking asylum. Their gender politics deal with textbook bias, math-science achievement scores, career opportunities, equal pay for equal work, child-care reform, abortion, and divorce. Their silence about women seeking asylum from sexual abuse and torture provides tacit approval of female persecution in the third world and parts of Eastern Europe.

There are other factors to consider with respect to female inequality and antifemale policies: poverty, illiteracy, corrupt governments, and the threat and dislocation of modernism. If democracy and education are to gain a stronghold in the Muslim world, and in other third-world countries, the role of women will become crucial. Although not all women are moderates or progressives (some choose traditional attire for religious reasons, some are steeped in Islamic fundamentalism and anti-Western sloganism, and some are candidates for terrorist missions), as a group they represent the symbols of change and modernization. However, as long as there is a struggle against the infidel, or against Western democracy and modernization, women will choose or be forced to forestall their own basic rights and freedom; traditional, religious, and nationalistic rhetoric will prevail.

Americans have a major stake in the struggle being fought over the minds and hearts of Islamic women and between the moderates and extremists of the Islamic world. With all the foreign aid and support we have given to Arab and Muslim countries, we find that we are misunderstood, perceived as a "big bully" and envied because of our prosperity and way of life. Similarly, it is not so easy to understand, according to Thomas Friedman, who, in the Muslim world, is moderate and extremist. "Failure to make this distinction jeopardizes our future relations with the Arab and Moslem world."[46] Part of the problem is that what few Muslims say in private, they refuse to say in public. They are victims of their own beliefs, religious teachings, as well as tribal and national customs.

Given this tragic history of rape and abuse, and lack of education and opportunities among women of the world, feminist literature can be interpreted as a huge scream against thousands of years of women wallowing and drowning in sorrow. How do we make the leap to the other side of the world—from bondage to freedom, from being ignored or wrongly perceived by most people to being given new worth and expression to neglected female virtues? Forget the great glamorous women—Ruth Bader Ginsburg and Madeleine Albright; Germaine Greer and Susan Sontag; Barbara Walters and Oprah Winfrey; or my favorite, Gloria Steinem— the symbols of female aspirations, rule breakers, icons, and legends. The idea is to break the chains of *all* women—of all races, religions, and nationalities—especially third-world women. To some extent, it means turning the world upside-down. It's a long road from an idea to reality, from traditional social callousness to modern ethics and just laws that protect sisterhood.

Only in a society, where men do not feel threatened, and where there is a strong belief in human rights, can women gain full freedom, full protection from discrimination and abuse, and full opportunity to achieve their human potential. I think Locke and Rousseau understood it by advocating that education be in accord with nature, and in their belief in natural law, which no human or divine authority could subvert. Henrik Ibsen wrote about it in *The Doll House* and *The Master Builder*, at a time when few people understood it; Babe Didrikson lived it on the playing field with her athletic prowess; and Eleanor Roosevelt tried to implement it on a worldwide stage as part of the preamble to the United Nation's charter. But Ibsen is not read in the third world, Didrikson is not known, and Roosevelt represents another era and another world for people outside the Western world.

It may be a man's world in the third world, but it is up to women to break the monopoly of men in the political, economic, and religious sectors. Most Muslims are moderate, lean toward some form of democracy and modernization, and accept the notion of education for women. Given the global village we live in—with the computer, cell phone, and satellite system—Western women need to assert, communicate with, and organize third-world women. There is a role for the United Nations and humanitarian organizations to play, and there is a role for American and other Western female educators and social activists to play, particularly at a professional association level and on the Internet highway. Some men are certainly willing and capable of helping, but what is really needed is an international Gloria Steinem to start a worldwide and peaceful female revolution. It is potentially a more powerful revolution—on a political, economic, and moral scale—than dreamed by Marx, Lenin, Che, or Mao, as it may reduce poverty, illiteracy, and the potential for war, increase democracy, modernization, and stability, and save the world from its own population time bomb.

Energy, Earth, and the Economy

By mid-2006, the price of crude oil settled above $75 a barrel, double the amount it was two years prior, and prices at U.S. gasoline pumps for premium topped $3.50 per gallon. Six months later crude oil and the pump price of gasoline had dropped one-third in price. Concerns over a possible Arab oil embargo involving Iran (which produces 10 percent of the world's oil supply) as a "weapon" against the West, as well as political disruptions and resource nationalism from other oil-producing countries, seem justified. The only question is when it will happen. In addition, OPEC members claim they are helpless in containing costs because of continuous worldwide demand for oil, especially from the West, China, and Japan; there is little extra oil to put on the market to soften prices.

Given the fact that the vast majority of oil-producing nations comprise a host of present or former "have not" countries, many with traditional resentment toward, and bad history with, the rich nations of the world, especially the West, it is feasible despite pipeline dips in 2006 to expect oil to reach $100 to $125 a barrel and gasoline prices at the U.S. pump to soar to $5 per gallon in a few years, which is still less than today's European prices. Of course, with declining prices of oil and gasoline, it is hard to get Americans to think about the worst-case scenario.

For the last thirty-five years, since the first oil embargo in 1973, there has been a constant struggle between oil-rich nations that consider the oil fields their property and the major oil companies that paid for the rights to the oil. The dominant role of the companies, nearly all from the United States, Britain, France, and the Netherlands, has been slowly eroding with the rise of resource nationalism from these non-Western countries. The age of colonialism has ceased, and the five countries from the Middle East that hold 60 percent of the world's oil supply have been growing increasingly unreliable and have served as potential staging grounds for terrorist activities against the West. Moreover, family ties and old clan and tribal allegiances intermingle with politics and business, adding to international instability and growing inequality between privileged groups that control the oil and the rest of the populace, which potentially threaten these countries' agreements with Western oil companies. Fuel prices cannot be contained or stabilized, short and simple. The escalating prices for oil are bound to impact U.S. inflation and its gross domestic product, as well as world economies. Higher energy prices are equivalent to a payment or debt; likewise, lower prices produce the effect of a pay increase or profit. Of course, there is little indication that policymakers can control the price of oil.

Uncontrollable energy prices have prompted U.S. companies to look for substitutes such as (safe) nuclear energy and coal, corn, sugar, wood-chip, and grass-related fuels, as well as alternatives related to wind, sun, water, and hydrogen. Coal seems to be the first alternative choice, or at least the most accessible, because of its immediate abundance. According to the World Energy Council, in 2004 the United States had 254 billion tons of coal in reserve and China had 115 billion tons, enough reserves to last through the twenty-first century.[47] The problem is, however, that fossil fuel (which includes coal) adds to global warming, toxic waste, and air pollution. Right now we are in a state of denial about how serious the problem is because of our dependence on oil and other fossil fuels that U.S. industries and corporate America depend on.

Even worse, energy and global warming problems are fueled by the geopolitics of rich versus poor nations, the West versus the non-West, as it is the wealthier and industrialized nations causing most of the greenhouse gases related to energy consumption and it is the developing and non-Western nations with oil-producing capacities. The people emitting greenhouse gases live in the rich nations of the West and Japan and in latitude zones that have moderate temperatures. But the effects of global warming will be felt the hardest at the North and South poles and by the majority of the poorer countries located nearer the equator where the temperatures are warmer. Moreover, the undeveloped and poorer countries do not have the resources to adapt to global warming caused by the developed and rich countries. Costal communities are threatened the most; in fact, thirteen of the seventeen largest cities of the world are coastal cities, totaling more than 100 million people, two-thirds of which are in poor countries.

To further compound the problem, we are in a war with the radical strain of Islam that is indirectly financed by oil revenues and our own consumption of oil. Every time we fill up at the gas pump, we are indirectly financing political terrorism on ourselves. We have become our own worst enemy. If we don't move away from our dependence on oil and shift to other energy sources, we are sealing our own demise. Moreover, as third-world countries attempt to move from undeveloped to developing status and developing countries move to industrial status, the people of the world will buy more cars and appliances and burn more fossil fuels, adding to global warming and the melting of the Artic and Antarctic polar areas. Moving beyond China and India, there are some thirty developing countries such as Brazil, Indonesia, and South Korea whose economies are growing annually at rates between 3 to 8 percent, and ten which grew twice as fast as the U.S. economy in 2006.

The critical issue is what can Americans do to satisfy their fuel needs, and to reduce our dependence on Middle-Eastern oil. Ironically, Brazil, which is a second-tier industrial nation, is energy sufficient, meeting its demand for fuel, through innovative methods of producing ethanol. It relies on sugarcane and stalks or forms of grass, not corn which is emphasized in the United States as a potential energy source. For thirty years, Brazil has poured research and development efforts into producing ethanol energy for its automobiles while the United States—the world's auto industrial hub—has lagged behind, producing bigger and more inefficient cars and burning more fossil fuel. Part of the problem has to do with the auto industry's indifference and lack of direction from the government, but one must also wonder what the role of the U.S. petroleum lobby has had on slowing down substitute fuels.

About 70 percent of the automobiles sold in Brazil, more than 1 million per year, have "flex-fuel" engines, designed to run on sugarcane-based ethanol, gasoline, or a mixture of alcohol and gasoline. For the same dollar invested, sugarcane ethanol currently produces 6.5 times more energy than corn-based ethanol.[48] Sugar-derived ethanol is also far superior in emitting less greenhouse gas, and the cost of producing a unit of energy from sugar-derived ethanol is as cheap as producing the same unit of energy from gasoline when it was at $35 a barrel.[49] (I am sure the reader can figure out the cost benefits of sugar ethanol when oil tops $105 a barrel.) So here we have a not so rich, not so industrialized, nation ahead of the richest, most industrialized nation in satisfying its fuel needs and reducing gas emissions. Ironically, the U.S. auto manufacturers have produced about 10 million "flex-fuel" cars out of about 240 million vehicles in use. And sadly, Ford has looked to Toyota for help in producing fuel-efficient cars. The issue here has little to do with innovative or entrepreneur ability, but rather government's role and motivation in resolving a national problem, and the freedom to do it without corporate pressure or interference from big oil and the auto industry.

Ideally what the rich nations and industrial world need to do is reduce their addiction to oil and learn to recycle industrial products to energy sources—to reuse what we make and return it back into the air, water, or soil as nontoxic nutrients that biodegrade safely. We must tax gas-guzzling vehicles, impose stiffer environmental regulations, and learn to recapture and reuse our energy output. In this way, the world's energy supply becomes limitless, while we also reduce or eliminate waste, pollution, and global warming. Wind energy is most promising (cheap and clean), but wind doesn't always blow when we need it. We need to learn how to store wind energy efficiently and use it when we need it most.

For the time being, we need to seriously consider a gasoline tax, say fifty cents per gallon in the United States, which could fund university-based research on fuel alternatives.[50] A fuel tax on inefficient automobiles, appliances, and heating/air conditioning equipment should also be considered by lawmakers. (See chapter 8.) Indirectly, the taxes serve as a means for reducing global warming and making us less dependent on foreign oil. While most Americans (85 percent) oppose a higher federal gasoline tax, they tend to favor a tax on gasoline that would reduce energy consumption and global warming (59 percent) and reduce dependence on foreign oil (55 percent).[51] Because increasing the gasoline tax is regressive, falling hardest on those who cannot afford it, it might be accompanied by a rebate or by lowering income-based taxes for low and average wage earners.

Going one step further on taxation, we might look at the top two hundred and fifty global energy companies conducting business in the United States, and tax their profits at the 1 or 2 percent level, as their revenues have dramatically increased in recent years partially at the expense of the American consumer. There are a host of foreign companies such as British Petroleum, Shell, and Citgo that are foreign-owned and earning huge profits (millions of dollars per week) in the U.S. market; that said, we should not overlook American companies such as ExxonMobil, ConocoPhillips, or Sunoco. Oil and gas companies only make up thirty-one of the top two hundred and fifty energy companies with average revenues of $62 billion and average profits of $5.3 billion in 2005.[52] We also need to look at the entire energy sector, including refineries and makers of chemicals and petroleum-based products such as asphalt, wax, and roofing material. We also need to look at all companies producing pollutants and global warming emissions and tax them for their dirty plants and engines—and push for global solutions, since we are a global village and breathe the same air.

ALL ROADS LEAD TO WASHINGTON, D.C.

Reversionary historians, or those with a strong Leftist bent have criticized traditional liberal scholars (such as David Halberstam and Arthur Schlesinger) and conservative scholars (such as Niall Ferguson and George Will) as being somewhat complacent and idealistic, taking the soft and safe road, describing the kinder and enlightened vision of America and not recognizing or discussing our brutal and predatory tendencies toward African Americans and American Indians, our imperialistic and colonial tendencies toward Latin America, and our mistreatment of immigrants, minorities, women, and gays.

Revisionary historians have also pointed out that wherever genocide occurred in the twentieth century, whether the victims were Armenians, Chinese, Jews, Cambodians, Croatians, Kurds, Tutsis, etc., the American government stood by and did nothing, despite their professed ideals, because it was not in their interests to intervene. These historians have also described the economic forces and gap in wealth between the rich, privileged, and capitalistic class over the common person, the less privileged, and the working class—a dichotomy that has existed since colonial America and has worsened over the centuries.

Going one step further, sort of a neo-Marxist interpretation, Boston University's Howard Zinn claims that the United States and former Soviet Union both devised their own political and economic methods for controlling their working and less privileged and poor populations, each with techniques that were idealized and distorted by their own "advocate" historians. Zinn, and other revisionary scholars, contend there is little consensus among historians today compared to the first half of the twentieth century, and many different interpretations now exist regarding how this nation is viewed both by its own scholars and by others across the oceans.[53]

We are at the juncture in time when the role of the United States, compared to any other civilization or country, has never been more dominant. A globalized perspective of the United States, based on Pax Americana, is the latest analysis of the changing interpretation of American history. As the road to idealism, purpose, and vision moves from Left to Right, the neoconservative narrative of the nation's history and global context have led to a growing militarism around the world, which includes the doctrine of preemption. No military power can challenge our global policy, cloaked in Wilsonian idealism if you believe in embarking on moral crusades, rooted in an empire more powerful than Rome or any other civilization if you are a realist.

This new level of "global consciousness" costs up to $450 to $500 billion a year in total military operations,[54] more than the rest of the entire world devotes to military spending, and is draining our economy. We are in perpetual war, and our bases and troops are stationed in nearly fifty countries.[55] We can move our planes and battleships all over the world through our political and economic alliances. Nothing like this has ever existed—such disparity in power and the ability for a nation to respond and mobilize to any far-reaching place in the world in a matter of hours in an emergency or days for a full campaign.

We were led into this new world order because the oceans no longer protect us, and we were led by a small group of "hawks" within the Bush administration, that is Dick Cheney, Donald Rumsfeld, and Paul Wolfowitz who originally worked together during the Reagan administration. They see the world through Henry Kissinger's perspective of world stability brought together by one superpower that is able to maintain international law and order. This coincides with the American belief that we are the moral and idealistic agent in world affairs, somewhat along Wilson's sentiments. (Ironically, Kissinger later claimed the war in Iraq was unwinnable.)

Actually, Richard Haass, the former president of the Council on Foreign Relations, claims that Kissinger's view of international order is rooted in the Congress of Vienna in 1815, after Napoleon was defeated, when the major powers of Europe carved up Europe. World stability, according to Haass, is largely determined when the mighty and powerful nations of any era can agree on the rules of order.[56] The G-8, the major industrialized countries of the world, is an attempt to deal with economic matters facing the world, but the international powers should include not only the United States, Western Europe, Russia, and Japan, but now also China and India.

Despite the fact that revisionary historians question this global view of America, this military perspective puts an economic burden on the American people, diverting resources that could be spent on health, education, and social programs. Most important, the United States cannot continue to "dis" its European partners, to do it alone, or create its own vision of the world by spreading democratic reform. Returning to Haass, America should simply keep out of the affairs of other countries, which sounds a little isolationist taken on its face, and it should not insist on any single democratic or capitalistic model. Democratic ideas that have worked on a nation-state level, or in the West, do not necessarily work on an international order. The history, culture, and people are different around the world. However, if you listen to more conservative advocates, such as George Will, the well-known journalist and Pulitzer Prize commentator, we are not exporting "Western" values but "universal" values, embraced by ordinary, God-fearing people, that "the masses of the world are ready for."[57]

Critics refer to the "hawks," along with Bush and his advisors such as Condoleeza Rice and Karl Rove as "chicken hawks," that is, people who never served in the military (or were consistently AWOL as in the case of Bush), and whose children have never served. These politicians see themselves as the Knights of the Round Table with the desire to refigure the world order. They determine war policy and send off poor, blue-collar, and working-class youngsters, along with minorities and recent immigrants, to fight the nation's wars (and to ensure that all roads will continue to lead to Washington, D.C.). There was a time, somewhat more idealistic and inspirational, during World War I and II, when sacrifices were expected from all social and economic groups.

If the wars in Iraq, Afghanistan, or anywhere else on the world stage are worth fighting—if it is a noble and patriotic venture, as the hawks and other conservatives claim—then it should be worth fighting with middle-class and upper-class blood. These soldiers should be added to their battle mix. All Americans of age, including youngsters born on second base and third base, should be serving the war effort, and not sitting on the sidelines moving money around on Wall Street or making an arms or oil deal that makes them more money at the expense of the less privileged. If it is not worth the lives and blood of all Americans, then we should be scaling down our Pax Americana policies and military efforts; we should be directing our energies to more peaceful endeavors where they would do the most good for the common people and public good.

Disagreement and Debate

Not every liberal or conservative critic speaks the same language. Neoconservative Pat Buchanan, in his book *America: A Republic, Not an Empire*, warns that America today has it backwards. We are not an empire, and we shouldn't act as one. Although the advantages of our military power is obvious, we still need our allies and friends in our Pax Americana view of the world. We must rely on international consensus and international organizations, not necessarily American might alone. We should have stayed out of Iraq; it was an unnecessary war—spreading us thin, exposing our limitations, and draining us economically.[58]

The American invasion of Iraq was supposed to be a quick military action, costing us very little in American lives and money, and winning us the gratitude of the international community—all of which, of course, is the opposite of what ensued. The war fused the *conservative* rationale, a matter of self-preservation and self-interest and the need to bring stability in a chaotic Middle-Eastern world, with a *liberal* slant, or a humanitarian argument to end tyranny and bring democracy to Iraq and then to spread it across the Middle East. The first argument reflected a realpolitik view of foreign policy and Hobbesian philosophy—a preemptive war based on the lessons of World War II and what the allies might have done to prevent the rise of Hitler and Nazism. The second position reflected Wilsonian idealism, making the world safe for democracy, and it was also formatted along Kantian principles of morality—or doing what is right. September 11 fused both arguments; more to the point, it bolstered the conservative view that Saddam Hussein was dangerous to the West because he must have had weapons of mass destruction or been in bed with Osama bin Laden, and it weakened liberal dissent by making criticism of the war seem anti-American and antipatriotic.

To Buchanan, however, not only did Bush and the conservatives both misjudge and botch the aftermath of the war, but the whole idea was based on a "pipe dream"—a form of "democratic imperialism," a silly belief that democratization and modernization would win the hearts and minds of the Moslem world, despite their belief in the Koran and its clash with reality. The conservatives or, more precisely, the "chicken hawks," believed the aftermath would be a "cakewalk"; the Iraq people would welcome the United States with flowers as liberators; the red-white-and-blue would be home in a few months and Iraq would govern itself. When things went wrong, the Bush administration and conservative commentators on television always found someone to blame; the *New York Times*, the ACLU, and Eastern liberals such as Dan Rather and John Kerry were prime targets. In the midst of defeat, Bush refused to give up his gun-slinging approach to diplomacy.

When Secretary of State Condoleezza Rice admitted to the administration making "tactical errors, thousands of them," in a 2006 statement in Liverpool, England, former Defense Secretary Rumsfeld quickly responded that she was "speaking figuratively, not literally." When initially six retired generals (and then a flood) publicly questioned Rumsfeld's invasion plans, postwar nonplans, and inadequate troop levels, as well as Cheney's "evidence" of a Saddam-Al Qaeda link and "evidence" of nuclear weapons,[59] Rumsfeld arrogantly responded on television, "Out of thousands and thousands of admirals and generals, if every time two or three people disagreed we changed the Secretary of Defense of the United States, it would be like a merry-go-round." When the president publicly admitted to errors in judgment, including but not limited to problems in training the Iraqi police and army, underestimating the strength and will of the insurgents, and abuse at Abu Ghraib, etc., one of his supporters responded: "My heroes have always been cowboys."[60]

Although the president and his advisors continued to emphasize that the overall purpose was sound and achievable, no one seemed to point out that their strategic plans might be flawed because the Bush administration consisted of a group of "chicken hawks," and the only experienced soldier in the administration, Colin Powell, was against the invasion of Iraq and subsequently resigned. None of these policymakers (except Powell) had ever been requested to execute a military mission or bury the results of a failed war plan. It took the Republican defeat in the 2006 Congressional election for Robert Gates, the former CIA director, to emerge from the Cold War shadows and move to the helm of the Pentagon, replacing Rumsfeld and signaling the restoration of a Bush I pragmatist.

It was our own ignorance and folly that led to defeat in Iraq, no matter how hard we try to dress up our exit strategy as "troop redeployment," "phased withdrawal," "troop surge," "military shift," and so forth. Not only did Bush and many members of Congress not know the difference between Shiites and Sunnis as he rushed pell-mell into war, but after the fall of Baghdad he refused to see the United States as occupiers, particularly Western occupiers in the Muslim world. As an imperial power, the United States has been humbled in Iraq by civil strife and by a network of insurgents and urban guerrilla fighters with minimal fire power. But we cannot simpy withdraw from Iraq, unless we wish to stir up the forces of hell in the Middle East.

What we must do now is seek a diplomatic solution, whether or not we like it or publicly admit it, including all the nations that border Iraq. In fact, if you are in the mood to face reality, Iran and Syria have more influence on what is happening today in Iraq than the 140,000 or 150,000 U.S. troops, a harsh fact for Bush II followers to accept. The problem with diplomacy is, of course, we don't know which government we are talking to—the moderates, extremists, or religious fundamentalists—or if they will be replaced or overthrown in the near future. A diplomatic solution four years ago would have been much better, given the fact that our razor edge today has been dulled and our enemies know that we are losing the war. The bottom line is the big and bold ideas of the neoconservatives, their conjured up geopolitical and military policies that negate common sense and common decency, have been much maligned. They are the same forces that stir within all powerful nations, although the slogans change as ideology changes, and they must be contained for the good of humanity.

David Fromkin's *Peace to End All Peace* best sums up why Iraq unraveled so quickly after the American invasion, and why it has cost so much in American lives, money, and international prestige. Besides the fact there was no real planning for Iraq governance or security, he emphasizes the religious, ethnic, and tribal differences of the country and cites an American missionary worker writing in 1920 to a British bureaucrat stumbling as an occupation administrator, somewhat like the way Paul Bremer did eighty years later. "You are flying in the face of four millenniums of history if you try to draw a line around Iraq and call it a country."[61] John Kerry in 2006 tried to make the same statement but fumbled when he tied Bush's education prowess, or lack thereof, to his inability to tell the difference between Sunnis and Shiites, the reason for the civil war in Iraq.

Edward Gibbon, Oswald Spengler, and Arnold J. Toynbee—European historians representing a three-hundred-year period—would have agreed with Buchanan and possibly with Fromkin, too. Having written extensively about military overreach, moral decline, economic drain, and political strife from within—in short, the downward spiral and fall of major empires, often much older than the United States—these historians certainly understood that no one imperial power can continue to run the world order. In fact, it can be argued that any single global order is exploitative and undemocratic for the countries that are not part of the super structure or on top of the order. These three historians saw eventual sadness and pathos in the growing isolation of empires mired in their own hubris and ideology. I don't see America that humbled or humiliated, for it is still the nation that most people around the world look to for hope and liberation. Still, it must face itself in the mirror and avoid the problems of imperialism that brought down Greece, Rome, and Old Europe.

The Class between Belief and Unbelief

The paradox is, however, that war has been declared on us by a radical form of Islam that is intent on destroying our way of life. Although there may not be the image of a mushroom cloud, as was the case in our fight with communism, Henry Kissinger's little ditty is worth repeating. "This [terrorism] is aimed at our existence." George Will is more explicit. "One maniac with a small vial of small pox spores can kill millions of Americans. . . . About 30,000 trucks cross our international borders" daily. It doesn't take a rocket scientist "to smuggle in a football-sized lump of highly enriched uranium sufficient to make a ten-kiloton nuclear weapon to make Manhattan uninhabitable for a hundred years."[62] Some of Will's prose may be construed as jingoism, but there is enough truth in the statements to get people's attention on 42nd Street and Broadway.

To be sure, the 9/11 strikes are vivid reminders that we are not dealing with people playing Scrabble or marbles and that our arsenal of military weapons cannot save our cities from terrorist attacks. Some critics claim there were plenty of warnings—Arab newspapers, U.S. intelligence briefs, CIA reports, and several incidents around the world in the last four decades, starting with the 1972 Olympics in Berlin. Still others might browse the library stacks and read the poets, playwrights, and journalists and recall the international tea-circles of spies and terrorists one hundred years ago in Europe, Russia, and the Ottoman Empire.

For example, there is Joseph Conrad's novels, *The Secret Agent* (1907) and *Under Western Eyes* (1911), which throw us into the psychic world of terrorists—people called conspirators, anarchists, extremists, and revolutionists. We meet terrorists strikingly similar to the ones we now face: educated, middle class, committed, and propelled by lofty delusions, people willing to use explosives and chemicals to achieve their objectives. Conrad's novels describe an underworld like the one we have inherited, where Eastern authoritarianism and religious fanaticism breed Eastern terrorism, where suicide bombers rant about the injustices of the West. Faith plunges the terrorist into ecstasy and paradise, into martyrism and heroism. One of Conrad's characters talks about this and asks, "Why should a man certain of immortality think of his life at all?" Here, then, is the preview of the enemy, his mystic world, driven by faith, ideology, and dogmatic baggage.

Some scholars who support a multicultural perspective, or see the world as a rose garden or feel they talk to Jesus Christ, fail to understand that a holy war for Muslims is a religious war and a religious war is difficult to stop or contain; it can go on for decades. To be sure, the history of religion takes the long perspective, amounting to centuries and going back to biblical times to support beliefs. Just as communism sought to bury the West, radical Islam is another form of aggression we are forced to contain. The war in Iraq feeds on American hostility and in turn fosters the notion of "the clash of civilizations." This hostility and these frustrations go back to the Crusades, the Spanish Inquisition (and the expulsion of Moslems and Jews), and the rise of European colonialism in the Middle East during the twentieth century.

The clash between infidels (the West) and jihads (holy warriors of Islam) is compounded by acute awareness that Americans have become, partially by design and partially by Old Europe's default, the sole defender (along with their "cousins" from Great Britain) of the West. People who lock themselves in false belief or false hope fail to grasp the new burden placed on the American people. The point is that, when you already feel left behind and already have an inferiority complex brought about by history, economic stagnation, and poverty, the slightest insult or perceived humiliation can produce anger and overreaction. I don't think it matters for many Moslems, whether they live in the suburbs of Paris or London, Kabul, or Karachi. When poverty and religious fanaticism mix in the local mosques or on the Internet it makes for a dangerous brew—personal rage, terrorist bombers willing to commit suicide, and holy causes and crusaders, all in the name of God or Allah.

You might also believe that Armageddon is coming, as most Bush supporters do,[63] bolstered by a rise of natural disasters such as earthquakes, tsunamis, and floods (including Katrina), pestilence such as AIDS, Asian flu, bird flu, and mad cow disease, and hunger and starvation signaled by crop failure due to climate changes and the warming of the earth. All these events are considered potent symbols of the end of the world, which is supposed to begin in the Middle East, the place where the Bible starts. If you are a true believer in religious ideology, then bin Laden is the agent of destruction, an anti-Christ figure, and Islamic terrorism is the intoxicating drug that the West must defend against in the twenty-first century, replacing Adolf Hitler and the twisted cross and Stalin and communist expansion in the twentieth century. For some readers, this may sound bizarre, almost as bizarre as a 2006 Associated Poll listing Bush as the number-one villain of the year, ranked even worse than bin Laden and Saddam Hussein.

Pretty scary! But if you are the kind of person who stumbles down the stairs in the morning, still slightly stoned, or if you enjoy psychedelic music and believe there are "ghost riders in the sky," then you should feel the hot breath, the sweat and mournful cries of those bastards (from the far-off East) as they die and go to hell. If you believe the Lord is on our side or there are some people without a soul, or if you are searching for a sign, some spirit or star ship, then you might believe the devil is descending upon us and we need to rid the world of him. Consequently, we need not to be wimpy moderns; rather, we are told by neoconservatives and extreme evangelists, we need to convert everyone to old-fashioned democratic beliefs laced with the meaning of religion. The problem is, not only are we going to become isolated from our allies with this kind of policy, we will also exhaust ourselves economically.

Who cannot say, with reason or certainty, why the walls are crumbling around us, why the oceans no longer protect us, and why the gods no longer seem to favor us. Your opinion is as good as mine; maybe you can speak like Sergeant Friday and cite the facts, nothing but the facts. And maybe there is someone from the far-off East, as well as God, who still loves us enough to forgive our blemishes and tell the world about our virtues. Maybe we can still live in a world of peace. Maybe the United States can make the world safe for democracy and even help third-world nations march toward democracy. I guess if you are a true believer or kind of person that sees the glass half full, then you still believe good guys always win and the likes of John Wayne and other cowboys will keep us safe and out of harm's way.

At the same time, we are unable to fathom why so many nations distrust or dislike the United States and why many of our old allies are unwilling to follow our lead in eradicating terrorism. Either our old allies and other democratic nations are ill-informed or afraid to act alongside America, asserts Stephen Walt, an international policy analyst at Harvard's Kennedy School.[64] Our allies seem to reject our arrogance and ignorance: 18 percent of the G-8 population claims they avoid U.S. brands such as McDonald's, Nike, and Coke.[65] The effects of globalization and mainly our do-it-alone international policies have led to an all-time low for favorable ratings of the United States in western Europe. Could it be that there is a conflict between American democratic principles and American foreign policy? Consider that other democratic nations, such as Britain, France, and the Netherlands, have been imperial powers and supersized colonizers of the less developed world. No wonder the meaning of globalization is often considered by critics to be a form of Western imperialism and colonialization.

Our own history books in school rarely mention our 115-year history of undermining and toppling dozens and dozens of governments, starting with the Hawaiian monarchy in 1893, and Cuba and the Philippines in 1898, and ending with present-day Iraq. Stephen Kinzer's *Overthrow* documents U.S. intervention around the world, especially in Latin America, Africa, Asia, and the former Ottoman Empire, under the guise of spreading democracy and freedom, words used by the Bush administration and almost every other administration in the twentieth century.[66] No wonder why the present U.S. intervention policy provokes worldwide anger, and why we have been called the "Big Bully," "The Great Satan," and the "Most Militarist Nation" of the world. Can Americans learn there is a difference between protecting democracy and promoting American interests, which usually boils down to big-business interests, or seeking control of the resources of undeveloped countries (sugar, rubber, oil, etc.)?

Then there is the possibility that clean drinking water may become the future resource for which people conspire and overthrow government leaders, to be replaced by puppets who are willing to play ball with fortune seekers and those who live a privileged life. The crises in the making has grown rapidly in the recent years, reflecting a soaring world population, sprawling cities, and a vast farm belt in third-world countries. All these demographic trends put strain on feeble and poorly maintained water supplies in nondeveloped and developing countries. At stake is the medical health of billions of people and the economic health of hundreds of poorer and developing nations in Latin America, the Middle East, Africa, and Asia. Conflict over clean water for drinking and water for farming is bound to become a fight between rich and poor nations, industrialized and nonindustrialized nations. With many governments unable to provide basic services to their people, the world will become very edgy; much of this new anger is expected to be directed at the "haves," especially the United States.

Could it be that the world just resents our imperial policies, resents a superpower or empire dictating the conditions of law and order to the world? It might also be that the world is not so neat and tidy, a world dominated by the *Superpower Myth* that "might makes right."[67] But that kind of policy moves the country off-kilter, away from its national purpose and national character, violating both its heart and soul and inspiring international resentment and subsequent vulnerability. Might makes right or any single answer to the world's multiple problems might make sense to the black-and-white idealism of Bush or others who feel that statecraft should supersede moral principle. But it makes little sense among those who envision a more complex and paradoxical world. For example, both Henry Kissinger, who served as Secretary of State under Nixon and Ford, and Zbigniew Brzezinski, who worked for Carter, believe the world is too complicated and cannot be interpreted by a single formula, one big idea or ideology.[68] We need a policy governed by moderation over Homeric glory, pragmatism over patriotism, strengthened alliances over stark, do-it-alone empire building.

We are in the midst of a war that will not end with the capture or death of bin Laden and his inner circle; it will only suit our sense of justice. Instead of draining our financial resources, and in turn lowering our standard of living, we would be better off taking a less smug posture and less militant policy and relying on regional alliances and offering economic benefits (which is less costly than fighting a protracted war). Right or wrong, since the towers fell, we cannot exit Iraq without dire consequences and we cannot rid the world of evil. Despite all our power—our planes, ships, and missiles—we have managed to show the world our limitations, as the number of jihadists pour into Iraq to fight the infidel (Americans). We stubbornly continue to fight a war based on our own distortions, obsessions, and Pax Americana view of the world order, and, thus, we divert our energies in waging a real war against the real enemy, which is terrorism.

To our surprise, also, we are learning that we are not all powerful; we are overstretched. We do not have unlimited resources; we are becoming financially drained. By whom? A group of religious zealots that control no state, no infrastructure, and no standing army, with no return address to respond or attack. To be sure, we are now in the first stages of a long war between Western *nations*, with traditional armies and infrastructure, and *networks*, with small units or cells and no infrastructure—only computers, propaganda, and weapons. The growing strength of networks will not only threaten our national security, but also hinder our economic growth because of military and antiterrorist spending, which leads to budget deficits.

NOTES

1. "New York City," Metro Channel, November 13, 2001.
2. Nathan Glazer and Daniel P. Moynihan, *Beyond the Melting Pot* (Cambridge, MA: MIT Press, 1963).
3. E. B. White, *Here Is New York* (New York: Little Bookroom, 1999), 14–15.
4. Roger Simon and Angie Cannon, "An Amazing Journey," *Newsweek*, August 26, 2001.
5. James O. Horton and Lois E. Horton, *Hard Road to Freedom* (New Brunswick, NJ: Rutgers University, 2001); David McCullough, *1776* (New York: Simon & Schuster, 2005).
6. Alan Taylor, *American Colonies* (New York: Viking Press, 2002).
7. Here I feel the presence of Yevgeni Yevuschenko, who saw himself and his ancestors "persecuted, spat on, and slandered" for centuries in Europe and wrote

about Belostock and Babi Yar (mass murderer and mass grave): "I'm every old man executed here, as I am every child murdered," he wrote.

8. Nathan Glazer, *We Are All Multiculturalists Now* (Cambridge, MA: Harvard University Press, 1997); Oscar Handlin, *The Newcomers* (Garden City, NY: Doubleday, 1959); Michael Novak; *The Unmeltable Ethnics*, rev. ed (New Brunswick, NJ: Transaction Publishers, 1996); Theodore Caplow, Louis Hicks, and Ben J. Wattenberg, *The First Measured Century: An Illustrated Guide to Trends in America, 1900–2000* (Washington, DC: AEI Press, 2000).

9. David E. Sanger, "In Leading Nations, A Population Bust?" *New York Times*, January 1, 2000, 8; Harold Hodgkinson, "The Demographics of Diversity," *Principal* (September 1998): 23–24.

10. Elisabeth Rosenthal, "European Union's Plunging Birthrates Spread Eastward," *New York Times*, September 4, 2006.

11. Ben J. Wattenberg, "Burying the Big Population Story," *International Herald Tribune*, May 18, 2001, 9.

12. Leslie Gaton, "Report on States," *New York Times*, February 2, 2001; Harold Hodgkinson, "Educational Demographics," *Educational Leadership* (January 2001): 6–11.

13. "Fastest Growing Countries," *New York Times*, January 1, 2000, 8.

14. Between 2000 and 2010, the Hispanic population should increase by 9 million compared to the black population increase of 3.9 million. See Hodgkinson, "The Demographics of Diversity."

15. Roger Cohen, "Cities: Audis and Cell Phones, Poverty and Fear," *New York Times*, January 1, 2000, 28; Wattenberg, "Burying the Big Population Story." If we add 80 million per year until 2025, the total approximates 8 billion people. Eighty percent of 8 billion is 6.4 billion; 75 percent is 6 billion.

16. Edmund L. Andrews and James Kanter, "Poor Nations Are Still Waiting," *New York Times*, July 4, 2006; Elizabeth Becker, "Poorer Countries Pull Out of Talks Over World Trade," *New York Times*, September 15, 2003; "The Rigged Game," *New York Times*, July 26, 2003; and Juliane von Reppert-Bismark, "How Trade barriers Keep Africans Adrift," *Wall Street Journal*, December 27, 2006. The G-8 nations, the most industrialized, are Canada, England, France, Germany, Italy, Japan, Russia, and the United States.

17. Keith Bradsher, "Ending Tariffs Is Only the Start," *New York Times*, February 28, 2006; John Zarocostas, "2007 Seen as a Potentially 'Defining Year," *New York Times*, December 27, 2006.

18. Jeffrey D. Sachs, *The End of Poverty: Economic Possibilities for Our Time* (New York: Penguin, 2005).

19. Moises Naim, *Illicit: How Smugglers, Traffickers, and Copycats Are Hijacking the Global Economy* (New York: Doubleday, 2006); Kenneth T. Walsh, et al., "Where Half the Money Is Off the Books," *U.S. News and World Report*, March 27, 2006.

20. Despite his crude slurs about women, gays, and minorities, and despite his fantasies that promote murder, rape, and incest, including a defense of the Columbine killers, and his overall offensive lyrics, Eminem has won numerous Grammy Awards from the Academy of Recording Arts and Sciences. Some people believe that a nation's greatness is measured not only by its economic and military

power but also by its artistic achievements, or what might be called the "quality" of its civilization. Put into report-card terms, I would rate American hard rock and metal music "A" for free expression and shocking the bourgeoisie, and "F" for its visual themes and portrayal of American life and values. I suspect a good number of younger folks and jet-setting swingers would argue that I'm merely part of the older Establishment and my views are humdrum and no longer relevant.

21. Allan C. Ornstein, *Teaching and Schooling in America: Pre and Post September 11* (Boston: Allyn and Bacon, 2005); Charles Passy, "War of the Worlds," *New York Times*, March 26, 2006.

22. Based on 1998 World Bank data; "Poverty and Globalization," Center for Global Studies Conference, St. Johns University, April 16, 2001; Allan C. Ornstein, "Curriculum Trends Revisited," in *Contemporary Issues in Curriculum*, 2nd ed., ed. A. C. Ornstein and L. Behar-Hornstein (Boston: Allyn and Bacon, 1999), 265–76; Virginia Postrel, "The Poverty Puzzle," *New York Times Book Review*, March 19, 2006. Also see Howard W. French, "Whistling Past the Global Graveyard," *New York Times*, July 14, 2002.

23. 1998 World Bank data; "Poverty and Globalization," Center for Global Studies Conference; Postrel, "The Poverty Puzzle"; French, "Whistling Past the Global Graveyard"; and Michael Wines, "Malnutrition Is Cheating Its Survivors, and Africa's Future," *New York Times*, December 28, 2006.

24. Gregory Clark, *A Farewell to Alms: A Brief Economic History of the World* (Princeton, NJ: Princeton University Press, 2007).

25. Stephanie Flanders, "In the Shadow of AIDS, A World of Other Problems," *New York Times*, June 24, 2001; Robert D. Kaplan, "A Nation's High Price for Success," *New York Times*, March 19, 2000, 15.

26. Caryl Phillips, *The Atlantic Sound* (New York: Alfred A. Knopf, 2000).

27. Michael Wines, "Africa Adds to Miserable Ranks of Child Workers," *New York Times*, August 24, 2006.

28. Rachel L. Swarns, "A Hint of the Coming Battle for Africa's Future," *New York Times*, July 14, 2002.

29. William Easterly, *The White Man's Burden* (New York: Penguin, 2005).

30. Todd S. Purdum, *A Time of Our Choosing: America's War in Iraq* (New York: Times Books, 2004).

31. See Stephen Graubard, *Command of Office* (New York: Basic, 2005).

32. Hernando de Soto, *The Mystery of Capital: Why Capitalism Triumphs in the West and Fails Everywhere Else* (New York: Basic, 2001).

33. William J. Broad, "U.S. to Vaccinate 500,000 Workers against Small Pox," *New York Times*, July 7, 2002.

34. Paul Ehrlich and Anne Ehrlich, *Extinction: The Causes and Consequences of the Disappearance of Species* (New York: Random House, 1981).

35. Stevenson and Cowell, "Bush Arrives at Summit, Ready to Stand Alone."

36. Peter Burrows and Marjeet Kripalani, "Cisco: Sold on India," *Business Week*, November 28, 2005, 50–51; Adam Aston and Burt Helm, "The Race against Climate Change," *Business Week*, December 12, 2005, 59–65.

37. Susan Jakes and Jodi Xu, "The Impact of Asia's Grants," *Time*, April 3, 2006, 61–62.

38. Nicholas D. Kristof, "Warm, Warmer, Warmest," *New York Times*, March 5, 2006; Andrew C. Revkin, "Yelling 'Fire' on a Hot Planet," *New York Times*, April 23, 2006.

39. Tom Siegfried, *The Bit and the Pendulum: From Quantum Computing to the M Theory—The New Physics of Information* (New York: Wiley, 2001).

40. Barbara Crossette, "Population Estimates Fall as Poor Women Assert Control," *New York Times*, March 10, 2002. Also see chapter 4.

41. Bob Herbert, " Punished for Being Female," *New York Times*, November 1, 2006.

42. Barbara Crossette, "Living in a World without Women," *New York Times*, November 4, 2001.

43. Salman Rushdie, "India and Pakistan Code of Dishonor," *New York Times*, July 10, 2005.

44. Although the exact numbers are sketchy, it is estimated that annually 2 to 3 million women are tricked or forced into the sex market against their will. Another 10 to 20 percent are abused by fathers or husbands; it is hard to agree on a percent because cases are underreported.

45. Anna Quindlen, "Torture Based on Sex Alone," *Newsweek*, September 10, 2001, 76

46. Thomas L. Friedman, "A Foul Wind," *New York Times*, March 10, 2002.

47. *Energy End Use Technologies for the 21st Century* (Washington, DC: World Energy Council, 2004).

48. Larry Rohter, "With Big Boost from Sugar Cane, Brazil Is Satisfying Its Fuel Needs," *New York Times*, April 10, 2006.

49. Norm Alster, "On the Ethanol Bandwagon," *New York Times*, March 26, 2006.

50. The World Energy Council, consisting of nearly one hundred countries, recommends that the United States should be investing about $4 billion per year on energy R&D, and forging new partnerships and incentives between government and industry. I would add a third partner, the university laboratory, which is the test-bed to the market.

51. "Americans on Gasoline Taxes," *New York Times/CBS News Poll*, February 28, 2006.

52. Platts Top 250 Global Company Rankings, March 20, 2006, www.top250 .platts.com.

53. Howard Zinn, *People's History of the United States*, rev. ed. (New York: Harper & Row, 1999).

54. "The Trillion-Dollar War," *New York Times*, August 20, 2005.

55. Emily Eakin, "All Roads Lead to D.C.," *New York Times*, March 31, 2002.

56. Richard N. Haass, *The Opportunity: America's Moment to Alter History's Course* (New York: Public Affairs, 2005).

57. George W. Will, "The Doctrine of Preemption," *Imprimis* (September 2005): 4.

58. Pat Buchanan, *America: A Republic, Not an Empire* (Washington, DC: Regnery, 1999).

59. The names are: Generals John Batiste, Paul Eaton, Gregory Newbold, John Riggs, Charles Swannack, and Anthony Zinni.

60. Thomas L. Friedman, "Condi and Rummy," *New York Times*, April 7, 2006; Jim Rutenberg, "Facing Tough Questions, Bush Defends War," *New York Times*, April 7, 2006.

61. David Fromkin, *A Peace to End All Peace* (New York: Henry Holt, 1989).

62. Will, "The Doctrine of Preemption," 2.

63. Approximately 77 percent of traditional evangelists and 53 percent of centralist evangelists, consisting of some 34 million people, believe the world will end in a battle at Armageddon between Jesus and the anti-Christ. See "Faith in America," *New York Times*, April 16, 2006.

64. Stephen M. Walt, *Taming American Power: The Global Response to U.S. Primacy* (New York: Norton, 2005).

65. William J. Holstein, "Erasing the Image of the Ugly American," *New York Times*, October 23, 2005.

66. Stephen Kinzer, *Overthrow: America's Century of Regime Change from Hawaii to Iraq* (New York: Henry Holt, 2006).

67. Nancy Solderberg, *The Superpower Myth* (Hoboken, NJ: John Wiley, 2005).

68. Zbigniew Brzezinski, *The Choice* (New York: Basic, 2004); Henry Kissinger, *Does America Need a Foreign Policy?* (New York: Simon & Schuster, 2001).

8

✣

Wishful Thinking: Recommendations and Solutions

B ooks and articles about almost every conceivable aspect of social and economic class have poured out by the hundreds over the last fifty years. It seems unlikely that major factual discoveries remain to be made, but as yet unsurmised summaries and solutions are becoming harder to distinguish. Obviously, another book about class must take off from available historical material and agreed-upon theories, but today the clash between a conservative's and liberal's methods for overcoming class differences (and related issues of mobility and opportunity, inequality and poverty, and social, health, and education programs) is dramatic, producing an utterly dysfunctional policy process.

What is an author to do? What solutions can he or she offer without being branded as on the Left or Right, and possibly dismissed as biased or slanted? Or is the author to merely state the facts and figures, like a statistician. But simply plucking high-end or low-end estimates to bolster an argument worries critics from both sides of the political aisle, as figures can be stretched and bent to fit a partisan perspective. A diligent author who is willing to steadily polish and revise his writings, and who sees all sides of an issue with uncanny impartiality, might in theory exist somewhere out in the countryside and reconcile opposing political and economic forces. But I don't think such a person is easy to find, much less exists today, that is, a person who can impartially argue both sides, given the fact that the debate over class differences (and related issues) in speeches, articles, reports, and books appears so one-sided, long on polemics, and hotly contested in the media and academia.

283

Most of us reading this book were "winners" in school. We learned to remember much and use it without prejudice, to examine both sides of an issue in our history and civics classes. In school, we exercised our memories and learned to appreciate the difference between facts and speculation, polite and critical writing. For me that was a lifetime ago, back in Arverne, a small town that no one probably knows but exists in my memory and on MapQuest. But there is something in my working-class background and sense of morality, where there should be no mystery as to where I stand with my recommendations and solutions. You don't have to be a wizard in philosophy or a super-duper psychologist to figure out my prejudices: to lift the average American's economic and social level, to enhance equality and equity, and to focus on people and not property. I guess you must also add I'm for taxing the top 10 percenters (of income and wealth), regulating markets, and cutting the toes off Wall Street hucksters.

In the spirit of egalitarian democratic faith, much of what I say here in this chapter, and elsewhere in the forefront of the book, is a cross between Jefferson's and Tocqueville's notion of democracy and John Galbraith's and Paul Krugman's economic and social ideas on how to improve the economy and society. But "swaddled" with an intention to be straightforward and honest, and to show that I still have a sense of wit and reality, I have started this last chapter, "oh dear," with the words "wishful thinking." Ah, what can I say? Somehow, the reader understands. On still another level, it's like asking the tooth fairy or genie for one or two wishes and being confident of the outcomes.

SWORD FIGHTING BETWEEN CONSERVATIVES AND LIBERALS

Conservatives in all political, social, economic, and education fields live in fear of being betrayed ideologically or branded as racist, mean-spirited, or some stooge of the military-corporate complex. They particularly distrust technocrats, experts, and educated elites with whom they are unfamiliar—including the press, academia, and Hollywood—and who they suspect will be seduced by the liberal establishment. To their credit, the conservatives made a leap and parachute drop from the Goldwater defeat in the mid-1960s, when they were branded as "cooks" and "crackpots," and landed on their feet. Over the years, especially since the Reagan era, they have assembled a host of activist judges and lawyers, television and radio commentators, magazine writers and think-tank thinkers—a mounting number of middle-brow second raters, according to liberal observers, whose chief virtue is they can be trusted to embrace the "party line." Regardless of whether you feel that conservatives are superficial or straight-and-narrow intellectuals, conservatives like to charge that liberals have no ideas and are "milquetoast" when it comes to defending the country.

On the other hand, liberals see those on the Right as lost in a "paleos" interpretation of history, that democracy can flourish in an unregulated market and in a world functioning according to Herbert Spencer's social and economic statistics. In such a world, Social Darwinism triumphs (the reason we are told why the United States strides as a colossal giant throughout the world) and the global economy is considered competitive enough to regulate itself. In this "brave new world," according to liberals, basic human rights and human dignity are at stake, especially among the lower 50 percent income bracket and even among the vast majority. The welfare state and various human services and social programs are up on the chopping block. The "rights revolution" and all entitlement programs are also at risk, especially those without obligations or duties, and other forms of government regulation are expected to be halted and reversed at the judicial and legislative levels.

Among conservatives "Reaganomics" became the guiding principles for policymakers. Despite growing debt, taxes are cut, especially among the richest members of society, with a few dollars thrown to the nonrich in order to appease them, and the buck (growing debt) is passed on to the next generation with the belief that entrepreneurship will stimulate the economy and the tax cuts will pay for themselves in terms of higher tax revenues. There is some truth to the logic that tax receipts do increase in a growing economy and thus reduce deficits, as they did in 2005. But the revenues were still far below what was predicted as recently as 2003 and far below historical norms (of revenues as a percentage of gross domestic product). The fact is that Reaganomics encourages more and more spending with the faulty logic that, with less taxation and more spending, everything will work itself out. It's nothing more than an empty promise, based on irrational mathematics. No one can really prove or disprove the theory, as we are projecting into the future and estimating a host of variables. Moreover, few people seem to care, because the burden is to be borne by the next generation. It should not come as a surprise that Bush II has latched on to Reagan's economics as a way to pay for the wars in Afghanistan and Iraq and for his Medicare benefits (to satisfy the baby boomer voters). It merely shows up as future government debt, figures that are shrugged off by average citizens who fail to grasp the size of the deficit and its future implications and obligations.

Seeking a Sane Policy

All of us—whether we believe in the Garden of Eden or not, whether we are sweet-tempered and modest or a little eccentric, or whether we consider ourselves conservative or liberal or just plain centrist—are skeptical about our nation's economic prospects. The great colossus is beginning to stumble, as the American people begin to recognize the economic mine-field onto which the nation is stepping. Competition with China and India, mounting trade deficits, the loss of manufacturing and subsequent loss of good paying jobs, the unstable price of fuel and its impact on the average American, the increasing cost of health care and college tuition, and the need to reform and fund Social Security, Medicare and Medicaid, and education are some of the policies that need to be worked out. If you have the stomach to think the unthinkable, then it is possible for the American standard of living to decline some 20 to 40 percent in the next twenty years![1]

Paradise seems lost in the United States. Something needs to be done; solutions need to be forged, but ideology splits Americans into warring camps and cultural warriors. Both liberal and conservative groups are burdened and bogged down by heavy dogmatic baggage, making it difficult to reconcile the warring camps. What makes matters worse is the new religious Right and faith-based movement in national politics, a most dramatic and unforeseen event that has become a potent force in the recent rise of conservatism and the crack in the wall between church and state. There used to be enough moderates, independents, and centrists to allow the system to work. The truth is that, in the United States, people are not as partisan as politicians, who get caught up on one side of the aisle and who we depend on to make policy.

Now history is a wonderful teacher, especially for skeptics who reconstruct skeletons to make a point or to one-up a rival critic, poet, or politician. There has been no limit to the spectrum of political discord, originally validated under the principles of free thought and free speech, beginning with the Jeffersonian forces squaring away at John Adams (the second U.S. president) and branding him in the nation's media outlets (then limited to pamphlets and newspapers) as an extremist, elitist, and pacifist and of dubious character. Under the tent of free speech and a free press, these were and still are nasty sentiments, especially for those who believe in the noble motives of "fairness" and "diversity of views." This short story is a reminder that Machiavellian principles have always prevailed in the political arena, even before Camelot, as the Greeks and Romans remind us. Although the reader may sense a touch of historical cynicism, one must be reminded that, at an earlier time in their lives, Jefferson and Adams were in the same political aisle as the principle authors of the Declaration of Independence and they were old (letter-writing) buddies in their declining years, much more "bud-like" than Clinton and Bush I appear to be.

I guess when it comes to political polemics, the line between truth and fiction, as well as political alliances and friendships, is not always easy to define. "A function of free speech . . . is to invite dispute," stated Justice William O. Douglas some fifty years ago, and "free speech, though not absolute, is . . . protected against censorship." But the supreme test of tact, especially in the twenty-first century with multiple media outlets and speedy web bloggers, is knowing what to include and what to exclude. There are not only sins of inclusion but also virtues of omission. Today, the current political debate is so intense, so lacking in discriminating or civil nuances, that the war between the pro-Right and pro-Left is worse than the *War of the Roses*, and for those who have tasted divorce there is not much worse than a marriage gone sour, full of emotional discontent.

Policymakers on both sides of the political aisle, today, are so openly hostile toward one another (like the Roses) that they don't even pretend otherwise. We cannot have a public dialogue on matters of policy without the major players appealing to their base of support and espousing partisan views. Not only is there minimal or no respect for diverse opinions but, even worse, we have stopped listening to one another. Moreover, the social and economic world is pretty intricate, full of paradoxes, competing interests, and pressure groups, and ideas like social justice, moral clarity, and equality and equity are subjective and provide little guidance for drawing bright ideas into messy reality. Just when we think we have the right formula or plan (i.e., to reform the tax code or improve health care and education) someone winks and blinks, challenges our assumptions or terms, and we got bogged down in the mechanics of actual governance.

The normal government policy assumes that a certain amount of politics enters into executive and legislative decisions, but it should not polarize the nation or allow ideology to determine policy. Since Nixon, and under the Reagan and Clinton administrations, government policies have become increasingly politicized, and it has become more apparent under the Bush administration. The vice president, cabinet members, and commission and agency executives appearing on television or reporting to Congress about important issues such as the war in Iraq and various other social and economic issues, have misrepresented data and misled the public—all in the name of party loyalty and ideology.

Instead of reporting data in an impartial and objective way, the information is shaped to coincide with specific policies and partisan views of the administration, to the extent that Bush's own appointees (Richard Clarke, counterterrorist chief; Paul O'Neill, Treasury Secretary; and Colin Powell, Secretary of State), once they left government "complained publicly . . . that the administration had repeatedly let politics trump sound policy analysis." Given the polarization between conservatives and liberals, the Bush administration and its appointees at all levels "see a lot of people as political enemies . . . trying to impede what they want to accomplish."²

The facts are rarely clean-cut, 100-percent proof, and, as long as there is some uncertainty or need for interpretation, ideology is going to play a major factor in how the information is presented to policymakers and the public. There is a point where many presidents skew the data (including Roosevelt, Kennedy, Johnson, and Reagan) or lie (Clinton and Bush II). Clinton's lies had something to do with morality and ethics, whether he had sex with a few women or whether he received favorable treatment in a business transaction as governor. Bush's lies involve the entire country and huge sacrifices and cost to the American people. The trouble is that Bush is so driven by conservative politics and faith-based initiatives he cannot understand how his policies have put ideology in favor of war and wealthy Americans at the expense of average Americans.

You don't need to be a British literacy expert with a predilection for gonzo prose to appreciate a spin of history—that since 9/11 there has been a revival of Orwell's *1984* and the notion of "disinformation" and "group think." You don't need to be a paperback genius or guru to explore the links of Bush's statements to V. S. Naipaul, the Nobel Laureate Indian novelist and author of *Half a Life*. When half the country feels that its political leaders are cherry-picking information, plotting, or lying, then it is hard to formulate prudent policy; everything must be filtered through a political and partisan view—not a healthy state for a democracy to function.

Some of us might say we are at the crossroads of democracy; political polarization and deliberate efforts to conceal information about the Iraq crusade and the economic health of the nation overshadow civil discussion and rational policymaking. As one Bush supporter put it, "I don't know if it's any one thing, as much as it is everything," helping to explain the downslide in Bush's popularity and trustworthiness ratings. There is a sense among Americans, including Bush proponents, that things have veered off course in America. A Harris poll released in late 2005 showed that 64 percent of Americans believed that the Bush administration "generally misled the American public on issues to achieve its own ends."³ (Of course, public opinion changes and one could question whether asking the American people how satisfied they are with the president's leadership or honesty has significance for anything real in the economy or in the world of military affairs or diplomacy.) As the 2006 congressional elections unfolded, the key issue was Iraq, to what extent the president had lied about nuclear weapons, and whether the United States should "stay the course." For liberals, the discussion went further: Does one country have the right to tell another sovereign country it cannot produce nuclear energy or build its military? Should the United States be hell-bent on spreading democracy in countries that are not ready for it, or whose traditions and local customs are antithetical to it? If only we could speak to the oracle for advice and comfort.

Extreme Views

It gets more messy and difficult to compromise and reach agreement on social and economic policies, or even to have a rational dialogue, when people of faith (some 85 percent of Americans are religious believers) move into "God's politics,"[4] and divide the world into "good" and "evil" or "us" and "them" (nonbelievers, wrong believers, and critics). As Europe grows more secular, socialist, and pacifist, America grows more religious, capitalist, and imperialist. Therefore, President Bush, the most overtly religious president in American history, a born-again Christian, pronounced to the world "you are either for or against us" in the war on terrorism. To Americans he said, "If you question my decision for going to war, you betray the troops in the battle." This kind of either-or thinking boxes people into an all-encompassing policy, which has been rejected by our European allies. Coupled with the Patriot Act which allows the president to round up terrorist suspects and hold them in jail without counsel, Bush's position represents an expansion of the president's powers, inching toward despotism and reminiscent of the Alien and Sedition Acts of the 1790s (which allowed the government to squash criticism and close down newspapers), the denial of habeas corpus during the Civil War (which permitted preemptive arrests), the Red Scare of 1919 (which allowed the government to round up leftist suspects who committed no crimes), and the McCarthy era of the 1950s (which focused on hunting down liberal intellectuals and filmmakers, branding them as communists, and forcing them out of work).

Elsewhere, Bush informed the world that he regularly speaks to Jesus and Jesus is the most influential person upon his political, social, and moral thoughts. This thinking is all well and good in church or at an old-time Billy Graham evangelist rally, or even at a modern-day Joel Osteen rally, the top TV preacher, but this type of messianism leads to self-righteousness and clouds political, social, and economic thought. Our Founding Fathers were well aware of this issue when they rejected all forms of a theocracy.

Conservatives, on the whole, are more optimistic than liberals about America's future, arguing that big business (left unrestrained) will grow the economy and provide jobs for the nation's working- and middle-class populace and the tax base to support future social, health, and education programs. (This is based on "trickle-down" economics, sort of a hoax promulgated by the economist Arthur Laffer, from Pepperdine University, and melded into Reaganomics and conservative free-market theories by disciples of Milton Friedman.) The more government programs and regulations rooted in Roosevelt's New Deal and Johnson's Great Society that we strike down, the theory goes, the more economic liberty to stimulate growth and the better off society in terms of political, social, economic, and education change. Similarly, the more entitlements and subsidies we eliminate, the more productive Americans will become.

In reverse or actually perverse logic, the more Congress extends billions of dollars worth of cuts or tax breaks and creates new ones for millionaires and corporations, the more the economy will grow. Bush wants to lock in this kind of legacy, which is as nonmainstream and nonprogressive as you can get in a rational world. It is sort of a winner-take-all philosophy, and/or having your cake and eating it too, based on a free-market economy, an economic system that rewards the strong and smart, the inventive and innovative, that is, those who supposedly keep the American engine running and thus provide the most benefits for society.

Liberals are less optimistic and more concerned about the need to maintain government regulation and business restraint, about the growing lack of mobility and inequality, the destruction of social programs and safety nets for the average and less fortunate populace, the shrinking of unions in numbers and influence, the transfer of good-paying jobs overseas, and job insecurity at home. They see the increasing plight of the majority of Americans tied to Reagan-Bush laissez-faire economics, where military and defense spending increases and human service spending decreases, big business goes unrestrained, and tax benefits go to the rich (top 10 percent) and superrich (top 1 percent).

Tax-Cut Theorists: Differences between the Political Left and Right

Liberal critics have referred to this type of economic theory as "voodoo economics," "hokum for the yokels" (or common people), or simply "fiscal instability." The advocates—what we might call the tax cut theorists—publicly refer to it as "supply-side economics," a term introduced by President Reagan's budget advisors such as Arthur Laffer and David Stockman, the latter who resigned after figuring out the theory was flawed. The insiders secretly refer to it as "starving the beast" (rooted in Hamilton's view of the "herd" or simply the masses in whom he had no faith). Proponents of tax cuts are not really concerned about budget deficits as evidenced by the mounting debt during the Reagan and Bush administrations, of which more than $2 trillion has been added since 2001 and which reached nearly $9 trillion by the end of 2006. Even worse, no one in power or making policy seems willing to face the unpleasant future in which coming generations will be required to pay this mounting debt, by raising taxes to exorbitant levels, by printing massive amounts of money which is bound to cause hyperinflation and wipe out pensions and savings, by forcing our children and grandchildren to delay retirement, or by eliminating other social programs related to health, education, etc.[5] I guess we can all choose our pick of poison, subject to Chinese approval, who own much of our debt.

According to Paul Krugman, the liberal economist from Princeton, tax-cut theorists realize budget deficits will mount but will also fulfill their hidden purpose: to shrink government's role, social programs, and entitlements. Or, as he puts it, "conservative heavy weights are using the budget deficit to call for cuts in key government programs [and] eventually achieve their true aim: shrinking the government's role back to what it was under [Republican] Calvin Coolidge."[6] In this connection, Alan Greenspan, the former head of the Federal Reserve, urges the government to reduce Social Security, Medicare, and Medicaid spending to maintain "fiscal stability." Although he is just about everyone's favorite economic guru, few people realize he is a disciple of Ayn Rand's philosophy that greed is good and it helps the economy and, therefore, so are tax cuts for the rich, which Greenspan helped sell to Congress in 2001 with Bush as president.

Although Bush was unsuccessful in 2005 in trying to reduce Social Security spending by privatizing it, Medicaid recipients (the poor, unemployed, and underemployed) are less likely to vote than Social Security or Medicare recipients, so they were the major target for federal cuts in 2005. Funds were also cut for food stamps, child support, and college loans (the beneficiaries of which are all unprotected and needy groups), as evidenced by the Republican vice president's tie-breaking vote that year in Congress to reduce aid to the neediest populace. In the meantime, tax cuts for the rich were saved and the majority of red voters remained indifferent because they have been bogged down trying to defend the war in Iraq and seduced by other economic and social issues ranging from affirmative action, jobs, pensions, gun control, gay-lesbian marriages, and expression of Christmas and God in public arenas.

In summing up the tax-cut package for 2006, Democrats accused Republicans of expanding tax relief to the very rich while cutting programs for the poor, although John Snow, Bush's former Treasury Secretary, praised the tax cut as "critical to sustaining our economic recovery and creating jobs"[7] (a supply-side interpretation of economics). Conservative economists argue that the tax breaks or extra money for top income-earners will be used to expand business, buy equipment, and conduct research and development—partially true and partially based on Cinderella fairy tales.

Few people recognize or are willing to admit that the politicians who make the laws have always been swayed by corporate giants and wealthy taxpayers, and therefore the laws favor them, at the expense of the poor and ordinary people, now including the middle class. We have always had tax breaks and loopholes for corporate America and the rich at the expense of those who need Medicaid, food stamps, decent jobs, infant education and headstart programs, college loans, etc. If ideology was not driving the nation's tax policy, the 2006 tax cuts could have saved more than $60 billion by eliminating $21 billion in special investment benefits for the wealthy, $14 billion in corporate tax loopholes, and $27 billion in write-offs for dependents of taxpayers earning $200,000 a year.[8] But that might lead to a newfangled country, whereby the super rich would have less money to buy their yachts, private jets, and art collections.

One must understand that not all dollars saved to finance tax cuts for the wealthy would have been spent wastefully by the government, as conservatives maintain. Most of the money cut for health benefits for the poor would have been recycled into the economy by physicians and pharmacists. Most of the money for food stamps would have been used to buy food and help employ people in food stores. Most of the money for college loans would have been used to further the education of less fortunate students and help build the nation's human capital, which has major implications for the future economy. In contrast, Robert Frank, an economist at Cornell University, maintains the tax cuts for the rich went to people that "already have everything they might reasonably need." The extra money might be used to buy "something special," say a bracelet or fur coat for the Mrs., but the idea is elastic and may not even happen or may "be little different than before."[9] Tax cuts for the rich do not always affect outcomes in the way supply-siders think; the cuts may also be used to buy something silly or extravagant, which does nothing more than help the rich achieve special status (i.e., buying a gold toilet seat or set of gold faucets or buying another classic car at the "bargain" price of one million dollars) and further divide the country along class lines. It's nice to go to Harvard and live in Greenwich or sail in the Hamptons, but what about the police in New York, the teachers in Chicago, or the nurses in Los Angeles? What about the soldiers in Iraq or Afghanistan? Do they count? Or are they pawns to be sacrificed in the game of life?

Off Center: Miles Apart

Liberals maintain that the right to a job, to food, clothing and housing, to health care and education, and to a decent quality of life during retirement are vital and necessary to life, rights that need to be protected by government and seen as an extension of Roosevelt's "Economic Bill of Rights" articulated in 1944 and Johnson's civil rights legislation of the 1960s. Conservatives argue that these areas of government undertaking exceed Constitutional limits because they were never enumerated and they lead to government meddling and bureaucratic inefficiency. In the end, these rights and entitlements alter our views of what role is expected of government and what responsibilities are expected of people. In short, free-market economists such as Milton Friedman want to move "in the direction of making people responsible for themselves and for their own care,"[10] sort of a new version of "survival of the fittest."

The overarching idea for conservatives is to return to nineteenth-century legislative and judicial doctrines that established severe limits on government power and to reduce government agencies, acts, and programs that inhibit big business and have come to be widely accepted in the twentieth century, especially since the Roosevelt administration. The conservative agenda is to strike down or reduce government administration, including Social Security, minimum wage, affirmative action, corporate pensions, and a host of environmental, clean air, health, and occupational safety agencies and acts that curb business or add to business costs. What these policies have in common is the attempt to come to terms with and adopt Reagan's social and economic agenda; even worse, it represents a single answer to the nation's economy based on a libertarian agenda. For liberals, however, such a perspective comes close to a throwback to the Gilded Age, when the captains of industry ruled with an iron fist, plundered the countryside, and fleeced the public.

Actually, the conservative platform is partially based on University of Chicago's Richard Epstein's legal, political, and economic theories,[11] perhaps more radical than Antonin Scalia's judicial views and Milton Friedman's free-market economy.[12] Epstein's views would eliminate many parts of the welfare state and put firm limitations on federal and state powers and rights that do not explicitly appear in the Constitution. His ideas have been fused with another conservative scholar, Michael Greve, who hangs his hat at the American Enterprise Institute. He has warned that judicial abandonment of Constitutional limits and the rise of employment, health, and public protection agencies have led to a regulatory maze of paper work, interfered with free enterprise, and caused unnecessary and costly lawsuits directed at big business. It has increased the cost of producing products and service, and has put Americans at a competitive disadvantage in the global economy. Never mind the possible return of the Gilded Age and the greed that goes with it. The need is to reconstruct the "Constitution Exile" and embrace federal and state deregulation—or risk a continuous decline of the American economy and erosion of jobs.

The liberal policy, expressed by Cass Sunstein, another law professor at the University of Chicago, fears that the Constitution is being railroaded, the conservative agenda is "fundamentally wrong," and that all government acts, programs, and policies, as well as regulatory commission boards and agencies, are now at risk. The confirmation of judges John Roberts and Samuel Alito in 2005 and 2006, both well-qualified on a formal basis but steadfastly conservative, represents a turning point—or more appropriately a radical swing to the Right—for how the Supreme Court will interpret the scope of civil, social, and education rights and health, environmental, and workplace protections that will affect Americans for decades. The overall American legal, political, and economic culture will most likely be transformed in the near future, and in a way that frightens Sunstein[13] and does damage to values liberals have long stood for. A conservative Supreme Court, coupled with Republican dominance in the White House or Congress, will likely tip the scale to laissez-faire economics and strike down much of the federal laws and social legislation that protects the rest of us from big business and provides us with safety nets necessary for a decent life. A conservative Supreme Court is likely to favor those with privilege and power over those who need the protection of the law: women, minorities, labor unions, the elderly, and gays and lesbians.

Finding the Center

Without trying to sound like a liberal alarmist or overeducated twit, Americans need to avoid religious dogma and ideological extremes from both the political Right and Left; it merely divides our nation. *Off Center*, by professors Jacob Hacker and Paul Pierson, describes how conservatives, since the Reagan administration and now with the Bush administration, gained control of the political system and neutralized political checks and balances; they have broadened the view of the president's power (somewhat like the old Federalist perspective). Liberals are not entirely innocent of such abuses, but they were never as guilty as the Right.[14] Presidents Johnson, Carter, and Clinton, as well as moderate Republicans Eisenhower and Ford, avoided fringe views and made attempts to communicate with congressional members from the opposing aisle in an attempt to achieve some "balance" and to reach a consensus (more along the lines of the old Jeffersonian Republicans).

Chris Mooney's book, the *Republican War on Science*, reports how federal positions in the areas of health, science, and technology have been filled under the Bush administration on the basis of ideology rather than expertise. The outcome is the politicization of research and knowledge on abortion, stem cell research, food and drugs, air and water pollution, global warming and industrial chemicals, and the war in Afghanistan and Iraq.[15] Although getting to the truth or distinguishing good science from faulty science is never an easy task, the demarcation should not be based on a researcher's party affiliation or ideology. The masking of truth and the bending of facts to suit a particular party line poses major problems for a democracy, especially if the truth is influenced by God or money and critics are branded as "ideologues," cowardly and unpatriotic, or "elitist liberals."

Today, however, the system is collapsing, and a class war is being waged against the bottom 80 or 90 percent of Americans who in the last thirty years have shared very little in the growth and prosperity of the nation. In fact, since the 1970s, corporations have been successful in rolling back union gains dating back to the 1935 National Labor Relation Act. Major employers in all sectors of the economy now treat their workers as disposable products or force them into wage cuts to keep their jobs. In the last twenty-five years, real wages, after inflation, fell 1 percent and the income of the richest 1 percent rose 135 percent.[16] For CEOs, it rose between 600 and 4,000 percent, depending on how you define compensation, whether you adjust for inflation, and which piece of research you prefer to believe. (See chapter 6.) Perhaps the most simple way of putting it is to say that most of those swell GM jobs, the model of post–World War II, no longer exists, but there still is an ocean of riches to be plucked by the super rich.

We cannot continue to go on like this for long and still call ourselves a democracy. The truth is that we must find the center. The vast majority of Americans are in the middle or just left or right of the center. Most Americans have become disenfranchised by ideology and by partisan politics that appeal to the far Left or far Right. For the past six years, the far Right was running the political show—with control of the White House, Congress, and the Supreme Court. Even worse, the rightist revolution barely stirred any notice among the common people who seemed confused and more involved in earning a living and making ends meet than in trying to piece together why they had not shared in the nation's prosperity. Add it all up. Corporate profits were estimated to run $9.5 trillion in 2006. As a percentage of gross domestic product, they were the highest they have been since the statistics were first kept in 1959, about 12.7 percent.[17] But all we hear from corporate America is that American workers are paid too much, even though, when adjusted for inflation, their wages are below what they were in 1972, when the first supply-side president (Nixon) was elected. Get with the program! Why shouldn't corporate America and the rich pay for their greatest share of government services? The people do not fully comprehend the growing economic divide; it seems like only a total crisis in the economy will generate party coalitions and the support needed to addresses the nation's social and economic problems.

Americans, in the past, have always managed to find the center; it's what has made this country free. Its political leaders have been able to balance excellence with equality, capitalist interests and free-market entrepreneurship with social reform and a progressive ethos. Its heroes have been presidents like George Washington and Abe Lincoln, folk people like Davy Crockett and Daniel Boone, and sport figures like Babe Ruth and Michael Jordan. Rarely have we looked to military or religious leaders, Wall Street tycoons, or corporate captains as our heroes—a tribute to our nation's sense of reality and civic balance. What we need today, however, is a national commitment—one purpose, one community—not a house divided by blue and gray, blue and red, white and black, rich and poor.

DONKEYS, ELEPHANTS, AND RICH PEOPLE

The conservative platform today is built on a shaky foundation, which includes faith in limited government and limited taxes, as well as religious morality. They include such groups as libertarians, antitax militants, Christian activists, and a glob of blue-collar populists, suburban soccer moms, and small business owners, bankers, and corporate personnel. All these groups do not have similar goals, nor do they represent a cohesive force. They are fused together by terrorist attacks in the United States and Europe, which Bush has emphasized in speeches to the public, similar to the way the anticommunist stand during the Cold War era united Americans. If we deal with social and economic reality, much of this voting block can return to the Democratic Party—and the political equivalent to liberal values. Hopefully, the political center can address the economic concerns of the working and middle class; it is probably the best way to slow down the new Gilded Age that is crippling the bottom 90 percent of Americans.

The terrorist attacks gave the Republican Party a great deal of leeway in which to encourage the public to ignore the economic home front. The grace period is hopefully coming to an end, signaled by the Democratic elected Congress in 2006. Americans need to wake up to the economic discomfort in their lives and related class issues gripping the country. Here I believe that minority groups, blue-collar workers, middle-class suburbanites, and even small business owners—what used to be called yeoman people, common people, and working people—should have sufficient common sense to vote in their best political and economic interests. It does not take a genius to figure out that taxes are needed to provide social, health, and education services and the money can be found by systematically taxing groups that can afford to pay more and closing up tax loopholes that favor the rich and big-business interests.

Political Lessons to Learn

No high-powered math or logic is needed to understand what needs to be done. The idea is to outmaneuver at election time large business groups and conservative Republicans, who have captured the gun-loving hunters, pick-up truck drivers, NASCAR dads, new immigrants, church-going people, working moms, and small business people—all who were once overwhelmingly Democrat—the war in Iraq should eventually become a nonissue. Democrats need to stick to "bread-and-butter" issues—jobs, wages, pensions, Social Security, health care, education, energy, etc.—and the larger concepts of equity, fairness, and progressive taxation. On the other hand, divisive social issues such as creationism, abortion, gay rights, and gun control should be avoided. When these issues surface, Democrats, centrists, and moderates need to state their position in thirty seconds, at most, and change the subject (and hammer home the kitchen issues).

The key is to focus on the needs and interests of average people, avoid left-wing politics, and remind Americans we are all in the same boat. It is important to show that wealthy and conservative groups have captured the political process and are exploiting it to their advantage at the expense of the majority of Americans. Moreover, they have duped average Americans—the silent majority, the common person, the wage earner, the blue-collar and white-collar worker—into believing that taxing the wealthy and corporate world, or redistributing wealth, is anti-American or somehow impedes the economy or American dream. In simple terms, people need to learn the facts and understand they have the power to effect change by electing politicians that will serve their interests; most important, the need is to encourage nonvoters to vote, as it is assumed that most of these people would vote their pocketbooks and thus Democrat. This is the most important target population, the millions of Americans who don't vote and would probably vote blue. In simple numbers, or pop-political clichés, that's about 50 percent of the people.

No one can predict the next congressional or presidential election, but the factions that splintered the Democratic Party need to recall the philosophy of Thomas Jefferson, reflected in the policies of Roosevelt and Johnson, who sought to protect the rights of workers from an unregulated market and expand the education and economic opportunities of poor, working, and minority groups. Their ideals are very different from the philosophy of Alexander Hamilton, reflected in the policies of Reagan (considered by one moderate conservative to be the most "overrated president" because he knew how to smile and communicate) and Bush II (considered by the same critic to be a "failed president").[18] Both presidents sought to strike down federal laws and federal regulations in order to foster laissez-faire economics and to use the courts to curb the social-welfare state. There are major differences between Democrats and Republicans, which need to be clarified when people with liberal values seek a coalition of interests that favors the average American, who is now struggling and seeing his or her standard of living in decline while the rich get richer.

Taken to its logical conclusion, the vast majority of us need to smarten up and vote blue by not getting hypnotized by or drawn into side issues such as family values, crime, abortion, gay rights, etc. and keep focused on our pocketbooks. The key issue is how wealth can be redistributed in an equitable way to reduce inequality and to reform and revamp social, health, and education programs. To be sure, the rise of Ronald Reagan in 1981 represented the resurgence of American conservatism, highlighted by the election of Bush II and followed by the rightward swing of the Supreme Court in 2005 and 2006. The conservative trend is further reflected in the invasion of Iraq to promote big business and oil interests and secure military bases under the pretext of nuclear weapons; the rising tide of evangelism and the marketing of God in schools and society; the global war between the so-called pluralist West and Islamic extremism; irresponsible tax cuts for big business and the rich; and the disgraceful and dangerous widening gap between the rich and the rest of us.

The Rise of the Nobility

There is good reason to believe that we are heading straight toward a political and economic system ruled by a financial oligarchy. In 1985, Donald Trump was ranked fifty-one among the Forbes 400 wealthiest people; his net worth was considered to be $600 million. By 2000, Trump was estimated to be worth $1.7 billion but ranked a mere 167,[19] indicating that the rich were getting richer relative to the average person working 9 to 5 whose income adjusted for inflation, according to estimates, remained flat during these fifteen years (and even longer).[20] In 1998, the average income of the thirteen thousand wealthiest families was three hundred times that of families with an average income. By 2004, it was nearly five hundred times greater than the average family.[21] In 1998, the average CEO's income (including salary, bonuses, and stock options) was about two hundred and fifty times greater than the average worker's in his or her company. By 2004 the average pay package for chief executives at big companies was about $10 million and four hundred to five hundred times greater than the average worker's.[22]

In view of pension and health insurance cuts being imposed upon low-level and average workers, this surge in CEO income is obscene. What we need is some agreed-upon ratio between what a CEO earns and what the average worker in the company earns, say twenty to twenty-five times, even fifty times. If the CEO's salary, bonuses, stock options, etc. totaled more than this ratio, the company would be taxed, in the same way major league baseball imposes a luxury tax on teams like the New York Yankees when they exceed the league's salary cap.[23]

One more plea for a liberal perspective and an analysis of data preventing its practice. Between 1998 and 2005, gross domestic product rose from

$8.7 billion to $12.2 billion, increasing every year, and 40 percent in seven years.[24] But median household income remained below what it was in 1998, once more indicating that the average American worker is not sharing in the prosperity of the nation and that gaps between the rich and rest of us are increasing. To put the issue in simple, layperson terms, growth rates of income and net worth are fastest for the group above the ninetieth percentile, and much faster for those in the top 1 percent.

The *power elites* who have the ability to make laws and stop these trends have become bogged down in partisan politics and ideology. The *corporate elites* who have a lot to say about politics behind the scenes are more concerned with amassing high salaries, stock options, and bonuses—and shifting taxes away from themselves to the rest of the populace. To be sure, most power and corporate elites are not given to sacrifice; rather they build their fortunes and pass it on to their descendents. This fact of life has been going on since the Gilded Age, with the Rockefellers, Duponts, Vanderbilts, and Mellons, and since the mid-twentieth century on a political level with the Roosevelts, Kennedys, and Bushes. Extrapolating events over the past few years, however, it is safe to conclude that the Bush dynasty has ended, with no sympathies for Jeb, not in this book.

Money and Politics

Today, money and politics often go hand in hand, witnessed by the rise of many millionaires elected to political office. In 2005 as many as twenty-five out of fifty governors and forty-five out of one hundred senators were millionaires, not to overlook a host of mega millionaires such as Tom Golisano (New York gubernatorial candidate), Al Cheechi (California gubernatorial candidate), and Blair Hull (Illinois senatorial candidate), each who spent $30 to $75 million of their own money but lost their bid for office.[25] Despite their defeat, the entry of mega millionaires into the political process who can finance their own campaigns and dramatically outspend their opponents represents a new precedent that clouds the democratic process with an economic variable. Given the elitist tendencies of our Founding Fathers (see chapter 2), few would care or have pause for concern about this new trend, as they believed the common people would be best served if the property and educated class ran the country.

On top of the political rich list was the sixth-ranked richest person, according to Forbes 400, Michael Bloomberg, the mayor of New York, who is worth more than $6 billion. Depending on the source you read, he spent between $70 and $80 million of his own money on his campaign in 2005, or about $200 per actual New York City voter. Then there is Jon Corzine, the senator from New Jersey who ran for governor and won in 2005 against Douglas Forrester, also a businessman and suburban mayor. Corzine's net worth was estimated at $260 million and Forrester's net worth was said to be a puny $50 million. The two candidates spent approximately $75 million, much of it on negative ads. In their last two political races, Bloomberg spent $130 million of his own money and Corzine spent $100 million.

There was a time when multimillionaires and successful business people did not want to run for office; they did not want to get involved in climbing the political ladder, knocking on doors, and shaking hands with people. But all that changed with the influence of television. Now wealthy people have new and instant political capital. They spend large sums advertising and reaching millions of people without political dues to pay, without running around and sweating. A new breed of wealthy people, in the tradition of the Rockefellers, has emerged, people who are ready to throw their hats in the political arena. These rich people may go out of their way to act humble and ordinary, but they are neither humble nor ordinary. The only good their entry into politics might serve is that, by having so much money, they may be sufficiently independent to avoid old party loyalties and clean up some of the political corruption—at least that is the image they try to portray without flaunting their money.

Like it or not, the role of money and its connection to political candidates seeking election or reelection to office is fast becoming the American norm. The Supreme Court has ruled that free speech allows people to spend as much of their own money as they want. Wealthy candidates are able to overwhelm nonwealthy candidates in the media. The standard candidate is forced to rely on rich contributors and special interest groups and thus become indebted and, if elected, bend policy to suit the interests of the rich and influence peddlers who helped fund their campaigns. With nonwealthy, underfinanced candidates, money provides the rich influence and access to the powerful as the cost of campaigns become more expensive. In the end, both trends can destroy our democracy—furthering the rise of a financial oligarchy.

Dreaming the Impossible Dream

Right now it is safe to say that the American standard of living and household income are the highest they have ever been, largely because of the growth in the female labor force, with wives as the second breadwinners in families; nonetheless, working- and middle-class income has stagnated for the last thirty years, while the rich and superrich continue to make more money and hoard society's gains. For this reason, there is a negative expectation among most Americans about the nation's future. The next generation is not moving ahead; rather it is behind the baby boomer's current living standards. On a global level, there seems to be more confi-

dence and greater economic prosperity, especially within the Asian rim
and parts of Eastern Europe and Latin America, and this is probably one
reason why democracy is spreading in these regions. Politically that helps
stabilize world affairs, but it doesn't help this nation economically grow;
in fact, the increased global competition puts American manufacturing in
jeopardy and leads to higher trade deficits, along with the loss of millions
of jobs as new plants are opened in China, the Philippines, and Mexico,
and/or other jobs are outsourced to India, Thailand, and Eastern Europe.
The danger to the American economy, particularly from trade deficits
and loss of jobs to other parts of the world, is illustrated by the increasing
frequency of discussion about reversing globalization and increasing protectionism.[26] Personally, I think the genie is out of the bottle, and it is
nearly impossible to stem the global tide.

Economic growth has characterized American society since the nation
was formed. This growth not only raises living standards and bolsters
liberal policies and democratic societies, according to Harvard economist
Benjamin Friedman, it also leads to social and cultural advancement and
improves human happiness.[27] As a nation, however, we have learned in
the last several decades that economic growth may not lead to social
mobility, opportunity, or greater equality. So much depends on how the
nation's growth and prosperity is distributed among the citizens, whether
we have progressive or nonprogressive government, good or bad public
policies.

In theory, there is nothing wrong with capitalism; in fact, we can link
the growth of capitalism to society's growth. But the key is how goods
and services are shared. If they mainly go to the capitalist class at the
expense of the masses or the majority of the populace, then society is
polarized and democracy is splintered. This is why we need unions, pensions, health care, schools, and other human services—to divide the
wealth of the nation in a fair and just way and to establish safety nets
for average Americans. You don't have to be a flaming liberal or Franklin
Roosevelt fan club member to recognize the need for these services; without them there is no viable democratic society, only "supply side capitalists" and free marketers, which translates into increased profits for a tiny
group of elites and a decline in the general welfare and standard of living
for the vast majority of Americans (the bottom 80 to 90 percent).

If the goal is greater equality, then redistribution of wealth based on a
progressive tax system is essential. (A 50 percent tax rate for those who
earn $500,000 a year and a 70 to 75 percent tax rate for those who annually
earn $1 million or more is not going to hurt anyone except those who can
afford to pay.) To put this thinking in reverse, why should the taxes on
the rich and superrich be lowered? (Who then is to pay for the nation's
services or debt?) And do you really think the majority of the superrich

care about those "poor bastards" on the other side of the divide? If the goal is equity (or opportunity), then more rights, entitlements, and social programs are required in order to level the playing field. (Of course, if you were born on third base, I don't think you want to level the playing field, or give someone better odds to compete with you.) If more people were able to get up at bat, more people (by the law of averages) would hit triples and home runs; there would be greater odds for more people to make it to Harvard or to Wall Street.

If the policy is to increase the number and percentage of people who can share in the social and economic pie, then it means we need to consider basic moral benchmarks and reduce our instincts toward greed, selfishness, and materialism, all hard to define, subjective, and contextual terms. Equality and equity lie deep in our history and folk memory; and, like Jefferson and Lincoln, they are part of our school assignments. These terms, like our presidential heroes, remain morally powerful ideas without having come to seem moralistic. Although they are obviously desirable goals, they are not easy to implement into policy because we tend to fracture in multiple voices and special interests. In the end, it means that as a society we move toward what John Rawls called "fairness and justice," what John Gardner refers to as balancing "excellence and equality," and what I prefer to call the "common good" or "public good," and what populist writers call "simply doing what is right."

REFORMING THE TAX CODE

I wish I could say how much pleasure this book has been for the reader so far, but, in truth, I'm sure it's been a bit of a slog, reading at times like a textbook, a history or civics lesson or a treatise in political and economic polarity. Having given you a wide-angle lens of politics, economics, and education, allow me now to give you a close-up set of recommendations and possible solutions at the risk of criticism from my peers and the public, especially from those of the conservative bent. I realize this is not going to be easy. I am faced with the supreme test of knowledge and objectivity: knowing what to include, what to exclude. So, here goes, a unique opportunity to examine some ideas about what needs to be done, a trillion-dollar moment of self-reflection on moving money from one group to another group, not necessarily a set of practical or doable policies.

It does not take rocket science to figure out that, in order to find money to pay for increased human services and to reduce inequality, we need to progressively increase taxes. Congress has the power of the purse and needs to exercise its power in order to provide necessary services and redistribute wealth. On the other hand, reducing taxes for the rich and the corporate sector as a means of stimulating the economy is an oversimplified solution and deceitful way of maintaining inequality. Moreover, it does not necessarily follow that tax cuts will stimulate economic growth or jobs. For example, the 1986 tax reform, under the Reagan watch, which sharply reduced taxes, led to the biggest real estate bust and second-largest banking bust in U.S. history. The tax rate dramatically increased during the Clinton administration, but the nation experienced a huge uptick in the economy and the largest surplus ever recorded.[28]

Of course, cleaning up tax loopholes and special preferences creates losers, but they tend to be wealthy people and corporations, which group can afford to pay more taxes. This group represents a solid conservative voting block, and Republican presidents and/or a Republican-controlled Congress rarely have the will to tackle this aspect of taxation. It would galvanize and provoke their own voters and a host of special interest groups to oppose the plan, the same groups that helped elect them into office. So, it falls on a Democratic administration to do what is fair and necessary for maintaining a decent life for average Americans.

Conservative disciples of the free market in business and banking, the same people who read the *National Review*, *Barrons*, and the *Economist* may not feel the masses represent the "herd," as did their guru Alexander Hamilton, but for all intents and purposes they do argue in print and in media that government regulation limits talent and destroys productivity, capitalism contributes to the common good, and making money drives the economy and produces jobs. This type of thinking is expressed nightly on CNBC with "Mad Money" and "On the Money" and in the morning with "Wake Up" and "Squawk Box." So where do we start? How do we encourage the talented to contribute to the common good and, at the same time, reduce greed and clean up the tax code and make it more progressive so that more people can share in the wealth of the nation?

1. *Reduce Taxable Income.* One idea that would garner public approval is to eliminate the federal tax on the first $35,000 to $40,000 earned by an individual and the first $50,000 to $60,000 earned by a household. For someone earning $40,000, the extra $10,000 (not paid in taxes) would have a much greater impact on the retail sector and the economy in general and make a major difference in the person's quality of life than for someone earning $200,000 and getting the same $10,000 benefit. It is safe to conclude that 100 percent of working- and middle-class Americans would benefit from and approve of this tax policy.

2. *Home Mortgages.* As many as 70 percent of tax filers receive no benefit from the mortgage deduction, even though between 67 and 69 percent of families are homeowners. In fact, 55 percent of the tax benefits went to the top 12 percent of taxpayers who earned $100,000 or more in 2002.[29] If

we totally scrapped the mortgage deduction, tens of billions of dollars could be used to lower taxes among average Americans or increase social, health, and education spending—or what some call human services. Such a bold idea would probably be defeated in Congress, so the next best idea is to limit the amount of deduction that can be taken for a home mortgage.

Rather than $1.1 million under current law, I would propose the mortgage deduction be limited to $500,000, which is beyond the average price of homes in the country. The only people negatively affected by this mortgage deduction would be the upper-middle and upper-class, the top 5 to 10 percent of American tax filers. Prices for homes would not fall across the board or across the country as predicted by bankers and real-estate salespeople who have their own selfish interests to protect. The proposal would only affect the top end of the market and a few states on the East and West coasts, as well as parts of Arizona and Nevada. Permitting a mortgage deduction tied to average prices of homes in a state or region of the country would also work but be confusing and constantly changing. It would lead to a maze of paperwork and misinformation, and favor high-income people. For these reasons, this idea is rejected, although it continuously appears in print as a "fair" concept that would prevent a potential panic or drop in home prices.

It would benefit the average American to change the tax deduction for mortgage interest to a flat tax credit. The advantage is that a tax credit is worth the same to everyone, regardless of income. A deduction, on the other hand, is worth much more to high-income people in the 35 percent tax bracket than people in the 15 to 20 percent bracket. Again, the only people opposing such a modification in the tax code would be the top 5 or 10 percent of the populace.

To put the benefit in precise terms, a tax filer with an adjusted income of $50,000 to $75,000 averaged a $524 deduction and someone earning $200,000 or more received an average of $5,036 in 2004.[30] The effect was ten times as great under the present system for the wealthier individual; in some cases it was more, say, involving a person with a new mortgage of $500,000 at 6 percent. The benefit was more than $8,000 or 15.5 times greater than the average homeowner's deduction of $524. What we need to understand is that the mortgage tax deduction was introduced forty-five years ago to encourage first time home buying among veterans and working people. The typical home purchase for decades was one and one-half baths, three bedrooms, and eighteen hundred to two thousand square feet. Instead, today, the subsidy has encouraged people to buy and build larger and more expensive homes, with three or four baths, four to five bedrooms, and four thousand to five thousand square feet—or just bigger with more goodies.

3. *Investment Income*. There is need to simplify the tax code and close up many of the investment loopholes for wealthy taxpayers. Capital gains, for example, are taxed at 15 percent and dividend income is no longer taxed, while salaries are taxed at more than twice the rate for capital gains. People who realize large capital gains and derive sizeable dividends are wealthy. Instead of lowering or eliminating these investment-related taxes, which favor rich taxpayers, there is need to increase these taxes to help reduce inequality.

Increasing taxes on profits will not necessarily reduce growth or investments; justification for investments is largely based on reward and risk factors, as well as financing and borrowing rates, not whether the tax rate on capital gains is 15 or 30 percent, or whether dividends are taxed or not, or whether capital gains are reduced. Nor is there any evidence that tax cuts summon outpourings of additional investment and risk taking. But there is evidence that tax cuts lead to federal deficits, which often result in reduced human services, including scientific research and education, which threaten the very basis of our long-term innovation and economic prosperity. Deficits that cause cuts in government programs that mainly serve poor and working people lead to increased inequality. Cynics argue that this is the only country that cuts taxes for the wealthy and cuts services for the needy. The need is to implement a progressive tax rate corresponding with increasing net profits and net dividend income or to create a higher flat tax for capital gains and dividends. Average working Americans don't receive this benefit or, if they do, it is minimal, as most, if not all, of their income is derived from salaries and wages and not investments.

Lowering taxes on investment income (capital gains and dividends) is bound to lead to higher taxes on salaries because all income is either investment income or earned income from salaries. To make up for the loss of tax revenue from investments, the government will eventually be forced to raise the taxes of 90 percent of taxpayers (who are wage earners) and give a large tax break to the top wealthy 10 percent. To be sure, the shift in the tax code (exempting or reducing tax on investment income) penalizes workers, including the middle class, who need to spend almost all they earn to keep their heads afloat. Lowering the tax rates on investment income as an incentive to take risks or create jobs, as conservatives claim should happen, only increases inequality between the rich who invest and the rest of us who spend what they earn and already pay a disproportionately higher percentage tax and have fewer deductions and other tax breaks.

To put it in simple terms, the tax breaks on investments are regressive and don't help the working and middle class. There is enough income inequality in America; these tax breaks merely increase inequality and shift the burden of debt to the next generation or what may be dubbed as the future "have nots." By lowering taxes on investments, we lower taxes for the rich who own most of the assets; we do not necessarily create more prosperity or stimulate the economy. What we really do is force workers to work harder and longer to keep up with growing inequality. If this is what the "supply-side economists" mean by productivity and growing economy, then their warped thinking is right.

Estate and Gifts Taxes

Tax rates for estates, trusts, and gifts, along with exclusion amounts and limits, have varied over recent years. They are skewed by certain credits, deductions, marriage status, and income and tax brackets. The measures, amendments, and laws miss the progressive mark, however, and allow the rich various tax loopholes to transfer wealth to the next generation and even skip a generation to grandchildren. The point is that there is a need to put a cap or ceiling, or a progressive limit, on the amount of money that can be transferred to descendents in order to prevent an entrenched oligarchy or Fourth Estate from emerging within the nation. Conservative politicians have linked minimum wage legislation to estate tax provisions eliminating the tax by 2015 on the first $5 million transferred. Estates up to $25 million would be taxed at 15 percent (as if they were capital gains), and estates in excess of $25 million would be taxed at 30 percent. The estimated cost to the government in lost revenue is about $300 billion over the next ten years, according to one estimate, and then higher after 2015.[31]

Allowing tax breaks on the transfer of wealth does not help the average American; it only leads to a "nobility class," which our Founding Fathers went to great length to avoid. Hence, we need to lessen the sense of entitlements, privileges by birth, and inherited wealth; otherwise, this nation will descend into moral decline and economic rot. Walt Disney, Michael Jordan, and Bill Gates (who is at the top of the Forbes list of billionaires) may be celebrities and folk heroes, and we can appreciate their aspirations and success. But should their descendents be given a free ride, and how long of a free ride, where no performance is needed to produce a paycheck? In the words of Warren Buffett, who gave away 85 percent of his $44 billion fortune, do we want to create the economic equivalent of "choosing the 2020 Olympic team by picking the eldest sons of the gold-medal winners in the 2000 Olympics"?

Whereas a net worth of $1 million would put you in the top 7 percent of American households in 2005,[32] a net worth of $5 million would put you in the top 1.5 percent. It is at this level where I would impose limits on the transfer of wealth, after which point wealth would be progressively taxed at 70 to 90 percent, whether or not the grantor is alive or dead. Consider that each million in capital invested conservatively in blue chip stocks and bonds would yield a 5 percent rate of return or $50,000, an amount more than the average household income, which was $44,000 in 2005. A total of $5 million inherited, with the same percent return, would produce real security—some $250,000 a year. How much more money does someone need to inherit?

The intent is to limit the disconnect between money and merit, money and the public good—eliminate gigantic inheritances and transfer of wealth that offer few marginal benefits to society and only increases inequality between the superrich and the rest of the people. First, consider the rich (top 10 percent) with their accounting tricks and the taint of avariciousness among the superrich (top 1 percent), the latter who often make their money at the expense of others or illegally—the Kenneth Lays of Enron, Bernard Ebbers of WorldCom, and Jack Grubmans of Smith Barney, not to mention the tens of thousands who don't get caught. Then consider members of the middle class, who have been downsized and outsourced and who are now struggling and becoming faceless drones and paper pushers in a system that no longer rewards their performance. The only way to strengthen democracy is to create a widely shared prosperity. Shrinking our middle class only weakens our political and economic system and reduces the value of an education, as these are the people who have traditionally depended on the schooling system for their mobility and advancement.

What it all comes down to is whether the common good will prevail over individual greed, materialism, and a me-me attitude or, alternatively, whether the rich and corporate giants will continue to trump the public interest. All of us in this country have the right to live the American dream, a concept rooted in the Declaration of Independence. This means that equality and opportunity must exist. However, increased inequality or reduced opportunity dampens the dream by further slanting the playing field against the average American and favoring inherited privilege.

Luxury Tax

Moralists often urge the wealthy to consider their lives and the lives of others and to adopt a more egalitarian posture toward the less fortunate. But the rich often respond that their own families would not be better off if there was more equality, that the differences in wealth allow them to purchase a personal aircraft, fancy cars, big boats, and expensive jewelry and furs, all of which distinguish them from average Americans who cannot afford these luxury items. These five high-priced items are now taxed, but the thresholds are high (and need to be lowered). Moreover, critics argue that the luxury tax raises little money; it is hard to administer, enforcing the regulations requires more resources than benefits derived, and the affected industries wind up losing jobs.[33] Of course, one needs to understand the critics and who they are—lobbyists and accountants that represent the wealthy and business people who sell luxury items to them.

Once we establish the fact that a person who buys a $100,000 boat or $50,000 car can afford an additional contribution to Uncle Sam, to help reduce the federal deficit, then the idea is to lower the thresholds or increase the tax rates, simplify the collection process, and expand the tax to include other luxury items such as expensive hotels, dining, cigars, liquor, and clothing. I would also curtail all tax loopholes that permit business exemptions and business write-offs for aircraft, boats, and cars. Finally, I would ask Congress to subject homes costing $1 million or more to a 5 to 10 percent excise tax, in addition to the normal transfer tax at the time of sale (which is determined by each state or local government body).

You might argue that taxing large homes is a fool's idea. But I don't believe such a policy in any way discourages home ownership, long considered an integral part of the American dream. It must be noted that one person's home may be another person's boat (or castle) or even an RV and, therefore, if we can tax expensive boats and RVs, even if purchased as a home, we should be able to tax expensive homes (as soon as the title or beneficiary is transferred).[34]

Cutting through all the criticisms, all the items I have added to the list for a potential luxury tax are purchased for personal enjoyment and status; they are not considered basic for one's life. Taxing these items, including expensive homes, would be progressive and achieve greater equity. To be sure, a family of four does not need a home with four and one-half baths and a three-car garage on a one- or two-acre lot; this is a luxury item. Of course, if everyone's home grows larger, the major effect would be to redefine what is an adequate dwelling and what is a luxury dwelling. Given this paradox, however, we should not pity the wealthy who are able to buy more and bigger things because they are adept at avoiding taxes. Ironically, the super rich (top 1 percent) claim they pay 35 percent of all income-tax payments, equal to more than what the bottom 50 percent pay.

No matter how we try to slice it, large and expensive homes, big boats, and fancy cars have more to do with status and conspicuous consumption and should be taxed. And, if we are honest with ourselves, so should someone who stays at the Ritz Carlton or Four Seasons and spends $1,000 a night for a two-bath, three-room suite overlooking a river or park in New York, Chicago, or San Francisco or anywhere else. The same holds true for expensive dining. Why should some corporate executive or salesperson be able to deduct $500 for dinner for two? Now, obviously, there are no popular taxes and a luxury tax can be criticized, from here to kingdom come, as unjust, counterproductive, and hard to enforce. These are all smoke screens for the rich and famous so they can continue their lifestyle and personal enjoyment without paying additional taxes, in their case a tax they can obviously afford if they are purchasing such high-priced items.

Windfall Tax

A windfall tax is an idea that has surfaced in connection with demonizing oil companies for price gauging and using these revenues to provide consumer rebates. A conservative view is that supply and demand dictates price and most of the demand is coming from China and India whose economies are growing at 7 to 10 percent annually.[35] Americans have a real need to reduce oil dependency, but oil companies have little motivation to invest their profits in ways that would advance those interests. A windfall tax on oil companies alone could produce an estimated $25 billion per year based on their 2005 profits, but a proposed formula, which centered around 50 percent of the profits on oil sales above $40 a barrel, failed to pass in Congress.[36]

It is easy for anyone with liberal stripes to zero in on the abuse of the free enterprise system at the expense of average Americans. But instead of looking for scapegoats or selecting a particular sector of the economy, I would suggest we look at *all* individuals and corporations that experience windfall profits on investments. For this tax not to effect small investors or dampen investment motivation in general, the limits should be set high; for example, a 5 percent tax on individual profits beyond 100 percent per year, starting at $500,000. Someone who invested $100,000 and made $300,000 profit in three years would not be affected because the $500,000 level was not achieved. However, someone who invested $100,000 and had a net profit of $700,000 in three years would pay 5 percent tax above $300,000, amounting to $20,000. Only wealthy investors who made large profits would be affected. This tax would not affect the average American nor reduce the incentive to invest.

For corporations, we might start the tax at $5 billion annual net income. Putting a $5 billion profit in perspective, the five largest oil companies earned $70 to $100 billion net income in 2005, depending on the source. Exxon's profit was the highest with $30 billion, and Chevron had $9 billion.[37] A 10 percent tax on Chevron's profits, after the $5 billion profit level, would generate $400 million. Fewer than two hundred companies would be affected by the tax because the ceiling would be set so high, but the idea is to target large companies with large profits. Depending on the economy, an additional $50 to $75 billion could be raised annually to fund needed human services. We could lower the criterion to a $1 billion profit margin and probably add another five hundred or more companies to the list, increasing the tax to about $200 to $250 billion—not a bad idea when we need to find ways to fund Social Security and health care for the onslaught of baby boomers.

I would also consider a tax on American casinos, which legally robs hard-working Americans of their money—about $80 billion a year. I'm sure the major casinos can afford to surrender 5 to 10 percent of their profits categorized under a windfall or luxury tax, or just simply for the grief it causes among gambling households.

Of course all this speculation is based on the belief that Americans are not timid nor indifferent, and they sincerely wish to preserve democracy and limit concentrated power and wealth in the hands of a few people. It also assumes that Hamilton was wrong—the majority (who he considered to represent the mob) are not stupid—and Jefferson was correct—checks and balances are needed to curb excessive power and wealth. To be sure, Alexis de Tocqueville's description of American democracy in the 1830s remains relevant today, despite the fact that so few American college graduates know who he is, can discuss his theories of democracy, and appreciate his cautionary tale about its fragility. Democracy needs a thriving, working- and middle-class population, where aspirations and dreams come true, where excellence is rewarded, and equality and equity are embedded in the hearts and minds of the people. Put in modern, working-class terms by contemporary economists, a nation's economic growth is tied to its workforce; a thriving workforce is the key ingredient to a nation's wealth, corporate profits, and gains in standard of living—all of which are crucial for the enhancement of democracy.[38]

Focus on Fuel

Thomas Friedman, the *New York Times* op-ed columnist, having shifted from the political Right to the Left in recent years, rhetorically claims that General Motors is the most dangerous company in America, with its emphasis on fuel-guzzling vehicles and that "the sooner this company gets taken over by Toyota, the better off our country will be."[39] Friedman's point is rhetorical, but Toyota is setting the standard for new auto technologies relating to fuel efficiency—gasoline-electric hybrids, low-pollution hydrogen cars, low-weight models, and flex-fuel cars that run on ethanol.

The ultimate display of U.S. indifference to fuel efficiency is that GM guaranteed for selected states a gas cap of $1.99 a gallon for one year in the form of a rebate if consumers bought one of their 2006 or 2007 gas-guzzlers such as a Hummer, several big SUVs, several trucks, and the Pontiac Grand Prix, Impala, and Monte Carlo sedans. This is their method for competing with the more fuel-efficient cars produced by Japanese rivals such as Toyota and Honda. You cannot fool most people most of the time; this is why Toyota in 2006 was worth $200 billion and GM $15 billion. It used to be reversed. Our political leaders, particularly Bush, are not willing to challenge Detroit automakers and force them to make fuel efficiency a top priority. GM, Ford, and Chrysler will continue to produce inefficient vehicles and remain tone death to the environment so long as the government or the people (who elect the government) refuse to take a firm stand.

The time has come to penalize Americans who buy gas-guzzlers and reward people for buying fuel-efficient automobiles. The new car and truck industry in America in 2006 amounted to approximately 64 million sales per year. We have the knowledge today to produce cars that easily get thirty-five miles per gallon.[40] Granted there is not going to be a "one-size-fits-all solution." But people need to be motivated to purchase smaller and more efficient cars, which in turn will motivate the American auto industry to produce and sell them.

The pocketbook is a key motivating device, and the states should eliminate the sales tax, as high as 8 to 9 percent in some states, on cars that average over thirty-five miles per gallon and trucks that average over twenty-five miles per gallon, inching up each year to fifty and forty miles, respectively, in the next five years. It is imperative for states with roads that have bumper to bumper auto traffic (California, Florida, Illinois, New Jersey, New York, etc.) to take the initiative to penalize gas-guzzlers and reward fuel-conscious consumers. If the states are unwilling to surrender the sales tax revenue for efficient cars, then the federal government might provide a tax deduction, reflecting the purchase price.

Those cars that do not reach the efficiency benchmark should pay a fine or a state or federal surcharge tax of 5 to 10 percent (in addition to the standard state sales tax). Right now a federal loophole permits bigger, heavier, and more inefficient cars and trucks to be produced by the "Big Three" automakers, one of Bush's corporate-favored policies. The impact of the reform proposal would not only improve the environment with fewer fuel-fossil emissions, but also would reduce oil consumption by eighty thousand to one hundred thousand barrels per day, an estimate calculated by the Union of Concerned Scientists. As a side benefit, it would help curtail the nation's trade deficit and fund fewer terrorist operations that are fueled by oil reserves from the Middle East.

Focus on Essentials

Income inequality is an economic and social ill, partially caused by regressive taxes, which discriminate against low- and moderate-income groups and favor the top 10 percent. It is further highlighted by U.S. law-makers who have refused to raise the minimum wage, presently $5.15 per hour, since 1997 and then vote for proposals that lead to deep cuts in social, health, and education spending. One of the most regressive taxes is the state sales tax on food, drugs, and clothing, some of the basic neces-sities of life. We need to follow the example of the state of Kansas, which has eliminated its sales tax on food. This concept needs to be extended to the cost of prescription drugs and clothing bought at tag sales at KMart or the Gap—or for items less than $100.

Since the economy emerged from its 2000–2001 recession, employment opportunities have remained subpar—below previous recoveries. Most of the growth in jobs, between 50 and 67 percent, depending on the report or economist you wish to believe, have been at the bottom-wage scale.[41] Both percentages undermine and shrink the middle class. Put in different terms, low-wage jobs are today's fastest growing job categories, and nearly 30 percent of our workforce is unable to provide for its basic needs. These people are in dire need of tax relief; instead, the federal govern-ment, under a conservative administration, has chosen to raise their taxes and reduce their social, health, and education benefits so it can provide tax relief for the rich.

Fortunately, the American people are smart enough not to be hood-winked by glib and gimmicky spoofs supporting regressive taxes. Elimi-nating the tax on food, drugs, and low-end clothing is a start in the right direction for slowing down the squeeze on moderate-income Americans. The money lost by the states can be made back by raising states taxes on annual household incomes above $200,000 or by increasing sales taxes on high-end purchases, such as homes above $500,000, expensive automo-biles, boats, jewelry, furs, etc.

Free College Tuition

Tuition costs and fees now exceed the borrowing limits of college stu-dents under the federal loan programs. Government loans, which had the best terms, made up 47 percent of all financial aid in 2005, but interest rates have increased under the Bush policy to offset deficit spending. Banks are taking advantage of these trends by expanding their student loan applications, and it is assumed that more students are doomed to be burdened with debt, as these interest rates are averaging 9 to 10 percent. We are so accustomed with debt as a society, and with most parents over-whelmed with their own debt, that we do not see it as a big deal if their children also take on debt. This perception is aggravated by the concern that parents need to plan their own retirement to avoid being a burden on their children.

We are in the midst of the beginning of a vicious cycle, caused by limited savings for retirement by the baby boom generation, increased college costs (exceeding the rate of inflation), and high interest rates and other burdens on private loans. It is a trend that now affects the middle class and is bound to worsen and affect more people up the economic ladder. One way to limit the effects of higher college tuition is for state lawmakers to consider free state-college tuition for resident high-school students with a "B" or better average and an agreed SAT or ACT test score, which could differ among the states and be set at the top 75 or 80 percentile within the state. More states need to think about ways of reducing the burden of debt for college students and their families. Here I would also argue for the need of the states and/or the federal government to reduce the burden of college loans by requiring banks to tie them to a lower index, such as the ten-year treasury note, which in 2006 hovered around 4.5 percent. A loan for 125 to 150 basis points above the ten-year treasury note would yield a 5.75 to 6.0 percent rate of interest, which is a fair profit for private financial institutions. These rates are obviously lower than the crippling rates of 10 percent currently offered.

In the meantime, several questions arise. How will the two-thirds of college students who have tuition debt, averaging $4,700 per year in payments for families with annual incomes of $33,600 or less in 2004, climb out of it?[42] Is it worth it to spend up to $160,000 to $200,000 in four years on private college tuition, room and board, and assume much higher student debt with higher payments than the average amount? Tuition alone at private colleges (averaging $22,218 in 2006–2007)[43] represented 20 to 25 percent of the mean income of the students' families. How much tuition help should the federal government, state governments, and colleges provide? To whom? Should financial need supersede merit or vice versa? If our goal is a diversified student population, will minority status be the prime criterion? If the goal is to further mobility for all classes, then will income trump academic merit? If our goal is to be globally competitive, then should merit exceed the notion of disadvantaged status? And if we consider the notion of reverse brain drain, how do we streamline immigration laws to assist foreign science and math students who graduate from American universities to obtain green cards? In the final analysis, we need to examine affordability and accessibility of higher education in context with the economy and global competition. And how do we ensure that U.S. multinational corporations, such as Cisco, Microsoft, G.E., and Wal-Mart, will not hire educated and skilled people in developing countries willing to work for less than half U.S. wages?

SAFETY NETS STRETCHED THIN

Most of us without a sense of history and proper benchmarks quickly forget the immigrant story, the Lady in the Harbor who welcomed the "huddled masses" who were denied opportunity in their native lands. This land is about dreams and opportunities, about the millions of Americans clawing their way into the middle class, and a melting pot of different races, religions, and languages coming together as a nation of many nations. It is the vagaries of *mobility*, an academic term that only sociologists and economists fully comprehend, a kind of looking-glass gloss supported by statistical data that most folks outside of academia don't fully understand, which characterizes so much of the story of America. For Joe or Jane Doakes, for all the Archie Bunkers, Homers, and Dorothys (of the *Golden Girls*), working in factories or waiting on tables, refusing to be poor, it is called economic opportunity. It is this spirit, the escape from poverty and the rise of the middle class, combined with the ideals of democracy, that make America great.

Despite our refusal to give up the middle class, we have entered a new era, with many Americans spiraling downward, teetering between the middle class and lower class, trying to hold on to the vestiges of their former world. We have been given a ticket to witness our own slow demise. What is causing this economic squeeze, this unwanted decline? Is it the slow evaporation of our "safety net"? Does it have something to do with globalization and the loss of American jobs to overseas competitors? As trade deficits grow and the American dollar declines, is there a new currency in the making—the North American peso? Can the shift of the tax burden from the rich to the rest of us, from investments to income, have something to do with the shrinking of the middle class? Is our decline related to our own personal responsibility or shift in family or cultural values?[44] Is luck a factor? Does it take nothing more than a series of bad personal decisions or choices that at the time appear to be perfectly reasonable to set in motion our economic decline? Quite simply, how we perceive this shift in mobility, and its cause, has something to do with our view of society and more precisely whether we lean toward the Right or Left.

From the halls of Congress and the White House, to the voting booths where Americans have the opportunity to make decisions about their future and their children's future, there is a denial, a repression, a false sense of reality about the economic outlook for most Americans. The looming shortfalls for pensions and health care in America are alarming, and there is a growing gap between promises and expectations on one side of the balance sheet and revenues and projections on the other side. A flood of retiring baby boomers, coupled with the reduction of private pensions and health-care plans, is already creating and will multiply economic hardship for tens of millions of Americans. It will cause federal spending on age-related benefits to skyrocket and consume most of the nation's economy.

Depending on the study we wish to cite, which often reflects partisan politics, the gap between promises and revenues will be $18 to $48 trillion over the next fifty years. Furthermore, the government is currently borrowing more than $200 billion a year from Social Security and Medicare funds[45] to finance its current budget deficits. As a matter of record, the U.S. annual deficit was about $300 billion in 2006, down about $20 billion from the previous year, with the cumulative red ink totaling some $9 trillion, which equals more than twice our annual output (GDP).[46] As we know, there is a limit or critical point when the ship sinks or the roof caves in. No one is able to predict our deficit limits, as history is no model because we have already passed all previous deficit figures. Meanwhile, the Republicans and Democrats and their associated economic advisors and news commentators squabble over who is to blame—whether the problem is largely related to foreign trade policies, the war in Iraq, taxes that favor the rich, or increasing entitlements to a growing elderly population. Peter Peterson, who is chairman of the Committee on Foreign Relations, blames both parties for not accepting responsibility and for creating "an undeclared war on the future . . . that is on our children."[47]

Peterson and other economists, such as Laurence Kotlikoff and Scott Burns, are convinced that economic growth cannot "bail us out" or make up the difference between government spending and revenues.[48] To put the problem in slightly different terms, we are living in an expanding retirement community, but fun in the sun is becoming very expensive. Our elected leaders prefer to ignore the problem and shift fiscal problems to future generations. They prefer to tell us what we want to hear and we fantasize about our retirement rather than face the future demographic tidal wave or what Kotlikoff and Burns have labeled "the coming generational storm."

In the meantime, the U.S. demand for consumption continues to bring in cheap imports from China and other Asian countries. Although Milton Friedman argued that the free-market system and unrestrained trade with China is beneficial for world stability and American growth, China boosted its foreign exchange reserves in the United States to $610 billion in 2004, up from $403 billion the previous year.[49] No one seems to want to face the possibility that China may very well become our future political and military enemy, threatening both Japan, Taiwan, and South Korea, and is already our long-term economic rival. What happens if it pulls the plug and stops financing our deficits? Interest rates will skyrocket, stocks and bonds would most likely plunge, and recession would soon follow.

Of course, Friedman believed it was in the best interest for China, which holds a huge and growing U.S. debt (interest Americans pay to China), not to upset the apple cart for it would overturn its own economic engine. But Friedman who looked and talks like everyone's favorite grandfather prior to his death, may not have had 100 percent of his marbles—a not so nice inference based simply on his ninety-plus years of thinking.

DEBT AND DECLINING BENEFITS

The big safety net programs—Social Security, Medicare, and Medicaid—represented 42 percent of federal spending in 2005. Based on demographic data and current rates of spending, by 2030 there will be no money left for any other human services, for parks, veterans benefits, environmental protection, highways and infrastructure, etc. According to government economists the total fiscal gap facing this country in the next thirty years is $60 trillion, which is considered to be a low-ball estimate by some experts outside of government. Without deficit reduction, the interest on the growing debt will amount to 33 percent of income tax dollars collected by 2015.[50] If we look to close the fiscal gap with higher taxes, it will require an immediate and permanent increase of the 80 percent tax in revenue—and we know this will not happen.[51]

When Alan Greenspan urged Congress to reduce future benefits on Social Security and Medicare, he was actually understating the problem that lies ahead. Isabel Sawhill, the director of the Economic Studies program at the Brookings Institution, points out that the number of retires is expected to double in the next thirty years, which means fewer dollars will be coming from payroll taxes and an increasing amount of dollars will be going out in retirement and medical benefits.[52] Medicare funds will starting running deficits (2013) and run out of money (2026) much quicker than Social Security reaches deficit levels (2013) and is exhausted (2044), because medical costs have been rising much faster than inflation and with increased population longevity the costs will soar.[53] Actually, Social Security benefits are much smaller and predictable than health care.

Social Security

Here are some disturbing and hard-to-swallow facts about the U.S. retirement population and the "golden years" ahead, which may likely become tarnished. In 2000, there were 35.5 million Americans age sixty-five and older. By 2030, we will have 70 to 75 million. During this thirty-year period, the dependency ratio—those sixty-five and older to those twenty to sixty-four (presumed willing and able to work)—will rise from 21 percent to 36 percent. In 1950, the number of workers per Social Security beneficiary was 16.5. By 2000 the ratio had declined to 3.4. In 2030, the number will be approximately two workers per beneficiary. This means that in thirty years (from 2000 to 2030), the cost of supporting one retiree rose 70 percent. In eighty years (from 1950 to 2030), the cost soared 800 percent.[54]

In order to try to keep up with increased Social Security costs, the employment tax on wages has increased from $3,000 in 1950 to $87,000 in 2003, a twenty-nine-fold increase. The choices needed to solve the mess we are in range from wishful thinking to glum news: (1) assume the economy will grow and federal reserves will match the revenues needed; (2) delay, reduce, or eliminate benefits for new retirees; (3) increase wages subject to Social Security tax; and (4) increase the Social Security payroll taxes on business and corporations.

The first option borders on fantasy. Government projections cannot be expected to resemble economic reality; they are only statistical models based on a few major variables and fail to consider unaccounted for and unpredictable variables. The second and third choices are antiprogressive and could damage America's safety net and entitlement program; they need to be implemented with caution. The fourth choice potentially increases production costs for goods and services on a global basis and limits America's ability to compete with other countries; in turn, conservative economists claim that this indirectly leads to manufacturing decline, outsourcing of jobs, and recession. This should be a last resort option. In short, the next generation is in for a huge awakening—a potential decline in their pension benefits and standard of living.

Bearing in mind my liberal tendencies, I would delay benefits until age sixty-eight for new retirees, saving about 5 to 10 percent of the cost for Social Security. It would be beneficial to lift the cap on payroll tax for Social Security and raise the wages subject to Social Security tax up to $200,000 or $300,000 per year in 2006 dollars, but exempt the first $50,000 in wages to help the common wage earner. Most controversial, we might reduce Social Security benefits for those people with private pensions—Keogh plans, 401(k) plans, IRA plans, etc. that are valued at more than say $1.5 million (in 2006 dollars) at the time of retirement. Finally, for the rising population over sixty-five still earning a gross income of $200,000 or more, instead of taxing their social security benefits, as we do now, we might think about eliminating their benefits entirely. Let's face it; they can afford to transfer their wealth to less fortunate Americans and strengthen America's economic future.

To conservative criticism—"screw the people who are lazy and don't work"—I would respond and call it giving money back to the country that allowed wealthy people the opportunity to earn their money and helping out the elderly in the coming age of limited prosperity. For the deer hunters of America who also want to put the "screws" on the so-called lazy and the less fortunate, I would ask them to calm down and stop shouting and stepping on their own toes. They need to get a grip on real issues and stop voting against their own self-interests; they are blinded by family and cultural values that are nothing more than small side shows and secondary issues that conservatives use to ignore or brush over economic issues.

The Pension Picture

The number of workers who can expect a pension plan from private sources is dwindling as large corporations on the verge of bankruptcy or reorganization curtail benefits or discover their pension funds are under-funded. Still other companies, in order to stay competitive, are freezing or eliminating them entirely for employees. For example, IBM claims it will save $3 billion over the next five years by freezing pensions for its current employees.[55] Company loyalty is gone; people are now on their own. Check with airline and auto employees if you need confirmation.

A traditional retirement plan promised a specific monthly benefit, in some cases an exact dollar amount, based on years of service and salary. Participants rarely made contributions to company plans, although some government plans required employee contributions. The participant was not expected to make investment decisions; knowledgeable fund managers made them. Most important, the traditional pension allowed individuals to create wealth in spite of themselves, part of a social contract (in the abstract) that existed between employers and employees.

Thus a typical pension that provided $50,000 a year (typical of the average teacher, policeman, or branch manager of a bank) to someone fifty-five or older was equivalent to approximately $1 million in savings earning a return of 5 percent. Moreover, many public-sector pensions added an annual cost of living adjustment in monthly payments to compensate for inflation, and many traditional plans (private and public) came with retiree health benefits that exceeded Medicare benefits. Many of these private plans are now evaporating, down from 91 percent in 1984 among companies with 1,000 or more employees to 61 percent in 2004. The number continues to fall—another 15 percent plan to eliminate contributions for new employees and 6 percent plan to freeze contributions for existing employees.

As for public pensions, huge shortfalls exist among state and local governments. The state plans, for example, have been calculated to provide $2.5 trillion but only $1.7 trillion has been set aside. Huge discrepancies exist between reported and funded plans, with Minnesota (49 percent), Kentucky (48 percent), and Maryland (50 percent) teachers being the most underfunded. As for city plans, the New York City pension fund gap in 2005 was $49 billion, more than twice the shortfall of the neighboring state of New Jersey.[56] In other words, public employees (teachers, social workers, policemen, judges, etc.) are being promised future benefits that might not be provided without big tax increases or big budget cuts. As most public law prohibits reducing pension benefits already granted, the cities and states are expected to trim future pension plans and skimp on salaries and health-care benefits.

With the new individual pension plans, such as 401(k) plans (the most popular), Keoghs and IRAs, the burden of retirement savings falls in the hands of employees, as well as the decision on how much to save and where to invest. Employers no longer have to worry about retirement benefits, appropriate funding and eventual payments, for employees. The result is that traditional pension plans have decreased by half, from 35 percent of the workforce in 1984 to 18 percent in 2004. Workers covered by 401(k) plans have soared from 7.5 million workers in 1984 to 42 million in 2001, according to the U.S. Employee Benefit Security Administration.

Most troubling, 25 to 30 percent of eligible workers choose not to participate in private pensions because their salaries are too low and they need the money for daily expenses. Another 20 to 25 percent choose not to participate because their employers don't participate or advertise the options available, and still others are too much in debt to put away retirement money.[57] Less than 10 percent contribute the maximum allowed by law and many cash out when they change jobs, leaving themselves with no retirement benefits. People trying to save for a home or pay their mortgage often strip their pensions or don't participate at all when times are tight.

When it comes to retirement, we have a new class of "haves" and "have nots," splitting along economic lines, generational differences, and the private versus public sector. Low- and moderate-income workers, including the struggling middle class, young workers, and private-sector workers are expected to come up short while better paid and older workers and public employees, who still have a traditional fixed-benefit pension, will fare much better. People today just don't realize the slim foundation they are standing on when it comes to retirement; they would rather not deal with it, especially if they are in their twenties or thirties. People who don't understand the stock market or fear it because of inside trading are now forced to take part in it. Many "do it yourself" plans are bound to lose money. All these trends may be great for investment companies and fund managers who earn commissions from investors, but it is doubtful if gambling on stocks will work for the average person.

Social Security traditionally provided about 40 percent of retirement income, but this is unlikely to continue as benefits are reduced and life expectancy increases—leaving the average American more dependent and desperate during retirement years and creating a new struggling and aging class of former working- and middle-class Americans. As the pension divide increases between those with traditional and guaranteed pension plans and those with individual and nonguaranteed plans, a good deal of resentment among workers with small or no pensions will most likely surface. It is also probable that city and state-run pension plans for municipal workers will come under attack and be reduced in the future for younger employees as pension costs increase and taxes are levied on the public to pay for them.

With traditional retirement plans being eroded, one strategy is to require all companies listed on the stock exchange that show profits for the year to increase Social Security taxes or pension contributions for the benefit of their workers. Companies often scream that they cannot continue to fund traditional pension and health benefits and remain competitive. However, here the focus is on profitable companies. During good times, corporations should be required to take care of their employees and honor the social contract that is supposed to exist between them. The bulk of benefits should not be earmarked for executives. If lawmakers would cap executive salaries, or at least insist on stockholders input, some of the remaining corporate profits could easily shift to the workers and stockholders—including improved retirement packages for employees.

Finally, as of 2005, there were approximately 50,000 private company retirement plans, but only 1.6 percent offered automatic enrollment. Studies show that automatic enrollment increases participation by 26 percent.[58] Common sense suggests the need for laws making enrollment automatic, so that more Americans will have a retirement fund.

The Health-Care Bubble

The American health care system—characterized by high costs, bureaucratic complexity, legal loopholes, and diminished services—is in a state of crisis and becoming a major financial burden on the national economy. It is a disgrace that a country with our resources continues to deprive some 46 million low-income wage earners of health insurance and deprive tens of millions of others of adequate health insurance. In fact, in many cases the present health-care system (the number-one reason for filing bankruptcy in America) forces bankruptcy on those who thought they had paid for adequate health insurance.

No one in America should have to bear the burden of catastrophic medical expenses, go bankrupt to avoid medical payments (a week in a hospital with a serious medical condition can cost more than $100,000 for those without insurance), or risk losing their life savings and assets or plot and shift them to their children in order to preserve their finances (commonly done before applying and receiving long-term care under Medicaid benefits).

Insurance is supposed to provide adequate protection so that no family or individual paying into the system is put into financial jeopardy because of an unforeseen health problem. Its purpose should not be profit or to maximize gains for insurance companies and managed health-care companies, but to protect the people of the country, especially those paying into the system. The fundamental concern of private enterprise is the bottom line, which is in direct opposition to a health care system, which should protect the nation's citizens or insured. Capitalism is fueled by profit, and one of the most successful, capitalist groups are insurance companies; generally, they have more assets and income than banks. A health care system is theoretically based on compassion and need, very different from the mission of free enterprise and corporate America.

Currently, two-thirds of Americans under sixty-five get health coverage on the job.[59] The insurance companies purposely erect a host of confusing and complex codes and jargon to slow down and limit patient reimbursement for legitimate expenses. Although they provide opportunity to contest reimbursement dollars, a thicket of organizational layers and personnel encourage patients to give up, or not even file. The insured usually experiences the battle of paperwork with unfriendly customer service employees whose mission is to say "no," "no," "no." The bottom line provides the incentive for insurance companies to say "no."

The private health care system is a zero-sum game. Insurance companies providing health benefits try to limit costs while maximizing profits and increasing premiums. For the many companies that provide insurance, there is no incentive to spend additional money on employee benefits. Increased benefits become too costly, and the companies eventually are unable to compete at home or on a global basis. For example, the cost of health care for employees and retirees at General Motors runs $5.2 billion annually and raises costs slightly more than $1,500 per car, one reason why the company is unable to compete with foreign competitors and is on the verge of bankruptcy. By contrast, Toyota spends $97 per car for health benefits in Japan.[60]

If the federal government was paying for a national health insurance program as in Japan and other G-8 (industrialized) counties, GM and other large U.S. corporations would be in better health and better able to compete. On the other hand, 46 percent of the children of Wal-Mart's employees are uninsured or on Medicaid. In its push for a healthy and therefore cheaper workforce, Wal-Mart executive memos recommend adding physical activity, like rounding up shopping carts, for all employees and discouraging the sickly from applying for jobs.[61]

General Motors, on one side, and Wal-Mart, on the other side of the health divide, represent the health-care dilemma facing all Americans. Reducing health benefits, and getting employees to share in these ballooning costs, lightens a company's balance sheet because it does not have to use cash flow to pay for such liabilities. Unquestionably, all Americans are entitled to full health coverage. But linking it to employment and putting the liability on the business sector raises the prices of goods and services; moreover, it discourages the creation of good jobs (both blue-collar, union jobs and white-collar jobs) and encourages outsourcing of such jobs. In the end, the American public is paying for health care—either in higher consumer prices or higher taxes or loss of good jobs. Keep in mind that whatever health insurance premiums GM and other companies are able to save, because of job reductions or as a result of reducing health employment costs, are transferred to those who pay for insurance or to taxpayers who pay for Medicaid and free emergency hospital care. Of course it's not only GM's problem. Just as companies have shifted pension responsibilities to their employees, the same shift is occurring with health care. When you start listening to what executives have to say about health costs, it feels that the auto industry is not alone, especially as global competition heats up.

The federal government needs to sort out the relationship between employment, health care, and the American people. One way for increasing business profits, jobs, and the health of the economy is to shift the health care responsibility onto the government or taxpayer who can afford the heavier burden. If we remain blind or deaf to this dilemma (expecting pension and health care costs to be absorbed by the private sector), then U.S. manufacturing will continue to decline (between 2000 and 2005 the United States lost about three million manufacturing jobs) and job cuts in other sectors of the economy including middle-class, white-collar jobs increasingly will be lost to the Asian market.

Lyndon Johnson was criticized as an "overreaching social engineer," when he introduced Medicare in 1966 to fortify his "Great Society" and originally taxed annual wage earnings up to $6,6000, the same amount Social Security was then taxed. The Clintons, Bill and Hillary alike, were labeled as "socialists" for trying to nationalize the American health care system some thirty years later; insurance lobbyists (with billions of dollars behind them) were hell-bent on protecting their interests and were successful in convincing Republican lawmakers that a universal health program would hinder free enterprise and lead to an inefficient, wasteful government program. Despite the fact that a recent (2004) survey by the Civil Society Institute (in Newton, MA) found 67 percent of American's believing there should be a guarantee of health care for all Americans,[62] conservatives continue to warn about socialized Medicare.

Unfortunately, today, because of partisan politics and the influence of insurance and drug companies, the American people still lack a national health care system for all people. We fail to recognize that the health-care systems of other nations (including Western Europe, Canada, and Australia) deliver better care for the majority of its people at much less cost. It does not take a magician or a mathematical genius to figure out that if we have one overall provider, who requires competitive bidding among subproviders or contractors for all services, it will force the "middlemen"—insurance companies, pharmaceutical companies, health equipment and supply companies, and hospitals—to sharpen their pencils and reduce costs. It's like the government taking on the role of Wal-Mart and forcing all its manufacturers, wholesalers, and suppliers to lower costs so they can pass the savings on to their customers.

If you are big enough like Wal-Mart, and the government is bigger, you can control the market, knock out or limit the middle contractors, and trim costs. With one overall health provider, we would have one set of papers to fill out, as opposed to an endless supply of forms for consumers who don't fully understand them, and one set of papers for doctors and pharmacists who are sensitive about time consumption. Choice is not the solution—not under the present Medicare system—with countless versions of premium payments, copays, deductibles, limitations, and methods of choosing doctors, drugs, and hospitals. Many people just find it dreadfully confusing to choose the best program for the money they can afford from a bewildering array of options and are frequently bounced from one computer to the next and one plan to the next.

Private Health Care

The health system in the United States is so complicated by a myriad of plans with different choices and options that most people find it dreadfully confusing to choose the best program if they have to make a choice; the only way to make sense of it is not to have to analyze it because you are not one of the 42 million Americans older or disabled and entitled to it, or one of the 20 million retirees with other coverage by a former company's or government's health plan. What is apparent and easy to grasp is that employers are reducing health benefits for employers older than sixty-five years and retirees who are eligible for either Medicare or Medicaid coverage. In fact the percentage of large companies (two hundred or more employees) offering retiree health benefits has declined from 66 percent in 1988 to 31 percent in 2005.[63]

Younger employees and new employees are no longer being provided full health coverage or are being asked to shoulder a larger portion of the costs in order for companies to maintain profits. It's a whole new world we are wrestling with, where companies and even government employers are asking: To what health-care benefits are workers entitled? What is their commitment to workers? Can these expenses be afforded? In the meantime, soaring Medicare costs loom on the horizon, due to the ever-increasing aging society, in which the number of eligible Americans entitled to coverage will double by 2030.

To compensate for companies trimming medical and dental benefits, new health-care laws allow individuals to invest their own money tax-free for current and future medical expenses not covered by insurance. By 2010 it is expected that 15 million Americans, or some 10 percent of those insured and who can afford it, will have health savings accounts—currently caped at $3,500.[64] These accounts should total some $75 billion, assuming the cap is raised to $5,000 by 2010, and you can bet your last dollar that the banks, insurance companies, and Wall Street will be offering consumers all kinds of accounts, accompanied by fees and commissions. It's another way for big business (U.S. financial giants) to pull money from the pockets of people on the street just trying to pay their bills.

The law is aimed at the high-end insured who can afford to put aside additional money for medical services, illustrating the bifurcation of the American health system along class lines, where one group can afford to pay for the top-tier health care. At the high-end of the health care system are those people who can afford specialists, special and preventative tests, and special drugs. On the other side of the divide are the uninsured and inadequately insured who are forced to opt for whatever limited services and participating doctors are available under their plan or under Medicaid. They are forced to wait in hospital emergency rooms and free clinics and be treated by resident physicians or those with minimal experience; they must learn to cope with additional frustration and pain. A two-tier system for higher education has existed since the colonial and post-colonial period. The question is whether we want to perpetuate a two-tier system of health care—one for the rich and one for the nonrich?

Medicaid

The federal government shares in the cost of, and provides the states with flexibility to modify (and limit) benefits and raise taxes to pay for, the Medicaid plan. Based on state politics and revenues the states have various plans. The plans are confusing and AARP representatives, insurance companies, and pharmacies are continuously explaining to consumers the changing Medicaid laws, which vary state by state. Some like New

York, Illinois, and Wisconsin are expansive because of liberal governors. Others in Arkansas, Mississippi, and Tennessee have limited benefits because they are more conservative, but the costs are still crippling because these states are poorer.

In the last ten years, Medicaid rolls have increased nationwide and the states have been squeezed by soaring costs and sluggish economies. The program consumes about 20 percent of the states' budgets. Moreover, more than half of the states do not require any local contribution, and those that do, with the exception of New York City, require a small percentage.[65] The outcome is that city and county government officials are not motivated to police the program or curb Medicaid fraud.

With states shouldering most of the financial burden, they are forced to either slash services in other areas, such as education, transportation, and infrastructure, or raise taxes. Poor states and states with a high percentage of Medicaid residents are forced to cut benefits, even if it means putting sickly and aged people at risk. The program also puts a burden on states that have had businesses leave, further shrinking the tax base. This problem became more apparent during the last recession, as the number of unemployed people increased and went on Medicaid.

As most states have budget deficits of their own, there is the reported draconian trend of cutting health coverage and benefits of people who have nowhere else to turn. Increasingly states are removing people from the program and/or reducing hospital and drug benefits with no process for appeal.[66] But the chief Medicaid problem is malfeasance and waste, compounded by inadequate monitoring of spending. Critics point out that Medicaid fraud is rampant with nonexistent and extra billed services from providers, and that the program serves many families with incomes well above the poverty level, which it was not originally designed to do. Drug prices are out of control because they were not prenegotiated.

In addition, there are continuous reports of mismanagement by state officials and by health-care organizations. Governors from various states have imposed restrictions and cutbacks in an effort to save money, to cut people and services from the program. But the longer the governors avoid dealing with this public expense, the more likely that the fiscal termites in the economic woodwork will bring down the state government budgets and force cuts in other social and education services they are responsible for providing or force higher taxes, which are already at peak levels in most states.[67]

Another issue tied to Medicare is that the middle class has used the program for long-term care by going to elder-care attorneys who figure out how to qualify and transfer assets to children or other kin and have the applicant become a ward of the state. Furthermore, some states give a spouse the right to refuse any financial obligation, leaving Medicaid responsible for home care and nursing home care. In 2006 Congress amended the law and curbed Medicaid planning (transferring assets), by reducing Medicaid coverage for nursing home residents if they had given away money to family members in the previous five years; recipients would lose coverage in an amount equal to what they had given away.[68]

Even worse is the overbilling by physicians, hospitals, and nursing homes, the latter of which averaged $62,000 a year nationwide and $94,000 in New York State in 2004, with some instances of overbilling topping $200,000 per year[69] (with 85 percent of the residents on Medicare). To be sure, the biggest problem is the need to cut costs, which can be achieved through tighter monitoring and investigation, as well as criminal prosecution of culprits, ranging from people who cheat and don't belong on Medicaid and those who overbill the government. We could probably cut costs $10 to $20 billion a year if we cracked down on the culprits.

What we need is a single government-financed health program incorporating Medicaid into the system and thus eliminating the fifty different plans that now exist. Our system of health care is shockingly confusing and inefficient, costing 350 percent more per person than the Canadian system, which most U.S. physicians consider to be first-rate.[70] It has become an insurance and pharmaceutical give-away plan, with limited competition. A single-payer system should be simpler and more efficient. Politically, this idea is impractical, given the influence of health insurance and pharmaceutical companies and the partisan outlook toward a national health-care program.

Hope is on the distant horizon; the majority of U.S. doctors are now lobbying Congress for an overall government-financed health program, with one set of instruction forms for all Americans and one set of medical reimbursement forms for physicians and pharmacies, which would limit confusion and time wasted by medical personnel, as well as the power of insurance companies. Instead of sitting on the sidelines, more health providers need to contain the cost and corruption linked to our present health programs and shift the focus from hospitals to physicians, with emphasis on prevention. Voters need to consider the number of uninsured Americans, including the working class (and their children) and middle class who are often forced to go bankrupt if they are inadequately insured. Much more ongoing policing and investigation, which could save billions of dollars on an annual basis, is needed. We need to limit the elder generation from "playing" the system by transferring their assets and becoming wards of the states in order to limit their own responsibility for long-term care. Despite AARP's objection to reducing coverage for such recipients, pressure groups need to take a progressive advocacy approach and not defend those who want to take advantage of the system.

Medicare

The new Medicare health plan, signed into law in 2005, expands coverage to millions of eligible Americans, but the basic program will cost $88.50 per month in 2006 compared to $58.70 in 2003—and withdraw an average of $120 a month per person. The premiums are deducted from Social Security checks, but the premiums paid to beneficiaries only cover about 25 percent of the actual cost.[71] Right now, workers and employers each pay 1.45 percent in Medicare taxes on salaries up to $219,417; when it began in 1966 the tax on Medicare was capped at $6,600. Those revenues, however, are inadequate; since 2000 Medicare benefits per beneficiary has increased 2.6 times faster than the amount workers pay into the program.[72] Getting a hold of these health expenditures should be a government priority; instead the health benefits were expanded in 2005/2006 by President Bush in order to attract voters from the graying population at the expense of the younger generation. But most people have not figured it out that the new Medicare program includes higher premiums and copayments and less payment for drug prescriptions for all beneficiaries, reducing costs $6.4 billion over five years. This was part of a $40 billion budget-cut package aimed at health, social, and education programs,[73] while the political Right continued to cut taxes for the rich and increase military spending.

The program also offers a wide variety of private-based plans with different premiums, benefits, exclusions, deductibles, and copayments—making for a daunting and confusing host of choices and decisions. The problem is that Medicare carries additional costs by allowing private insurance companies to provide the various plans at a profit. To meet the approval of conservative lawmakers, the plan had to include private insurance policies, which tend to shortchange the American people by pressuring doctors to choose fewer and cheaper medical devices and diagnostic tests, generic drugs, and reduced hospital care. The result is that the elderly and disabled will have to continue to fight for equal health-care treatment in society. The alternative is a uniform government program, with only one or possibly two options, designed to eliminate the profit of the insurance companies, simplify the paperwork, and cost considerably less per person if we use the Canadian, Australian, or British yardstick. Of course, we cannot use the word "socialism" in context with health care, despite the fact that it seems to be working in the rest of the Anglo world.

Payment could be made by employees under sixty-five who get health coverage on the job. Right now, wage-earners get their health coverage tax-free, costing the government approximately $126 billion in uncollected annual taxes. If workers received high-cost health insurance benefits paid by employers, they should be taxed in part on the value of their benefits. For example, a basic family policy costs employers about $10,800 a year.[74] The worker participating in any plan that costs above the average could be taxed on the value of the more generous benefits in excess of the average cost.

Right now, these costly health insurance policies are provided to high-paid managers and executives and union members and government workers in generous health plans. But most of the benefit that goes untaxed overwhelmingly favors wealthy workers in higher tax brackets. This is only one way to consider how the government can find the tax revenues to pay for rising medical costs and give people more control over insurance companies that seek to provide coverage for a profit and maximize the bottom line. It is the insurance industry—with its premiums, deductions, exclusions, and copayments—that has created a health crisis in which the growing elderly, disabled, and poor population and many wage earners are now at risk and have to tolerate diminished services.

The health of the nation's citizens should not be in the hands of the private sector. Reform has never been a priority of big business. It is time for the American public to understand that health is part of the human services sector, along with education, unemployment insurance, welfare, etc., and should be the responsibility of the public sector. Medicare is bound to be more expensive if decisions are made by the private sector because business is in the business of making money. Ultimately the health care of the nation falls on the government anyway, and the public pays for it directly and indirectly. This is not like trying to explain the unexplainable; in simple terms, the government needs to find a way to raise revenues and make more demands on people who can afford to pay so that all Americans can share in the benefits of Medicare and technological and medical advances.

A PERSONAL PERSPECTIVE

Americans are hustlers, dreamers, and innovators. Nothing in our historical experience as a nation has prepared us for the future decline in the American standard of living or the growing cleavage between the rich (the top 10 percent) and the majority populace. Only when an epoch passes can historians, writers, or reformers look back and decide what was distinctive about it, what led to the outcomes of that period. In the early 1930s, no one could be sure when the Great Depression would end, and in the early 1940s no one could determine exactly the outcome of the Great War in Europe, just like today no one can tell us precisely how much higher will the ratio climb between what a CEO earns and a worker in a company makes (current estimates range between 300 to 525 to 1), how many more manufacturing jobs America will lose to China and the Asian rim, or how many more high-paying white collar jobs will be outsourced to India.

By 2020 or thereabouts, economic opportunity, social mobility, and an expanding gross domestic product—defining characteristics of the American nation—may have withered away to the point where Americans may finally awaken to the need to curb the capitalistic appetite that we now have and to put more effort (greater government regulation, disclosure methods, and indictments and longer criminal sentences) to stop the ruthless quest for profits among many captains of industry. What was once considered to be a passing period in our history, those robber-baron millionaires who broke the lives of workers and laws of the land, the many men that Teddy Roosevelt labeled as the "malefactors of great wealth," is still with us as part of the MBA culture and American business ethos. It's reflected today in what I call the age of Enronism, characterized by Wall Street and business and banking fraud.[75] It is reflected in the out-of-control salaries of the top paid CEOs in the country, who sometimes earn the equivalent of 10 percent of the total corporate earnings of their companies,[76] and complain that American workers who average about $16.50 an hour are overpaid.

So long as we have the view that people like Bill Gates, Michael Dell, and Steve Jobs, along with their descendents, are entitled to all their wealth because they founded highly successful companies, and that all the other CEOs like Michael Eisner of Disney World or Jim Kilts of Gillette deserve the hundreds of millions they make for managing a big company, and that all the entertainers and athletes earn what is reasonable for singing a three-minute song or shooting a basket through a hoop, then the millions they make will continue to create an economic imbalance that will cause the rest of the people to struggle to live day by day and to make ends meet.

In this regard, the superrich will drive up the prices of whatever they want, because money is no limitation, making such things too expensive for the average person to afford. So long as we hold on to the conservative belief that it is the "personal responsibility" of individuals that should define economic outcomes, and that the government role should be minimal, we are doomed to a bleak future characterized by vast inequalities that threaten democracy. Blinded by the myth of equal opportunity, Americans continue to defend an economic system that has led to great fortunes for a few, often built on deceit, dishonesty, and fraud, despite the pious denials of free-market and supply-side pundits. No question that some of the business titans have become rich the honest way and have returned their fortunes to the community, but most of them are not philanthropists or Santa Claus; their fortunes create a growing schism between the rich and the growing struggling class and shrinking middle class in America.

Food for Political Thought

Of course, there is nothing inevitable about the dark side of the economy, and everything could be written off by conservative pundits as a figment of my imagination, sort of a liberal and loony way of distorting reality, obscuring the truth, and screwing up the American economy. I hope the conservatives are right and I'm proven wrong. More to the point, a few changes in our tax system and pension and health-care system could drastically change the scorecard. The binoculars of the not-so-distant future might hopefully reveal a more progressive view of society, one that subscribes to greater equality and social mobility, as well as the redistribution of wealth. To move the hands of fate in the right direction, we need to discard the old thinking that treats taxation of wealth as a sin and introduce aggressive tax policies aimed at inherited privilege and power—particularly those descendents of eight- and nine-figured millionaires and ten-figured billionaires.

Although I'm not an insider of the political or religious processes shaping America, I can speak about the intellectual and academic world. From my perspective, no one does a better job today explaining the liberal agenda and conflict between liberals and conservatives that is still unfolding than Paul Krugman and Robert Reich. But they are outnumbered ten to one by conservatives, business leaders, and bankers, as well as authors and media talk-show hosts, and, therefore, trying to get their ideas across to the American people is like trying to describe a forest while racing through it on horseback at the thick of the night.

Consider just one conservative group, the *American Compass*, a reading club for America's intellectual Right with 2005–2006 titles such as: Fred Barnes, *Rebel in Chief: How George W. Bush is Redefining the Conservative Movement and Transforming America*; Paul Kengor, *God and George W. Bush*; Michael Deaver, *Why I am a Reagan Conservative*; Bryon York, *The Vast Left Wing Conspiracy*; Ben Shapiro, *Porn Generation: How Social Liberalism is Corrupting Our Future*; Peter Schweiszer, *Do as I Say: Profiles in Liberal Hypocrisy*; Michael Malkin, *Unhinged: Exposing Liberals Gone Wild*; Bernard Goldberg, *100 People Who Are Screwing Up America*; Ann Coulter, *How to Talk to a Liberal (If You Must)*; Thomas Sowell, *Black Rednecks and White Lib-*

erals; Herman Cain, *They Think You're Stupid: Why Democrats Lost Your Vote and What Republicans Can Do to Keep It;* Edward Klein, *The Truth about Hillary;* Mark Levin, *Men in Black: How the Supreme Court Is Destroying America;* Michael Medved, *Right Turns;* Gary Rosen, *The Right War? The Conservative Debate on Iraq;* John Gibson, *The War on Christmas: How the Conspiracy to Subvert Our Most Sacred Holiday Is Worse Than You Thought;* and Jonathan Foreman, *A Pocket Book of Patriotism.*

In all, hundreds of "books you can believe in," which parrot the conservative view of America, are published regularly—far outstripping books representing the liberal perspective—making me wonder if the liberal tide is going to take shape and form, or recede from the natural life of politics. The content is repetitive: unflinchingly righteous as to American power; abrasive dialogue against anyone who criticized the war efforts in Iraq; melodramatic polemics against liberalism; heightened support of old-time religion under the guise of moral reform; and tax cuts for the rich under the banner of stimulating the economy. In a nutshell, some of their ideas don't make any more sense than scenes in a Fellini movie or the *Twilight Zone.* But to look for logic is to miss the point. Many of their ideas are based on faith and fantasy, not reason or reality.

Wise men say only fools make quick judgments, but no matter how you slice it the war of words is still being won by the political Right. Given this trend, our children's future is at stake. The story is still unfolding, but trying to change the economic system or explain how the conservative agenda—the combination of big business, religious evangelists, and superpatriots—is turning the political winds and the mood of the country to the Right, for the benefit of the rich (the top 10 percent) and superrich (the top 1 percent) and at the expense of the common people (which includes the middle class), falls on deaf ears. The 2006 elections provide a ray of hope, but the crucial issue was Bush's failed policy in Iraq, which in parts of the country was dubbed the "Bush drag," not the economy and the inequalities that undermine our nation.

Trying to explain this conservative shift and how it has transformed the country has been sensationalized by conservative commentators as some left-wing, socialistic plot, a screw-up notion that defies conventional wisdom and ridicules the values that made America great. Fueling the common impression in the war of words among conservative ideologues that the critical needle has swung past personal bias and political indulgence toward personal attacks and brick bats hurled at the Left, the liberal platform is considered by people like Ann Coulter (columnist and radio commentator), Newt Gingrich (former congressman and political commentator), and Pat Robertson (evangelist and television spokesman) to be anti-American and anti-Christian. They play to a political base far to the Right with the intention that, if they push the Republican Party to the extreme side of the political process, including but not limited to Congress and the Supreme Court, there will be a compromise at the right center.

No doubt we need a liberal wake-up call, based on coalition building on issues including a progressive tax policy, a more equitable Social Security and health-care system for all Americans, and safety nets for low-income, modest income, and disabled and elderly people. The country needs to be driven less by political ideology, less by verbal pistol-whippings, and more by the kinder and informative side, less by partisan politics and more by cross-party and middle-of-the-road coalitions. The country cannot continue to favor high-income taxpayers; it must invest in all Americans. We know that the present Social Security system does not provide sufficient benefits for a comfortable old age and benefits are now shrinking to compensate for military spending; the system must provide a basic level of income for all old people to live with dignity. For the vast majority of retired Americans for whom Social Security comprises more than half their income, a decent level of benefits is needed and is the difference between living in destitute circumstances or with dignity. Similarly, the country does not need an incomprehensible health insurance package that is a minefield for consumers but a goldmine for insurance and drug companies, rather Congress needs to enact a cost-effective, uniform, or standardized program, administered directly by the government.

Despite my dissatisfaction with the present economic system, and despite my own biases and dreamy views of what should be, when the workday ends, I can still be drinking buddies with people like William Buckley (conservative spokesman and founder of the *National Review*) and David Brooks (conservative columnist for the *New York Times*), just as actors dueling with swords or pistols onstage may troop off to the bar for a beer when the curtain falls and the lights are turned off. This is why first and foremost I believe in America.

But feeling the winds of reality, like a cold-winter snap from the heartland, I sometimes feel like a beaten warrior, battered and bruised, sensing that the conservative mood is rolling over me and my outnumbered comrades in arms. In the twilight of my academic career, after more than forty years of crossing swords with a wide range of philosopher-kings, I now feel more like one of the last Spartans fighting the good fight outside the gates of imperial Rome, one of the last brave hearts fighting for a hard and cold country against the English invaders, or one of the last of the Mohicans waging a war for a way of life and a land in which my ancestors once flourished. We know these warriors from old novels and old movies, where they are all trying to hold on to their romantic dreams and all registering their noble objections before succumbing manfully to overwhelming odds, the inevitable force of power, the inexorable will of fate.

This, and perhaps also a little self-righteous and egotistical, is how I feel as conservative bills in Congress have rolled over the American people in the first six years of the Bush administration. And as I wrestle with my desire to speak out against powerful financial and political interest groups, the captains and chieftains of big business and big government—supported by the religious Right, superpatriots, and the people in pickup trucks and deer-hunting orange—seem still in control. Yet it is the last group, the one most easily dismissed by the political Left, that holds the cards for a change. Mocked as bitingly hopeless and helpless, a combination of Archie Bunker, Homer Simpson, and Al Bundy, all rolled up and left-behind as politically incorrect, little more than cavemen, and not the type to invite for a jolly evening in the theater, they are the potential wrecking crew of the political Right. More concerned about the recent economic success of minority groups, they have overlooked the abuse of big business and the assault of a conservative government in the form of policies that favor the rich. They may never go to Harvard or Yale, and they may never go on to wealth, fame, or privilege, but they can be redeemed by the political merger of the political Center and Left. Instead of criticizing their values and virtues, we need to restore them to the old-fashioned Democratic Party, when blue-collar and ethnic Americans overwhelmingly voted blue.

Given a messy dissatisfaction over the radical shift to the Right since the Reagan administration, and now with a conservative Supreme Court, I feel left alone with only a few drinking buddies who fully understand. Certain things just don't seem to change. Since the days of Pharaoh, some seven thousand years ago, when the workers were pushing stones uphill, the captains and chieftains, the noble and wealthy class, have been running the show and pushing the buttons. Although two thousand years ago the church seeped into our souls, it has not changed the social order. Despite the sense of religious righteousness that has been thrusted on humanity, the same privileged people continue to maintain systems of social stratification, waging a class war and keeping down the common people. However, America is the symbol of the new world, the New Athens—the only country to provide vast opportunities for the disenfranchised, the masses, and the common people who have come from the four corners of the world to start a new life. We are the hope for humanity, where plain people can transcend class distinctions and find their way to the top.

But today a class war is being waged against the bottom 80 or 90 percent of Americans who in the last twenty-five to thirty years have shared very little in the growth and prosperity of the nation. We cannot continue along this path much longer and call ourselves a democracy. Although arguments are rarely settled in American politics, we must find the Center. The vast majority of Americans are in the middle or just left or right of the Center. Most Americans have become disenfranchised by ideology, and by partisan politics that appeals to the far Left or far Right. The far Right has been running the political show in the early years of twenty-first century—with control of the White House, Congress, and the Supreme Court—although there is now a crack in its core with a Democratic Congress. Even worse, the conservative revolution barely stirs any notice among the common people who seem confused and more involved in earning a living and making ends meet than trying to piece together why they have not shared in the nation's prosperity.

A Final Comment

The need is for Americans to remember that most of the social and economic reforms of the nineteenth and twentieth centuries were based on liberal thought, supported by party coalitions that addressed our social and economic problems. To restore the liberal model, Peter Beinart, the editor of the *New Republic*, contends that liberals need to "first conquer their ideological amnesia" and then "conquer their ideological weakness."[77] I would introduce a third consideration: Liberals must break the conservatives' old habit of painting them as anti-American or anti-patriotic and weak on defense—a ploy rooted in the 1960s and 1970s, which associated liberals first as "radicals" and later as "soft on Communism." Americans seem to forget it was the Roosevelt and Truman doctrines, bolstered by George Marshall and the Marshall Plan and George Kennan's foreign policy, that won World War II, rebuilt Europe, and contained Communism. Then there is a fourth consideration: economic inequalities and the fact that many Americans, if not the majority, can barely stay afloat, much less get ahead. Prosperity should not be limited to the top 10 percent; we are all in it together. This message needs to be hammered home in forceful prose—not the language of Aeschylus or Euripides.

We haven't had a major upheaval since the Civil War. What this country needs is a Third Revolution that softens the hidden depths of inequality gripping the social and economic fiber of our nation. The rights and needs of the vast majority should trump the sentiments and privileges of the new nobility. This is not fluff nor an exercise in feeble fatality, but rather thoughts rooted in the intellectual weaponry of the Enlightenment, which were transferred and mixed into our nation's history, political phrases, and legal statutes. Here I should reinstate the mini-portraits and maxims of John Locke, Jean-Jacques Rousseau, and Immanuel Kant, the major personalities of the Enlightenment, as well as the words and pronouncements of U.S. presidents Thomas Jefferson, Abraham Lincoln, Franklin Roosevelt, and Lyndon Johnson, ideas from the hilltop, statesmen searching for a way to connect with and improve the dignity of the masses.

Our tale is an epic story, rooted in Greek philosophy and Roman laws, lofty ideas based on a social contract between government and the people—nothing more and nothing less. The long story of our nation's spirit and soul, four hundred years of achievement and what we aspire to be, is fused with a search for social and economic justice. It is mirrored in the title of this book, *Class Counts*, in which terms like equality and equity, mobility and opportunity, dreams and hopes, what is and what should be, take on new and emotional meanings.

NOTES

1. Assuming you are able to process basic economic data, some unpleasant facts and trends can be obtained by reading Jagadeesh Gokhale and Kent Smetters, *Fiscal and Generational Imbalances* (Washington, DC: AEI Press, 2003); James J. Heckman and Alan B. Krueger, *Inequality in America* (Cambridge, MA: MIT Press, 2003); Laurence Kotlikoff and Scott Burns, *The Coming Generational Storm* (Cambridge, MA: MIT Press, 2004); and Robert Schiller, *The New Financial Order* (Princeton, NJ: Princeton University Press, 2003).

2. David E. Rosenbaum, "Politics as Usual, and Then Some," *New York Times,* November 20, 2005.

3. *Wall Street Journal,* November 25, 2005.

4. Jim Wallis, *God's Politics* (San Francisco: Harper, 2005).

5. Jagadeesh Gokhale and Laurence J. Kotlikoff, *Does It Pay to Work?* (Washington, DC: American Enterprise Institute, 2005); Gokhale and Smetters, *Fiscal and Generational Imbalances*; and Kotlikoff and Burns, *The Coming Generational Storm.*

6. Paul Krugman, "The Tax-Cut Zombies," *New York Times,* December 23, 2005. Since Krugman writes a regular opinion column for the *New York Times,* his critics can discount what he has to say as *New York Times* liberalism or plain off-center.

7. Edmund L. Andrews, "House Completes Vote on Tax Cuts for $95 Billion," *New York Times,* December 9, 2005.

8. "The Shape of Taxes to Come," *New York Times,* November 19, 2005.

9. Robert H. Frank, "Tax Cuts for the Wealthy: Waste More, Want More," *New York Times,* December 2005.

10. "Free to Choose: A Conversation with Milton Friedman," *Imprimis* (July 2006): 4.

11. Note that Scalia and Friedman were also professors (law and economics) at the University of Chicago.

12. Richard A. Epstein, *Takings: Private Property and the Power of Eminent Domain* (Cambridge, MA: Harvard University Press, 1985).

13. Cass Sunstein, *Radicals in Robes: Why Extreme Right-Wing Courts Are Wrong for America* (New York: Basic, 2005). In the past twenty-five years, since 1980, there has been a major shift, what Sunstein calls a "genuine revolution in constitutional thinking," from a *liberal* perspective when the Court was headed by Chief Justice Warren Burger to a *moderate* perspective during the years headed by Chief Justice William Rehnquist, due to the influence of Justices Anthony Kennedy and Sandra Day O'Connor, and now to a *conservative* perspective, headed by Chief Justice John Roberts, due to the efforts of Republican Presidents Ronald Reagan and George H. W. Bush.

14. Jacob S. Hacker and Paul Pierson, *Off Center: The Republican Revolution and the Erosion of American Democracy* (New Haven, CT: Yale University Press, 2005).

15. Chris Mooney, *The Republican War on Science* (New York: Basic, 2005).

16. Paul Krugman, "Wages, Wealth and Politics," *New York Times*, August 18, 2006.

17. Ben Stein, "My Country; Right and Wrong," *New York Times*, August 6, 2006.

18. Thomas L. Friedman, "Thou Shall Not Destroy the Center," *New York Times*, November 11, 2005.

19. Timothy L. O'Brien, *TrumpNation: The Art of Being Donald* (New York: Warner Books, 2005).

20. Benjamin M. Friedman, *The Moral Consequences of Economic Growth* (New York: Knopf, 2005); Robert Reich, *Reason: Why Liberals Will Win the Battle for America* (New York: Knopf, 2004).

21. James T. Patterson, *The United States from Watergate to Bush v. Gore* (New York: Oxford University Press, 2005).

22. Gretchen Morgenson, "How to Slow Runaway Executive Pay," *New York Times*, October 23, 2005.

23. See Joseph Nocera, "Disclosures Won't Tame CEO Pay," *New York Times*, January 14, 2006.

24. *Bureau of Economic Analysis* (Washington, DC: U.S. Department of Commerce, August 2005), table 1.1.5. GDP is listed up to 2004 at $11,734 billion, and 2005 is projected, based on previous figures, from 1975 to 2004.

25. Patrick D. Healy, "Pity the Rich in Politics," *New York Times*, November 13, 2005.

26. Alan Greenspan, cited in Heath Timmons, "Greenspan Points to Danger of Rising Budget Deficits," *New York Times*, December 3, 2005.

27. Friedman, *The Moral Consequences of Economic Growth*.

28. Alice M. Rivlin and Isabel Sawhill, eds., *Restoring Fiscal Sanity: How to Balance the Budget* (Washington, DC: Brookings Institution, 2004).

29. Edmund L. Andrews, "Echoes of 1986?" *New York Times*, November 6, 2005.

30. *The President's Panel on Federal Tax Reform* (Washington, DC: U.S. Treasury Department, 2005).

31. Carl Hulse, "House Approves Wage Increase Linked to Tax Breaks," *New York Times*, July 30, 2006.

32. Daniel Akst, "Pity the Billionaires," *New York Times*, April 3, 2005.

33. Elda DiRo, "Luxury Tax, Federal Taxation," *CPA Journal* (October 1991): 3–6.

34. The information in the parenthetical suggests more than a sale, including a

gift or a transfer of an asset or an inheritance which could be implemented for purpose of avoiding taxes.

35. "America and China: Partners, If not Friends." *New York Times*, November 20, 2005; "India: Growth Rate of 7.5% Is Forecast," *New York Times*, November 30, 2005.

36. Nick Schulz, "Demagogues and 'Windfall' Taxes," *Washington Times*, November 4, 2005; "The Windfall Profit Tax," *International Herald Tribune*, November 9, 2005.

37. CNN, "The Windfall Profit Tax," on *Money*, November 17, 2005.

38. See Gregory Clark, *A Farewell to Alms: A Brief Economic History of the World* (Princeton, NJ: Princeton University Press, 2006); Rodolfo E. Manuelli and Ananth Seshadri, *Human Capital and the Wealth of Nations* (New York: Society for Economic Dynamics, New York University, 2005).

39. Thomas L. Friedman, "A Quick Fix for the Gas Addicts," *New York Times*, May 31, 2006.

40. The Chevy Areo averaged thirty-five miles per gallon, as reported in 2005.

41. The most optimistic report is "More Jobs, Worse Work," published in 2004 by Stephen Roach, an economist for Morgan Stanley. However, Mr. Roach represents Wall Street—certainly no friend to the average American investor considering retirement or his child's college tuition. Wall Street favors insiders and institutional clients, short and simple, so the reader cannot trust the low-end number of 45 percent. Sadly, 67 percent seems more likely to represent the percent of low-end jobs.

42. *Trends in Student Aid* (New York: College Board, 2005).

43. Mary Beth Marklein, "College Aid Is Up, but Tuitions Are Too," *USA Today*, October 25, 2006.

44. Personal responsibility and family/cultural values (single mothers, divorce, abortion, gay rights, school prayer, etc.) have become a new obsession and stand-in issues for traditional values that conservatives now associate with economic outcomes instead of dealing with larger societal issues related to class, race, gender, and education.

45. Edmund L. Andrews, "Fearing the Gap Will Become a Chasm," *New York Times*, March 2, 2004; Isabel V. Sawhill, "The Danger of Deficits," *USA Today*, August 16, 2005.

46. These figures are projections based on 2005 data and include a jump in revenues due to corporate profits for 2006.

47. Peter G. Peterson, *Running on Empty* (New York: Farrar, Strauss, & Giroux, 2004).

48. Laurence J. Kotlikoff and Scott Burns, *The Coming Generational Storm* (Cambridge, MA: MIT Press, 2005).

49. Clyde Prestowitz, *Three Billion New Capitalists: The Greatest Shift of Wealth and Power to the East* (New York: Basic, 2006); John W. Miller, "EU to Get Tougher on China Trade," *Wall Street Journal*, October 24, 2006.

50. Alice M. Rivlin and Isabel Sawhill, eds., *Restoring Fiscal Sanity 2005* (Washington, DC: Brookings Institute, 2005).

51. Austan Goolbec, "In Retirement Planning There Is Nothing Certain," *New York Times*, November 19, 2006.

52. Sawhill, "The Danger of Deficits."

53. Andrews, "Fearing that a Gap Will Become a Chasm."

54. Laurence J. Kotlikoff and Scott Burns, "The Perfect Demographic Storm," *Chronicle of Higher Education*, March 19, 2004.

55. "The Pension Gap," *Newsday*, April 9, 2006.

56. Mary Williams Walsh, "Public Pension Plans Face Billions in Shortages," *New York Times*, August 8, 2006; Mary Williams Walsh and Michael Cooper, "City Gets a Sobering Look at Possible Pension Trouble," *New York Times*, August 20, 2006. Also see *New York Times*, December 29, 2006, C1, C6.

57. Democratic Senator Dianne Feinstein, on CNN's *Larry King Live*, June 21, 2006, estimated that 50 percent of the U.S. workforce had no pension and relies solely on Social Security.

58. Based on a 2005 Fidelity Institutional Retirement Service report and a 2004 report by the Investment Company Institute.

59. Nicholas D. Kristof, "Medicine's Sticker Shock," *New York Times*, October 2, 2005.

60. Kristof, "Medicine's Sticker Shock"; Paul Krugman, "Bad for the Country," *New York Times*, November 25, 2005; and Andy Rooney, cited on *60 Minutes*, January 5, 2006. If we add GM's pension costs, then the number is $2,000 per car.

61. "Inside Wal-Mart, a Larger Debate," *New York Times*, October 28, 2005.

62. Lee Walczak and Richard S. Dunham, "I Want My Safety Net," *Business Week*, May 16, 2005, 25–31.

63. Milton Fradenheim and Robert Pear, "A Drug Benefit Conundrum," *New York Times*, November 4, 2005.

64. Eric Dash, "Wall Street Senses Opportunities in Health Care Savings Accounts," *New York Times*, January 27, 2006.

65. Richard Pérez-Pena and Michael Luo, "As Medicaid Rolls Grow, Costs Take a Local Toll," *New York Times*, December 13, 2005.

66. Shaila Dewar, "In Mississippi, Soaring Costs Force Deep Medicaid Cuts," *New York Times*, July 2, 2005; Bob Herbert, "Curing Health Costs: Let the Sick Suffer," *New York Times*, September 1, 2005.

67. For the year 2002–2003, Nassau County (NY) residents paid $8,389 per household in property taxes. Residents in Bergen (NJ) paid $6,268, and in Fairfield (CT) they paid $5,690. More than 50 percent of households in these counties report difficulty in paying mortgage payments and property taxes. See Bruce Lambert, "Property Taxes Push Residents to Limit," *New York Times*, January 26, 2006.

68. The provision does not take effect if the money was given to charity or to a grandchild's college tuition.

69. Jane Gross, "The Middle Class Struggle in the Medicaid Maze," *New York Times*, July 9, 2005; Richard Perez-Peña and Michael Luno, "As Medicaid Rolls Grow, Costs Take a Local Toll," *New York Times*, July 9, 2005.

70. Kristof, "Medicine's Sticker Shock."

71. George Peristein, Transit Worker Board member, cited in Steven Greenhouse and Sewell Chan, "Transit Workers in Deal to Share Health Plan Cost," *New York Times*, December 28, 2005.

72. Kotlifoff and Burns, *The Coming Generational Storm*.

73. Sherly Gay Stolberg, "House Approves Budget Cuts of $39.5 Billion," *New York Times*, February 2, 2006.

74. Howard Glerkman and Rich Miller, "Eyeing a Tax on Company Benefits," *Business Week*, December 12, 2005, 49.

75. In 2005, eight out of ten of the largest financial and investment companies on Wall Street, such as Morgan Stanley, Merrill Lynch, and Citigroup settled legal suits and paid penalties totaling $1.4 billion because of conflicts of interest and misleading and fleecing the public. Between 2004 and 2005, sixty of the top five hundred companies had to restate their earnings, a combined value of more than $3 trillion, which is an enormous part of the corporate world. See John C. Bogle, *The Battle for the Soul of Capitalism* (New Haven, CT: Yale University Press, 2006).

76. Nocera, "Disclosure Won't Tame CEO Pay."

77. Peter Bernart, *The Good Fight: Why Liberals—and Only Liberals—Can Win the War on Terror and Make America Great Again* (New York: Harper Collins, 2006).

Index

Xenophon, 23

Yemen, 250
Yevuschenko, Yevgeni, 277–78n7
Young, Michael, 100, 101

Yugoslavia, 260

Zakaria, Fareed, 31
zero tax, ix
Zinn, Howard, 268
Zinni, Anthony, 29

About the Author

Allan Ornstein is a professor of education at St. John's University. Professor Ornstein's doctorate is from New York University. He is a former Fulbright-Hayes Scholar and Screening Committee Member of the Commission and author of more than four hundred articles and fifty books on education and social issues. Professor Ornstein's books have been published in four different languages, and three of his textbooks—*Foundations of Education*, 10th ed.; *Education Administration: Concept and Practices*, 5th ed.; and *Curriculum Foundations, Principles, and Issues*, 4th ed.—are leading books in their respective fields. You may want to Google Mr. Ornstein for more information on his textbooks, or this particular book.